*The Texas Panhandle Frontier*

*Number* 12

*The M. K. Brown Range Life Series*

# The Texas
# Panhandle Frontier

FREDERICK W. RATHJEN

UNIVERSITY OF TEXAS PRESS

AUSTIN AND LONDON

*Publication of this book was assisted by*
*a grant from the Andrew W. Mellon Foundation.*

Library of Congress Cataloging in Publication Data

Rathjen, Frederick W                    1929-
  The Texas Panhandle frontier.

  (The M. K. Brown range life series, no. 12)
  Bibliography: p.
  1. Texas Panhandle–History. 2. Frontier and
pioneer life–Texas. I. Title.
F392.P168R37            917.64'8            73-7602
ISBN 0-292-78007-9

For Betty

# CONTENTS

# ILLUSTRATIONS

# PREFACE

This study in regional history is personal as well as professional, since I was born in the Texas Panhandle and have spent more than half my life there. The germinal idea for this book emerged and evolved while I was a student of the late H. Bailey Carroll. Dr. Carroll introduced me to the local-state-regional approach to history, and through him I acquired an appreciation of its potentialities for serious historical inquiry, a fascination for Texas and frontier history, and some measure of the Carroll doctrine that in historical scholarship "no document, no history" is the name of the game. From Dr. Carroll, an erudite, urbane gentleman, I also came to understand that the local, the regional, indeed the commonplace, contain the universal—that regionalism and provincialism are not the same thing; or put another way, that to be a Texan is to be the heir of distinguished cultural and historical traditions that breed dignity and gentility in Texans who will learn and understand.

The intellectual and emotional seeds planted and carefully nurtured by Dr. Carroll were cultivated by two other outstanding thinkers to whom I would like to pay tribute. In one scintillating summer I settled the Great Plains and explored the Great Frontier with Walter Prescott Webb, whose stimulating teaching helped mature my thinking on regionalism, enlarged my concept of the frontier and its possibilities for scholarly consideration, and quietly personified his conviction that one need not fear an idea—original or otherwise—or the consequences of having one.

The second is a man I never met or, as far as I am aware, even saw. Only through his books did I know Roy Bedichek, whose lovely *Adventures with a Texas Naturalist* is, in my view, the finest expression of a mind deeply involved in a physically defined entity, but in no discernible way its captive; and this rare combination of qualities constitutes, I suspect, the only really efficacious premise for regional studies.

The persons to whom I owe particular thanks are legion and include a myriad of friends—many of them non-academicians—who have remained interested in me and the study.

I would like to express special gratitude:

To my mother, Mary McGee Rathjen, whose own American frontier heritage of many generations manifested itself in her unswerving determination that no adversity should stand between her son and access to higher education; and my father, Fred W. Rathjen, Sr., a self- but highly educated immigrant shoemaker at whose knee I received my first instruction in both history and intellectual integrity;

To the colleagues with whom I have worked in the History Department of West Texas State University, who, to borrow a phrase from Dr. Webb, "believe that he works best who is let alone," but particularly to Dr. Ima C. Barlow, whose confidence in this study has never wavered though my resolution often has, and to Professors Peter L. Petersen and Garry L. Nall, who—taking time from their own work—have been my sounding boards when ideas refused to jell and my literary critics when words refused to express what I wanted them to say;

To a host of librarians and archivists who contribute their lives to other persons' success, but especially to Dr. Llerena B. Friend and Chester V. Kielman of the Eugene C. Barker Texas History Center, The University of Texas at Austin; Mrs. Fay B. Crain and Mrs. Claire R. Kuehn of the Panhandle Plains Historical Museum; and Mrs. Mary Burke and Miss Bertie May Williams of the West Texas State University Library;

To the Committee on Organized Research, West Texas State University, for two grants to finance research, and to Duane F. Guy, Head of the West Texas State University History Department; Dean Theodore D. Freidell, and Vice-President Ray A. Malzahn for arranging a reduced teaching load to facilitate preparation of the manuscript for publication;

To Professor Charles E. Nelson for his excellent map work;

To my wife, Elizabeth S. Rathjen, and sons, Eric and Kurt, who have awaited completion of this study with understanding and patience;

And finally unique and special thanks are due to Dr. Joe B. Frantz, whose sparkling courses immeasurably enriched my graduate study, and who, upon Dr. Carroll's death, assumed supervision of my work and has provided the kind of guidance, help, and backing that only a genuine friend and gentleman could.

*The Texas Panhandle Frontier*

# 1. Physiography

The Texas Panhandle, as the term is commonly applied and as defined for purposes of this study, includes the northernmost twenty-six counties of the state.[1] The area is separated from Oklahoma by the one-hundredth meridian on the east and by parallel 36°30' on the north. The 103rd meridian separates the Panhandle from its western neighbor, New Mexico, and the region's southern boundary coincides with the southern line of Childress, Hall, Briscoe, Swisher, Castro, and Parmer counties. In area, the Panhandle comprises 25,610 square miles.[2]

While located within the political boundaries of Texas, the Panhandle is geographically a part of the vast interior region of North America, the Great Plains.[3] The Great Plains rest upon a marine rock sheet, the Permian

[1] These counties are Armstrong, Briscoe, Carson, Castro, Childress, Collingsworth, Dallam, Deaf Smith, Donley, Gray, Hall, Hansford, Hartley, Hemphill, Hutchinson, Lipscomb, Moore, Ochiltree, Oldham, Parmer, Potter, Randall, Roberts, Sherman, Swisher, and Wheeler.

[2] For area and other data pertaining to individual counties, see "Counties, Cities and Towns of Texas," *Texas Almanac*, 1970-71, pp. 239-352, from which this figure is computed.

[3] The basic work on the geological history of the Great Plains is Willard D. Johnson, "The High Plains and Their Utilization," *Twenty-First Annual Report of the United*

red beds, which emerged from swampy plains as the Rocky Mountains were thrust upward, and which slants eastward from the base of the Rockies. Because of their great elevation, the mountains caught immense amounts of moisture that formed large streams.[4] Charging eastward toward the marine rock sheet, these rivers eroded the mountains and carried their loads of eroded materials into the lower elevations. Here, deprived of steep gradient and moisture supply, the streams spread out, dropped the debris washed from the mountains, and choked their beds. As their beds became choked, the streams sought new ones, which in turn were similarly choked. As the process continued, stream beds crossed and recrossed, and a network of interlacing, aggrading streams built up a vast, flat debris apron or alluvial deposit about three hundred feet thick stretching eastward from the foot of the mountains for hundreds of miles, and from Texas' Edwards Plateau, in the south, northward to Canada.[5] But even as nature's forces were at work building up the Great Plains, the forces of erosion began to modify the landscape, and to produce a most startling feature, the High Plains. On the east, the climate was sufficiently humid to produce a cover of tall grasses, which, luxuriant though they may have been, were not able to protect the land from erosion. Water

---

*States Geological Survey*, Part IV (1899-1900), pp. 609-741; and *Twenty-Second Annual Report of the United States Geological Survey*, Part IV (1900-1901), pp. 635-669. An excellent exposition of Johnson's rather technical work is to be found in Walter Prescott Webb, *The Great Plains*, pp. 10-17, upon which the following discussion is based, except as otherwise noted. An account that combines scientific exactness with exceptional literary quality is W. C. Holden, "The Land," in *A History of Lubbock*, ed. Lawrence L. Graves, pp. 1-16. See also Frank Bryan, "The Llano Estacado: The Geographical Background of the Coronado Expedition," *Panhandle-Plains Historical Review* 13 (1940): 21-37; Neven M. Fenneman, *Physiography of Western United States*, pp. 11-30; and William D. Thornbury, *Regional Geomorphology of the United States*, pp. 287-289, 300-309. For more specific treatment of the geology of the Texas Panhandle, see West Texas State University Geological Society, *Geology of Palo Duro Canyon State Park and the Panhandle of Texas*; Charles N. Gould, *The Geology and Water Resources of the Eastern Portion of the Panhandle of Texas* (U.S. Geological Survey Water Supply and Irrigation Paper, No. 154), hereinafter cited as Gould, *The Geology of the Eastern Panhandle*; and Gould, *The Geology and Water Resources of the Western Portion of the Panhandle of Texas* (U.S. Geological Survey Water Supply and Irrigation Paper, No. 191), hereinafter cited as Gould, *The Geology of the Western Panhandle*. Gould's studies do not include Childress, Hall, Briscoe, Swisher, Castro, and Parmer counties.

[4] Holden, "The Land," in *A History of Lubbock*, ed. Graves, pp. 2-3. Holden speculates that many of these streams "may have been larger than the Mississippi today, and some may have been comparable to the Amazon."

[5] Ibid., p. 3.

erosion chopped away at the surface of the land and reduced its elevation, eventually creating an abrupt escarpment.

On the western side of the massive alluvial deposit, the Pecos River inched northward from the Rio Grande and affected geologic development in two important ways. First, the Pecos "beheaded" the streams that flowed from the mountains across the Texas Plains, except for the Canadian River, leaving their beds devoid of water; and, secondly, the drainage system developed by the thieving Pecos, aided by wind erosion, cut down the surface of the alluvial deposits in the west.[6]

Erosion on both the eastern and western sides of the Plains left a middle section standing substantially higher than the adjacent areas. This central area, the High Plains, was largely protected from erosion by two factors. One, a sod grass cover produced by semiarid climatic conditions kept drainage systems from developing and thus inhibited erosion. Second, calcium-bearing water, trapped in buried river beds, worked its way upward by capillary action and, upon reaching the air zone just below the surface, evaporated and left a calcareous caprock. This caprock was far harder than either the top soils above it or the sedimentary strata below. The exposed caprock on both sides of the High Plains was affected by water and wind erosion, and the High Plains gradually narrowed, becoming characterized by precipitous escarpments caused by the fact that the caprock is very substantially harder than the underlying sedimentary strata.[7]

Whereas the western edge of the High Plains is essentially straight, the eastern edge is made remarkably irregular by deep canyons that stab far into the heart of the High Plains. The most conspicuous canyons, from north to south, are Palo Duro, Tule, Quitaque, Casa Blanca, and Yellow House.[8] Stream erosion is responsible for these abrupt gashes in the High Plains, and each canyon testifies to what might have happened to the High Plains had the Pecos not stolen its streams.[9]

The Texas Panhandle is located in the south-central part of the Great Plains of North America and is a composite of the features found in the Great Plains region. More than three-fourths of the Panhandle is located

[6] Ibid., p. 3-5.
[7] Ibid., p. 5.
[8] Bryan, "The Llano Estacado," p. 22.
[9] Danny Johnson, "Some Geomorphical Speculations about Palo Duro Canyon," in *Geology of Palo Duro Canyon State Park and the Panhandle of Texas*, by West Texas State University Geological Society, p. 31; Gould, *The Geology of the Western Panhandle*, pp. 10-11.

upon the High Plains, and the region's most striking physical features are the eastern escarpment of the High Plains and the incredible flatness of the High Plains above the escarpment.

The tilt of the Great Plains downward from the mountains is clearly apparent in the Panhandle. The lowest point in the region is in Childress County in the southeastern corner, where minimum elevation is sixteen hundred feet. The maximum elevation is forty-six hundred feet in Dallam County in the northwestern corner. Changes in elevation are most dramatic in counties affected by the High Plains Escarpment or the Canadian River Valley. In Briscoe County, which is heavily affected by the escarpment and which contains Tule Canyon, elevation jumps from a minimum of twenty-one hundred feet to a maximum of thirty-three hundred. Similarly, there is an increase of eleven hundred feet in Armstrong County, and one of eight hundred feet in Randall County. Comparable variations occur in counties affected by the Canadian River. For example, in Roberts County minimum elevation is twenty-five hundred feet, but the maximum is thirty-two hundred. Elevation rises from three thousand feet to thirty-eight hundred in Potter County, and from thirty-two hundred to forty-two hundred in Oldham County.[10]

The drainage of the Texas Panhandle is a small part of the massive, intricate drainage system of the Mississippi River. Northern Panhandle streams flow into either the North Canadian or Canadian rivers, which are tributaries of the Arkansas River, while the drainage from the southern Panhandle is tributary to the Red River (see fig. 1).[11]

The Panhandle's main tributaries to the North Canadian are Wolf Creek, which rises in western Ochiltree County and flows eastward through Lipscomb County into Woodward County, Oklahoma; Palo Duro Creek, which flows from southwest to northeast across Hansford County, and joins Beaver Creek in Beaver County Oklahoma; and Coldwater Creek (also known as Rabbit Ears Creek), which rises near the Rabbit Ears Mountains in northeastern New Mexico and flows toward the southeast through

[10] Elevation data are taken from "Counties, Cities and Towns of Texas," *Texas Almanac*, 1970-71, pp. 239-352.
[11] Gould, *The Geology of the Eastern Panhandle*, pp. 40-41. The North Canadian is also known as the North Fork of the Canadian River. Figure 1 is based on the official highway map published by the Texas Highway Department. Stream courses as shown in figure 1 have been approximated from county highway maps available from the Texas Highway Department.

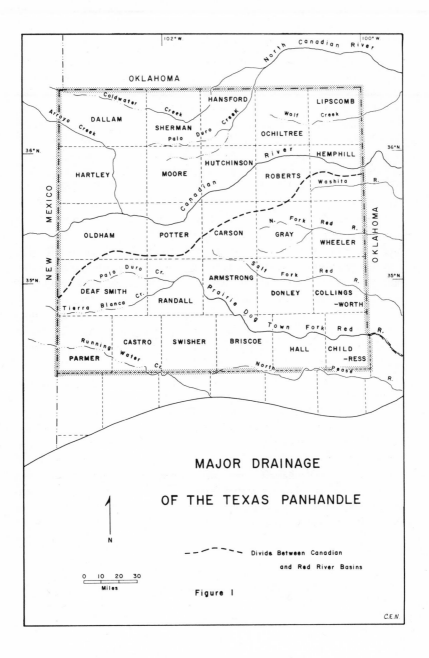

MAJOR DRAINAGE

OF THE TEXAS PANHANDLE

N

– – – – – Divide Between Canadian
and Red River Basins

0  10  20  30
Miles

Figure I

C.E.N.

Dallam and Sherman counties, then cuts sharply to the northeast across Hansford County into Beaver Creek, Oklahoma.[12]

The Panhandle's largest stream, in terms of both volume and drainage area, is the Canadian River. The Canadian, the only stream that flows completely across the Texas Plains, is the sole survivor of the headhunting of the Pecos.[13]

The Canadian River rises among the mountains of northeastern New Mexico and flows generally southeastward to a point north of Tucumcari Mountain where its direction turns toward the northeast. Maintaining its generally northeasterly course, the river crosses the Texas Panhandle and enters Oklahoma.[14] More specifically, the Canadian enters the Panhandle at the midpoint of western Oldham County and describes a northerly arc through Oldham and Potter counties, terminating just above the center of Potter County. Thence, the river's course describes a much larger arc tilted toward the northeast, and crosses Hutchinson and Roberts counties. In northeastern Roberts County, the course turns to the southeast, crosses Hemphill County, and passes into Oklahoma at about the middle of the eastern Hemphill County line.

The Canadian River Valley, cut through the High Plains, averages about six hundred feet in depth, and varies from twenty to thirty-five miles in width. The slopes of the valley are quite irregular because of the dissections of numerous tributary streams. The flood plain ranges up to four miles in width, while the usually sand-choked riverbed varies from two hundred yards up to three-fourths of a mile in width.

The waters of the Canadian are usually turbid and sometimes, especially when on a rise, red. The redness is derived from red clays over which the Canadian flows in its upper courses.[15] Notwithstanding the turbid character of its waters, the Canadian is fed by numerous tributaries throughout its course in the Panhandle. These tributaries account for the very rugged sides of the river valley since they have cut down through the escarpment to the floor of the valley. Few of these tributaries, which enter on both sides of the river, exceed twenty-five miles in length. Some flow when

[12] Ibid., pp. 41-42.
[13] Holden, "The Land," in *A History of Lubbock*, ed. Graves, pp. 3-4.
[14] Gould, *The Geology of the Eastern Panhandle*, p. 42.
[15] Among the New Mexicans and Indians, the Canadian was historically known as "Red River."

there is rain, but many are fed by sweet Tertiary springs.[16] Description of the physical characteristics of the Canadian River is not adequate to convey the real character, indeed the personality, of the stream. Charles N. Gould makes the point clearly and with proper regard for the niceties of language:

> Canadian River is perhaps more treacherous than any other stream of the plains. The stream is either dry or a raging torrent. The river may have been dry for weeks at a time, when suddenly, without warning, a wall of water several feet high rushes down the channel, sweeping everything before it, and for a number of days the river continues high, then gradually subsides. Following this period of abnormal flow the sand in the stream becomes "quicksand," or loose sand which appears firm but gives way suddenly under foot, rendering the stream extremely dangerous to cross. Many a herd of cattle has been mired in Canadian River, and every year loaded wagons and even teams are abandoned.[17]

Many Panhandle pioneers, especially cattlemen, would have endorsed Gould's description, but doubtless in far more forceful language.

The most spectacular drainage pattern in the Texas Panhandle is that related to the Red River. Prairie Dog Town Fork, which flows through Palo Duro Canyon, is the main headstream of the Red River and is formed near the center of Randall County by the confluence of Palo Duro[18] and Tierra Blanca creeks. These streams rise in the High Plains of eastern New Mexico and flow into Deaf Smith County on the north and south sides of the county respectively. From their origins to a point near the center of Deaf Smith County, these creeks depend solely upon rainfall for their waters. About twenty-five miles inside Texas, however, their beds cut into Tertiary deposits and springs begin to feed them. At their point of confluence just northeast of the town of Canyon, Palo Duro and Tierra Blanca creeks form Prairie Dog Town Fork, which flows eastward through

---

[16] Gould, *The Geology of the Eastern Panhandle*, pp. 11, 42-43, and *The Geology of the Western Panhandle*, pp. 9-10, 48-49. The Tertiary springs to which Gould refers are from the Ogallala Formation.

[17] Gould, *The Geology of the Eastern Panhandle*, pp. 42-43.

[18] Not to be confused with the Palo Duro Creek of Sherman, Moore, Hansford, and Ochiltree counties, which flows into the North Canadian.

the increasingly deep and vivid Palo Duro Canyon and is increasingly fed
by Tertiary springs. Near the eastern boundary of Randall County, Prairie
Dog Town Fork receives the waters of several other creeks that drain
southeastern Randall and Swisher counties. Among these are Timber, Sunday, and Ceta creeks;[19] and, of course, Tule Creek of Swisher and Briscoe
counties. All of these have cut their own canyons, but only Tule Canyon is
obviously separate from the Palo Duro. From the eastern Randall County
line, Prairie Dog Town Fork proceeds eastward through Armstrong,
Briscoe, Hall, and Childress counties, receiving additional tributaries along
the way and eventually forms the Texas-Oklahoma boundary.[20]

In addition to Prairie Dog Town Fork, four other main branches of the
Red River originate in the Texas Panhandle. Beginning on the north, these
are the Washita River, North Fork, Elm Fork, and Salt Fork.

The Washita River rises in the High Plains Escarpment in Gray County,
and flows eastward through Hemphill County into Roger Mills County,
Oklahoma, and is fed by clear, sweet Tertiary springs. While a river of
some consequence in Oklahoma, the Washita is a small creek in the Panhandle.[21]

North Fork rises on the High Plains in Carson County, descends the High
Plains Escarpment in Gray County, and flows through lower Wheeler
County into Oklahoma. The bed of the North Fork is largely sand-choked,
and its northern and southern banks, east of the Gray-Wheeler County
line, are characterized by red-bed bluffs and sand dunes, respectively. Notwithstanding its sand-choked character, the North Fork is fed by fresh
water through several tributaries.[22]

Elm Fork rises from Tertiary springs located in sand hills along the High
Plains Escarpment, and drains northern Collingsworth and southern
Wheeler counties. Elm Fork quickly reaches red beds where gypsum and
salt corrupt its waters before the stream passes into Greer County, Oklahoma.[23]

Salt Fork is a typical Plains stream. Rising on the High Plains in Carson
and Armstrong counties, Salt Fork crosses Donley and Collingsworth
counties in a southeasterly direction. The stream cuts into Tertiary forma-

[19] Gould, *The Geology of the Western Panhandle*, pp. 49-50. Gould's investigations
did not include Swisher County and Tule Creek.

[20] For more detailed discussion of Prairie Dog Town Fork east of Randall County,
see Gould, *The Geology of the Eastern Panhandle*, pp. 12, 44-45.

[21] Ibid., pp. 12, 43.

[22] Ibid., pp. 12, 43-44.

[23] Ibid., pp. 12, 44.

tions about ten miles from its source and shortly receives water from Tertiary springs. Farther east the bed widens, cuts into red beds, and becomes sand-choked and treacherous. From central Donley County, Salt Fork, like North Fork, is characterized by red bluffs on its north bank and sand hills on its south bank. From southeastern Collingsworth County, Salt Fork enters Greer County and finds its way to the Red River.[24]

The topography of the Texas Panhandle may be divided into two categories: the High Plains and the Eroded Plains.[25] The severe breaks along the High Plains Escarpment divide the two (fig. 2).[26]

The surface of the High Plains is flat and drainage is, as characterized by Gould, "for the most part wholly undeveloped."[27] In the absence of developed drainage, rainfall either evaporates, sinks in, or collects in playa lakes,[28] which in the interior are fed by immature stream beds, or draws.[29] Playa lakes are shallow, circular depressions caused by "ground settlement," and vary in diameter from a "few feet" to "hundreds of rods." They vary considerably in the dependability of their water supply, and their occurrence is quite irregular. In some areas playa lakes are few and are separated by many miles, while in other areas they occur very frequently.[30]

The High Plains are divided by the Canadian River and the portion south of the river is known as the Llano Estacado or Staked Plains. The High Plains north of the Canadian exhibit the same characteristics as the Staked Plains, but the area has no distinguishing name.[31]

The escarpment that marks the boundary of the High Plains and the transition to the Eroded Plains is in many places abrupt, and especially so along the Canadian River and branches of the Red River, and presents a distinct cliff from two hundred to five hundred feet above the Eroded Plains. In most places, however, and particularly along the smaller streams,

---

[24] Ibid.

[25] Ibid., p. 8. Various terms are applied to the area east of the High Plains Escarpment. "Eroded Plains" is considered to be most descriptive for purposes of this study, and will be used throughout.

[26] The irregular line that divides the High Plains and the Eroded Plains approximates the limit of the Ogallala Formation, which coincides with the High Plains.

[27] Gould, *The Geology of the Western Panhandle*, p. 8.

[28] Ibid., pp. 8-9.

[29] Gould, *The Geology of the Eastern Panhandle*, p. 45.

[30] Ibid., p. 45.

[31] Ibid., p. 8. For a discussion of the derivation of the term Llano Estacado or Staked Plains, see H. Bailey Carroll, ed., *Gúadal P'a: The Journal of Lieutenant J. W. Abert, from Bent's Fort to St. Louis in 1845*, pp. 74-75, footnote 209.

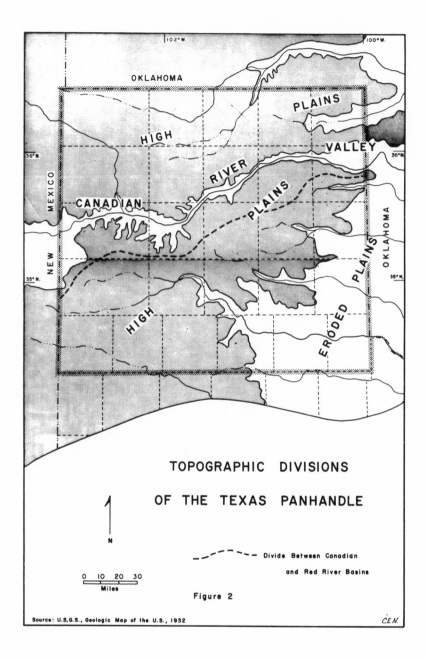

TOPOGRAPHIC DIVISIONS

OF THE TEXAS PANHANDLE

— — — — Divide Between Canadian
and Red River Basins

Figure 2

Source: U.S.G.S., Geologic Map of the U.S., 1932

C.E.N.

the descent is more gradual and stretches over five to six miles.[32] Areas dominated by the escarpment are commonly known as breaks, and are marked by "bad-land erosion forms, short ridges, steep talus slopes, isolated conical hills, butresses, peaks, and numerous V-shaped valleys, which on becoming larger develop into impassable canyons." The escarpment is most dramatically developed along the Canadian River and in Palo Duro Canyon,[33] where there is an almost sheer drop of seven hundred to eight hundred feet from the level surface of the High Plains.[34]

The Eroded Plains, which lie east of the escarpment, cover much of the southeastern portion of the Panhandle. The upper strata (Tertiary and Pleistocene rocks) that compose the High Plains have been removed from the Eroded Plains, and the streams have exposed the Permian red beds. While not as conspicuously level as the High Plains, the Eroded Plains exhibit more gently rolling contours than do the badlands of the escarpment. The streams have cut valleys averaging three miles in width and from one hundred to two hundred feet in depth in the Eroded Plains, and the stream valleys are rather steep sided. The divides are rolling and well drained. Ranges of hills and mesas, such as the Rocking Chair Mountains north of Elm Fork and Antelope Hills in eastern Hemphill County and western Oklahoma, are to be found. These elevations are characterized by relatively hard upper strata that have inhibited their erosion.[35]

The soils of the Texas Panhandle are predominantly associations of Reddish Chestnut soils, but substantial portions of the region are covered by associations of Lithosols (Relatively Sparse Vegetation) and Lithosols and Shallow Soils (Arid-Subhumid). A small portion of the region is covered by an association of Brown soils.[36]

Reddish Chestnut soils cover most of both the Eroded Plains and the High Plains of the Panhandle except for the extreme northwestern corner of the region, and are represented by the Zita-Pullman, Greensburg-Pullman-Richfield, Miles-Vernon, Amarillo, and St. Paul-Abilene soil associations. Reddish Chestnut soils are developed over a large area of grassy

[32] In general, the High Plains Escarpment is quite abrupt from Armstrong County southward and more gentle from Armstrong County northward.

[33] Gould, *The Geology of the Eastern Panhandle*, pp. 9-10.

[34] Gould, *The Geology of the Western Panhandle*, pp. 10-11.

[35] Gould, *The Geology of the Eastern Panhandle*, pp. 10-11. For a description of the Panhandle written from a somewhat different point of view, see Elmer H. Johnson, *The Natural Regions of Texas*, pp. 113, 116, 122-123, 126-129, 141-143.

[36] See map, "Soil Associations of the United States," U. S. Department of Agriculture, *Yearbook of Agriculture*, 1938, *Soils and Men*.

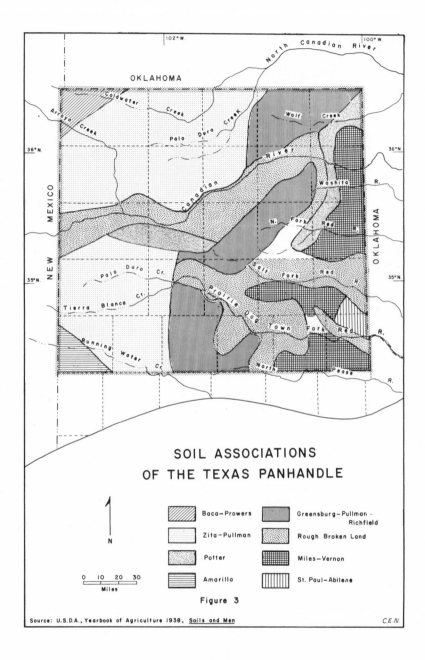

102°W.

North Canadian River

100°W.

OKLAHOMA

Coldwater Creek

Arroyo Creek

36°N.

Wolf Creek

Palo Duro Creek

36°N.

NEW MEXICO

Canadian River

Washita R.

N. Fork Red R.

OKLAHOMA

35°N.

Palo Duro Cr.

Salt Fork Red R.

35°N.

Tierra Blanca Cr.

Prairie Dog Town Fork Red R.

Running Water Cr.

North Pease R.

R.

SOIL ASSOCIATIONS
OF THE TEXAS PANHANDLE

N

| | | |
|---|---|---|
| Baca–Prowers | | Greensburg–Pullman–Richfield |
| Zita–Pullman | | Rough Broken Land |
| Potter | | Miles–Vernon |
| Amarillo | | St. Paul–Abilene |

0  10  20  30
Miles

Figure 3

Source: U.S.D.A., Yearbook of Agriculture 1938, Soils and Men

C.E.N.

plains that extends from southern Kansas southward through Oklahoma and Texas to the Gulf of Mexico. Their climate is warm-temperate and semiarid or subhumid. These soils are typically dark reddish brown and friable at the surface. Subsoils are reddish brown to red in the upper part, where they are heavier and tougher than at the surface, and are grayer and highly calcareous in the lower part. Vegetation native to Reddish Chestnut soils is primarily grass with occasional growths of brush and small trees. Small shin oaks are found in the sandier areas. Inherent fertility of Reddish Chestnut soils is relatively high, but crop production is restricted by limited rainfall and a high evaporation rate. Agricultural use includes production of cotton, grain, sorghums, wheat, and livestock grazing.[37]

Lithosols and Shallow Soils (Arid-Subhumid) are represented in the Panhandle by the Potter association, which are comparatively light-colored and shallow. The larger areas of Potter association soils are found in the Canadian River Valley in the west-central Panhandle, and more or less between the High Plains and Eroded Plains in the northeastern part of the Panhandle. Often they are associated with both broken land and smoother areas that have deeper and darker soils. The surface color of Potter soils is grayish brown, brown, or light brown and the texture is fine. Subsoils are gray or yellow and grade into white chalky carbonate of lime at a depth of one or two feet. Potter soils are extensively eroded, hold moisture poorly, of little productivity, and useful mainly for grazing.[38]

Lithosols and Shallow Soils (Relatively Sparse Vegetation) are characteristic of the arid West and occupy rough, broken country. They are shallow, stony, often highly calcareous, and are dependent largely upon underlying bedrock for their character. The soils of this type present in the Panhandle are designated simply "Rough Broken Land"—a synonym for the commonly used term, "badlands." In such areas water erosion is excessive and soil is poorly developed and useful largely for grazing. Remnants of the upper strata that have survived erosion, or alluvial deposits which are to be found scattered about in Rough Broken Land, support growths of grasses and shrubs, which furnish grazing and sometimes trees. The broken nature of the land has a value of its own, however, because of its scenic and recreational value, and because it protects livestock during severe weather. The Rough Broken Land of the Panhandle lies in the valley

[37] Ibid., p. 1085.
[38] Ibid., pp. 1125-1126.

of the Canadian River, the valleys of Red River tributaries, and along the High Plains Escarpment.[39]

Brown soils occupy a vast portion of the western Great Plains, but are only slightly represented in the Panhandle by the Baca-Prowers association, which occupies approximately the northwestern one-third of Dallam County. Brown soils are climatically located in a temperate, semiarid area, and produce a native cover of short grass, bunch grass, and shrubs. Surface soils are brown, but subsoils shade into light gray or white at depths of from one to two feet. Grazing and dry farming, mostly small grains and sorghums, are the primary uses of Brown soils.[40]

The soil associations of the High Plains include the Baca-Prowers, Zita-Pullman, Greensburg-Pullman-Richfield, and Amarillo. The parent material of all of these except the Amarillo is the Ogallala formation,[41] a Pliocene deposit. Amarillo soils, which occupy only about the southwestern one-third of Parmer County, are derived from Quaternary deposits[42] and are thus of more recent origin than other soils of the High Plains.

Soil associations found in the Eroded Plains include Miles-Vernon, St. Paul-Abilene, and Potter. All of these except the Potter soils are derived largely from the red beds[43] of the Permian period. Potter soils, found near Rough Broken Land in both the Eroded Plains and the Canadian River Valley, are derived from chalky calcareous clays, marls, and caliche[44] which are probably younger than the Permian red beds, but older than the Ogallala soils of the High Plains.

Rough Broken Land is found in the valley of the Canadian River, along the High Plains Escarpment, and along the tributary streams of the Red River, and its soils are derived from the red beds[45] of the Permian period. In many places, indeed, the red beds are clearly exposed with little soil development present.[46]

Rainfall in the Panhandle averages about 21.5 inches per year in the three eastern tiers of counties, and drops to about 18.5 inches per year in the two western tiers. The region may be classified, therefore, as subhumid

[39] Ibid., pp. 1127-1128.
[40] Ibid., pp. 1088-1089.
[41] Ibid., "Soil Associations of the United States," and pp. 1089, 1088, and 1086.
[42] Ibid., p. 1085.
[43] Ibid., p. 1087.
[44] Ibid., p. 1126.
[45] Ibid., p. 1128.
[46] In connection with the soils of the Panhandle, see also W. T. Carter, *Soils of Texas* (Texas A&M Agricultural Experiment Station Bulletin No. 431), and William T. Carter, Jr., *Reconnaissance Soil Survey of the Panhandle Region of Texas*.

to semiarid. Heaviest precipitation occurs in the late spring and summer months, and the least occurs from November through March.[47] Annual averages, however, do not imply certainty of rainfall and in many years actual rainfall drops substantially below the average and drouth conditions prevail. Drouth, a constant threat, has had a profound, continuing influence upon the history of the land.[48] Hail, a form of moisture wholly destructive in its effect, may be expected to fall on at least two days of each year throughout the Panhandle, and may be expected on four or more days per year in the upper portion of the region.[49]

The winter months in the Panhandle are characterized by northers and occasionally, by blizzards. A norther is a rush of cold air from the north or northwest into a warmer area. It may carry moisture, and is accompanied by strong winds and sudden, sometimes spectacularly great, drops in temperature.[50] Blizzards are more frequent in the northern Great Plains, but are far from strangers to the Texas Panhandle. Whereas a norther may be an annoyance, a blizzard is invariably a catastrophe. Blizzards are characterized by extreme cold and very high winds that drive snow and ice particles before them, and are the cause of widespread suffering and economic losses—especially among livestock.[51] The winter of 1883, for example, was characterized by blizzards that lasted "days at a time" and "swept cattle into ravines and against drift fences where they froze to death by the thousands."[52] Many contemporary Panhandle residents vividly recall the blizzards of March 1957 and February 1971.

[47] Data on precipitation are extracted from U.S. Department of Commerce, Weather Bureau, *Climatography of the United States No. 86-36, Decennial Census of United States Climate—Climatic Summary of the United States—Supplement for 1951 through 1960, Texas*, pp. 2-81. While this source doubtlessly contains the most authoritative and accurate precipitation data, it should be noted that the period of record in some counties is quite short (fourteen years in Childress County, twelve years in Dallam and Swisher counties, eleven years in Hutchinson County), and averages given are therefore probably slightly lower than the actual averages since they are heavily affected by the severe drouth of the 1950's. For comparison see the climatic summary for Texas in U.S. Department of Agriculture, *Yearbook of Agriculture*, 1941, *Climate and Man*, pp. 1129-1135.

[48] An interesting study of the influence of drouth on West Texas generally is W. C. Holden, "West Texas Drouths," *Southwestern Historical Quarterly* 32 (October 1928): 103-123.

[49] U.S. Department of Agriculture, *Yearbook of Agriculture*, 1941, *Climate and Man*, p. 730.

[50] Robert De Coury Ward, *The Climates of the United States*, pp. 378-380.

[51] Ibid., pp. 380-382.

[52] Ernest Cabe, Jr., "A Sketch of the Life of James Hamilton Cator," *Panhandle-Plains Historical Review* 6 (1933): 20.

July temperatures vary from average highs of ninety-two degrees in Dallam County, in the northwestern corner of the Panhandle, to ninety-nine degrees in Childress County in the southeastern corner. January temperatures vary from average lows of eighteen degrees in Dallam County to twenty-six degrees in Childress County. Correspondingly, the growing season varies from 178 days in Dallam County to 217 days in Childress County,[53] and averages 195 days for the entire region.

The groundwater resources of the Panhandle are to be found primarily in Blaine Gypsum and Quaternary Alluvium in the Eroded Plains, and in the Ogallala Formation in the High Plains. Blaine Gypsum is composed of anhydrite, gypsum, shale, and dolomite, and is subject to easy erosion by chemical weathering. Gypsum beds are therefore frequently cavernous, and collapsed caverns, or sink holes, are common in some areas, especially in Collingsworth County. At the outcrop, Blaine Gypsum ranges in thickness up to about 250 feet and, in the subsurface, the minimum thickness is about two hundred feet. Saturated thickness, however, varies substantially. The Blaine Gypsum is overlain by Dog Creek Shale and is underlain by Flower Pot Shale, both of which are aquicludes.

Blaine Gypsum is recharged by precipitation on the outcrop. Precipitation infiltrates directly into the acquifer or percolates into it from streams above the water table, a process rendered easy by fractures in the gypsum. Discharge occurs "in low places in or near stream valleys where the water table intersects the land surface."

The usefulness of Blaine Gypsum ground water for domestic and industrial purposes is decidedly limited by its high mineral content, especially sulfates and, in some instances, chlorides. The suitability of Blaine Gypsum water for irrigation depends upon the degree of salinity and sodium present, and the character of soil and crops which are irrigated.[54]

The Quaternary Alluvium is composed of remnants of the Seymour Formation, other sediments of Quaternary age, and some wind blown materials which exhibit similar hydrologic characteristics. Many Quaternary Alluvium deposits are small, but some, especially in the Panhandle counties of Wheeler, Collingsworth, and Hall are sufficiently large to have

[53] "Counties, Cities and Towns of Texas," *Texas Almanac*, 1970-71, pp. 239-352.
[54] E. T. Baker, Jr.; A. T. Long, Jr.; R. D. Reeves; and Leonard A. Wood, *Reconnaissance Investigation of the Ground-Water Resources of the Red River, Sulpher River, and Cypress Creek Basins, Texas* (Texas Water Commission Bulletin 6306), pp. 85-87. This source considers the Eroded Plains as a part of a larger area that is designated "Osage Plains" and includes a substantial area of north Texas lying adjacent to the Red River.

hydrologic significance. Quaternary Alluvium was deposited on stream terraces where its topography is essentially flat but slopes gently both toward and down the stream, or in channel fills where its topography is rolling.

The waters of Quaternary Alluvium come from precipitation on the surface, and, in the flood plains of streams, from stream flow. Natural discharge ordinarily occurs along streams through springs and seeps.

Water from the Quaternary Alluvium is "very hard" but is probably suitable for industrial use if formation of scale, as in steam boilers, is not objectionable. Public water supply utilizes some Quaternary Alluvium waters, but most is applied in irrigation.[55]

Almost all of the High Plains of Texas is underlain by the Ogallala Formation of the Pliocene epoch. The Ogallala consists of clay, silt, gravel, caliche, and most importantly, sand, which composes at least half of the Ogallala's saturated material. The thickness of the Ogallala ranges from zero to approximately nine hundred feet.[56] The irregular thickness of the Ogallala derives from its deposit upon an erosional surface of "considerable relief."[57] Contrary to persistent myth, the only source of recharge to the Ogallala is precipitation upon the surface and the annual amount of recharge is almost insignificant—certainly less than one inch.[58] The degree of recharge is influenced by several factors such as permeability of soils, amount of precipitation, topography, and character of caliche beneath the surface, but most precipitation is lost to evaporation, runoff, or transpiration.[59] The lakes of the High Plains probably contribute little recharge to the Ogallala because of silt accumulations in lake bottoms.[60] The gradient of the Ogallala is to the southeast and drops about ten feet per mile. Unless diverted locally by streams or wells, water moves through the formation a few inches a day

[55] Ibid., pp. 90-92, 93.

[56] Ibid., p. 106.

[57] Jack De Spain and James L. Hughes, "Underground Water Resources of the High Plains of Texas," in *Geology of Palo Duro Canyon State Park and the Panhandle of Texas*, by West Texas State University Geological Society, p. 38.

[58] Ibid., pp. 39-41; Baker et al., *Reconnaissance Investigation* p. 106; and Texas Board of Water Engineers, *Reconnaissance Investigation of the Ground Water Resources of the Canadian River Basin, Texas* (Texas Board of Water Engineers Bulletin 6016), p. 11. De Spain and Hughes report that in the High Plains south of the Canadian River "*water is being pumped out of the acquifer over 500 times as rapidly as it is being replenished.*"

[59] Baker et al., *Reconnaissance Investigation*, p. 106; Texas Board of Water Engineers, *Reconnaissance Investigation of the Ground Water Resources of the Canadian River Basin*, p. 11.

[60] Texas Board of Water Engineers, *Reconnaissance Investigation of the Ground Water Resources of the Canadian River Basin*, p. 11.

toward areas of natural discharge such as springs or seeps along the High
Plains Escarpment and along stream channels that have cut into the saturated
zone, or water-table lakes such as those found in Donley County. The
amount of natural discharge probably about balances the recharge.[61] Notwithstanding their characteristic chemical content and "hardness," Ogallala
waters are acceptable for domestic use, irrigation, and for most industrial
uses.[62]

The economic importance of Ogallala waters to the High Plains of the
Panhandle is immense. In the High Plains lying within the Red River Basin,[63]
in 1959, 960,000 acre-feet of water were pumped from the formation by
7,800 major wells. Of this amount, 940,000 acre-feet were for irrigation and
the remainder went to public supply and industrial use.[64] The Ogallala
formation is unconfined in most of the Canadian River Basin and therefore
will not rise in wells above the level at which it is found. In some areas,
however, the Ogallala is confined and will rise, and local artesian conditions
may occur.[65] Ground water is the sole source of water for all uses in the
Canadian River Basin, and since 1953 irrigation has consumed increasing
amounts. The depth to ground water in the High Plains north of the Canadian
has been an inhibiting factor in the development of ground water resources
for irrigation, but the drouth of the 1950's, which drastically reduced the
profits of dry land farming, stimulated development of irrigation.[66]

While the Ogallala formation is by far the most important water bearing
formation in the High Plains, other formations are of some significance in the
Panhandle. The Dockum Group, consisting of Triassic deposits,[67] is the only

[61] Baker et al., *Reconnaissance Investigation*, p. 106; Texas Board of Water Engineers, *Reconnaissance Investigation of the Ground Water Resources of the Canadian
River Basin*, pp. 11-12.
[62] Baker et al., *Reconnaissance Investigation*, p. 106; Texas Board of Water Engineers, *Reconnaissance Investigation of the Ground Water Resources of the Canadian
River Basin*, p. 14.
[63] The Red River and Canadian River basins in the Panhandle are separated by the
divide between the drainage of the two streams. The Red River Basin includes all of
the southern Panhandle except for a small portion of the southwestern corner. The
Canadian River Basin covers all of the northern Panhandle. See figure 1.
[64] Baker et al., *Reconnaissance Investigation*, p. 107.
[65] Texas Board of Water Engineers, *Reconnaissance Investigation of the Ground
Water Resources of the Canadian River Basin*, p. 11.
[66] Ibid., pp. 16, 19.
[67] De Spain and Hughes, "Underground Water Resources of the High Plains of
Texas," in *Geology of Palo Duro Canyon State Park and the Panhandle of Texas*, by
West Texas State University Geological Society, p. 44.

secondary acquifer in the High Plains portion of the Red River Basin. The Dockum Group was probably laid down as inner-channel and flood-plain deposits and consists of shale, crossbedded sandstone, and conglomerate. Most waters from the Dockum Group are so highly mineralized as to be of very limited use, but in localized instances they are suitable for public water supply.[68]

In the Canadian River Basin, Cretaceous, Jurassic, and Triassic rocks underlie the Ogallala in the central and western parts of the area and hold significant quantities of water.[69] Water from the Cretaceous rocks, and some from the Jurassic and Triassic rocks, is qualitatively suitable for most uses.[70] Permian deposits which underlie the Ogallala in the eastern part of the Canadian River Basin locally contain fresh water, but in most places Permian water is saline and not suitable for most uses.[71]

The native vegetation of the Texas Panhandle is primarily grasses, and the region may be subdivided, as usual, into two parts for the purpose of examining native vegetation: the Eroded Plains and the High Plains.[72]

The Eroded Plains lying east of the High Plains Escarpment are a part of a larger region characterized by the surface exposure of the Permian red beds. In the eastern Panhandle, soils derived from parent Permian rock and Quaternary sandy-gravel soils are found.[73] On sandy-gravel soils "there is a scrubby growth of mesquite and catclaw,"[74] but in the entire area there is at present no grass of first-rank importance. Hairy grama and buffalo grass are of second rank; purple and Roemer's three-awn, tumblegrass, blue grama, and three-awn grama are third rank; tumble love grass, hairy *Triodias*, elongate *Triodias*, covered spike drop-seed, long awned, Wright's three awn, plains three-awn, curly mesquite, slim-spike windmill grass, windmill grass,

---

[68] Baker et al., *Reconnaissance Investigation*, pp. 113-114.

[69] Texas Board of Water Engineers, *Reconnaissance Investigation of the Ground Water Resources of the Canadian River Basin*, pp. 1, 6.

[70] Ibid., p. 14.

[71] Ibid., pp. 6, 14.

[72] Benjamin Carroll Tharp, *Texas Range Grasses*, pp. 7-8; see map following page 8. Tharp divides Texas into eighteen major vegetation regions. Two of these are represented in the Panhandle: the Mesquite Savanna of which a subdivision, the True Savanna, coincides with the Eroded Plains and covers all or parts of the eastern Panhandle counties of Lipscomb, Hemphill, Gray, Wheeler, Donley, Collingsworth, Hall, and Childress; and the High Plains, which covers the remainder of the Panhandle.

[73] Ibid., p. 64. These soils include Miles-Vernon, St. Paul-Abilene, and Potter associations.

[74] Ibid.

black grama, Texas grama, and sandbur are of fourth rank; and thirty species are fifth rank.[75]

The dark rich soils of the High Plains[76] originally supported a mantle of short grasses in which the dominant grasses were probably blue grama and hairy grama. Buffalo grass was of secondary importance. Even before white men appeared on the scene, however, the great buffalo herds had so overgrazed the area that the buffalo grass had become the chief dominant grass, and the gramas had been reduced to secondary importance. The cover of buffalo and grama grasses protected the High Plains from wind erosion, and it was not until the plow arrived that the short grass cover was broken and the surface opened to wind erosion.[77] When the High Plains were virgin, the sinks or depressions present on their surface had a grass cover distinctly different from the surrounding areas. Dense, practically pure stands of western wheat grass stood waist high in these depressions, and furnished hay to pioneer ranchers. Intensive grazing destroyed these stands, but their remnants may still be seen in protected places such as railroad right of ways.[78]

The valley of the Canadian River, in certain areas, contains soils which are sufficiently sandy "to support extensive stretches of hair-leaved sand sage." Other areas which have stiffer soils once carried mixtures of side-oats grama, three-awn grama, hairy grama, sweet bluestem, covered spike dropseed, and other grasses. Frequently, these grass stands have been depleted and have given way to "worthless and unpalatable weeds" because of intensive grazing.[79]

The canyons along the High Plains Escarpment are characterized by the presence of woody species. The most prominent of these is Pinchot's juniper, which is "distributed in open savanna both upon slopes and upon the irregularly eroded canyon floor." Where moisture conditions are right, other species are also to be found, including cottonwood, hackberry, mesquite, elm, wild china, willow, and plum. Scrub oak, grape, and stretchberry are found along the base and face of the High Plains Escarpment.[80]

A great variety of wildlife species are native to the Panhandle. New Mex-

[75] Ibid., p. 66.
[76] Ibid., Baca-Prowers, Zita-Pullman, Greensburg-Pullman-Richfield, and Amarillo associations.
[77] Ibid., pp. 60-61.
[78] Ibid., p. 62.
[79] Ibid.
[80] Ibid., p. 60; see footnote 5.

ican sheepmen who lived in the vicinity of Tascosa found the pristine Canadian River Valley supplied with an abundance of wild life including blue and bobwhite quail, some prairie chickens, waterfowl, and numerous antelope and white-tailed deer. Coyotes and lobos (wolves) were very numerous, and buffalo "watered by the thousands at the river and creeks," grazed on the plains in the summer, and sought the protection of the breaks in winter. The Canadian was well supplied with fish and "was no more than twenty feet wide. . . . It was deep and there was always cold, clear water running between high steep banks."[81] A later resident of Tascosa found blacktailed deer and wild turkey in the area, and credits the Canadian with "the finest channel cat fish."[82]

An early resident of the Hansford County area found the northern Panhandle so infested with lobo wolves that the county paid a two-dollar bounty on each wolf head. So numerous were the lobos, however, that wolf hunting became a lucrative business, and the county was compelled to stop bounty payments to protect its treasury.[83]

The buffalo of the plains are, of course, legendary. They evoked awe in virtually every one who left a record of having seen them, and, when Thomas S. Bugbee established a ranch in the Panhandle in 1876, the buffalo could be shot from the front door of the Bugbee ranch house.[84] For two years Bugbee had to hire men to drive the buffalo from his range in order to protect the grass for his cattle.[85]

Joint occupants of the plains with the buffalo were the antelope. By January 1888, in Carson County, the buffalo were gone, and "the sole occupants of the great plains were thousands of antelope, scattered far and wide wherever one went."[86] Large numbers of antelope remained in the Panhandle until the early 1890's when market hunters greatly depleted the herds.[87]

---

[81] José Ynocencio Romero, "Spanish Sheepmen on the Canadian," ed. Ernest R. Archambeau, *Panhandle-Plains Historical Review* 19 (1946): 56-57.

[82] John Arnot, "My Recollections of Tascosa Before and After the Coming of the Law," *Panhandle-Plains Historical Review* 6 (1933): 60.

[83] Cabe, "A Sketch of the Life of James Hamilton Cator," p. 21.

[84] L. F. Sheffy, "Thomas Sherman Bugbee," *Panhandle-Plains Historical Review* 2 (1929): 132.

[85] Ibid.; John Arnot, "The First Cattlemen in the Canadian and Adjacent Territory" (MS, Earl Vandale Collection, Archives, University of Texas at Austin), p. 15.

[86] J. C. Paul, "Early Days in Carson County Texas," *Panhandle-Plains Historical Review* 5 (1932): 76.

[87] H. T. McGee, "Some Panhandle and Plains History" (MS, Earl Vandale Collection, Archives, University of Texas at Austin), p. 1.

Many small animals including rabbits, raccoons, wildcats, the ubiquitous prairie dogs[88] and beaver[89] are native to the Panhandle.

The arrival of Europeans in the Panhandle-Plains area implied no immediate change for its rich wildlife endowment except in one important and unusual respect. The Spaniards contributed a new species to the wildlife complex of the area: the horse. Spanish horses originated in the desert regions of Africa, were brought to the Iberian Peninsula by Moorish invaders, and came to America with Spanish explorers. As various expeditions penetrated the southern Plains, horses either escaped or were deliberately set free, and, finding a natural home in the great semiarid grasslands of North America, multiplied into large herds.[90] Not only did the Spanish horse enhance an already rich endowment of wildlife, but this new creature was destined to play a more significant historic role than was any native creature except, perhaps, the buffalo.

From the foregoing discussion of physiography, certain basic facts about the Texas Panhandle emerge clearly. The region divides into two natural areas, the High Plains and the Eroded Plains which are separated by the High Plains Escarpment. Each of these subdivisions displays unique features common to itself. Each has a certain unity in topography, drainage, soils, native vegetation, and ground water which, at least locally, distinguishes it from the other. Nevertheless, local variations notwithstanding, the one overpowering fact about the physiography of the Texas Panhandle is its essential sameness. Both High Plains and Eroded Plains are the products of the same geological forces, with the exception of the effect of the erosive forces, that whittled down the surface of the Eroded Plains and left the High Plains standing; both are essentially flat, the High Plains being very flat and the Eroded Plains being gently rolling; the High Plains has practically no drainage system while the Eroded Plains has no drainage system of particular use to man as a source of domestic water, irrigation, or transportation; the soils of the two areas exhibit similar characteristics (the exception being the Rough Broken Land common to the areas dominated by the High Plains Escarpment and the river courses); native vegetation common to both areas is grass; and, in both High and Eroded Plains,

[88] Floyd V. Studer, "Some Field Notes and Observations Concerning Texas Panhandle Ruins," in *Archaeology of the Arkansas River Valley*, by Warren King Moorehead, p. 133.

[89] W. S. Mabry, "Early West Texas and Panhandle Surveys," *Panhandle-Plains Historical Review* 2 (1929): 36-37.

[90] L. F. Sheffy, "The Spanish Horse on the Great Plains," *Panhandle-Plains Historical Review* 6 (1933): 81-82.

irreplaceable ground water, despite its varying quality, must be relied upon by man for his domestic and industrial needs, and, where possible, for agriculture as well. Weather phenomena vary little, and from the point of view of annual precipitation, the most important weather feature of all, the entire region hovers on the dividing line between subhumidity and semiaridity.

As compared to the environment found, for example, in Indiana, Kentucky, or East Texas, the Panhandle was hostile to many American pioneers, and the characteristic of subhumidity implied especially serious difficulties for the agricultural phase of the Westward Movement. Nevertheless, the Panhandle was entirely hospitable to many who visited the region while it retained its pristine condition.

In 1601 the Spanish explorer and colonizer Don Juan de Oñate led an expedition along the Canadian River. Pronouncing it "one of the best rivers which we have seen in all the Indies,"[91] the chronicler of the expedition wrote of the Canadian:

> Each day the land through which we were travelling became better, and the luxury of an abundance of fish from the river greatly alleviated the hardships of the journey. And the fruits gave no less pleasure, particularly the plums, of a hundred thousand different kinds, as mellow and good as those which grow in the choicest orchards of our land. They are so good that although eaten by thousands they never injured anybody.
>
> Proceeding . . . God was pleased that we should begin to see those most monstrous cattle [buffalo] called *cibola*. . . . The flesh of these cattle is very good, and very much better than that of our cows.[92]

Nearly three centuries after Oñate visited the Panhandle, Anglo-Americans found the land equally attractive. W. S. Mabry, who entered the Panhandle with a surveying party in 1873, recalled:

> We walked from ten to twenty miles a day, giving us ravenous appetites. After eating hearty meals during the day, we would sit around

[91] Herbert Eugene Bolton, ed., "True Account of the Expedition of Oñate toward the East, 1601," in *Spanish Exploration in the Southwest, 1542-1706*, p. 252.

[92] Ibid., pp. 253-255. This journal of the Oñate expedition also describes animal herds "consisting of deer which are as large as horses. They travel in droves of two or three hundred and their deformity causes one to wonder whether they are deer or some other animal." This observation would seem to suggest the possibility of elk living in substantial numbers along the Canadian.

the campfire at night and toast buffalo humps and marrow bones, eat a big part, go to bed on the ground in the open, and awake the next morning feeling fine.

The wild turkey were fat, and a favorite dish was to slice the breast and drop the slices in a frying pan of hot grease making delicious turkey breast steaks.[93]

Just as the Panhandle was good to Oñate and Mabry, so also did the men who trailed cattle from the Panhandle to the northern ranges fare well: "Time was no object then, for the cattle improved on the fine grass and water along the way. Deer, antelope and wild turkey furnished ample food for the men."[94]

[93] Mabry, "Early West Texas and Panhandle Surveys," p. 37.
[94] Paul, "Early Days in Carson County Texas," p. 78.

# 2. The Aborigines

"Northwest Texas is a region replete in the romance of a forgotten people."[1] So wrote Floyd Studer in 1931 with specific reference to the people of Antelope Creek Focus, which lies within the Canadian River Valley. Studer could as well have written that Northwest Texas is a region replete in the romance of many forgotten peoples, for the prehistoric people who left the ruins designated Antelope Creek Focus were relatively late occupants of the Panhandle region. They were preceded by others who had their day upon the Plains; lived, perhaps flourished, for a time; and eventually passed into oblivion.

While it is not possible to say precisely when men first arrived in North America, doubtlessly the original Americans immigrated from Asia at least fifteen thousand years ago and entered the continent during the Pleistocene epoch, or Ice Age, by way of the Bering Land Bridge. Though alternately emerging and submerging according to climatic oscillations and consequent degrees of glaciation, the Land Bridge at one time stretched

[1] Floyd V. Studer, "Discovering the Panhandle," *Panhandle-Plains Historical Review* 4 (1931): 7.

about fifteen hundred kilometers from the eastern Aleutians to a northern limit in the Arctic Ocean.[2] Environmental unity between the Old World and the New permitted free movement of various animals—mammoth, bison, reindeer, musk-ox, elk, brown bear, and others—across the northern regions of the continents.[3] Roving bands of scavenger-hunter people, adapting to the harsh Land Bridge environment, supported themselves from the roaming herds, followed their quarry as the animals dispersed over North America, and slowly populated a new continent to become the forebears of the American Indians. Of the cultural traits of these first Americans little is known, but nomads who lived in the northern latitudes of Asia and America inferentially must have developed weapons, crude butchering tools, an acquaintance with fire and fuel (perhaps rendered fat), shelter, and clothing that probably included crude boots and mittens.[4]

From the Bering region, various routes into the heart of the continent were open and indeed southeasterly migration may have been forced by increasing frigidity of climate toward the end of the Late Pleistocene. Except for periodic blockage by glaciers from the Canadian Shield and the Rocky Mountains, an unobstructed trail from Alaska to the southern Plains seems probable.[5] This probability is reinforced by the known significance of the High Plains to the study of early man in America. "The oldest radiocarbon dates for archaeological discoveries which demonstrate, beyond any doubt, man's presence in the New World fall in the range of 10,000 to 9,000 B.C. These dates and discoveries come from the southwestern United States."[6]

[2] W. S. Laughlin, "Human Migration and Permanent Occupation in the Bering Sea Area," in *The Bering Land Bridge*, ed. David M. Hopkins, pp. 410, 417; Hans Jürgen Müller-Beck, "On Migrations of Hunters across the Bering Land Bridge in the Upper Pleistocene," ibid., pp. 380-381.

[3] E. A. Vangengeim, "The Effect of the Bering Land Bridge on the Quaternary Mammalian Faunas of Siberia and North America," ibid., p. 285.

[4] Laughlin, "Human Migration and Permanent Occupation in the Bering Sea Area," ibid., pp. 421-422. Archaeological evidence from northern Eurasia indicates that sufficient adaptation to cold climate and technological development had occurred to equip men for the Bering migration. See Müller-Beck, "On Migrations of Hunters across the Bering Land Bridge in the Upper Pleistocene," ibid., pp. 398-399.

[5] Müller-Beck, "On Migrations of Hunters across the Bering Land Bridge in the Upper Pleistocene," ibid., p. 399. Müller-Beck believes the first hunter-migrants crossed the Land Bridge about 28,000 years ago and that convenient routes southward remained open for several thousand years thereafter. In connection with the foregoing discussion, see also Waldo R. Wedel, *Prehistoric Man on the Great Plains*, pp. 46-50.

[6] Gordon R. Willey, *An Introduction to American Archaeology: North and Middle America*, p. 29.

When men first arrived in the High Plains region, they probably found a much more humid environment than is presently characteristic of the area. Certainly they found the greatest concentration and variety of big-game animals in the history of the Plains, including such Pleistocene mammals as the elephant, horse, camel, and ground sloth.[7] The arrival of the first big-game hunters in the southern Plains initiates man's occupation of the region of the Texas Panhandle. With their arrival begins the study of the archaeology of the southern Plains.

The chronology of southern Plains archaeology may be divided into four major periods, each characterized by a particular tradition. These are the Paleo Indian Period, which dates from about 9000 B.C. to about 4000 B.C. and is characterized by the Big-Game Hunting tradition; the Archaic Period, which dates from about 4000 B.C. to 0 and is characterized by the Plains Archaic tradition; the Woodland Period, which dates from 0 to about A.D. 1000 and is characterized by the Plains Woodland tradition; and the Plains Village Period, which dates from about 1000 to 1800, is characterized by the Plains Village tradition, and extends well into the historic period. These periods and traditions tend, of course, to overlap, and, except for the Big-Game Hunting tradition which developed locally, were affected substantially by eastern woodland influences.[8]

The remains of early man's big-game hunting civilization are scant if for no other reason than that men who lived by hunting and depended on their own locomotion perforce had few possessions not related to subsistence. Knowledge of these men, therefore, derives from a few game kills and campsites where stone and bone tools were left, probably accidentally.[9] It is nevertheless definite that big-game hunters inhabited the southern Plains before the extinction of large Pleistocene mammals which included bison larger than the historic form, horses, and several kinds of elephants. With the remains of such animals the artifacts of their human contemporaries are most often found; the evidence of earliest human habitation of the South Plains is especially found in association with the remains of the Columbian mammoth.[10] Several kinds of elephants were present during Pleistocene time, but the Columbian mammoth is the one most closely associated with the artifacts of early man. Standing thirteen or fourteen feet high at the shoulder and possessing curved tusks as long as

[7] Wedel, *Prehistoric Man on the Great Plains*, pp. 47-48.
[8] Willey, *An Introduction to American Archaeology*, pp. 313-315.
[9] Wedel, *Prehistoric Man on the Great Plains*, p. 54.
[10] Ibid., pp. 279-281.

he was tall, the Columbian mammoth was an imposing animal by any standard and must have been challenging quarry for primitive hunters. There is no evidence to indicate that mammoths were taken by pits, traps, poison, fire drives, or communal drives. Rather, individual animals—those ill or crippled, mired in water holes, or otherwise incapacitated—were sought and attacked, probably with reasonable safety to the hunters.[11]

The artifact most consistently found among the remains of Pleistocene elephants, and by which the elephant hunters are identified and classified, is the Clovis Fluted point, which Wedel describes as follows:

> Clovis Fluted points vary somewhat in details, but all are leaf-shaped in outline, fairly heavy in cross section, with parallel or slightly convex edges and a concave base. On one or both sides they have a broad, shallow channel or flute, that runs from the base about half way to the tip. The edges above the base are usually blunted by grinding. In length, these points range from one and one-half to about five inches, and their width is about one-third to a little less than one-half of the length. The flaking is not remarkable for either fineness or precision.[12]

Clovis Fluted points take their name from a site on Blackwater Draw near Clovis, New Mexico, where they were first found. The site contains over twenty "blow-outs," or "dry basins hollowed out by wind action."[13] Excavation of the Blackwater Draw blow-outs, which began in 1932, eventually revealed skeletal remains of extinct bison, horses, camels, and especially of mammoths with which Clovis points were clearly associated. The evidence found at Blackwater Draw indicates that man hunted mammoths in the area near the end of the Pleistocene and at a time of heavy rainfall and reduced temperatures.[14]

In 1933, a year following the initial Blackwater Draw excavations, an important discovery of Clovis Fluted points in association with mammoth skeletons was made in the Panhandle near Miami in Roberts County. Deep plowing exposed bone fragments, and subsequent investigation uncovered parts of at least five dismembered Columbian mammoth skeletons in what was apparently a filled-in pond. Among scattered skeletal parts, three projectile points and a scraper were found in clear association with mammoth bones. Perhaps disease, hunger, or drouth brought the animals to a diminishing water hole where some died of natural causes, while others were

[11] Ibid., pp. 58-59.
[12] Ibid., p. 54; see also H. M. Wormington, *Ancient Man in North America*, p. 42.
[13] Wormington, *Ancient Man in North America*, p. 47.
[14] Ibid., pp. 47-49; see also Wedel, *Prehistoric Man on the Great Plains*, p. 56.

killed by hunters.[15] The evidence of the Miami site would seem to establish unquestionably the presence of prehistoric elephant hunters in the Panhandle.

The period in which Columbian mammoths were the object of the prehistoric hunt was evidently short. A leading student of Panhandle geology and archaeology places the arrival of man in North America at the close of Pleistocene Ice Age, which brought about profound changes in the fauna of the Panhandle region. Warm-blooded, milk-producing mammals, which dominated the landscape in earlier times, were unable to cope with colder, harsher climatic conditions and both time and environment ran out on them. The close of the Pleistocene, then, "was indeed the time of great dying."[16] If Johnston's estimates are correct, it would seem that man arrived in the South Plains just barely in time to find the last of the mammoths, which were hunted with Clovis Fluted points. Perhaps man hastened the demise of the mammoths, but the basic reason for their disappearance from the South Plains would surely seem to be climatic change.

With the mammoth gone, the big-game hunters were forced to turn to other species that managed to adapt more successfully to changed environment and therefore to last somewhat longer. Fortunately, there was an abundance of smaller grazing animals, especially bison. Several forms of bison inhabited the southern Plains, but archaeological evidence indicates that the form known variously as *Bison taylori*, *Bison antiquus*, or *Bison occidentalis* was most frequently hunted. This prehistoric bison was larger than his modern counterpart and had larger and straighter horns. Though not abundant, the remains of the bison hunters are more plentiful than are those of their predecessors, the elephant hunters. Campsites and the sites of mass kills produce the most substantial archaeological data, but individual projectile points are found from the prairie provinces of Canada southward through the Great Plains into Texas and New Mexico.[17]

[15] Wedel, *Prehistoric Man on the Great Plains*, pp. 55-56; Wormington, *Ancient Man in North America*, pp. 44-47; Dee Ann Suhm and Alex D. Krieger, "An Introductory Handbook of Texas Archeology," *Bulletin of the Texas Archeological Society* 25 (1954): 65.
[16] C. Stuart Johnston, "Prehistory in the Texas Panhandle," *Panhandle-Plains Historical Review* 10 (1937): 82-83.
[17] Wedel, *Prehistoric Man on the Great Plains*, p. 60. *Bison antiquus* and *Bison taylori* are synonymous, but *Bison occidentalis* is a distinguishable form. *Occidentalis* ranged contemporaneously upon the Great Plains with *antiquus*, but appears to have been a later arrival and to have been the surviving species from which the historic form, *Bison bison*, derived. See Morris F. Skinner and Ove C. Kaison, "The Fossil

The artifact most closely associated with the earliest of the bison hunters is the Folsom Fluted point, which takes its name from Folsom, New Mexico, near where the artifacts were first found in association with articulated bones of extinct bison.[18] In 1926 paleontologists from the Denver Museum of Natural History discovered projectile points among the bones of extinct bison, and three seasons of excavation eventually produced nineteen projectile points associated with bones of twenty-three extinct bison. Though controverted for a time, the association of the projectile points was eventually recognized, and the Folsom site thus achieved a rare significance because of its suggestion that man's habitation in North America was much older than had been previously thought.[19] Folsom Fluted points are best described by Wedel:

> The points, known as Folsom Fluted, are generally smaller and lighter than the Clovis Fluted . . . and often show more painstaking workmanship on the part of the ancient flintsmith. They are more or less leaf-shaped in outline, broadest toward the tip which is either rounding or tapering, and have a concave base. The base frequently has two sharp rearward projections and sometimes a small nipple-like protuberance in the center. Highly characteristic is a broad groove on one or both faces which runs from the base for two-thirds or more of the distance toward the tip, and results in two lateral ridges paralleling the edges of the blade. In cross section, this gives a biconcave appearance to the points. The edges have a fine secondary retouching, after which the base and the edges for about one-third of the length of the blade were blunted. In length, Folsom Fluted points range from less than one inch to about three inches.[20]

Doubtlessly, a close relationship existed between Clovis Fluted points and Folsom Fluted points, nor did the two necessarily exist independently of each other in time. Rather, the Folsom points appear to have been a specialized type that evolved from the Clovis in the High Plains. Clovis points may have persisted in some localities for a long time after Folsom points emerged, and all specimens are not necessarily more ancient than Folsom points.[21] Since their discovery, Folsom Fluted points have been

*Bison* of Alaska and Preliminary Revision of the Genus," *Bulletin of the American Museum of Natural History* 89 (1947): 149, 171.

[18] Wedel, *Prehistoric Man on the Great Plains*, p. 60; H. M. Wormington, *Ancient Man in North America*, p. 23.

[19] Wormington, *Ancient Man in North America*, pp. 23-25.

[20] Wedel, *Prehistoric Man on the Great Plains*, p. 61.

[21] Wormington, *Ancient Man in North America*, pp. 30-31.

found in many locations, either in excavations or on the surface where erosion has exposed them, but the greatest number has been found in the High Plains.[22] Accordingly, the Panhandle and adjacent areas have been productive of Folsom Fluted points. In 1943 the Lipscomb bison quarry, located eleven miles southwest of Lipscomb, in Lipscomb County, was reported. Here were found a number of artifacts among fossil bison skeletons, including Folsom points, scrapers, knives, and flakes. The Lipscomb bison quarry yielded fourteen articulated bison skeletons and nine skulls. The situation of the skeletons in the quarry would seem to indicate that the animals were somehow concentrated in a depression and were there killed by men. Ashes and charcoal were found among the bones, and some indications of hearths were present. Some bones showed signs of having been split and cut.[23] Just as the Miami site established the presence of prehistoric elephant hunters in the Panhandle, the Lipscomb bison quarry would seem to establish that prehistoric bison hunters inhabited the area as well.

While not in the Panhandle, the Lubbock site, located in the valley of Yellow House Draw, is of special significance to this study because it was the first of the Folsom sites to render material suitable for radiocarbon dating and thereby to provide a specific clue as to the age of Folsom points. The Lubbock site, excavated by Texas Memorial Museum in 1948, 1950, and 1951, produced charred bones containing four Folsom points which, by radiocarbon dating methods, yielded a date of 9,883 ± 350 years ago. Freshwater snail shells from the Lubbock site produced a date of 9,300 ± 200 years ago.[24]

A highly important site just south of the Panhandle is the Plainview site located near the city of the same name. This site was discovered accidentally when in 1944, a pit dug to obtain road building materials revealed a bed of bison bones. In 1945 the Texas Memorial Museum began excavations and found remains of about one hundred bison "which appear to be of the same species as those of the Folsom type station." Twenty-two artifacts were found in association with the bones, and eighteen of them were whole and fragmentary projectile points of a distinctive type designated as Plainview points. Plainview points bear a general resemblance to

[22] Ibid., p. 29; Johnson, "Prehistory in the Texas Panhandle," *Panhandle-Plains Historical Review* 10 (1937): 83.
[23] Wedel, *Prehistoric Man on the Great Plains*, p. 62; Wormington, *Ancient Man in North America*, p. 40.
[24] Wormington, *Ancient Man in North America*, p. 40.

Folsom points, but are unfluted. The most reliable Carbon 14 samples taken from the Plainview site produced a date of 9,170 ± 500 years ago.[25]

The number of skeletons found at the Plainview site, and the fact of their closeness to each other, may suggest they were stampeded into a water hole along a stream, that they became disabled, and were then attacked and killed by hunters. Notwithstanding their reputedly wide distribution, little is known about the people who made and used Plainview points or associated tools.[26]

By way of generalization, it may be said that the users of Clovis points hunted elephants in the South Plains before eleven thousand years ago and that Folsom and Plainview points were used to kill bison probably after about ten thousand years ago.[27] In no site have anatomical remains of the early big-game hunters been found, and therefore nothing is known of their physical characteristics.[28] It is believed that the big-game hunters killed their game with hand-held spears or projectiles thrown by atlatls (devices for throwing darts or javelins) and that bows were not developed until long after the big-game hunters had passed from the Plains.[29]

Considering the lapse of time involved and the considerable physiographic changes that have occurred, it would seem that perhaps remarkably much is known of the first inhabitants of the South Plains and Panhandle. Absolutely, of course, this knowledge is very limited. What is known is best summarized by Wedel:

> Beyond the fact of their existence, and some understanding of the sort of hunting and butchering equipment they possessed and of the animals upon which they largely subsisted, we still know little about these early hunters. They were probably present only in comparatively small numbers and in scattered groups; but the wide dispersal of their characteristic weapon points and other tools indicates that the people, though limited to travel on foot and not known to have had dogs as possible beasts of burden, may have roamed over considerable distances in search or pursuit of their quarry. Most of the artifacts that have survived from this remote period are of stone, and consist of knives, scrapers, choppers, and other implements primarily designed for the chase and for processing the products of the chase. Their

[25] Ibid., pp. 107-108.
[26] Wedel, *Prehistoric Man on the Great Plains*, pp. 64-65.
[27] Ibid., p. 281.
[28] Ibid., p. 78.
[29] Wormington, *Ancient Man in North America*, p. 29.

weapon points were of several distinctive kinds, and often show high competence in flint working. Grinding stones are rare or absent at most of these early sites; but it seems likely that some use must have been made of roots, berries, and seeds in season, and perhaps of small game when the larger animals were for any reason not readily obtainable.[30]

Generally, the termination of the Big-Game Hunting tradition coincides with the decline of the Pleistocene animals, but the tradition persisted longer in the Plains than elsewhere, lasting until about 4000 B.C., with the modern bison being the major object of the hunt.[31]

The reasons for the extinction of the Pleistocene mammals are obscure, and various explanatory theories have been advanced, some of which attribute extinction substantially to the activities of man.[32] While dogmatism is out of place in the effort to explain events so far removed in time, and with such limited evidence available, it would seem that the answers to these questions must ultimately be found in climatic change. Given the vastness of the land and the immensity of Pleistocene herds, it does not seem reasonable that a relative handful of primitive hunters, however skillful and courageous, equipped with very elementary weapons, could have been a primary factor in the destruction of Pleistocene wildlife.

As the Big-Game Hunting tradition faded from the Plains, it was replaced by the Plains Archaic tradition, which coincides with the Archaic Period dating, in the Plains, from about 4000 B.C. to about the time of Christ.[33] In its broadest aspects the Archaic tradition is an "abstraction synthesized from numerous archaeological assemblages of artifacts and site contexts." The tradition refers primarily to the eastern woodland and river valleys and comprehends a culture that relied upon small game, fish, and wild plants for its subsistence. There are many regional variations, and description presents greater difficulties than does description of the earlier Big-Game Hunting tradition. Remains of Archaic cultures are found throughout eastern North America, and from the Atlantic extend westward into the Plains. On the western edge of the Plains, the Archaic tradition tends to merge with the Desert tradition.[34]

The southern Plains reflect strong Eastern Archaic influences as revealed

---

[30] Wedel, *Prehistoric Man on the Great Plains*, pp. 281-282.
[31] Willey, *An Introduction to American Archaeology*, p. 38.
[32] Wedel, *Prehistoric Man on the Great Plains*, pp. 75-77.
[33] Willey, *An Introduction to American Archaeology*, p. 315.
[34] Ibid., p. 60.

in the various archaeologic phases such as the Grove and preceramic Fourche Maline, in Oklahoma; the Carrollton and Elam of north-central Texas; and the Edwards Plateau culture of central Texas, which is strongly oriented toward the Eastern Archaic tradition while exhibiting some Desert culture traits. The Edwards Plateau culture appears to have begun before 4000 B.C. and to have been long-lived.[35]

The remains of the Archaic tradition just outside the Texas Panhandle, in northeastern New Mexico and the Oklahoma Panhandle, indicate that Plains Archaic people lived by a combination of hunting large and small game and food gathering. In caves south of Kenton, Oklahoma, refuse heaps yield bones of bison, deer, antelope, rabbit, and of other animals. There are remains of vegetal items such as wild seeds, acorns, maize (corn), and squash. In one cave, corncobs with sticks inserted in the butts were found. Other artifacts include sandals of yucca leaf, coiled basketry fragments, skin bags, wooden fire drills, and triangular snares. The evidence indicates that the weapon common to these people was the spear thrower; evidence of the bow and arrow is absent as is evidence of pottery, grooved axes, or other polished-stone artifacts. Similar, though more scanty, remains have been found in extreme north-eastern New Mexico, but it may be that these early New Mexicans were a nomadic hunting and gathering people who predate the Kenton, Oklahoma, cave dwellers.[36]

It would appear to be widely believed among archaeologists that the Texas Panhandle is a fruitful area for investigation of the Plains Archaic tradition and, indeed, the impression is substantiated by an archaeological survey of the region conducted by the Panhandle-Plains Historical Museum since 1952.[37] There is, however, a remarkable paucity of published reports.

Archaic sites in the Panhandle reflect considerable variety in both kind and in the nature of remains. This variation is accounted for by the length—several thousand years—of the Archaic Period, which was great enough to permit substantial change even in a slowly developing culture.[38] Therefore the two Archaic sites reported from the Panhandle are not necessarily to be construed as typical. Little Sunday site lies in eastern Randall County on the northwest rim of Little Sunday Canyon, a tribu-

---

[35] Ibid., p. 316. Wedel, *Prehistoric Man on the Great Plains*, pp. 133-137.

[36] Wedel, *Prehistoric Man on the Great Plains*, pp. 134-135.

[37] Jack T. Hughes, "Little Sunday: An Archaic Site in the Texas Panhandle," *Bulletin of the Texas Archeological Society* 26 (1955): 55.

[38] Ibid.

tary to Palo Duro Canyon. The site is situated in a heavily eroded area in a patch of soil protected by sod. Remains are found buried in the soil, and the site, at the time of reporting, yielded 160 artifacts—158 of chipped stone and two of shell. Of the 158 stone artifacts collected, 146 are chipped implements and twelve are grinding tools; seventy-nine of the chipped stone implements are unifacially flaked and sixty-seven are bifacially flaked.[39] The artifacts found at Little Sunday and the general situation of the site indicate that its inhabitants located their open camps on canyon rims, and used hearth rocks and pebbles for stone boiling. The presence of large numbers of dart points, hide scrapers, choppers, and milling stones indicates a subsistence based on hunting and gathering. The materials from which the artifacts were made indicate that the people who made them were resident in the area and not itinerants, since the artifacts are predominantly of local materials. Some, however, are of materials that indicate roaming or trading to the north, southeast, and west. The physical features of Little Sunday site and the general character of its cultural remains indicate an age bracket of between 2000 B.C. and A.D. 1000, with the actual age of the site probably falling somewhere between these extremes.[40]

A second Archaic site, designated the Twilla site, is located about five miles east of Turkey in southwestern Hall County, and is especially significant because it contains bison bones of more recent vintage than the Pleistocene and is the only such site so far reported in the Panhandle. Many of the bones, largely those of cows and calves, are articulated, and none indicate the presence of the large, Pleistocene bison. The bone layer, covered by eroded materials from above, is located on the east side of a heavily eroded arroyo, and reaches a thickness in excess of one foot.[41]

The Twilla site has produced two corner-notched projectile points closely resembling large points that are most common to the Edwards Plateau but that extend northwestward into the Plains. Points of this type and similar ones occur frequently on sites that also produce points affiliated with the Big-Game Hunting tradition, thus suggesting the possibility of some continuity between the earlier Big-Game Hunting tradition and the following Plains Archaic tradition.[42] Limited investigation of the Twilla site indicates that men of the Plains Archaic tradition used the

---

[39] Ibid., pp. 56-59.
[40] Ibid., pp. 72-73.
[41] Curtis D. Tunnell and Jack T. Hughes, "An Archaic Bison Kill in the Texas Panhandle," *Panhandle-Plains Historical Review* 27 (1955): 63-65.
[42] Ibid., pp. 66-67.

arroyo as a corral or possibly as a fall for the entrapment of modern bison; then proceeded to dispatch their game with darts tipped with barbed points and to butcher the animals with retouched flakes. A precise age for the kill must be determined by Carbon 14 dating, but the characteristics of the points found and the surrounding geologic features indicate an age for the site falling somewhere between the possible extremes of 4000 B.C. and A.D. 1000.[43]

Two other Archaic sites, located in southern Donley County, upon casual observation bear a strong resemblance to the Twilla site. None of the three, however, indicates the presence of camp sites, and therefore do not produce camp debris, which might be highly significant were it present. The absence of camp sites may be caused simply by geologic change that has either destroyed or deeply buried them.[44]

The beginning of the Plains Woodland tradition coincides approximately with the beginning of the Christian era and is signaled by the appearance of pottery derived from the Eastern Woodland. Although little is known about the Woodland tradition in the southern Plains, the period is significant, not only because of the appearance of pottery, but more importantly because of the probable introduction of maize agriculture. Although the introduction of agriculture implies no more than a subsistence economy, it nevertheless signifies a transition from a food-gathering economy to a food-producing economy. This transition, in turn, laid the basis for a firmer hold upon the land than was possible for mere food gatherers.[45] Most pottery bearing sites in the southern Plains are related on a variety of grounds to the Plains Village tradition which began about 1000, and the people who inhabited the southern Plains during the Woodland Period (0 to A.D. 1000) appear to have remained culturally, to a large extent, in the Archaic tradition. Exceptions are to be found on the edges of the southern Plains, notably in Oklahoma and in northeastern New Mexico and southeastern Colorado, where pottery remains have been found.[46] Another exception, however, would appear to be the only Woodland site reported from the Texas Panhandle, the Lake Creek site.

Lake Creek site, in eastern Hutchinson County, is situated on the west bank of Lake Creek, a tributary of the Canadian River, on a small bench

[43] Ibid., pp. 69-70.
[44] Ibid., pp. 68-69.
[45] Willey, *An Introduction to American Archaeology*, pp. 315-317; Wedel, *Prehistoric Man on the Great Plains*, p. 285.
[46] Willey, *An Introduction to American Archaeology*, p. 318.

between the main stream and a tributary draw. The eastern and southern sides of the bench are steeply eroded, are about twenty feet high, and seep-fed bogs lie along the bases.[47] Hughes described the site as "an attractive camping place for small groups of prehistoric Indians, situated as it is on a small bench very close to spring water but well above flood level, in a sheltered part of a little valley with plenty of timber, game, and other resources."[48]

A total of 154 items were collected from Lake Creek site. One hundred three came from the general surface and fifty-one from a test trench. Fifty-three objects were of chipped stone and forty-five of these are Alibates flint, a significant local material.[49]

The evidence indicates that the Lake Creek site was occupied for a time, abandoned, and reoccupied for a short time when the surface had its essential present appearance. The test trench almost certainly produced remains of the earlier period of occupation, and excavation revealed various sorts of stone implements, including "one light triangular point," various animal remains, and most significantly, "eight corded sherds of Woodland ware [and] one plain sherd of Pecos valley 'brown ware.' "[50] Dating of the Lake Creek site is somewhat indefinite, but pottery from the Pecos Valley, known to have been manufactured from about 950 to 1300, is present. Moreover, a date well before 1300 is suggested by the similarities of Woodland pottery and light to heavy corner-notched points from Lake Creek to Woodland archaeological complexes of known age.

The relationship of Lake Creek site to the Woodland tradition is best characterized by Hughes: "The trait assemblage is suggestive of a local complex which has passed from a late pre-pottery [Archaic] stage of development into an early pottery [Woodland] stage, largely through the

---

[47] Jack T. Hughes, "Lake Creek: A Woodland Site in the Texas Panhandle," *Bulletin of the Texas Archeological Society* 32 for 1961 (1962): 65-66.

[48] Ibid., p. 82.

[49] Ibid., pp. 68-69. Alibates flint comes from quarries located about thirty-five miles north of Amarillo in northern Potter County. Horizontal beds of characteristic red-banded agatized dolomite (flint) outcrop for a length of about 3/4 mile along Alibates Creek, a tributary of the Canadian River. Artifacts of this material have been found widely in Texas, central and western Oklahoma, eastern Colorado, and western New Mexico, and appeared in artifacts as old as Folsom and as recent as early historic. See James B. Shaeffer, "The Alibates Flint Quarry, Texas," *American Antiquity* 24 (October 1958): 189; Suhm and Krieger, "An Introductory Handbook of Texas Archeology," *Bulletin of the Texas Archeological Society* 25 (1954): 71; and Wedel, *Prehistoric Man on the Great Plains*, pp. 153-154.

[50] Hughes, "Lake Creek: A Woodland Site," p. 82.

borrowing of a Woodland tradition of pottery-making." Two other significant points relative to Lake Creek site remain to be made. First, the
presence of Woodland and Puebloan sherds in clear association indicate
channels of "cultural exchange between the Plains and the Southwest at an
early date." And secondly, the use of local flint for most of the chipped
stone artifacts found at Lake Creek indicates a resident group.[51]

The Plains Village Period, and the tradition of the same name, begins
about A.D. 1000 and terminates at 1800, when the native peoples of
North America become fully historic. The period may be subdivided into
two parts: one, from 1000 to 1550, prior to European contacts; and two,
from 1550 to 1800, a protohistoric time of initial contact with, and assimilation by, people of European origin.[52] Plains Village culture had spread
over the area by about the beginning of the twelfth century and dominated the Plains for from three hundred to five hundred years. Of all
remains of aboriginal cultures in the Plains, those of the Plains Village
tradition are best known to archaeology, and especially are the late cultures of the Texas-Oklahoma area fruitful objects of archaeological
study.[53]

The Plains Village tradition represents very substantial cultural advance
over earlier plains traditions. Notably, man developed a successful agriculture, and while hunting continued to be a quite significant factor in his
economy, the cultivation of maize, beans, and squash became equally, if
not more, important. Moreover, the technology of prehistoric man reflects
considerable development over previous traditions as is shown by far more
substantial homes and more elaborate ceramic work. The Village tradition
was most firmly established in the eastern half of the Plains and shows
strong influences from the eastern woodland. It is not to be supposed,
however, that the Plains Village tradition was a mere extension of eastern
culture westward. On the contrary, it is a culture exhibiting clearly eastern
characteristics, including agriculture, which were refashioned and adapted
to a Plains environment and fused with earlier Plains cultural traditions.
Neither was the Plains village tradition confined to the eastern Plains, for
in the south-central Plains are to be found such significant cultures as
those of the Washita River and Custer phases of central Oklahoma, the
Upper Republican phase of western Kansas and Nebraska, the Henrietta
phase of north-central Texas, and the Antelope Creek phase of the Cana-

[51] Ibid., pp. 83-84.
[52] Willey, *An Introduction to American Archaeology*, pp. 313, 317.
[53] Wedel, *Prehistoric Man on the Great Plains*, p. 139.

dian River valley.[54] The consistent occurrence of archaeologically significant cultural remains in river valleys is far from coincidental, because the
Plains river valleys provided primitive man, no less than modern man, with
access to water and wood, shelter from the elements, game, convenient
travel routes, and, in the case of agricultural peoples, cultivable lands.[55]

Of the interrelated Plains Village cultures in the southern and central
Plains, the one most important to the Texas Panhandle is that designated
as Antelope Creek Focus located along the Canadian River and its tributary streams.[56]

The ruins now comprising Antelope Creek Focus were first investigated
in 1907 because of the curiosity of a fifteen-year-old schoolboy, Floyd V.
Studer, who lived at Canadian. While attending Canadian Academy, Studer
persuaded one of his teachers, T. L. Eyerly, to lead a group of interested
students to a "buried city" on Wolf Creek in Ochiltree County. Thus were
the Antelope Creek ruins discovered, and in subsequent years Studer
brought them to the attention of leading archaeologists. Surveying,
mapping, photographing, and digging of the ruins became a life-long avoca-
tion for Studer,[57] whose labors are clearly recognized by professional
archaeologists.[58]

The life of Antelope Creek culture may be dated rather definitely from
1350 to 1450 by the presence of datable potsherds derived from trade
with the Puebloans to the west. During this century, Antelope Creek
people may be presumed to have been at their cultural height.[59] Some
evidence suggests that trade relationships between Antelope Creek people
and the Puebloans were established as early as 1300, and the general

---

[54] Ibid., pp. 285-286; Willey, *An Introduction to American Archaeology*, p. 320,
324. See map, p. 312.

[55] Wedel, *Prehistoric Man on the Great Plains*, p. 29.

[56] Several terms have been used to designate this archaeological complex. In the late
1920's and early 1930's the term "Post Basket Makers" was in vogue and appears in
much of the literature of that period. "Texas Panhandle Pueblo Culture" was once a
professionally used term and is presently used outside academic circles. The term is
deficient, however, because it implies more of a relationship to the puebloes to the
west than can be demonstrated. "Antelope Creek Focus" is the most authoritative,
accurate, and current term and is therefore used here.

[57] Floyd V. Studer, "Archeology of the Texas Panhandle," *Panhandle-Plains Historical Review* 27 (1955): 87-89.

[58] Alex D. Krieger, *Culture Complexes and Chronology in Northern Texas with
Extension of Puebloan Datings to the Mississippi Valley* (University of Texas Publication No. 4640), p. 17.

[59] Ibid., p. 47.

culture may have been established well before trade relations with the
Pueblos were established. On the basis of available evidence, Krieger re-
gards 1300 as a "reasonable" beginning date for Antelope Creek culture.[60]
Studer, also drawing his conclusions from datable potsherds found in the
ruins, dates "occupancy within the period of about 1200 to 1400 A.D."[61]

Antelope Creek ruins were once taken as evidence of an eastward extension of Puebloan peoples occurring shortly after the time of Christ. More
recent research has dispelled this view and shown the ruins to be of much
more recent vintage.[62] Antelope Creek people are now considered to have
been, not Puebloan, but pottery-making Plains people who first appeared
in the central plains shortly after 900 and who worked their way into the
Canadian River Valley about two or three centuries later.[63] The theory of
a Plains origin of Antelope Creek Focus is supported by the clear cultural
similarities between Antelope Creek Focus and Upper Republican Aspect
of western Nebraska. These similarities are described by Krieger: "The
economic life, [of Antelope Creek culture] based jointly on agricultural
[sic] and hunting, use of bone hoes, many artifacts of bone, antler, and
chipped stone, carved elbow pipes, pipes of stone, and the making of a
single pottery ware, utilitarian and cord-marked, all point to affiliation
with central Plains cultures, especially Upper Republican."[64] As the plains
agriculturalists pushed westward, however, they did contact Puebloans
who were expanding eastward. Then there ensued a process of "selective
borrowing," which is manifested in the Canadian River Valley by the
architectural features of Antelope Creek Focus. Except for architectural
patterns, however, Antelope Creek culture borrowed "almost nothing
from eastern Puebloans."[65]

Probably the most distinctive feature of Antelope Creek Focus is its
characteristic architecture. Dwelling units appear to have centered around
a "starting core" onto which additional rooms were added, without apparent pattern, until a block of one-story rooms was developed. While some
walls were constructed of unshaped stones held together by adobe mortar,
the most conspicuous method of wall construction was by the vertical
placement of large slabs in parallel rows with the interior filled with adobe

[60] Ibid., p. 47-48.
[61] Studer, "Archeology of the Texas Panhandle," pp. 94-95; see also Wedel, *Prehistoric Man on the Great Plains*, p. 144.
[62] Wedel, *Prehistoric Man on the Great Plains*, p. 143.
[63] Studer, "Archeology of the Texas Panhandle," p. 94.
[64] Krieger, *Culture Complexes and Chronology in Northern Texas*, p. 73.
[65] Ibid.

and rubble, thus producing a wall which was a structure in itself. Some horizontal masonry apparently served to strengthen walls. There is some evidence that rooms were constructed in pits, but the point is not conclusively established. The larger rooms were rectangular, varied in size from ten by twelve feet to twenty-two by twenty-four feet, were more carefully planned and built, and apparently were actual dwelling rooms. Smaller, odd-shaped rooms were less carefully planned and built and were apparently supplementary to the larger ones. Roofs, generally considered to have been flat, but possibly dome-shaped, were supported by four central posts.

Villages were located on promontories, mesa tops, and steep terraces along the Canadian River and its tributary streams and were situated primarily with a view toward defensibility. Streams or springs were usually to be found within one or two miles of village sites, but defensive considerations took precedence over convenience to both water and fields. From six or eight, up to perhaps as many as eighty dwelling units comprised a village, but no particular pattern of village layout appears to have existed. Indications are that many villages were occupied simultaneously and that they contained substantial populations.

The economy of Antelope Creek culture was based on maize cultivation and hunting of game animals, particularly deer, bison, and antelope. The cultivation of beans and squash and the practice of irrigation may be inferred, but direct evidence of these is not present. Small animals and birds were hunted and wild plant foods probably were used, but no evidence of the use of fish is present.

The most commonly found agricultural implement among Antelope Creek ruins is the bison scapula hoe, while other implements fashioned from bones or chipped from quartzitic pebbles have been less commonly found. Food was stored in slab-lined cists, either round or oval in shape, and located both in and outside of homes. Cists were carefully chinked to protect stored food from rodents.

Implements relating to the preparation of food include metates and manos fashioned from sandstone slabs, hammerstones of quartzitic material used for crushing, and pottery. Antelope Creek pottery was exclusively utilitarian, globular and round-bottomed in form, with exteriors vertically cord-marked.

Cutting and scraping implements include variously shaped chipped knives, snub-nosed and side scrapers, mussel shells with serrated edges, and fleshing tools fashioned from the humerus of bison or deer. Other implements include drills made from chipped flint or bone, chipping instruments made of bone and antler, and hammerstones of flint or quartzite. Charred pieces of coiled basketry apparently woven from willow rod have been found in several ruins.

The major weapon of Antelope Creek people would appear to have been the bow and arrow, as is indicated by numerous triangular projectile points that range in length from one-half to one and one-half inches and are finely flaked on both faces. Some use of the atlatl is suggested by the presence of a few dart points that are broad, thick, and from two and one-half to three inches long. Spears and lances appear not to have been used by the people of Antelope Creek.[66]

In summary, the known traits of Antelope Creek people would seem to suggest that they developed a reasonably advanced degree of primitive culture. In addition to hunting big-game animals, they understood and used rudimentary agriculture; their plain but substantial architecture produced an apartment-house type of dwelling, which would appear to imply a reasonably cohesive social organization; their technology enabled them to produce well-made projectile points, plain but thoroughly utilitarian pottery, and other items and tools essential to a simple hunting-farming society; the location of villages on promontories, mesas, and terraces reflects an intelligent apprehension of defensive measures and perhaps implies some degree of military organization. In short, the cultural traits of Antelope Creek Focus indicate a considerable social and economic advance over previous primitive civilizations in the Panhandle region. Moreover, so far as is known, the people of Antelope Creek Focus were the first to establish a sedentary existence based in large part upon agriculture in the subhumid Texas Panhandle. Three and one-half centuries elapsed after the arrival of the first Europeans in the Panhandle region before white men duplicated that achievement.

The precise time and exact reasons for the demise of Antelope Creek culture are obscure. It is generally believed, however, that the culture disappeared from the Canadian River valley during the middle years of the fifteenth century because of disease, drouth, or the attacks of more war-

[66]The foregoing description of Antelope Creek Focus cultural traits and artifacts is taken from Krieger, *Culture Complexes and Chronology in Northern Texas*, pp. 41-46, a thorough and authoritative summary of the available data. See also Floyd V. Studer, "Archeology of the Texas Panhandle," pp. 89-94; Floyd V. Studer, "Some Field Notes and Observations Concerning Texas Panhandle Ruins," in *Archaeology of the Arkansas River Valley*, by Warren King Moorehead, pp. 131-141; and Suhm and Krieger, "An Introductory Handbook of Texas Archeology," pp. 66-73.

like tribes. Quite possibly, a combination of these factors drove the Antelope Creek farmers from the Canadian.[67] In any case, it is certain that the first historic documents of the Panhandle, those of the Coronado expedition that visited the region in 1541, include no description of an Indian civilization resembling that of Antelope Creek Focus. It is possible, of course, that Coronado simply did not visit the area occupied by Antelope Creek culture. On the other hand, it seems likely that the Spaniard did get close enough at least to have heard of a culture so elaborate and well established had it been present in 1541. The Spaniards were far too observant to have missed such a report and far too greedy for gold not to have investigated such an intriguing possibility as the towns of Antelope Creek Focus would have posed.

The principal tribes that historically possessed the Panhandle region were the Apaches, Comanches, Kiowas, and Kiowa Apaches.[68] The Apaches, the first of the tribes to be recorded in historical documents of the Panhandle region, were surely present shortly after 1500.[69] Of Athapaskan linguistic stock, they are therefore members of the most widespread of all North American Indian linguistic families. Geographically, the Athapaskans consist of Northern, Pacific, and Southern divisions, with the Apaches comprising a large segment of the Southern division. Since Athapaskans showed a strong tendency to borrow culture traits from other groups, it is not possible to describe an Athapaskan culture, or indeed, even to say whether one ever existed.[70] From their homeland far to the north, the Athapaskans who came to be known as Apaches worked their way southward, probably on the Great Plains and along the eastern flank of the Rockies, and appropriated considerable areas of the Southwest. Some Apaches moved into the areas already occupied by Pueblo Indians, while others gravitated toward the High Plains and came to be the Eastern, or Plains, Apaches.[71]

The first historic record of the Apaches is that of the Coronado expedition that in 1541, somewhere south of the Canadian River on the Llano

[67] Krieger, *Culture Complexes and Chronology in Northern Texas*, pp. 48-49; Studer, "Archeology of the Texas Panhandle," pp. 94-95.

[68] Jane Holden Kelley, "Comments on the Archeology of the Llano Estacado," *Bulletin of the Texas Archeological Society* 25 (1964): 9; Wedel, *Prehistoric Man on the Great Plains*, p. 131.

[69] Dolores A. Gunnerson, "The Southern Athabascans: Their Arrival in the Southwest," *El Palacio* 63, nos. 11-12 (November-December 1956): 346; Wedel, *Prehistoric Man on the Great Plains*, p. 289.

[70] Frederick Webb Hodge, ed., *Handbook of American Indians North of Mexico*, Part I, pp. 108-109.

[71] W. W. Newcomb, Jr., *The Indians of Texas from Prehistoric to Modern Times*, pp. 104-105; Wedel, *Prehistoric Man on the Great Plains*, p. 289.

Estacado, met a tribe designated Querechos. The Querechos, according to Pedro de Castañeda, the historian of the Coronado expedition, "lived like Arabs," followed the "cows," upon which they depended for subsistence, and used tents made from tanned buffalo skins.[72] Continuing his journey across the Staked Plains, Coronado came upon a second tribe whom the Spaniards called Teyas. The Teyas, like the Querechos, were buffalo hunters and maintained a comparable way of life.[73] The Querechos were in all likelihood Apaches, and the Teyas may have been.[74] Coronado found these Apaches in full possession of the Panhandle region, and went his way, leaving them masters of the land. In the aftermath of the Coronado venture, Spanish interest in the Southwest waned and was not to revive until late in the sixteenth century. When the Spaniards turned their attention to New Mexico, however, various expeditions explored to the east and found the Apaches still very much in possession of the area of the Panhandle. Various names were applied to these Apache bands including Vaqueros, who were probably the same as the Querechos, Escanjaques; and Faraones, who reminded the Spaniards of the hordes of Pharaoh. The name "Apache" was first applied by Don Juan de Oñate, who visited them on the Canadian River in 1601.[75] By about 1700 these names disappear from the spanish documents and are replaced by what Newcomb calls a "confusing welter of names which often cannot be associated with later Apache peoples." The Querechos, however, are the probable forebears of the Lipan Apaches of later times, although the connection is "somewhat tenuous." The Faraones appear to be related to the well-known Mescalero Apaches.[76]

Before 1700, Apache raiders from east of the Rio Grande wreaked havoc among the Spanish settlements, and Pueblo Indians of New Mexico and

[72] George Parker Winship, "The Coronado Expedition, 1540-1542," *Fourteenth Annual Report of the Bureau of Ethnology*, Part I, p. 504.

[73] Ibid., pp. 507-508.

[74] Gunnerson, "The Southern Athabascans," pp. 346-363, is an elaborate analysis of the evidence identifying the Querechos and Teyas as Athapascans. See also Newcomb, *The Indians of Texas*, p. 105; Wedel, *Prehistoric Man on the Great Plains*, p. 289; and Albert H. Schroeder, "A Re-Analysis of the Routes of Coronado and Oñate into the Plains in 1541 and 1601," *Plains Anthropologist* 7 (February 1962): 7-9. Schroeder agrees that the Querechos were Apache, but thinks it probable that the Teyas were Caddoans. Schroeder makes the interesting suggestion, however, that the Teyas may have been direct descendants of the people of Antelope Creek Focus.

[75] Herbert Eugene Bolton, ed., "True Account of the Expedition of Oñate toward the East, 1601," in *Spanish Exploration in the Southwest, 1542-1706*, pp. 252-253.

[76] Newcomb, *The Indians of Texas*, pp. 105-107.

would appear to have been maintaining their hold upon the southern Plains. During the early decades of the eighteenth century the appearance of undisputed Apache domination remained, for Plains Apaches, especially the Faraones, continued to terrorize the Spanish frontier. Indeed, the Spaniards had good reason to be reminded of the hordes of Pharaoh. The days of Apache domination were numbered, however, and shortly forces far beyond their control and probably their comprehension combined to drive them from the southern Plains. In the first place, Apache raids into New Mexico brought retaliatory strikes from the Spanish that fell far short of conquest, but that undoubtedly weakened the Apaches. Second, during the first half of the eighteenth century, the Comanches invaded the southern Plains and proceeded to make war upon and to dispossess the Apaches. Third, the Wichitas, who lived to the east of the Apaches and were their enemies, acquired French equipment and, desiring Spanish horses, proceeded more boldly to prosecute war upon the Apaches. Thus the Apaches, confronted with enemies on all sides, were especially crushed between Spanish and Comanche power.

Some Apache bands were destroyed by their enemies while others retreated from the Plains and scattered over the southwest. The Jicarilla Apaches sought refuge among the Pueblos hoping—fruitlessly—for Spanish protection, were drastically reduced, and their remnants eventually acquired a Pueblo-type culture. Other Plains Apache groups, newly mounted on Spanish horses, retreated into Texas and Mexico and became the hated Lipan Apaches of more recent Texas history.[77] It is well known that even after having been driven from the Plains, the Apaches made plenty of trouble in Texas and Mexico, and in Arizona and New Mexico were among the very last of the American Indians to be pacified. The recorded history of the Plains Apaches, however, is a tale of cultural and tribal degradation. Newcomb goes straight to the essence of Apache history when he says, "From the proud and independent warriors Coronado met in the sixteenth century they became the skulking, beggarly riffraff of the Texas frontier."[78]

The Comanches who drove the Apaches from the Plains are of the Shoshonean linguistic family, which covered a geographical area exceeded only by those occupied by the Algonquin and Athapaskan families. The linguistic relatives of the Comanches include such tribes as the Hopis,

[77] Ibid., pp. 107-109.
[78] Ibid., p. 131.

Shoshonis, Bannocks, Utes, Snakes, and Crows. Because of the large area occupied by Shoshoneans and the environmental variations within their area, their culture varied considerably.[79] The Comanches, however, were the only purely Plains Indians among the Shoshonean peoples.[80]

Linguistic and cultural similarities indicate a close kinship between the Comanches and Northern Shoshones, and Comanche tradition indicates tribal origins somewhere north of the headwaters of the Arkansas River. Taken together, these factors suggest that the Comanches originated probably in the mountains of Colorado and Wyoming. Sometime in the seventeenth century the "proto-Comanches" made an acquaintance with horses, and by 1700 were in eastern Colorado and western Kansas. By 1750 the Comanches were in control of the South Plains.[81]

A combination of factors encouraged the Comanches to move toward the South Plains: Some animosity developed between the Comanches and the Shoshones and the two separated. This changed relationship with former friends does not necessarily imply a positive reason for the Comanches to have moved, but rather is more likely to mean that the Comanches lost incentive to remain in their original homeland. The more powerful Blackfeet and Crows, armed with French muskets, intruded upon the Comanches and put pressure upon them to move southward. Yet it is probably going too far to say that the Comanches were "driven" to the south against their will, for the history of the Comanches in Texas—if it is relevant to the point—surely indicates that the Comanches were not likely to be "driven" anywhere by anyone. Relative to the Blackfeet and Crows, therefore, the Comanches' movement southward would seem to be more of a territorial adjustment than an enforced evacuation. The Comanches were among the first Plains Indians to acquire horses, the value of which was readily apparent, and doubtless the chance of being closer to the source of supply counted heavily in the incentive to move southward. Finally, acquisition of the horse made a thoroughly buffalo-hunting economy not only possible, but a rich and highly attractive way of life for the Comanches. The buffalo-rich South Plains were consequently even more enticing.[82] On balance, the Comanche migration to the South Plains would seem to have been motivated by a simple fact: the South Plains

[79] Hodge, ed., *Handbook of American Indians*, Part II, p. 555.
[80] Ibid., Part I., p. 327.
[81] Newcomb, *The Indians of Texas*, pp. 156-157; Ernest Wallace and E. Adamson Hoebel, *The Comanches, Lords of the South Plains*, pp. 6-9.
[82] Wallace and Hoebel, *The Comanches*, pp. 9-11.

provided utmost attraction as a place to live. Having found the South Plains to their liking, the Comanches proceeded to dispossess the Apaches and make the land their own to be held against all challengers.

By 1836 the borders of Comanche territory were firmly established on the north at the Arkansas River; on the west from the headwaters of the Arkansas southward near Taos and Santa Fe; on the southwest by the Pecos River; on the southeast by the white settlements along the Balcones Escarpment; and on the east by the Cross Timbers, just west of the ninety-eighth meridian. This area, about four hundred miles wide and six hundred miles long, was Comanche domain.[83]

The Kiowas, who became the partners of the Comanches in the South Plains, are linguistically unique among the Indians of the area; they "speak a language related to Tanoan, and Tanoan-Kiowa appears to belong to the Uto-Aztekan family of languages." Other Tanoan-speaking Indians are Puebloans who live along the Rio Grande in New Mexico and who live closer to the Plains than other Puebloans. The Kiowas, however, are the only Plains people who speak Tanoan.[84]

Although Kiowa prehistory is largely unknown,[85] tribal tradition and legend place the tribe's origins near the sources of the Yellowstone and Missouri rivers in western Montana. While a mountain people, the Kiowas hunted small game with the bow and arrow, used domesticated dogs, knew nothing of the buffalo, and had a tribal association with the Sarsis. According to legend, a tribal dispute over the spoils of the hunt led to a parting of ways among the original group, and the victorious faction moved eastward out of the mountains into the Black Hills to become the historic Kiowas. The Kiowas shared the Black Hills with the Crows, with whom they intermarried to some degree and from whom Kiowas learned the ways of the Plains. By about 1765 the Kiowas had acquired horses, had learned the use of buffalo skin tepees, and had become, in short, Plains Indians. The Kiowa Apaches (who are historically associated with the Kiowas) moved eastward with the original Kiowa migration, the two tribes having always been associated and a single tribal group for practical purposes, except linguistically. When the Kiowas lived in the Black Hills, the Comanches lived to the south of them, and about 1775 the Dakotas drove the Kiowas and Comanches further south, the Kiowas coming to inhabit the area of the upper Arkansas River and pushing the Comanches

[83] Ibid., p. 12.
[84] Newcomb, *The Indians of Texas*, p. 194.
[85] Ibid.

south of the Arkansas. About 1790 the Kiowas and Comanches made peace with each other in New Mexico through an intermediary friendly to both tribes. This peace was not only permanent, but developed into something of an alliance between the Comanches, Kiowas, and Kiowa Apaches who, operating together, expropriated the South Plains.[86]

A considerable gap exists between Kiowa tradition and what is accepted among scholars. The Tanoan linguistic connection of the Kiowas suggests a southwestern origin of the tribe, but one must choose between the equally plausible possibilities that the Tanoan-speaking Puebloans were formerly nomads who took up a settled existence, or that the Kiowas were originally Puebloans who adopted a nomadic existence. While the presence of the Kiowas as far north as the Yellowstone may be demonstrated, it is doubtful that the Kiowas remained in the north for an appreciable length of time. About 1780 the Kiowas and their Kiowa Apache allies were in the Black Hills, but were driven out by the invading Dakotas and Cheyennes. They were ranging between the forks of the Platte River by the early nineteenth century and by 1832 had passed through eastern Colorado and were ranging along the Arkansas River. In their southward migration the Kiowas met the Comanches, and warfare of long duration ensued. But consistent with Kiowa tradition, peace was effected about 1790 and thereafter, the Comanches, Kiowas, and Kiowa Apaches functioned as close and effective allies.[87]

The Kiowa Apaches were Athapaskans who in the view of early scholars were never associated with any of the three Athapaskan divisions but were associated with the Kiowas before the legendary Kiowa migration southward.[88] This view, of course, coincides with Kiowa tradition. More recent scholarship inclines toward the view that the Kiowa Apaches were connected with one of the Athapaskan divisions. Newcomb plausibly suggests that the Kiowa Apaches were originally eastern or Plains Apaches who became separated from their relatives when the Comanches intruded into the South Plains. As an isolated and vulnerable group, an attachment to

[86] Mildred P. Mayhall, *The Kiowas*, pp. 6-14.
[87] The foregoing summary is extracted from Newcomb, *The Indians of Texas*, pp. 194-195, but see James H. Gunnerson and Dolores A. Gunnerson, "Apachean Culture: A Study in Unity and Diversity," in *Apachean Culture History and Ethnology*, ed. Keith H. Basso and Morris E. Opler (Anthropological Papers of the University of Arizona Number 21), p. 14, which differs in some details.
[88] Hodge, ed., *Handbook of American Indians*, Part I, pp. 109, 701; James Mooney, "Calendar History of the Kiowa Indians," *Seventeenth Annual Report of the Bureau of American Ethnology*, Part I, p. 247.

the more powerful Kiowas was effected, and thus the Kiowa Apaches achieved their historic identity. Since the Kiowas probably numbered no more than two thousand persons and the Kiowa Apaches even fewer, the alliance benefited both.[89] An alternate point of view contends that the Kiowa Apaches were the northernmost of the Southern Athapaskans and emerged onto the northern Plains and into history about 1700 under the name of Gattacka—a term that appears in French and Anglo, but not in Spanish, records. At about the same time the Kiowas and Kiowa Apaches became associated.[90] The impression that the Kiowa Apaches retained their Athapaskan tongue while becoming thoroughly confederated with the Kiowas appears to be well established and uncontroverted.

The pioneer American anthropologist, Clark Wissler, isolated eleven Indian tribes, including the Comanches, Kiowas, and Kiowa Apaches, as culturally typical Plains tribes and described their characteristics.[91] The Plains historian, Walter Prescott Webb, related the culture characteristics of the Plains Indians to environment, and elaborated their culture traits as defined by Wissler. According to Webb, the Plains Indians were (1) nomadic and nonagricultural, (2) dependent almost exclusively upon the buffalo for sustenance, (3) exceedingly warlike, (4) users of beasts of burden, (5) users of weapons peculiarly well adapted to warfare and hunting on horseback, and (6) users of a sign language developed from the need for friendly communication over long distances.[92]

As Webb sees them, these traits were the product of cultural adaptation to a stern environment, but were drastically enhanced by the Indians' acquisition of the horse. "Steam and electricity have not wrought a greater

---

[89] Newcomb, *The Indians of Texas*, pp. 108, 194.

[90] Gunnerson and Gunnerson, "Apachean Culture," in *Apache Culture History and Ethnology*, ed. Basso and Opler, p. 19. See also Charles S. Brant, "The Culture Position of the Kiowa Apache," *Southwestern Journal of Anthropology* 5 (Spring 1949): 56-61; and Brant, "Kiowa Apache Culture History: Some Further Observations," ibid., 9 (Summer 1953): 195-201.

[91] Clark Wissler, *The American Indian*, pp. 218-222.

[92] Walter Prescott Webb, *The Great Plains*, pp. 48-84. For elaboration of the culture traits of the Indians treated in this study, several works are pertinent. Clark Wissler, *North American Indians of the Plains*, and Robert H. Lowie, *Indians of the Plains*, apply to the whole plains culture area. Wallace and Hoebel, *The Comanches*, and Mayhall, *The Kiowas*, deal extensively with both the history and culture of their respective subject tribes. In connection with the Kiowas see also Mooney, "Calendar History of the Kiowa Indians," *Seventeenth Annual Report of the Bureau of Ethnology*, Part I, pp. 141-468, and H. Bailey Carroll, ed., *Gúadal P'a: The Journal of Lieutenant J. W. Abert from Bent's Fort to St. Louis in 1845*, pp. 65-67, 77. The Apaches are best treated in Newcomb, *The Indians of Texas*, pp. 103-131. Not di-

52 *The Texas Panhandle Frontier*

revolution in the ways of civilized life," says Webb, "than the horse did in the savage life of the Plains."[93]

On most points Webb's view of the culture of the Plains Indians appears to be quite valid in the light of recent anthropological investigation. Two points, however, merit clarification: the alleged exceptionally "warlike" character of the Plains Indians and the exact derivation of their cultural traits. That the Southern Plains tribes were worthy military opponents and the scourge of the southwestern frontier is implicit in Chapter 7 of this study. But recent scholarship simply does not sustain the notion that the Plains Indians were exceptionally fierce, warlike, and cruel.[94]

The second point in Webb's concept of Plains Indian culture that deserves further consideration is the matter of the precise relationship among environment, the horse, and culture traits. It is important to understand that the problem does not relate to culture patterns in historic times, but rather to what produced the culture in the first place. Sharply disputing Webb's view, Mildred P. Mayhall argues flatly that their was no Plains culture before horses arrived and that without them there would have been no such culture.[95] Waldo Wedel approaches the problem more cautiously, pointing out "that the final period of Plains Indian supremacy" derived from environment and the "historic accident" of the arrival of horses among the Plains Indians.[96] Still, assuming

---

rectly relevant to the early Apaches of the Panhandle but nevertheless helpful is Andree F. Sjoberg, "Lipan Apache Culture in Historical Perspective," *Southwestern Journal of Anthropology* 9 (Spring 1953): 76-98. The Apaches may be disqualified as purely Plains Indians because of their rather early departure to the periphery of the Plains and their partial reliance on an indifferent agriculture.

[93] Webb, *The Great Plains*, p. 53. It has been commonly believed that the first horses available to the Indians and the parent stock of the wild horse herds of North America were either lost or abandoned by early Spanish expeditions. Recently this view has been seriously challenged. See Frank Gilbert Roe, *The Indian and the Horse*, pp. 35-55.

[94] Newcomb, *The Indians of Texas*, p. 349, cites Webb's characterization as an example of "wild, unsubstantiated claims." Another authority, Harold E. Driver, *Indians of North America*, pp. 374-375, observes: "Most instances of torture on the Plains and Prairies seem to have been derived from the East in the historic period." Webb, of course, had nothing like the fine ethnological studies of recent years to work with and drew his conclusions largely from the works of Richard I. Dodge. A critical reading of Dodge's sensationalized treatment (which would have delighted William Randolph Hearst) indicates that the officer was more concerned with appeal to his Victorian readership than with accurate reporting. See, for example, Richard Irving Dodge, *Our Wild Indians: Thirty-three Years' Personal Experience Among the Red Men of the Great West*, pp. 523-541.

[95] Mayhall, *The Kiowas*, p. 285.

[96] Wedel, *Prehistoric Man on the Great Plains*, p. 291.

the availability of dogs as beasts of burden, Wedel believes that the pedestrian nomadism of the Querechos and Teyas might have existed all over the Plains for centuries before Coronado arrived in 1541.[97]

Since the Querechos and Teyas are the first aboriginal Plainsmen of whom there is historic record, they are crucial to the resolution of the problem of horses' relationship to historic Plains culture. Were these peoples new arrivals seeking an established culture to adopt? or was their culture mature and well established? Dolores A. Gunnerson, an exceptionally close student of Southern Athapaskan prehistory, observes: "The highly integrated life of the Teya-Querecho—growing out of the Plains environment and in turn adapted to it—almost qualified the High Plains east of the Pecos, in 1541, as a 'culture area.' For the material culture of the 'dog-nomads' was the forerunner of Plains 'horse culture' and, for the purposes of the Teyas and Querechos, it was probably as effective."[98] Mrs. Gunnerson's conclusions leave little doubt as to the maturity and stability of Plains culture as of 1541 and, all things considered, Webb's concept of historic Plains culture as a product of environment that was enhanced to a revolutionary degree by the addition of horses, would appear to be in no jeopardy.

With the flowering of the nomadic life of the historic Indians, the cultural history of aboriginal man in the South Plains had come full cycle. From very humble beginnings as pedestrian hunters of Pleistocene mammoths and bison, aboriginal man in the South Plains made his slow way to the agriculturally oriented Antelope Creek culture, and from thence moved into his period of greatest cultural development as the splendid, proud, mounted warrior and hunter of historic bison or buffalo. This culture flourished from early in the eighteenth century through much of the nineteenth only to be overwhelmed by the more numerous, better organized, and equally determined Anglo-Americans who were backed by a burgeoning industrial civilization.

[97] Ibid., pp. 302-303.
[98] Gunnerson, "The Southern Athabascans," p. 347.

# 3. The Spaniards

Not long after Christopher Columbus discovered the New World, the Spaniards established themselves in the West Indies and from there spread the tentacles of empire to the north and west. Florida and Mexico were soon known to them, and in 1519 Alonso Alvarez de Piñeda discovered and mapped the coast of Texas. While Piñeda explored the Texas coast, Cortés conquered the Aztecs and established the Spanish Empire in Mexico. Once secure in Mexico, the Spaniards began to push northward, inching their frontier toward the southwestern portion of what is now the United States. In time, rumors of the land farther to the north reached Spanish ears, largely through contacts with northern Indians. Learning that the Spaniards wanted to hear tales of riches in those lands, the Indians were accommodating.[1] It was, in fact, the yarns of an Indian slave, con-

[1] Herbert E. Bolton, *The Spanish Borderlands*, pp. 79-80. Most useful for the New Mexico background of this chapter are Hubert Howe Bancroft, *History of Arizona and New Mexico, 1530-1888*, and Ralph Emerson Twitchell, *The Leading Facts of New Mexico History*. Less thorough are Warren A. Beck, *New Mexico: A History of Four Centuries*, and Cleve Hallenbeck, *Land of the Conquistadores*. The best work from the Texas point of view is Carlos E. Castañeda, *Our Catholic Heritage in Texas*.

cocted for the delight of his master, which led Nuño de Guzmán, governor of Pánuco, Mexico, in 1530 to lead an expedition north seeking the Seven Cities, alleged by the slave to be rich in silver and gold. Although no riches were discovered, Guzmán founded Culiacán, the capital of Sinaloa; Compostela; and Guadalajara, the first city in New Galicia.[2]

Guzmán's apparent gullibility in taking seriously the tales of an Indian slave makes somewhat more sense in the light of a European legend of seven exotic New World cities made more credible by the possibly independent existence of a similar legend among the Indians of Mexico.[3] Besides, the immense wealth that the Spaniards had found among the Aztecs doubtless made it easy for them to infer that it was to be found elsewhere—especially since they wanted wealth so badly.

While the Guzmán adventure of 1530 did not find the Seven Cities, it did revive the legend, which was dramatically reinforced six years later when three Spaniards and a Negro slave appeared at Culiacán insisting that they were survivors of the Narvaez expedition lost eight years earlier.

The very formidable expedition of Pánfilo de Narvaez landed on the coast of Florida in April 1528. Plagued by continuing disaster, remnants of a once powerful force were eventually cast ashore upon an island off the Texas coast. Of these, only four, Andrés Dorantes de Carrança, his slave Estévan (or Estévancio), Captain Alonzo del Castillo Maldonado, and Álvar Núñez Cabeza de Vaca, were destined to reach civilization again. These survivors remained prisoner-slaves of the coastal Indians for six years, then escaped, made their way westward, and arrived among their countrymen in western Mexico in the spring of 1536.[4]

The Cabeza de Vaca route to Mexico evidently passed far to the south of the Texas Panhandle, but the fugitive's reports were to have vast implications for the region.[5] Cabeza de Vaca's narrative is quite cautious; he was

[2] Bolton, *The Spanish Borderlands*, pp. 79-80. Frederick W. Hodge, ed., "The Narrative of the Expedition of Coronado by Castañeda," in *Spanish Explorers in the Southern United States, 1528-1543*, ed. Hodge and Theodore H. Lewis, pp. 285-287. Guzmán's conquest of New Galicia was characterized by extreme barbarism.
[3] A. F. Bandelier, *The Guilded Man*, pp. 125-128.
[4] Hodge, ed., "The Narrative of Alvar Nuñez Cabeza de Vaca," in *Spanish Explorers, 1528-1543*, ed. Hodge and Lewis, pp. 12-126. Fanny Bandelier, trans., *The Journey of Alvar Nuñez Cabeza de Vaca and His Companions from Florida to the Pacific, 1528-1536*.
[5] For a summary of the findings of various students of the Cabeza de Vaca trail, see Cleve Hallenbeck, *Alvar Nuñez Cabeza de Vaca: The Journey and Route of the First European to Cross the Continent of North America, 1534-1536*, pp. 243-306, and pp. 103-241 for Hallenbeck's own study of the route. Morris Bishop, *The Odyssey of*

careful to distinguish between that which he had *seen* and that of which he had merely *heard*, and, as Hodge observes, "there is no blatant announcement of great mineral wealth."[6] Nevertheless, Cabeza de Vaca's story bestirred Spanish interest in the land to the north, directly inspired the Coronado expedition, and possibly influenced the De Soto expedition.[7]

More specifically, the legend of the Seven Cities would seem to have been made more real to the Spanish mind by the experiences of Cabeza de Vaca and his companions. Accordingly, the first Viceroy of New Spain, Don Antonio de Mendoza, laid careful plans for a reconnaissance to determine whether a full-scale expedition to find the Seven Cities was justified. A Franciscan, Friar Marcos de Niza, was selected to lead the reconnoitering party, and Estévan, now the property of Viceroy Mendoza, was order to serve as the friar's guide.[8] Traveling northward, Friar Marcos eventually reached the Cíbola region in 1539, but was unable actually to enter the Seven Cities because of the murder of Estévan by local Indians.[9] Friar Marcos did get near enough to the Seven Cities to examine them from a hilltop, apparently a discreet distance removed from the villages. Having thus observed the Seven Cities, Friar Marcos hastened homeward to file his report with the viceroy.[10] Friar Marcos' report caused great excitement among the citizens of New Spain, and potential explorers clamored for the commission to lead a full-scale expedition to open the new lands of which Friar Marcos reported.[11] Eventually the honor was conferred upon Francisco Vásquez de Coronado, governor of New Galicia.[12]

---

*Cabeza de Vaca*, is the best biographical study of Cabeza de Vaca. The best recent account of Cabeza de Vaca's adventures in the Southwest is Thomas F. McGann, "The Ordeal of Cabeza de Vaca," *American Heritage* 12 (December 1960): 32-37, 78-82.

[6] Hodge, ed., "The Narrative of Alvar Nuñez Cabeza de Vaca," in *Spanish Explorers, 1528-1543*, ed. Hodge and Lewis, p. 8.

[7] Ibid.

[8] George Parker Winship, "The Coronado Expedition, 1540-1542," *Fourteenth Annual Report of the Bureau of Ethnology*, Part I, pp. 354-355; cited hereafter as, Winship, "The Coronado Expedition." The legend of seven cities appears to have been vague until the time of Cabeza de Vaca. His reports seem to have given definite form to the concept of seven cities of great mineral wealth somewhere in the Southwest, and the reports of Friar Marcos de Niza appear definitely to have galvanized the idea of Seven Cities of Cíbola.

[9] Herbert Eugene Bolton, ed., *Spanish Exploration in the Southwest, 1542-1706*, p. 5, identifies the Seven Cities as the Zuñi pueblos. These pueblos were located in west central New Mexico.

[10] Winship, "The Coronado Expedition," pp. 361-367.

[11] Ibid., pp. 362-373.

[12] Ibid., p. 373.

Francisco Vásquez de Coronado, born at Salamanca in 1510, was apparently educated along the proper lines for a socially prominent young Spaniard. He came to New Spain with Don Antonio de Mendoza when De Mendoza assumed the viceroyalty. Coronado served De Mendoza ably and became something of a protégé of the viceroy, married well, rose quickly in the imperial hierarchy, and by 1540 was governor of New Galicia, New Spain's northwestern frontier province.[13] By temperament, training, and experience, Coronado would appear to have been an excellent choice to lead an expedition into the northern wilderness. The expedition itself, by the most reliable testimony, consisted of about 250 cavalrymen, seventy footmen, about one thousand Indians, and an abundance of supporting equipment, including livestock and light artillery.[14]

Coronado's army marched from Compostela on February 23, 1540, and arrived at Culiacán a little over a month later.[15] Since Culiacán was the last outpost of civilization, from that point the army seems to have dispensed with pomp and settled down to the serious business of campaigning in a hostile land. By July 1540, the Spaniards approached Zuñi—the Seven Cities of Cíbola—and by the seventh had attacked, conquered, and occupied the pueblos. Food—good food—badly needed by the army, was found in quantity, but there was no mineral wealth.[16]

Using Zuñi as a base of operations, the Spaniards turned their energies to exploration. During these explorations the Grand Canyon of the Colorado was discovered and the first Europeans made their way eastward toward the High Plains. Exploration eastward was led by Don Hernando de Alvarado, who reached Tiguex on the Rio Grande, near present Bernalillo, on September 7. Recognizing Tiguex as more desirable winter quarters than Zuñi, Alvarado recommended to his commander that the army winter there, and then moved eastward.[17]

Alvarado's expedition to the east was not a casual undertaking but a direct response to the appearance of an Indian chief at Cíbola whom, because of his conspicuous mustache, the Spaniards called Bigotes, "Whiskers." A man of friendly disposition, Bigotes exchanged gifts with Coronado, told of the "cows," and invited the Spaniard to visit his home-

[13] George P. Hammond and Agapito Rey, *Narratives of the Coronado Expedition 1540-1541*, pp. 1-3.
[14] Winship, "The Coronado Expedition," pp. 378-379.
[15] Ibid., pp. 382-384.
[16] Ibid., pp. 388-389.
[17] Ibid., pp. 389-391.

land. Accordingly, the captain-general commissioned Alvarado to lead an advance party of twenty men to explore to the east, giving him eighty days in which to execute the commission. Following Bigotes' lead, Alvarado reached the fortress-pueblo of Acoma in five days and Tiguex, where he was welcomed, three days later. He then proceeded to Bigotes' province, Cicuye, or Pecos. Alvarado's visit to Cicuye was to have fateful implications, for here the Spaniards made contact with the Indian slave called El Turko—the Turk—"because he looked like one." Taking the Turk as a guide, Alvarado traveled eastward along the Canadian River, according to Bolton, "nearly to the Texas Panhandle."[18] A few buffalo were seen, but Alvarado quickly lost interest in them because of the Turk's continuous stories of a populous land far to the east where gold and silver were commonplace. So mesmerized with the Turk's yarns did the Spaniard become that he turned back to report these alleged glories to his captain-general. Upon reaching Tiguex, Alvarado found that, pursuant to his recommendation, the army was establishing winter quarters there.[19]

Quivira! What visions of wealth that term must have inflamed in the Spanish imagination! Coronado, clearly under the spell of the Turk's description of Quivira,[20] set out to explore that exotic place, according to Coronado's own testimony, on April 23, 1541.[21] Traveling eastward, Coronado's army bridged a swollen stream, probably the Pecos, entered and crossed the Staked Plains where the Querechos and Teyas were encountered, and encamped in a "ravine" on the eastern edge of the Llano Estacado, probably Palo Duro Canyon. At this point the Spaniards reflected upon their circumstances and found them none too good. Provisions had dwindled alarmingly, and the Turk's story and directions seemed increasingly implausible. Coronado resolved therefore to send the bulk of his army back to the relative safety of Tiguex and, with only a picked force, to make a dash for Quivira. Reluctantly, the army turned back, and the captain-general found his Quivira—a series of squalid Indian villages—probably along the Arkansas River in central Kansas. The Turk admitted that he had lied and that his stories of wealth were designed to lure the Spaniards into the plains, where, he thought, they would surely perish, or

---

[18] Herbert E. Bolton, *Coronado: Knight of Pueblos and Plains*, p. 189. Bolton's location of Alvarado's trail along the Canadian seems entirely reasonable, and, as Bolton indicates, it is doubtful that Alvarado entered the Panhandle.
[19] Winship, "The Coronado Expedition," pp. 390-391, 490-492.
[20] Ibid., p. 493.
[21] Ibid., p. 580.

become so depleted that they could be easily conquered if they returned to the pueblos. The Turk was put to death, and Coronado, doubtless in disillusionment and the bitterness of failure, returned by a much more direct route to Tiguex.[22]

The impression that the Panhandle region, and especially the Llano Estacado, made upon the Spaniards, was profound indeed. These were not ordinary men, but were men of experience—urbane explorers. Pedro de Castañeda characterizes them as "the most brilliant company ever collected in the Indies to go in search of new lands."[23]

Those who left written records do not appear to have been particularly startled by the basic nature of these new lands, that is, by their semiarid, desert-like qualities. But with the vastness of the plains, their rank grass cover, the incredible flatness of the Llano Estacado, the absence of landmarks, the immensity of the buffalo herds, and Indians "who lived like

[22] Ibid., pp. 504-512. The route followed by Coronado on his thrust into the plains has been the subject of much investigation and much disagreement. Virtually all investigations place Coronado's outward trail at least in the vicinity of the Panhandle and south of the Canadian River. In addition to Winship, "The Coronado Expedition," see the following: Bolton, *Coronado*; David Donoghue, "The Route of the Coronado Expedition in Texas," *Southwestern Historical Quarterly* 32 (January 1929): 181-192; Hodge, ed., "The Narrative of the Expedition of Coronado by Castañeda," in *Spanish Explorers, 1528-1543*, ed. Hodge and Lewis, pp. 329ff.; W. C. Holden, "Coronado's Route across the Staked Plains," West Texas Historical Association *Yearbook* 20 (1944): 5ff.; Albert H. Schroeder, "A Re-Analysis of the Routes of Coronado and Oñate into the Plains in 1541 and 1601," *Plains Anthropologist* 7 (February 1962): 2-23, which argues Coronado passed through the Panhandle, but north of the Canadian River; Waldo R. Wedel, "Coronado's Route to Quivira 1541," *Plains Anthropologist* 15 (August 1970): 161-168, which refutes Schroeder's argument; and J. W. Williams, "Coronado: From the Rio Grande to the Concho," *Southwestern Historical Quarterly* 63 (October 1959): 190-220, which advances the interesting idea that the expedition crossed only the southwestern corner of the Panhandle, encamped probably in Quitaque Canyon, and turned southeast, terminating the journey southeast of Sterling City on the North Concho River. Donoghue is of the opinion that Coronado never went beyond the Panhandle, but found Quivira on the Canadian River in Hutchinson and Roberts counties. This view of the location of Quivira is flattering to the Panhandle, but the location of Quivira in Kansas is more plausible, as demonstrated by Bolton and Holden. Moreover, the archaeological evidence supports a Kansas location for Quivira. See Gordon R. Willey, *An Introduction to American Archaeology: North and Middle America*, p. 327; Waldo R. Wedel, *Prehistoric Man on the Great Plains*, pp. 104-107; and especially Waldo R. Wedel, "After Coronado in Quivira," *The Kansas Historical Quarterly* 34 (Winter 1968): 1-17.

[23] Winship, "The Coronado Expedition," p. 477. Interestingly, Castañeda goes on to observe, "But they were unfortunate in having a captain who left in New Spain estates and a pretty wife, a noble and excellent lady, which were not the least causes for what was to happen."

Arabs," the Spaniards were profoundly affected. While the Spaniards encamped in the canyon on the eastern edge of the Llano Estacado, a frightful hailstorm, apparently a new experience, occurred and injured horses, destroyed equipment, and battered bewildered men. The necessity to subsist on buffalo and the ease with which men who strayed from camp were lost must surely have challenged the mettle of the cavalier tradition.[24] So incredible did Castañeda regard the things he reported that, "I dare to write of them," he says, "because I am writing at a time when many men are still living who saw them and who will vouch for my account."[25]

Upon his return, Coronado went into winter quarters at Tiguex, apparently intending to visit Quivira again in the spring. The general was injured in a fall from a horse, however, and the serious injuries he sustained, coupled with other factors, caused him to lead his army homeward.[26] The explorer had nothing to report in terms of the expressed objectives of his mission, and one perceives a gloomy sense of failure in Coronado's own documents.[27]

After returning to Mexico, Coronado settled into the routine of an imperial official, experiencing the usual vicissituede of such a position. In time, he was beset by ill health that possibly derived from the riding accident at Tiguex in 1541. He died on September 22, 1554, at the age of only forty-four.[28]

Notwithstanding his failure to find wealth in Cíbola or Quivira, Coronado's achievements were truly great. The mere fact that he explored such a vast territory and got his men home to tell about it is, in itself, something of an achievement. This was done, moreover, with remarkably little loss of life among his command and its Indian allies. Finally, Coronado made significant contributions to Spain's eventual occupation of the Southwest and to Europe's knowledge of North American geography.[29]

One aspect of the Coronado expedition that remains to be noted is the story of Fray Juan de Padilla, four lay brothers, a few Negro slaves, and Andrés do Campo, a Portuguese soldier, who remained in New Mexico to seek converts among the Indians. Fray Luís de Escalona and a slave established themselves at Cicuye, the home of Bigotes—and were never heard

[24] Ibid., pp. 504-507, 526-528, 540-544.
[25] Ibid., pp. 541-542.
[26] Ibid., pp. 530-539.
[27] See Coronado's letter to his king, ibid., pp. 580-583.
[28] Bolton, *Coronado*, pp. 403-405.
[29] Ibid., pp. 395-401.

from again. Fray Padilla, do Campo, and others returned to Quivira because of the priest's conviction that missionary prospects among the Quivirans were good. Quite possibly, this party crossed the Texas Panhandle north of the Canadian River. Although Fray Padilla worked successfully for a short time, he was set upon by hostile Indians and murdered. Do Campo and two Indian lay brothers, Lucas and Sebastián, were later captured and made slaves. Do Campo individually, and Lucus and Sebastián together, eventually escaped and made their separate ways to Pánuco, where they reported the death of Fray Juan. The escape and flight of these fugitives are strongly reminiscent of the achievements of Cabeza de Vaca and his companions, and are hardly less spectacular.[30]

After Coronado's return to New Spain, Spanish interest in northern lands subsided and forty years elapsed before it was renewed. Those four decades did not find the Spaniards idle, however, and the course of imperial development was to bring Spaniards back to the Southwest. Explorers, missionaries, miners, cattlemen, and soldiers crept northward, gradually establishing new frontier outposts including Santa Bárbara at the head of the Conchos River, a tributary to the Rio Grande. Santa Bárbara was destined to be of especial significance to the American Southwest because it opened a new route, the Conchos River, to the area. About 1579 an Indian captive at Santa Bárbara told of a populous land to the north where the inhabitants wore cotton clothing and enjoyed bounteous supplies of food. This report fired the imagination of Fray Agustín Rodríguez, a Franciscan lay brother. Having secured permission from the viceroy, the friar organized an expedition of three friars, sixteen Indian servants, and nine soldiers commanded by Francisco Sánchez Chamuscado.[31]

The Rodríguez-Chamuscado party set out from Santa Bárbara on June 5, 1581, followed the Rio Conchos to the Rio Grande, then followed the Rio Grande upstream, eventually reaching Coronado's old headquarters near Bernalillo.[32] Subsequent exploration led the expedition eastward "because they wished to go find the cows." In the plains, buffalo were found, as was "a rancheria of naked Indians . . . going to kill cattle for their food." The Spaniards killed buffalo, jerked the meat, and returned to

[30] Ibid., pp. 336-340, 358-360; Winship, "The Coronado Expedition," pp. 400-401.
[31] Bolton, ed., *Spanish Exploration, 1542-1706*, pp. 137-138. The most comprehensive documentary treatment of Spanish activity in New Mexico after Coronado and before the conquest is George P. Hammond and Agapito Rey, *The Rediscovery of New Mexico, 1580-1594*.
[32] Bolton, ed., *Spanish Exploration, 1542-1706*, p. 138.

the pueblos.[33] Thereafter, the clerics remained among the pueblos while the soldiers returned to Nueva Vizcaya. Reports of the expedition excited the interest of the viceroy, who, with royal backing, began laying plans for permanent occupation of New Mexico.[34] Viceregal interest in colonizing New Mexico doubtlessly intensified through the fact that the friars remained among the Indians of the area, but while news that the missionaries had been slain removed some of the urgency from the program, it was far from sidetracked. The real reasons for it were far broader and more fundamental.

The wheels of colonial administration turned very slowly, however, and no official contract for the colonization of New Mexico was made until 1595. Meanwhile, individuals undertook to explore, and possibly to colonize, New Mexico upon their own initiative. Most notably, Antonio de Espejo, a wealthy Mexican citizen, and Fray Bernaldino Beltrán led an expedition in 1582, apparently in hopes of finding alive at least one of the friars who remained in New Mexico with Fray Rodríguez. The deaths of the friars were verified, however, and Espejo turned to exploration. Espejo's interest lay in the Rio Grande and Pecos River areas and in the land to the west, and he did not, therefore, play a direct role in Spanish exploration of the Panhandle region.[35] Espejo found rich ores in Arizona and was, in general, attracted by the prospects of New Mexico. He therefore entered the competition for the colonization contract and applied directly to his king.[36]

Among others who led unauthorized expeditions into New Mexico were Francisco Leyva de Bonilla and Antonio Gutiérrez de Humaña who about 1593 remained a year among the pueblos, and then explored eastward, perhaps crossing the Panhandle and continuing eastward, possibly as far as the Platte River. The expedition ended in tragedy, however, because the leaders quarreled and Humaña killed his colleague and later perished himself at the hands of Indians.[37] By the 1590's colonization of New Mexico,

[33] "Declaration of Pedro de Bustamante, 1582," in ibid., pp. 147-148. It is difficult to locate this eastward thrust other than to say that the Spaniards were east of the Pecos and in the High Plains. See Hammond and Rey, *The Rediscovery of New Mexico*, pp. 91-92.

[34] Bolton, ed., *Spanish Exploration, 1542-1706*, pp. 138-139.

[35] Ibid., pp. 163-166. Hammond and Rey, *The Rediscovery of New Mexico*, pp. 208-211, place Espejo in the area of present Pecos, Texas, and to the southwest of that point.

[36] "Letter of Espejo to the King, 1584," in Bolton, ed., *Spanish Exploration, 1542-1706*, p. 195.

[37] Ibid., pp. 200-201.

a project that had become bogged down in jealousy, intrigue, and administrative lethargy,[38] acquired a new urgency. The mythical Strait of Anian, it was rumored, had been found by the English pirate, Francis Drake, who had reputedly sailed home through the strait in 1579 after sacking Spanish ships in the Pacific. If the Englishman had in fact found the Strait of Anian and if the English occupied its shores, then Spain's position in the New World would be seriously jeopardized. Therefore, the colonization of New Mexico achieved a special urgency as a means to Spanish discovery and occupation of the Strait of Anian. Moreover, in 1588 the great Spanish Armada was destroyed and with it went Spain's domination of the seas. New Spain, consequently, became essential to Spain's security in the New World and the expansion of overseas dominions came to be regarded as a means of making good the loss of the Armada. It was no coincidence, therefore, that in 1595 contracts were issued for the conquest and colonization of both California and New Mexico. "The two expeditions," says Bolton, "indeed, were regarded as parts of the same enterprise."[39]

Juan de Oñate, awarded the contract for the conquest and colonization of New Mexico, and appointed governor, *adelantado*, and captain-general of the province, was a distinguished son of New Spain whose ancestors had participated significantly in the conquest. Political changes and harassment by his disappointed rivals delayed Oñate's departure until early in 1598, but on February 7 he led four hundred men, 130 of whom were accompanied by their families, toward New Mexico. The expedition was well equipped and was supported by eighty-three baggage carts and more than seven thousand head of livestock.

On April 30, at a point on the Rio Grande below El Paso, Oñate took formal possession of New Mexico in the name of his king. The Rio Grande was crossed at El Paso on May 5, thus establishing that strategic point in southwestern travel. By early fall of 1598, Oñate had established both political and religious authority in New Mexico, and the area thus became the northernmost province of New Spain.[40]

Having accomplished his immediate goal, Oñate turned to his secondary but scarcely less important objective, exploration. A preliminary expedition of sixty men led by Vicente de Saldivar Mendoca set out for the

---

[38] Ibid., pp. 199-200.
[39] Bolton, *Spanish Borderlands*, pp. 169-170.
[40] Bolton, ed., *Spanish Exploration, 1542-1706*, pp. 200-203. George P. Hammond and Agapito Rey, *Don Juan de Oñate: Colonizer of New Mexico, 1595-1628*, is the definitive collection of Oñate documents.

buffalo plains on September 15, 1599, and several days later reached the Rio de la Magdalene—the Canadian River.[41]

The apparent major purpose of Saldivar's expedition was to reach the main buffalo range, and, if possible, to capture specimens. Fifty-one leagues (125 to 140 miles) east of Pecos, buffalo were found in superabundance and Saldivar halted to capture them. A corral with long wings was built of cottonwood logs. So large was the corral, so great the number of buffalo in the vicinity, and so awkward the buffalos' appearance, that the Spaniards expected to capture ten thousand head with no trouble.[42] Apparently, it never occurred to Saldivar and his compatriots that their plan might not work—until they tried it! For several days every means that could be contrived was tried to get buffalo into the corral, but not one was captured. The enterprise must have been an exercise in sheer frustration for the Spaniards—and doubtless would have been a delightful comedy of errors to a detached observer had one been present. Efforts to capture calves were no more successful for, while they could be captured, they soon died either from their exertions while resisting or from the rough handling necessary to their capture. As hunters of buffalo the Spaniards were more successful. They collected over a ton of tallow, and found the meat of the buffalo much to their liking.[43]

While the buffalo of the Panhandle seem most to have impressed the Saldivar party, the Canadian River Valley was found to be very hospitable, and the Indians of the area were found to be living as they had been when Coronado visited them almost sixty years earlier.[44]

The exploration of Juan de Oñate across the Panhandle to Quivira, executed in the summer and fall of 1601, was a part of a much larger program of exploration carried out pursuant to the terms of Oñate's contract for colonization of New Mexico. More specifically, however, Quivira seems, in itself, to have had a strong fascination for Oñate, which was reinforced by the dream of Christianizing its people. Oñate led a party of seventy picked men who were backed by ample supplies, livestock, and four artillery pieces.[45]

After several days' journey from Galisteo, Oñate struck the Canadian

[41] "Account of the Discovery of the Buffalo, 1599," in *Spanish Exploration, 1542-1706*, ed. Bolton, pp. 223-224.
[42] Ibid., p. 227.
[43] Ibid., p. 228.
[44] Ibid., p. 230.
[45] "True Account of the Expedition of Oñate toward the East, 1601," in *Spanish Exploration, 1542-1706*, ed. Bolton, p. 251.

River at a point Bolton locates "just below the sharp turn to the east."[46]
As the explorers travelled eastward, the land became more hospitable,
water was easily found, and, once the plains were ascended, the trail
became easier. Fresh fish and wild fruits permitted the Spaniards to live,
apparently sumptuously, off the land. Buffalo were common and duly
impressive, as usual. Heavy rains slowed the march at one point and led
Oñate to the quaint observation that "such . . . are very common in those
plains." Indians, whom Oñate called "Apaches," were frequently encountered in considerable numbers, but the contact with them was entirely
amiable.[47]

Oñate appears to have turned northeast just west of Antelope Hills, or at
a point about on the one hundredth meridian, and proceeded onward to
Quivira, or in Bolton's estimate, to the site of Wichita, Kansas.[48]

With the conclusion of the Oñate exploration into the Panhandle, the
first phase of Spanish activity in the region ended. This initial phase,
exploration, had been highly successful in that Spanish explorers had been
able to go where they pleased, and their reports, taken together, contained
quite comprehensive, accurate descriptions of the region. Certainly any
subsequent Spaniards interested in the region had only to read their own
documents to find out what was there. As the initial phase of the Spaniards' activity in the Panhandle ended, their presence in New Mexico was,
for the time being, secure, and the Panhandle became the hinterland of
New Mexico. Thus was established the orientation of the Panhandle
toward New Mexico. The Spaniards, on the other hand, developed no
immediate interest in occupying the region and, as things turned out, never
was the Panhandle to be really important to the Spaniards except as it
related incidentally to some other objective. Had the Spaniards been inclined to occupy the Panhandle, however, the early eighteenth century was
the propitious time, because the indigenous Indians were not yet mounted.
But, even if there had been any Spanish interest in occupying the Panhandle at the opportune moment, it seems likely that it would have been
smothered by the glowing possibilities for trade and converts among the

[46] Ibid., p. 252, footnote 3.
[47] Ibid., pp. 251-255.
[48] Ibid., pp. 255-256. Hammond and Rey, *Don Juan de Oñate*, II, pp. 751-757
accepts Bolton's view, but the idea that Oñate reached central Kansas is disputed by
some. See Carlos E. Castañeda, *Our Catholic Heritage in Texas*, I, p. 194, which
contends that Oñate "could not have been beyond the northern Canadian in the
vicinity of Beaver County, Oklahoma." David Donoghue, "The Location of Quivira,"
*Panhandle-Plains Historical Review* 14 (1940): 46, agrees with Castañeda.

Jumanos of the San Angelo area. Until the great New Mexican Indian uprising in 1680, and the appearance of Frenchmen on the Texas coast five years later, Spanish activity in Texas was directed toward the Jumanos, and for a number of decades the objective that brought Spaniards into or near the Panhandle was the Jumanos of west-central Texas.

In July 1629, fifty representatives of the Jumanos appeared at old Isleta, near present Albuquerque, requesting that Christian missionaries be sent to baptize their people and to instruct them in matters relating to the Christian faith. The Jumanos had been converted, their emissaries claimed, by a beautiful woman dressed as a nun who had miraculously appeared among them, taught them, and exhorted them to seek Christian missionaries.[49] Subsequent investigation proved to Spanish satisfaction that Mother María de Jesús de Ágreda, abbess of a well-known convent in Spain, had been transported bodily, miraculously, and in "ecstasy" to New Mexico to instruct many tribes, including the Jumanos, in the Christian faith. These visits, which began in 1620, numbered in excess of five hundred.[50]

Fray Juan de Salas, Fray Diego López, and three soldiers accompanied the Jumano emissaries to their homeland. They crossed the plains and passed through Apache country along a course slightly south of east from Isleta and eventually reached, probably, the Middle Concho. The Spaniards were joyously received by the Jumanos and were visited by representatives from neighboring tribes who claimed also to have been visited by "the Woman in Blue" and requested missionaries. After a time the missionaries took leave of the Jumanos, but promised to return, and, so impressed were they with the opportunities for converts, to bring additional missionaries. Some of the Jumanos followed the fathers back to New Mexico, where San Isidoro Mission was established for them. By 1632 the neophytes had tired of mission life, however, and drifted back to Texas.[51] Father Salas returned to his Jumanos in 1632 and found them probably on the Concho River. Again they were friendly and seemed inclined toward Christianity. Father Salas remained only a short time apparently, but Fray Juan de

[49] Herbert E. Bolton, "The Spanish Occupation of Texas, 1519-1690," *Southwestern Historical Quarterly* 16 (July 1912), 8; Castañeda, *Our Catholic Heritage in Texas*, I, pp. 200-201.

[50] Charles Wilson Hackett, trans. and ed., *Pichardo's Treatise on the Limits of Louisiana and Texas*, II, pp. 463-499. See especially pp. 492-493. Castañeda, *Our Catholic Heritage in Texas*, I, pp. 195-200. It is implicit in the documents quoted in *Pichardo's Treatise* that the Spanish considered West Texas as a part of New Mexico and had no concept of West Texas as a part of the area to the east.

[51] Castañeda, *Our Catholic Heritage in Texas*, I, pp. 200-203.

Ortega remained among the Jumanos for six months before returning to New Mexico. Why he left and how he returned are not known, and there is no record of further Spanish contact with the Jumanos for another eighteen years.[52]

In fact, until 1650 there is record of only one *entrada*, and this one probably passed through the Panhandle north of the Canadian River and does not appear to have related to the Jumanos at all. In 1634 Captain Alonso de Vaca set out from Santa Fe and traveled three hundred leagues eastward until he reached a large river beyond which, he concluded, was Quivira. The captain turned back, however, and did not enter Quivira. Practically nothing appears to be known about the De Vaca journey or the reasons for it. Two possible motives are plausible, however: continuing Spanish curiosity about Quivira, and a desire to open contact between Santa Fe and Havana by way of the mouth of the Mississippi.[53]

Whatever may have been Spanish ambitions relative to Quivira or the Mississippi, they did not forget the Jumanos of the Concho country, and in 1650 contact with the Jumanos was renewed by Captains Hernán Martín and Diego del Castillo. Departing Santa Fe, this party, including soldiers and Christian Indians, traveled two hundred leagues to the "river of nuts [the Concho] where the nation of the Jumanos lived." Martín and Castillo stayed six months as guests of the Jumanos, found pearls of indifferent quality in the river, and explored about fifty leagues to the east and met the Tejas, who were found to be friendly.[54]

The pearls brought back by Martín and Castillo and the newly made contact with the Tejas excited considerable interest among the Spanish and encouraged further exploration of the Jumano country. Accordingly, in 1654 an expedition of thirty soldiers and two hundred Christian Indians led by Sergeant Major Diego de Guadalajara left Santa Fe for the Concho. Guadalajara remained for some time on the Concho, and sent an exploring party thirty leagues beyond the Jumano country, where a band of hostile Indians was defeated. Two hundred prisoners were taken and a rich supply of buffalo and deer skins was seized.

Fearing his force too small to explore further among hostile Indians, Guadalajara returned to Santa Fe, but his expedition along with that of

[52] Ibid., pp. 203-204.
[53] Bolton, ed., *Spanish Exploration, 1542-1706*, p. 313; Castañeda, *Our Catholic Heritage in Texas*, I, p. 204.
[54] Bolton, ed., *Spanish Exploration, 1542-1706*, p. 314; Castañeda, *Our Catholic Heritage in Texas*, I, pp. 204-206.

Martín and Castillo (both purely military in character) gave the Spaniards a clearer knowledge of the Tejas and of the Jumanos and their land.[55]

While there is no record of further Spanish contact with the Jumanos until 1683-1684, it is reasonable to believe that the Jumanos were visited regularly by Spanish parties for trade and friendship purposes, and that these visits were made with complete safety.[56] In a broader sense these expeditions are significant as indicators of Spanish excellence in exploration and of Spanish knowledge of West Texas and especially of the Llano Estacado. That this knowledge was rather complete is indicated by the fact that in order to cross the Llano Estacado, knowledge of fresh water holes was imperative—and the Spaniards crossed the Staked Plains at will.

Spanish contact with the Jumanos was disrupted by the pueblo revolt of 1680, but was reestablished in late 1683 when a baptized Jumano, Juan Sabeata, appeared at El Paso before the governor of New Mexico, Domingo Gironza Petris de Cruzate, and the Reverend Fray Nicholás López, *custodio* and ecclesiastical judge of New Mexico. Speaking for himself and several other chiefs, Sabeata requested Spanish trade, missionaries, and help against the Apaches. El Paso then became the point from which contact with the Jumanos was renewed, and as a consequence the La Junta area, which surrounds the confluence of the Rio Conchos and the Rio Grande, was developed as a center of missionary activity for local Jumanos and as a base of contact with the Jumanos of the San Angelo area. A new trail to the Jumano country, far south of the old trail from Santa Fe, was opened along the Rio Grande, the Pecos, Horsehead Crossing, and the Middle Concho.

In 1684 an expedition led by Father López and Captain Juan Domínguez de Mendoza reached the Jumano country. So promising did the possibilities appear that Father López and Captain Mendoza hastened to Mexico City to enlist the aid of the viceroy in establishing Spanish authority and colonies among the Jumanos.[57] The dreams of Father López for a great missionary effort among his Jumano friends were not to be realized, although it is likely that they would have been except for the appearance of the French on the Texas coast. But when word reached Spanish authorities of the activities of Robert Cavelier, Sieur de La Salle, they turned

[55] Bolton, ed., *Spanish Exploration, 1542-1706*, p. 314; Castañeda, *Our Catholic Heritage in Texas*, I, pp. 206-207.

[56] Bolton, ed., *Spanish Exploration, 1542-1706*, p. 314.

[57] Bolton, ed., *Spanish Exploration, 1542-1706*, pp. 314-318; Castañeda, *Our Catholic Heritage in Texas*, II, pp. 312-328.

eastward and bent their not inconsiderable efforts first to driving La Salle away—a feat that harsh fate accomplished for them—and then to establishing missions among the Tejas of East Texas so as to enforce Spanish territorial claims with the fact of occupation.

The revolt of the New Mexican Indians in 1680, which forced the Spanish population to retreat to the El Paso region, not only forced a shift in the approach to the Jumanos but obviously terminated for the time being Spanish activity in the Panhandle region. The reconquest of New Mexico was begun in 1692 by Governor Diego de Vargas, and was carried out initially with amazingly little bloodshed. Continued resistance to Spanish authority led to bloody campaigns against the Indians, however, and not until 1698 was the province entirely secured.[58] Completion of the reconquest, approximately coinciding as it did with the beginning of the eighteenth century, marks the arrival of both change and a certain definiteness in the New Mexico-Texas Panhandle relationship. While the relationship emerged over many years, its more or less permanent character comes into historical focus about 1700 and resolves into an odd dichotomy of beneficial commerce on the one hand and vicious warfare on the other.

Trade between the Plains nomads and the river valley Puebloans predates European intrusion by countless years and the arrival of Spaniards simply enlarged that commerce.[59] By 1700 Spanish commercial ties with the Panhandle were strong, but their opportunities for a physical grip on the region were rapidly slipping away. Theretofore the Spaniards had entered the region at will: they could come, go, do as they pleased, or ignore the region as they were wont. By approximately 1700, however, in addition to commercial benefits, the Panhandle implied active hostility toward New Mexico with which the Spaniards had to contend. This hostility arose from

[58] The most basic documentary work relative to the pueblo revolt is Charles Wilson Hackett and Charmian Clair Shelby, *Revolt of the Pueblo Indians of New Mexico and Otermín's Attempted Reconquest 1680-1682*. The revolt and reconquest are treated in the following secondary works: Bancroft, *History of Arizona and New Mexico, 1530-1888*, pp. 174-223; Beck, *New Mexico*, pp. 73-89; Herbert Eugene Bolton, *The Spanish Borderlands*, pp. 178-181; Charles Wilson Hackett, "The Revolt of the Pueblo Indians of New Mexico in 1680," *Quarterly of the Texas State Historical Association* 15 (October 1911): 13-147; Hallenbeck, *Land of the Conquistadores*, pp. 142-185; Twitchell, *The Leading Facts of New Mexican History*, I, pp. 354-413. In connection with the Spanish retreat to, and the origins of, El Paso see Charles Wilson Hackett, "Retreat of the Spaniards from New Mexico in 1680, and the Beginnings of El Paso, I," *Southwestern Historical Quarterly* 16 (October 1912): 137-168, continued in ibid., 16 (January 1913): 259-276.

[59] For an extended treatment of this commerce to 1700, see Charles L. Kenner, *A History of New Mexican-Plains Indian Relations*, pp. 3-22

two threats, each far larger than the Panhandle itself. These were, one, French intrusion into Spanish territory from the north and east, and two, the raids of hostile Indians upon the settlements and pueblos in New Mexico for which the Panhandle was one important breeding ground. These two problems were not unrelated to each other, and New Mexico had to absorb their combined force to protect the northern provinces of Coahuila, Chihuahua, and Sonora.[60]

While the eighteenth century appears to have been the period of greatest Spanish concern with French intrusion and Indian raiding, the seventeenth portended both, since documentary evidence indicates Apache raids upon the converted Pueblo Indians before 1639. At this time, however, the Spaniards appear to have been able to cope satisfactorily with the situation.[61] After the lapse of another thirty years, the Apache problem was more difficult, as shown by the following: "In the year 1672, the hostile Apaches who were then at peace rebelled and rose up, and the said province [New Mexico] was totally sacked and robbed by their attacks and outrages, especially of all the cattle and sheep. They killed, stole, and carried off all except a few small flocks of sheep which were saved by the vigilance and care of some of the inhabitants."[62]

Similarly, as early as the 1680's the Spaniards found indications of French intrusion in the West Texas area. In 1684 the Mendoza-López expedition discovered a French flag in possession of Indians on the Pecos River.[63] This flag, in Castañeda's view, proved "that French traders had been as far as the Pecos by 1684, or that the Indians of this region traded with the French to the east either directly or through other tribes."[64] Father López, either taking seriously the presence of the French flag or realizing that he had a telling point in support of Spanish colonization in

[60] Hallenbeck, *Land of the Conquistadores*, p. 195.

[61] Petition [of Francisco Martínez de Baeza. Mexico, February 12, 1639], in Adolph F. A. and Fanny R. Bandelier, *Historical Documents Relating to New Mexico, Nueva Vizcaya, and Approaches Thereto, to 1773*, trans. and ed. Charles Wilson Hackett, III, p. 119, hereinafter cited as Hackett, ed., *Historical Documents Relating to New Mexico*.

[62] Petition [of Fray Francisco de Ayeta. Mexico, May 10, 1679], ibid., p. 302.

[63] "Itinerary of Juan Domínguez de Mendoza, 1684," in Bolton, ed., *Spanish Exploration, 1542-1706*, p. 330.

[64] Castañeda, *Our Catholic Heritage in Texas*, II, p. 321. Although it seems improbable that French traders reached the Pecos in the 1680's, indirect contact with Indians that far west is entirely plausible.

the Jumano country, invoked the threat of French intrusion in his pleas to the viceroy.[65]

By 1700, then, there was indication of the troubles that the eighteenth century would bring to Spanish New Mexico. The Spaniards could not anticipate the extent of these troubles, nor could they have anticipated a new factor that was to add immeasurably to their miseries: the arrival from the north of the Comanches, hitherto unknown in New Mexico. Thereafter, the Comanches were entirely too well known in New Mexico, for they soon appropriated the South Plains, including the Texas Panhandle.[66]

Officially, of course, raiding could not be condoned—but neither could it be entirely stopped and trade was important. So as an informal but conscious "policy," the Spaniards, somewhat akin to the barkeeper who recognized his patrons' right occasionally to shoot up the saloon, appear to have accepted a certain amount of plunder, destruction of life and property, and kidnapping as a condition of the trade relationship. This is not to imply, obviously, that they made no attempt at defense and Spanish efforts to protect their settlements against Indian raids, and French ingress occasionally led them into the Panhandle. Similarly, French attempts to establish trade with New Mexico led them through the Panhandle on isolated occasions.

The first known Spanish campaign against Apaches—Faraones in this case—was undertaken in July 1702 by Governor Pedro Rodríguez Cuberó. Cuberó campaigned southeast of Santa Fe with success,[67] but information on the campaign is scanty, and only by inference may it be located in the Panhandle. The inference is not unreasonable, however, because it is well known that the Panhandle was a Faraone stronghold.

The degree of Governor Cuberó's success is not ascertainable, but it was not so great as to halt Faraone raids for long, and although other Spanish campaigns were launched against them after 1702, their raiding into New Mexico continued. In the spring of 1715 an especially audacious Faraone attack upon the Picuríes and Taos pueblos brought more determined,

---

[65] Letter of Fray Nicholas López to the viceroy [1686] in Hackett, ed., *Historical Documents Relating to New Mexico*, III, p. 362.

[66] Alfred Barnaby Thomas, trans. and ed., *After Coronado: Spanish Exploration Northeast of New Mexico, 1696-1727*, p. 26. Ernest Wallace and E. Adamson Hoebel, *The Comanches: Lords of the South Plains*, pp. 6-9.

[67] Thomas, ed., *After Coronado*, pp. 14, 23.

although not necessarily more effective, Spanish retaliation. Two expeditions campaigned east of Santa Fe with no results. The second of these was led by General Don Juan Paez Hurtado, who shortly thereafter embarked on a third and more ambitious campaign to the east.[68]

A council of war met on July 23, 1715, at Santa Fe and after apparently extensive investigation agreed that an offensive against the Faraones was necessary because of their deviltry among the pueblos. September was the choice time for the campaign because pasturage would be good and, hopefully, the Indians could be caught unaware in their *rancherías* to which they presumably would have returned to harvest their maize crops sown the previous April.[69] Hurtado led a command of soldiers, settlers, and pueblo Indians that aggregated 237 men supported by 275 horses and mules.[70]

On August 30, 1715, Hurtado set out from Picuríes pueblo and traveled eastward, reaching Rio Colorado (the Canadian) on September 5. The Spaniards proceeded along the Canadian and in all likelihood penetrated well into the Panhandle. Much evidence of the recent departure of the Faraones was found—but no Faraones. "I presume," wrote Hurtado, "that . . . they had had news that the Spaniards were to set out in search of them." Considering the absence of the Faraones and his diminishing supplies, Hurtado resolved to return to report to his governor. This the officer did, without having fired a single angry shot.[71]

By 1717 Comanche raids upon the New Mexican settlements appear to have become constant and very severe. Many children appear to have been carried away into captivity. Smarting under these attacks, the Spaniards, according to tradition, prepared a campaign that met with unusual success.

According to legend, Don Juan de Padilla and Don Carlos Fernández, both aggressive soldiers and proven Indian fighters, and Don Pedro Pino led the expedition into the Llano Estacado by way of Anton Chico. While the main force was camped in a "beautiful valley," scouts reported the presence of a large encampment of Comanches a few leagues ahead. Marching at night so as to be ready for a dawn attack, and letting their long hair hang freely and painting their faces red so as to look like Indians,

[68] Ibid., p. 23. Hallenbeck, *Land of the Conquistadores*, pp. 204-206.
[69] Council of War, July 23, 1715, in Thomas, ed., *After Coronado*, pp. 84-85.
[70] Ibid., editorial note 35, p. 266.
[71] "Diary of the Campaign of Juan Paez Hurtado against the Faraone Apache, 1715" in Thomas, ed., *After Coronado*, pp. 94-98. Thomas places the point at which Hurtado turned back as "some distance north of the present town of Amarillo, Texas." See editorial note 43, p. 266.

the Spaniards approached a Comanche camp of "hundreds of tepees." Charging to the war-cry of "Santiago," the attacking Spaniards caught the enemy entirely by surprise and were apparently taken at first for a returning war party. In the ensuing battle hundreds of Comanches were slain, seven hundred were taken prisoner, and most captives from the Spanish settlements were found and liberated.[72]

At most, the legend of the Padilla-Fernandez expedition may indicate increasing Spanish concern with the Comanche problem. About the same time (the second decade of the eighteenth century) the French threat to New Mexico increased. French interest in New Mexico—"this Promised Land," as Bolton says they thought of it—was based on the belief that the province was rich in gold and silver (a serious misapprehension), and a desire to tap a rich trade and get quicker access to the Pacific Ocean. Two obstacles blocked French contact with New Mexico: (1) exclusive Spanish trade policies and (2) Indian tribes that stood between the westernmost French settlements and Spanish territory. In the French view the natural approaches to New Mexico were the Missouri River (thought to rise in the Southwest) and the Arkansas River, both blocked by the Comanches, and Red River, blocked by the Apaches. Actually, the problem of passage was not so much with the Plains tribes, but with their eastern neighbors who were unenthusiastic about the prospect of traders placing French weapons in the hands of their Plains enemies. The French, therefore, sought to make peace among the Indian tribes. Accordingly, French outposts were established on the Red, South Canadian, and Arkansas rivers in 1718 and 1719. These French posts, clearly in territory claimed by Spain, were much nearer to New Mexico than any previous ones.[73] Establishment of these outposts was a part of a larger picture of French activity in southern Louisiana and along the eastern border of Texas, while Spanish colonization of East Texas was in large part stimulated by the French presence in the area. In order to strengthen the ties between San Juan Bautista, the Spanish outpost on the Rio Grande near Eagle Pass, and East Texas, a new Spanish settlement was established at San Pedro Springs on the San Antonio River in 1718.[74]

[72] The foregoing account is taken from Twitchell, *The Leading Facts of New Mexico History*, I, p. 431, footnote 439. Twitchell reports this incident as "tradition." Hallenbeck, *Land of the Conquistadores*, p. 207, reports as much of the story as has been related above as fact, but without documentation. More recent scholarship concludes that the incident never occurred. See Kenner, *New Mexican-Plains Indian Relations*, p. 29, especially footnote 26.

[73] Herbert E. Bolton, "French Intrusions into New Mexico, 1749-1752," in *Bolton and the Spanish Borderlands*, ed. John Francis Bannon, pp. 150-151.

[74] Bolton, *The Spanish Borderlands*, pp. 225-226.

In the next year, 1719, the French attacked the East Texas Spanish missions in the comic opera Chicken War and aroused Spanish fears for the security of their whole northern frontier. Captain Diego Ramón, from Texas, wrote to Governor Antonio de Valverde of New Mexico warning him that a French attack on the governor's province was imminent.[75] Actually, Governor Valverde needed no warning that the French threatened his province. While campaigning against the Comanches—whom he did not find—in the fall of 1719, Valverde met a Poloma (Apache) on the Napestle River (the Arkansas) who bore a gunshot wound suffered in battle. When questioned, the Indian described being attacked by French, Pawnees, and Jumanos and told Valverde of French towns among the enemies of the Apaches whom the French supplied generously with firearms.[76]

The disaster of the Chicken War in the east and the discoveries of Valverde in the west combined to impress deeply upon the Spaniards that counteraction was essential to protect their interests against the French. Their eastern countermeasures, the brilliant and highly successful work of the Marquis de San Migual de Aguayo, were not destined to be matched in the west. A carefully planned, well-equipped, and expertly manned expedition led by Colonel Don Pedro de Villasur left Santa Fe in midsummer 1720, heading for the Jesús María River (which Thomas identifies as the South Platte), where the French were thought to be located. The river was reached on August 6, with no sign of the French. Crossing the Jesús María, Villasur led his command to the San Lorenzo River (the North Platte), crossed it, and shortly found a large village of Pawnees. Unable to obtain peaceful contacts or to discover anything about the presence of Frenchmen, Villasur fell back across the San Lorenzo and made camp. The Spanish camp was attacked at dawn the next day with calamitous results. Only a handful of Spaniards and forty-eight of their Indian allies managed to escape and eventually to report their tale of catastrophe and death to Sante Fe.[77]

[75] Castañeda, *Our Catholic Heritage in Texas*, II, pp. 330-331.
[76] Thomas, ed., *After Coronado*, pp. 26-33, 110-133. Thomas believes that Valverde's route to the Arkansas lay well to the northwest of the Texas Panhandle. The Chicken War occurred in June 1719, when M. Blondel, commander of French forces at Natchitoches, Louisiana, by order of his governor, Celeron de Bienville, hurled an army of seven men against the Spanish mission of San Miguel de Linares de los Adaes (near present Robeline, Louisiana). The French invaders captured a lay brother, one soldier, and the mission chickens, which reputedly fought valorously to uphold the honor of Spanish arms.
[77] Ibid., pp. 33-39, 133-137. Thomas places the site of Villasur's defeat near the present North Platte, Nebraska (see editorial note 152, p. 278), and believes that

The destruction of Villasur's command left New Mexico's defenses sorely depleted and even more exposed, as Governor Valverde reported to the viceroy, to the incursions of the "great number of heathen, the Utes, Comanches, and Apache tribes of Faraones, [who] invade the kingdom with death and robbery."[78]

As part of their countermeasures against the French, the Spanish attempted to make peace with the Apaches. A major objective of the Aguayo program in East Texas was to make friends with the Apaches and to persuade them to come to the missions. Aguayo failed in this objective and was frequently harassed by the Apaches, but felt that the presidio at Los Adaes would prevent a French alliance with the Apaches. In August 1723, however, Apache raiders, under cover of a dark, stormy night, raided the San Antonio presidio and captured eighty horses. Captain Nicolás Flores y Valdez, commander of the presidio, pursued the raiders and finally attacked and defeated them, probably near the present city of Brownwood, on September 24. Stolen horses were recovered, and twenty women and children captives and much plunder were taken. Interrogation of a prisoner squaw revealed that the Apaches raided San Antonio to get items—especially horses and captives—for trade with other Spaniards "far to the north." In other words, the Apaches had learned shrewdly to play San Antonio and Santa Fe against each other. Captain Flores now undertook to use his Apache prisoners as a bargaining point with which to effect peace with the Apaches. These efforts failed, and no peace was secured.[79]

The general pattern of Spanish relationship to the Panhandle region that was established by 1700 and solidified during the next three decades remained essentially intact for as long as Spain retained her empire in the southwestern United States. The details vary, and, in addition to the Indian and French threats, those of the English and Americans were eventually added.

As the eighteenth century progressed, the Indian problem, at least in the

---

Villasur's outward route was approximately that followed by Valverde in 1719. Castañeda, *Our Catholic Heritage in Texas*, II, p. 332, says, on the other hand, "the expedition to the Panamas, undertaken in 1720, passed through a portion of North Texas, at least, being one of the first to traverse the region of the Panhandle in the vicinity of Amarillo. But more significant than this fact is the possibility that Jesús María may be either the present day Red River or the Arkansas." Hackett, ed., *Pichardo's Treatise*, I, pp. 186-213, contains extensive documents relating to the Villasur disaster.

[78] Valverde to Valero, Santa Fe, October 8, 1720, in *After Coronado*, ed. Thomas, p. 166.

[79] Castañeda, *Our Catholic Heritage in Texas*, II, pp. 189-201.

eastern New Mexico area, lay increasingly with the Comanches. There were occasional periods of peace, but they were inevitably terminated by renewed hostilities. Periodic campaigns against the Comanches occasionally resulted in considerable military success, but it is very difficult to locate any of these definitely in the Panhandle. The French continued to trade with the Indians and to try to establish trade contacts with the Santa Fe area. In general, the French continued to regard the Arkansas and Missouri rivers as the preferable routes to Santa Fe. Only occasionally did some French *voyageur* cross the Panhandle along the Canadian River as did Paul and Pierre Mallet, who first appeared at Santa Fe in 1739.

In 1754 the North American colonies of England and France began the French and Indian War, which initiated a chain of events destined to alter drastically the imperial structures of North America. Spain joined that conflict on the side of France in 1761, and, in the peace settlements that followed the English victory, acquired title to Louisiana. England, on the other hand, acquired French Canada and Spanish Florida. France thus was eliminated as a colonial power on the continent. The cession of Louisiana to Spain resulted in no mass exodus of Frenchmen; rather, they gave their allegiance to Spain and many of them served Spain loyally and ably. Spanish authorities did not always find it easy to trust Frenchmen, however, and in some instances their suspicions doubtless had justification. The transfer of Louisiana to Spain, however, introduced a new threat to New Mexico because English territory now lay adjacent to that of Spain. English activities relative to New Mexico, much like those of France, came largely from the upper Mississippi Valley and Canada and therefore passed to the north of the Texas Panhandle.

The territorial alignments in North America effected in 1763 were drastically altered twenty years later when the Treaty of Paris of 1783, which formally terminated the United States' War for Independence, recognized the Mississippi River as the western boundary of the United States—much to the annoyance of America's European allies. Although England did not vacate her outposts south of the Great Lakes for a number of years, Spain's eastern neighbor was now the United States, and the problem of English ambitions was complicated by the Americans whose territory now extended to the Mississippi and of whose restlessness the Spaniards were acutely aware. If the American presence on the Mississippi was a thorn in the Spanish side, salt was rubbed into the wound in 1803 when Napoleon Bonaparte, having forced Spain to re-cede Louisiana to France in 1800, sold the entire province to the United States. The boundary provisions of the Louisiana Purchase Treaty were so vague as to be almost nonexistent, and almost immediately American actions reinforced Spanish fears of American intentions.

Regardless of their real motives and regardless of the role of the United States government in them—or the lack of a role—such occurrences as the Lewis and Clark expedition, the Pike expedition, and the activities of filibusters such as Philip Nolan caused the Spanish to be greatly fearful of American territorial covetousness of, and possible violence toward, their land.

Spanish efforts to adjust to and to protect their interests in the face of the rapid changes that occurred after 1754 were made with a decaying, corrupt, unbelievably inept administrative system. Nevertheless, the last activities of the Spaniards in the Texas Panhandle occurred in connection with these efforts. These terminal activities were in the area of exploration and were, in general, intended to open direct communication between Santa Fe and San Antonio and various points in Louisiana.[80] Although differences can be seen between latter-day Spanish explorations and those of the sixteenth century, it may still be said that the Spaniards left the Panhandle region as they had entered it nearly three centuries earlier: as successful explorers.

In 1786 the first of a series of expeditions designed to establish direct routes between San Antonio and Santa Fe was undertaken by Pedro Vial. A Frenchman by birth, Vial's life before 1786 is obscure, but it is apparent that he had lived and practiced his gunsmithing trade among the Indians

[80] The best summary of the imperial relationships discussed in the foregoing paragraphs is Noel M. Loomis and Abraham P. Nasatir, *Pedro Vial and the Roads to Santa Fe*, which, because of the documents included, is also fundamental to the remainder of this chapter. The maps must be used cautiously, however, because they consistently err in identifying all important stream courses. Interested readers not familiar with West Texas-New Mexico geography should trace the routes given by Loomis and Nasatir against contemporary maps. The Indian problems are best covered in the works of Alfred Barnaby Thomas, trans. and ed., *After Coronado; Forgotten Frontiers: A Study of the Spanish Indian Policy of Don Juan Bautista de Anza, 1777-1787*; *Teodoro de Croix and the Northern Frontier of New Spain, 1776-1783*; and *The Plains Indians and New Mexico, 1751-1778*, which include both summary texts and documents. Many pertinent documents are to be found in *Historical Documents Relating to New Mexico* and *Pichardo's Treatise*, ed. Hackett. Generally pertinent are the works of Herbert Eugene Bolton, "French Intrusions into New Mexico, 1749-1752," in *Bolton and the Spanish Borderlands*, ed. Bannon, pp. 150-171; *Athanase de Mézières and the Louisiana-Texas Frontier, 1768-1780*; *Texas in the Middle Eighteenth Century*; *The Spanish Borderlands*; Castañeda, *Our Catholic Heritage in Texas*, IV and V; and Henry Folmer, *Franco-Spanish Rivalry in North America, 1524-1763*.

before he offered his services to Spanish authorities at San Antonio to explore a route to Santa Fe. The Frenchman in Spanish service left San Antonio on October 4, 1786, according to his journal, with one companion and one packhorse.[81]

Traveling northward from San Antonio, Vial wove a snake's-back trail to the Taovaya villages on the Red River, and then followed the Red westward. Near, or just west of, the one hundredth meridian Vial appears to have veered toward the northwest so as to reach the divide between the Red and Canadian watersheds and to have traveled toward Santa Fe along the southern tributaries of the Canadian River, thus avoiding the rough country of the High Plains Escarpment and of the Canadian River Valley. Vial entered Santa Fe on May 26, 1787—seven and one-half months after leaving San Antonio.[82]

Pedro Vial, so far as is known, was the first man to travel from Bexar to Santa Fe by way of the Texas Panhandle, and though his route was circuitous, especially in the lower part, he proved that such a route was feasible. Promptly, a retired corporal, José Mares, left Santa Fe for Bexar in an effort to shorten the trail blazed by Vial.

Mares, accompanied by two other men, left Santa Fe on July 31 and headed straight for the Llano Estacado, which he crossed, apparently along Tierra Blanca Creek, and emerged at Tule Canyon on the eastern side. Descending the High Plains Escarpment, Mares continued toward the southeast for a time and then swung back toward the Taovaya villages, which were visited. From the Taovaya villages, Mares continued to San Antonio.[83]

Mares remained in San Antonio until January 18, 1788, when he set out

---

[81] Loomis and Nasatir, *Pedro Vial*, pp. 264-268. Among the extant copies of the journals of Pedro Vial, José Mares, and Francisco Amangual there is more or less variation, probably because of copyists' errors. Loomis and Nasatir have published collations of the various versions. The locations of the trails, as reported in this study, are the estimates of Loomis and Nasatir and are tentatively accepted as accurate.

[82] "Diary of Pedro Vial, Bexar to Santa Fe, October 4, 1786, to May 26, 1787," in ibid., pp. 268-285; pp. 282-284 pertain to Vial's route across the Panhandle. The Taovaya villages that figured so prominently in the explorations of Vial and Mares were located on the Red River near present Spanish Fort, Montague County, Texas. See also Castañeda, *Our Catholic Heritage in Texas*, V, pp. 150-155.

[83] "Journal of José Mares, Santa Fe to Bexar, July 31 to October 8, 1787," in Loomis and Nasatir, *Pedro Vial*, pp. 289-302; pp. 290-295 contain the account of travel through the Panhandle. See also Castañeda, *Our Catholic Heritage in Texas*, V, pp. 155-158.

on the return journey to Santa Fe. Avoiding the Taovaya villages, Mares took a much more direct route and approaching the Panhandle from the southeast, apparently crossed the region over much the same trail he had followed the previous fall.[84]

With a direct route between San Antonio and Santa Fe established, it remained to establish direct communication between Santa Fe and Natchitoches. Not surprisingly, Pedro Vial was chosen to blaze that trail. Three cavalrymen were assigned to escort Vial as far as the Taovaya villages and were commanded by Santiago Fernández, who was also appointed to keep the diary for that segment of the journey. Francisco Xavier Fragoso was designated to keep a diary of the entire trip. Three New Mexicans completed the party.[85] Vial entered the Panhandle south of the Canadian River, descended Palo Duro Canyon, followed Prairie Dog Town Fork of Red River to the main Red, and proceeded on to the Taovaya villages. On his return journey to Santa Fe, Fernández crossed the Panhandle by essentially the same route.[86] Vial continued on to Natchitoches, thence back southwest to San Antonio, and finally in August 1789, approached the Panhandle, which he evidently crossed along Tierra Blanca Creek and arrived at Santa Fe on August 20.[87]

In 1792 Vial set off on a third major exploration, this time heading for St. Louis in order to establish a direct road between Santa Fe and the Illinois country. Taking leave of Santa Fe on May 21, Vial headed for the Canadian River, which he appears to have followed across the Panhandle as far as the present site of Borger and perhaps as far eastward as present Canadian. Vial then turned to the northeast and the Arkansas River.[88]

[84] "Itinerary and Diary of José Mares, Bexar to Santa Fe, January 18 to April 27, 1788," in Loomis and Nasatir, *Pedro Vial*, pp. 306-315; pp. 312-314 pertain to Mares' trail through the Panhandle. See also Castañeda, *Our Catholic Heritage in Texas*, V, pp. 158-161.

[85] Loomis and Nasatir, *Pedro Vial*, p. 318.

[86] "Diary of Santiago Fernández from Santa Fe to the Taovayas and Return to Santa Fe, June 24-July 21, 1788, and July 24-December (August?) 17, 1788," in ibid., pp. 319-321, 324-325; pp. 326-327 contain Loomis' and Nasatir's estimation of the trail's location. The discrepancy in the terminal date of the journal, i.e. "December (August)" is occasioned by the fact that while Fernández arrived at Santa Fe on August 17, he did not sign the diary until December 17.

[87] "Diary of Francisco Xavier Fragoso from San Antonio to Santa Fe, June 25 to August 20, 1789," in ibid., pp. 365-366. See also, Castañeda, *Our Catholic Heritage in Texas*, V, pp. 161-170.

[88] "Diary of Pedro Vial from Santa Fe to St. Louis, May 21 to October 3, 1792," in Loomis and Nasatir, *Pedro Vial*, pp. 373-376.

Returning to Santa Fe in the next year, Vial retraced his outbound trail across the Panhandle.[89]

Pedro Vial's trail blazing, as effective as it was, was not destined to benefit the Spaniards who had sponsored his expeditions. Rather, the Americans, whom the Spaniards so greatly feared, were to appropriate the trail from St. Louis to Santa Fe and turn it into a major artery of commerce. Indeed, the nineteenth century brought major American expeditions into the western portion of the continent and into territory that the Spaniards clearly considered to be their own. One of these, the expedition of Lieutenant Zebulon M. Pike, inspired the last Spanish thrust down the Red River.

Pike left St. Louis on July 15, 1806. Aware that he was heading westward, Spanish authorities hastened to intercept him. Lieutenant Facundo Melgares, leading a force of over six hundred men, marched 233 leagues down the Red River. He then turned north to the Republican River, arriving there one month before Pike and therefore too early to intercept the American. Melgares negotiated with the Pawnees, who agreed to stop Pike and returned to New Mexico. As things turned out, the Spaniard failed either to halt the American or to erect an effective Pawnee barrier against him.[90]

Eventually, the Pike expedition was apprehended by Spanish soldiers in the valley of the Rio Grande, but Pike's presence so deep in New Mexico raised grave questions as to the security of the Spanish northeastern frontier. It was Spanish interest in securing their northeastern borders by direct communication between the two points that produced their last expedition between San Antonio and Santa Fe.

By the end of March 1808, Captain Francisco Amangual—sixty-nine years old at the time—was on his way from San Antonio in command of a force of two hundred men. Amangual was to establish a road between two extreme Spanish outposts, and to make friends with the Indians of the intervening territory.[91]

Amangual moved in a generally northwesterly direction, passed the ruins of the presidio on the San Saba, and sighted the High Plains Escarpment on May 12.[92] The captain appears to have moved more or less parallel to

[89] "Pedro Vial from St. Louis to Santa Fe, June 14-November 16, 1793," in ibid., pp. 402-404.
[90] Loomis and Nasatir, *Pedro Vial*, pp. 237-238.
[91] Ibid., p. 461.
[92] "Diary of Francisco Amangual from San Antonio to Santa Fe, March 30-May 19, 1808," in ibid., p. 485.

the escarpment for several days and to have mounted the Llano Estacado at a point west of Quitaque on May 22.[93] Amangual headed several canyons on the eastern side of the Llano Estacado, crossed Tierra Blanca creek probably in Randall County, and continued northward to the Canadian River. Plagued by all of the vagaries of springtime weather in the Plains, Amangual fought his way westward through the breaks of the Canadian and passed out of the Panhandle and on to Santa Fe, which he reached on June 19.[94] Amangual rested his command at Santa Fe for three months before returning to San Antonio by way of El Paso.

The explorations of Vial, Mares, and Amangual were a fitting swan song to the long history of Spanish activity in the Texas Panhandle, for they were in the finest traditions of the epic explorations of the sixteenth century. In some ways, in fact, the latter-day explorers may have been superior to their predecessors. Coronado was able to go wherever he wanted to go—by force, with an army at his back. Pedro Vial did likewise, but he traveled with, at most, small parties, and relied upon his skill as a frontiersman, his knowledge of the Indians, and his wits to secure passage through hostile territories. José Mares was similarly effective, and Francisco Amangual, who commanded an expedition of two hundred men, displayed singular qualities of leadership in getting his command across West Texas with minimum losses. Unlike Coronado's expedition, Amangual's was supported by wheeled vehicles, which implied far more difficult problems with the terrain than had confronted Coronado. The Indians, moreover, were unmounted and easily intimidated in Coronado's time. The Comanches with whom Amangual had to contend were mounted and clearly aware that they need not be intimidated by any mere sojourner in the heart of Comanchería.

These expeditions tell a great deal also about Spanish knowledge of southwestern geography, especially of the Llano Estacado. José Mares crossed the Llano with no great difficulty attributable to environment; yet he was the first Spaniard, so far as is known, since the Martín-Castillo expedition of 1650 to cross the Llano proper.[95] In other words, notwithstanding the passage of 137 years, the Llano Estacado held no mysteries for the Spaniards. That they respected the area for the immense dangers it could present seems implicit enough, but the Spaniards were not terrified

[93] Ibid., p. 493.
[94] Ibid., pp. 493-508.
[95] Vial had crossed the Panhandle the previous year, but through the Canadian River Valley. Mares marched across the Plains in the vicinity of Tierra Blanca creek.

of the Llano Estacado as Anglo Americans later appeared to be. Moreover, there were no mysteries among the Spaniards as to the sources of the Red River and the Canadian River (known to them as the Colorado), and they clearly understood the relationship between the two streams. Anglo Americans remained thoroughly confused about these matters, particularly so about the sources of the Red River, until 1852, when the redoubtable Randolph B. Marcy discovered anew what the Spaniards had known for years.

The journals of the latter-day explorers are of considerable historical interest; especially is this true of Amangual's, which is by far the most elaborate. Among other things, these journals establish clearly the fact of Comanche domination of the South Plains in the late eighteenth and early nineteenth centuries, for Vial, Mares, and Amangual were virtually overrun by Comanches who made periodic trouble for the explorers. The explorers, to their credit as frontiersmen, avoided really serious difficulty and often used Comanches effectively as guides.

For almost three centuries the Texas Panhandle was Spanish territory; yet in that entire period the Spaniards found nothing in the region really to interest them. When they did enter the area, they almost always did so because of something on the other side, so that the Panhandle was an intervening barrier that had to be crossed. Similarly, the French and the English who approached the region from the east were interested in New Mexico, or, casually, in trade with the Indians of the Panhandle region, but not in the Panhandle per se. Relative to the great interplay of imperial relationships then, the Panhandle was an area where the vanguards of empire touched, but otherwise was lost in the backwash of imperial ambition.

Culturally speaking, the Panhandle is an old region—one of the oldest in the United States when judged by the standard of early contact with European influences. In this respect it predates East Texas—except for the remnants of the Narvaez and De Soto expeditions—by well over a century. By the time La Salle had bestirred the Spaniards to action in East Texas, they knew and had named "practically every place of interest in West Texas."[96] The European influences that came so early to the Panhandle were brought from the west first by Coronado, and the region's orientation toward the west and specifically toward New Mexico was firmly

[96] W. C. Holden, "Indians, Spaniards, and Anglos," in *A History of Lubbock*, ed. Lawrence L. Graves, p. 27.

secured by Oñate. In the Spanish view, the Panhandle was part of New Mexico. The orientation of the Panhandle eastward and its status as a part of a political entity centered toward the east is of relatively recent origin, a departure from historic precedent, and, for that matter, unnatural from a physiographic point of view.

Notwithstanding the fact that the Panhandle was Spanish "property" for almost three hundred years, Spanish influence upon subsequent development is severely limited and confined almost solely to place names such as Amarillo, Palo Duro, Tule, Tierra Blanca, and the like. In any other respect, there is little reason to believe that regional history after Spain's demise would have been any different had Spaniards never seen the Panhandle.

The year 1821 marks an historical watershed in Panhandle history. In that year the Mexican Revolution finally succeeded and the Spanish Empire, while holding on a little longer, went the way of the British and French empires in what is now the United States. Spain, therefore, departed from the Panhandle. In the year 1820 Anglo-Americans entered the region when the party of Major Stephen H. Long explored the Canadian River. Long's entry marks the beginning of the first phase of Anglo-American appropriation of the region and its gradual reorientation toward the east.

# 4. The Middle Nineteenth Century

While the period from 1821 to 1874 is primarily significant in the history of the Texas Panhandle because of Anglo-American exploration of the region, it is nevertheless true that during this time a number of other events occurred, some indigenous and others far removed, of historic significance or interest.

On December 19, 1836, the Congress of the newly born Republic of Texas defined the boundaries of the republic. Ultimately basing their territorial claims upon the Right of Revolution, the Texans laid their eastern and northern boundaries along the line of the Florida Purchase Treaty of 1819-1821, which had defined the boundary between American Louisiana and the Spanish southwest,[1] and claimed the Rio Grande, from mouth to source, as their boundary on the south and west.[2] Although exceedingly ambitious, these territorial claims were entirely legitimate and mark the first effort actually to orient the Panhandle region toward the east and

[1] William M. Malloy, comp., *Treaties, Conventions, International Acts, Protocols and Agreements between the United States of America and Other Powers, 1776-1909*, II, pp. 1652-1653.
[2] Ernest Wallace and David M. Vigness, eds., *Documents of Texas History*, p. 125.

Anglo-American Texas. The Texans did nothing to enforce these boundaries in the New Mexico area, however, until the Texan Santa Fe Expedition of 1841.

Mirabeau B. Lamar, the highly nationalistic[3] second president of the Republic of Texas, designed his policies to strengthen the republic's independence and to establish it in the community of nations. Accordingly, Lamar was anxious to make good Texas' boundary claims and promoted the Texan Santa Fe expedition to that end. Additionally, it was hoped, the expedition would establish commercial connections between Santa Fe and the Texas coast. Lamar acted under at least two important illusions: (1) he had understood that the citizens of Santa Fe would welcome Texan government, and (2) he thought Santa Fe to be only about four hundred miles from Austin.

On June 21, 1841, the expedition marched confidently out of its camp. As is well known, the fate of the expedition was a far cry from the realization of the high hopes with which it left Austin. By August 30, a point at the foot of the Llano Estacado had been attained, and the expedition was in critical circumstances when it made camp near the confluence of Los Lingos and Quitaque creeks. In fact, so desperate had conditions become that resolute spirit and action were demanded. Accordingly, on the night of August 30, the leaders had to confront squarely some basic realities and to make basic decisions. Naturally the camp on Los Lingos and the Quitaque was thereafter named Camp Resolution. "The surrounding circumstances called for a tremendous amount of resolution on the part of the Pioneers. Hostile Indians, shortages of supplies, and a lack of knowledge of the surrounding topography all but overwhelmed the expedition."[4]

The leadership decided to send a party of one hundred chosen men, mounted on the strongest horses, on a dash to the New Mexican settlements from which aid could be sent back to the main party remaining at Camp Resolution. Although division of the force was recognized as dangerous, the risk was accepted as necessary in view of the crisis surrounding the expedition.[5]

Captain J. S. Sutton was placed in command of the advance party and,

[3] Dorman H. Winfrey, "Mirabeau B. Lamar and Texas Nationalism," *Southwestern Historical Quarterly* 59 (October 1955), pp. 184-205.

[4] H. Bailey Carroll, *The Texan Santa Fe Trail*, p. 133. See also Noel M. Loomis, *The Texan-Santa Fe Pioneers*.

[5] George Wilkins Kendall, *Narrative of the Texan Santa Fe Expedition*, I, pp. 210-211.

with only about an hour of sun in the western sky, it left Camp Resolution on August 31. After a "brisk trot of two hours," the Sutton party, as it came to be called, made camp for the night.[6] On September 1 Sutton led his men onto the Llano Estacado and turned northwestward. In the following days Quitaque and Tule canyons were crossed; Tierra Blanca Creek was reached near the Randall-Deaf Smith county line, where diminished supplies were replenished by killing a buffalo; the western escarpment of the Llano was descended near Glenrio, New Mexico; and the Canadian River was reached west of present Logan, New Mexico, on September 8. When four days later a group of Mexican traders were overtaken, three were hired to return to Camp Resolution and guide the main body of the expedition to the New Mexican settlements.[7]

After the departure of the Sutton party, the men left at Camp Resolution endured many hardships. Hostile Indians killed two men; the weather was inclement; and dissatisfaction, discouragement, and confusion permeated the camp. Some thought that the Sutton party surely had perished. The Mexican guides sént back by Sutton were, therefore, enthusiastically received when they arrived at Camp Resolution, which was even more enthusiastically abandoned on September 18. On the twentieth the Llano was ascended west of present Quitaque, and the pioneers proceeded across Briscoe and Swisher counties, reaching Tierra Blanca Creek on September 23 at a point about fifteen miles east of present Hereford. Sticking to the main branch of Tierra Blanca Creek, the expedition passed out of the present Texas Panhandle on the twenty-fifth.[8] Eventually reaching the Santa Fe area in disorganized groups, the ragged, hungry, demoralized Texans were at the mercy of Mexican authorities and easily taken into custody. Made prisoners, the pioneers were sent to Mexico City in a barbarous overland death march. Though grandiose in concept and intent, the expedition ended dismally and totally failed to secure the western territorial claims or the trade of Santa Fe to the Republic of Texas.

The Republic of Texas made no further direct effort to secure actual possession of the New Mexican area, but the Mexican War, following Texas' annexation to the United States, seemed to guarantee Texas' claims. United States forces led by General Stephen Watts Kearney oc-

---

[6] Ibid., pp. 215-216.
[7] Carroll, *Texan Santa Fe Trail*, pp. 137-142. Carroll's authoritative study of the route of the Texan Santa Fe Expedition is followed throughout this study.
[8] Ibid., pp. 148-153.

cupied Santa Fe, and President James K. Polk was entirely sympathetic to Texas' claims. As General Kearney moved his main forces on to southern California, he left Colonel John M. Washington in command at Santa Fe. Colonel Washington was opposed to slavery, and therefore to the expansion of Texas' political control to the Santa Fe area. The soldier, moreover, was a Whig and President Polk was a Democrat—reason enough in Washington's mind to obstruct the policies of his commander-in-chief. He therefore ignored the president's instructions to assist Texas in fixing its authority in the New Mexico area. President Polk, moreover, was succeeded by the successful Mexican War general, Zachary Taylor, a Whig, who opposed Texas' territorial claims and who would appear further to have borne a personal hostility toward anything Texan.

In view of the foregoing circumstances, failure of the momentous efforts of Texans to secure their territorial claims is hardly surprising. But the question of the western land claims continued as an exceedingly warm issue in Texas politics during the administrations of George T. Wood and P. Hansborough Bell, the second and third governors of the state, respectively. Both advocated Texas' right to the western territories with uncompromising vigor, and on two occasions Texans sent commissioners to Santa Fe to organize the area politically under the jurisdiction of Texas. On both occasions, however, the military authorities obstructed the Texans' efforts. Public opinion in Texas became increasingly inflamed over this apparent breach of faith on the part of the United States. Threats of armed action and even of secession became frequent. An adequate settlement and a graceful retreat from violence was available, fortunately.

Another problem deriving from Texas' annexation was the public debt of the republic, which had remained the responsibility of the State of Texas. Wishing to retain her public lands, Texas agreed also to retain responsibility for the republic's debt and to apply the public lands, so far as necessary, to settle the debt.[9] What the terms of annexation failed to take into account, however, was that the debt of the republic was in two parts: the ordinary debt, for which no funds had been pledged, and the preferred debt, for which the tariff revenues of the republic had been pledged. Upon annexation, not Texas but the United States collected those revenues. Since the United States now received tariff revenues formerly payable to the Republic of Texas, had the United States there-

[9] Resolution Annexing Texas to the United States in *Documents of Texas History*, ed. Wallace and Vigness, pp. 146-147.

fore also acquired responsibility for the debt to which those revenues had been pledged? Thoughtful persons in Congress began to feel that the United States might be legally responsible and that the national government might have to pay at least the preferred debt.

In 1850, therefore, Texas' relationship with the Union was clouded by two specific problems: the state's claim to western territories which was, in effect, disputed by the United States, and the debt of the former Republic of Texas for which the state was responsible under the terms of annexation, but for which many felt that the national government was responsible in morality and law. These controversies became related to the much larger controversy of slavery in all of its ramifications. Americans generally, for example, tended to react to Texas' western land claims in terms of their attitude toward slavery and expansion of slave territory. By 1850, in fact, the slavery question had acquired such heat that it posed a threat to the Union, and from the south threats of secession became more frequent and more serious. Fearing that the days of the American Union were numbered unless some accommodation could be reached, Senator Henry Clay, the Great Compromiser, worked out the system of proposals that came to be known as the Compromise Measures of 1850 and submitted them to the consideration of Congress. After tempestuous debate, and despite the strenuous opposition of President Taylor, the Compromise Measures were eventually enacted into law in five separate bills. One of these, written by Senator James A. Pearce of Maryland, provided for the surrender of Texas' land claims north and west of the present boundary in return for ten million dollars with which Texas was to settle its public debt. By the time the Compromise Measures had actually been enacted, President Taylor had died in office and was succeeded by Millard Fillmore. President Fillmore, although not overly friendly toward Texas but anxious to compromise the slavery issue, signed the Compromise Measures into law in September 1850. Texans, on the other hand, despite much extravagant talk about the righteousness of their territorial claims, had the good sense to recognize a notable deal when they saw one and accepted the provisions of Senator Pearce's legislation. Appropriate legislation was passed by the legislature and was signed into law by Governor Bell on November 25, 1850.[10] The specific boundaries fixed by the Pearce Bill created the politi-

[10] H. P. N. Gammel, comp., *The Laws of Texas, 1822-1897*, III, pp. 832-833. Relative to the Compromise of 1850, see Holman Hamilton, *Prologue to Conflict: The Crisis and Compromise of 1850*.

cal-geographical entity known presently as the Texas Panhandle. These boundaries were described specifically as follows:

> [The] boundary on the north shall commence at the point at which the meridian of one hundred degrees . . . is intersected by the parallel of thirty-six degrees thirty minutes . . . and shall run from said point due west to the meridian of one hundred and three degrees . . . thence . . . due south to the thirty-second degree of north latitude; thence on the said parallel of thirty-two degrees . . . to the Rio Bravo del Norte; and thence with the channel of said river to the Gulf of Mexico.[11]

Although the compromise boundary accepted by Texas in 1850 was considerably short of the territorial claims of the republic, the state still possessed a vast public domain. Very gradually, the West Texas area was brought under the physical control of the state and eventually, as settlement progressed, was organized politically. For many years West Texas was thought of as the Bexar Land District, which, as far as can be determined, never existed as a matter of law in Anglo-American times, but as a geographical concept of the public mind of Texas.[12] In 1874, however, the Bexar Land District, whatever its character, was displaced by the creation of five land districts. The Panhandle was distributed between the Jack Land District, which covered all of the Panhandle lying south of Prairie Dog Town Fork and west of the 101st meridian, and the Clay Land District, which contained the remainder of the region. These land districts were attached to the counties from which they took their names for surveying purposes.[13] The Jack and Clay land districts were apparently of little significance, and the legislature even ignored their existence in 1876 when it created numerous counties from their areas. The Panhandle counties so created were named to honor Texas heroes from various periods in the state's history, and their boundaries were specified. Since there was no politically significant population in the Panhandle when its counties were created, the ten eastern ones were attached to Clay County "for judicial, surveying and

[11] The Texas-New Mexico Boundary Act in *Documents of Texas History*, ed. Wallace and Vigness, p. 181.
[12] The concept of the Bexar Land District probably derived from the Mexican subdivision of Texas into departments or districts of Nacogdoches, Bexar, the Brazos, and the like.
[13] Gammel, comp., *Laws of Texas*, VIII, pp. 164-165.

all other purposes" and those remaining were similarly attached to Jack County.[14]

While Texas was in the lengthy process of establishing a permanent western boundary and extending its political jurisdiction over the enclosed area, events in the Panhandle, except for formal exploration, continued to be oriented toward New Mexico. Much that happened was directly related to some form of commercial venture; such was the case with Josiah Gregg, the famous Santa Fe trader.

Gregg's presence in the Panhandle in 1840 had curious antecedents. Political instability in Mexico during the 1830's was often characterized by upheaval, mob action, and looting. Foreign nationals whose Mexico City shops were looted filed damage claims against the Mexican government. In late 1838, France delivered an ultimatum to Mexico demanding that the claims of French nationals be settled immediately. The demand was reenforced by a blockade of the port of Vera Cruz. Mexico, lacking funds with which to pay, ignored the demand and French troops landed. Eventually, English mediation succeeded in adjusting the matter and the Pastry War—taking its name from the fact that the looting of a French baker's shop had touched off the affair—ended. In the meantime, however, Chihuahua, which depended on the port of Vera Cruz for imported goods, found the flow of commerce halted by the French blockade. Gregg, who had previously been active in the Santa Fe trade, saw great commercial possibilities in bringing goods overland from the United States for sale in Chihuahua.

Having made one round trip in 1839, Gregg was anxious to complete another before the flow of imports resumed from the coast. A more southerly route was desirable since earlier pasturage would permit him to start sooner. Gregg resolved to seek a trail south of the Canadian River.[15] Although Gregg's motive was purely commercial, he blazed the Fort Smith-Santa Fe Trail which attained wide fame. Largely because of the publicity given the route in *Commerce of the Prairies*,[16] at least twenty trains of California gold seekers used it, as did the explorer Captain Randolph B. Marcy in 1849. Gregg's trail was favored as a transcontinental railroad by some, while others advocated it as a transcontinental wagon

---

[14] Ibid., pp. 1070-1073, 1076-1078.
[15] Josiah Gregg, *Commerce of the Prairies: The Journal of a Santa Fe Trader*, p. 306.
[16] Ibid., pp. 305-318. *Commerce of the Prairies* was first published in 1844.

road.[17] Nevertheless, little use was made of the trail before 1849 because of the suspicion of Mexican officialdom toward any traveler who arrived in New Mexico by way of Texas. As a general matter, little love was lost between New Mexico and Texas, while the Texas Santa Fe expedition of 1841 no doubt heightened Mexican hostility. On the other hand, the fate of the Texan Santa Fe pioneers served as ample warning of the fate awaiting Anglo-Americans who arrived in New Mexico from Texas. After the Mexican War and acquisition of New Mexico by the United States, no political obstacle remained to the use of Gregg's trail. Heavy travel did not come before the summer of 1849, however.[18]

On March 10, 1840, Gregg's caravan, led by a Comanche guide, crossed the 103rd meridian, penetrated six miles into the Panhandle, and camped on a tributary of Trujillo Creek in Oldham County.[19] During the night the party was attacked by a band of Indians identified as Pawnees. Gregg's men sprang from their bedrolls, weapons ablaze, and fought their attackers for about three hours. Although spectacular, the engagement was of astonishingly little consequence in loss of property or life. None of Gregg's party was killed and only two were wounded, one in the hand and the second, a rather indolent, corpulent Italian nicknamed Dutch, shot in the head. The bullet penetrated Dutch's hat and scalp, but glanced off his skull leaving a messy but not serious wound. "Although teachers not unfrequently [*sic*] have cause to deplore the thickness of their pupil's skulls," observed Gregg, "Dutch had every reason to congratulate himself upon possessing such a treasure." Because snow and rain fell for several hours after the battle, the Indians' trail was obliterated and no estimate of their losses could be made by the whites.[20]

From his camp on Trujillo Creek, Gregg moved across the Panhandle proceeding from creek to creek and passed into United States territory on March 23. For approximately the western half of the journey, Gregg remained well away from the Canadian. Through the eastern half of the Panhandle, however, he traveled very close to the bed of the river. Wood

[17] Ibid., p. 214. Ernest R. Archambeau, "The Fort Smith-Santa Fe Trail Along the Canadian River in Texas," *Panhandle-Plains Historical Review* 27 (1954): 3. Archambeau's authoritative study identifies Gregg's exact route within the Panhandle. Note especially Archambeau's map following page 25.
[18] Archambeau, "The Fort Smith-Santa Fe Trail," pp. 9-10.
[19] Ibid., p. 4.
[20] Maurice Garland Fulton, ed., *Diary and Letters of Josiah Gregg: Southwestern Enterprises, 1840-1847,* p. 48; Gregg, *Commerce of the Prairies,* pp. 308-311.

was adequate and although a couple of dry camps were necessary, Gregg normally had little trouble in finding good water. Doubtlessly he was tapping the Tertiary springs that characterize the tributaries of the Canadian. Several of Gregg's campsites later became well-known landmarks or were heavily used by later travelers. Among these were the campsite of March 11, in present Oldham County, which Gregg referred to as Agua Pintada or Agua de Piedras, known later as Rocky Dell Creek; probably Tecovas Springs in southwestern Potter County, where camp was made on March 13; Wild Horse Lake in present north Amarillo, which was Gregg's camp on March 14; and on March 16 the caravan "nooned" on Antelope Creek in present Carson County at a well-watered spot that later became a common stop for travelers on the Fort Smith-Santa Fe Trail, and from 1877 to 1887, a stop on the Mobeetie-Tascosa stage line.[21]

The journey of the caravan across the Panhandle was reasonably eventful, and several of Gregg's observations are of interest. On March 12 the trail ascended the High Plains Escarpment and followed for an indeterminate distance across the Llano Estacado, which Gregg found "almost as firm and more smooth than a turn-pike." On Friday, March 13, "an extraordinarily cold" norther blew all night and stampeded Gregg's sheep and goat herds across the Llano Estacado, which swallowed them forever.[22] The hospitality that nature could provide in the Panhandle became evident to the caravan on March 16 while on Antelope Creek. Not only was good water found in abundance, but also deer, wild turkey, "partridges," and many buffalo.[23] On March 19, 1840, while on a creek he called "Quagmire," Gregg encountered what must have been one of the greatest frustrations in the life of a Santa Fe trader. He confided to his diary:

> Oh what mulish animals are mules! Many of these silly brutes, when they get their feet into sticky mud over the hoof, conclude they are mired and immediately fall down; and even when lifted up again they will not stand, but quietly permit themselves to be dragged out of the mud by the ears or tail; and even then it is sometimes necessary to strangle them to make them get up.[24]

Later in the 1840's, Bent, St. Vrain and Company, one of the great

[21] Archambeau, "The Fort Smith-Santa Fe Trail," pp. 4-9.
[22] Fulton, ed., *Gregg's Diary*, pp. 52-53.                     [23] Ibid., pp. 53-54.
[24] Ibid., p. 55. Archambeau, "The Fort Smith-Santa Fe Trail," p. 8, identifies Gregg's Quagmire Creek as the stream shown on modern maps as either Tallahone Creek or Walnut Creek in present Roberts County.

trading firms of the American West, followed Josiah Gregg into the Panhandle while attempting to tap the Comanche-Kiowa trade. From its main post, Bent's Fort, located on the Arkansas River near present La Junta, Colorado, the company established many satellite outposts, including Fort Adobe on the Canadian River in present Hutchinson County, Texas.[25] Although little is known about Fort Adobe, a few points emerge from its obscure history.

The best evidence indicates that no actual fort existed before 1846,[26] although Kiowa tradition says that Fort Adobe was built and operated as early as 1843 by a Bent agent known to the tribe as K'odal-aka-i, or Wrinkled Neck.[27] Doubtlessly, trade was conducted on the Canadian before 1846 by the Bents or their agents either from tepees or log structures. Experience soon showed that a log building was inadequate protection from cantankerous Indians, and the annexation of Texas obviated the Bents' reluctance to place a private fort in territory considered by the government of New Mexico to be Mexican. Ceran St. Vrain and William Bent, therefore, brought Mexican adobe makers to the Panhandle and built "a stout fort eighty feet square with walls nine feet high."[28]

By 1848 use of Fort Adobe had been terminated by widespread Indian hostility. A tenuous peace was made in the fall, however, and William Bent tried to reopen the isolated post. No less a frontiersman than Kit Carson was hired to lead the party, which reached Fort Adobe only to have Jicarilla Apaches steal the horse and mule herd and force an almost immediate withdrawal. Burying trade goods and buffalo robes that had been acquired, Carson and his men set out afoot for Bent's Fort on the Arkansas, packing their gear on two mules that had been tied inside Fort Adobe. Kiowas attacked the Party, but were driven off by a cool defense that made the potential booty more expensive in casualties than it was worth.

Comanche protestations of friendship and desire for trade encouraged

---

[25] David Lavender, *Bent's Fort* is the definitive work on the Bent-St. Vrain enterprise. See also Frank McNitt, *The Indian Traders*, pp. 25-43.

[26] Lavender, *Bent's Fort,* p. 405, note 10.

[27] James Mooney, "Calendar History of the Kiowa Indians," *Seventeenth Annual Report of the Bureau of American Ethnology, 1895-1896,* Part I, pp. 280-281, 283; Mildred P. Mayhall, *The Kiowas,* pp. 152-154.

[28] Lavender, *Bent's Fort,* pp. 246-247. C. B. McClure, ed., "The Battle of Adobe Walls, 1864," *Panhandle-Plains Historical Review* 21 (1948): 18, locates Fort Adobe "on the Section line between sections One and Two, Block G, Houston and Great Northern Survey, Hutchinson County, Texas." According to McClure, the fort was located on the stream known since as Bent's Creek.

William Bent to make another effort to establish amicable commercial relationships at Fort Adobe. Wishing also to recover the goods abandoned by Carson, Bent sent a party of twelve led by a trusted man, Dick Wootton. Arriving on the Canadian, Wootton's party found the Comanches so arrogant that the whites barricaded themselves in the adobe walls and admitted only two or three Indians at a time. Soon, even that could not be risked and a window was cut in the wall of the fort and trade conducted through it. Offended, the Comanches began taking pot shots at the window. A senior chief finally pacified his people, after which Wootton conducted profitable transactions in what he later called "the most hazardous trading expedition I ever had anything to do with."[29]

Thoroughly put out with the conduct of the Comanches toward the Wootton party, William Bent decided to make one final effort at Fort Adobe. In the spring of 1849 he led the last expedition to the fort, only to have Indians kill part of his stock. That did it! Bent blew up the interior of Fort Adobe, leaving only the exterior walls standing, and withdrew forever from the Indian trade of the Texas Panhandle.[30]

While the Bents failed, traders of a different breed, the Comancheros, dealt successfully with the tribes of the southern Plains. Trade between the Plains and pueblos far predates historic times, thus the Comanchero trade is simply an extension of an earlier development. More specifically, the Comanchero trade, so famous in the middle nineteenth century, assumed its peculiar form after 1786 when a peace treaty between the Spaniards and the Comanches was effected. Seemingly simple, innocuous individuals, the Comancheros included both pueblo Indians and persons from the frontier villages of Spanish New Mexico.[31] For decades their transactions swapped the products of the river valleys for the products of the Plains—horses, mules, meat, and buffalo robes.[32] Though often risky and tending to ebb and flow with the pulsations in Indian relations, the Comanchero trade continued for almost a century.

By about the middle of the nineteenth century, however, the character of the business changed substantially. Theretofore harmless enough, the trade became ominous about 1850 and its implications far reaching, especially in view of the dislocations accompanying the Civil War. As Anglo-American settlement in Texas progressed, the Indians learned of the

[29] Lavender, *Bent's Fort*, p. 310.
[30] Ibid., pp. 308-310.
[31] Charles L. Kenner, *A History of New Mexican-Plains Indian Relations*, p. 78.
[32] Ibid., p. 86.

commercial value of horses and raided both the Texas and Mexican frontiers to obtain horses for themselves and to secure animals for trade to the Comancheros. A bit later, an increased demand for cattle in New Mexico accelerated raiding and between roughly 1850 and 1870 thousands of head of livestock passed from Texas to New Mexico, having been stolen by Indians, traded to Comancheros, and sold finally to New Mexican ranchers. Similarly, trade items from New Mexico came to include firearms and whiskey, so that the character of the trade became unsavory. As the reputation of the trade worsened, the Comancheros acquired the hatred of those who suffered from it—especially Texans. While the conditions and circumstances surrounding the trade changed more than the Comancheros themselves, it is plausible that as profits rose less innocent persons were attracted. On the other hand, many respectable New Mexican ranchers who needed livestock doubtlessly welcomed and supported the contraband business.

During its earlier years, the Comanchero trade would appear to have been haphazard and ill-organized, but when commerce in stolen stock grew to significant proportions, definite meeting times and places were arranged—not the least reason for which was the necessity to transact business far from the settlements of either the losers or buyers of stolen property. Surely a place more adapted to clandestine transactions than the Staked Plains could hardly be imagined, and the Panhandle region became a major trading ground.[33] Texas horses and cattle changed hands on the south Plains at Cañon del Rescate—the canyon of ransom—or Yellow House Canyon, near Lubbock; at the site of Old Tascosa; on Mulberry Creek, in what was later the JA range; and at Las Tecovas springs located just northwest of Amarillo and the most active of the latter three sites. To the southeast, Indians of different tribes, renegade Anglos, and Mexican traders "gathered in the valley of the Tongues, where their negotiations called for the use of many languages, or *lenguas*—tongues." Thus was named the stream, Las Lenguas.[34]

Near Las Lenguas, in the area of Quitaque Creek, raiding bands of Indians gathered "and separated their captives to lessen the danger of escape and to insure more rapid assimilation."

Here mothers and children, torn from homes in Texas and Mexico,

---

[33] Ibid., p. 97. J. Evetts Haley, "The Comanchero Trade," *Southwestern Historical Quarterly* 38 (January 1935): 157-161.

[34] Las Lenguas Creek, also known as Linguist Creek or the "Linguish," is located in southeastern Briscoe County and flows into Motley County.

were scattered with the splitting of tribal bands, rarely to be ransomed by the traders. In that wild region it was known as a spot of heartache, of grief, and tragedy, and the Mexicans appropriately referred to it as Valle de las Lagrimas—the Valley of Tears.[35]

The Comanchero trade lasted as long as there were Indians in the Plains to supply livestock to New Mexico. Once the Indians were subdued and confined to the reservations, however, the basis of the trade collapsed, and the Comancheros and their dangerous, lucrative game retreated into historical shadows.[36]

The Civil War gave the Comancheros their greatest opportunity because of the attendant inability of either the United States or the Confederacy to police their activities. By the same token, the Indians of the Plains could be effectively disciplined by neither of the warring factions. Out of this general situation developed the circumstances that led to the first formal Anglo-American military engagement in the Panhandle—the First Battle of Adobe Walls, fought on November 25, 1864. More specifically, the engagement was an outgrowth of the policy of the United States Army to protect the commerce of the Santa Fe Trail and to subjugate the Indians and confine them to reservations. During the Civil War federal forces available for such tasks were indeed scanty, so that the Indians depredated freely.[37] In fact, on June 27, 1864, Governor John Evans of Colorado Territory appealed to the friendly Indians of the Plains to accept protective custody at various Army posts so that they might not be mistaken for hostiles. "The war on hostile Indians will be continued," Governor Evans declared, "until they are all effectually subdued."[38]

Almost three months later, Comanches were reported to have killed five persons at Lower Cimarron Springs and to have raided a wagon train and stolen cattle belonging to a Santa Fe citizen.[39] General James H. Carleton,

---

[35] Haley, "The Comanchero Trade," pp. 163-164.

[36] Ibid., p. 174. Kenner, *New Mexican-Plains Indian Relations*, p. 206. Because of its nature the Comanchero trade left little documentary material and Kenner's excellent account is probably as conclusive as is possible. See especially his chapters 4, 8, and 9.

[37] McClure, ed., "The Battle of Adobe Walls, 1864," pp. 18-19.

[38] John Evans to the friendly Indians of the Plains, June 27, 1864, *The War of the Rebellion: A Compilation of the Official Records of the Union and Confederate Armies*, Series I, Vol. XLI, Part I, p. 964, hereafter cited as *War of the Rebellion*.

[39] James H. Carleton to Christopher Carson, August 15, 1864, ibid., Part II, p. 723. Clearly, the transfer of New Mexico from Spain to Mexico to the United States had altered the Plains Indians' attitude toward the area not one whit.

commander of the Department of New Mexico, ordered that no passes to leave be given to reservation Indians, and inquired of Kit Carson, "Will 200 Apaches and Navahoes go with troops to fight Comanches, in case of serious troubles with the latter Indians?"[40]

The general's inquiry suggests that he had already considered a campaign against the Comanches as something more than a theoretical possibility; a month later details were substantially formulated. On September 18 Carleton directed the renowned scout to lead two hundred Utes and several cavalry and infantry units against the "Kiowas and other Indians." The General's real strategic objective, however, was "to have the Utes commit themselves in hostility to the Indians of the plains, that there may be less chance for them to join in any league which the latter Indians may attempt to make for a general war by all the Indians between the mountains and the Missouri upon the whites."[41]

Carson quickly acknowledged Carleton's communication and proposed specific procedures and objectives. The scout endorsed the general's "plan of compromising the Utes and Apaches with the Indians of the plains," but apparently envisioned more of a campaign than the general had in mind. "You, as myself, are fully aware that it will require a strong force to attack their [the Plains Indians'] villages and be successful," wrote Carson, "and therefore I hope you will provide me with a necessary force, so that I can give the Indians of the plains a sound drubbing." To provide such "necessary force" Carson proposed the enlistment of three hundred Navahos from Fort Sumner.[42] The general, though, remained committed to a campaign of limited objectives, that is, to cripple the Plains tribes and commit the mountain tribes against them. Insufficient forces forbade more extensive objectives, thought Carleton.[43]

Since obtaining an Indian force turned out to be more difficult than either Carson or Carleton had anticipated,[44] the expedition did not begin officially until October 22, when appropriate orders were issued.[45] Perhaps by then the general's attitude toward the campaign had hardened, for he wrote to Carson, "I have given you more men than you asked for

[40] Ibid.
[41] Carleton to Carson, September 18, 1864, ibid., Part III, pp. 243-244.
[42] Carson to Carleton, September 21, 1864, ibid., pp. 295-296.
[43] Carleton to Captain Cyrus H. De Forrest, September 24, 1864, ibid., p. 35.
[44] McClure, ed., "The Battle of Adobe Walls, 1864," pp. 23-31.
[45] General Orders No. 32, Department of New Mexico, *War of the Rebellion*, Series I, Vol. XLI, Part IV, pp. 198-199.

because it is my desire that you give those Indians, especially the Kiowas, a severe drubbing."[46]

Departing Fort Bascom on November 12, in command of fourteen officers and 321 enlisted men of the California and New Mexico Volunteers and seventy-five Ute and Apache Indians, Carson marched down the Canadian toward Fort Adobe (old Bent's Fort), which he intended to use as a depot for operations against the Plains tribes. On November 24 camp was made at a stream about thirty miles west of the old Bent trading post, which Carson called "Adobe Fort." Reports from advance scouts convinced the colonel that hostile Indians were near. Immediately, Carson advanced fifteen miles with his mounted troops and mountain howitzers, encamped briefly, and resumed his advance two hours before daybreak.

About an hour after resuming the downstream march, a party of Indians was sighted on the opposite side of the river. Sending a detachment in pursuit, Carson continued downstream with his main force and quickly discovered a large Indian camp about five miles ahead. After preliminary skirmishing, Carson drove through the village of about 150 lodges, intending to destroy them later. Fighting his way downstream four more miles through sharp resistance, Carson assumed a defensive position around old Bent's Fort. From a village of some 350 lodges located about three miles downstream, "at least 1,000 Indian warriors, mounted on first class horses," attacked Carson's command. Although the whites' horses were jaded and the men must have been near exhaustion, they repulsed several Indian charges. Their artillery may very well have saved the command from being overrun.

Carson resolved to retrace his march and to destroy the village through which he had passed earlier in the day so that it could not be removed by the Indians under cover of darkness. Under constant attack, which included an Indian effort to burn the command by igniting the dry grass, the whites successfully regained the village and destroyed it. Again, their artillery easily may have been the decisive factor in the successful retreat. Seeing the village aflame, the Indian attackers—principally "Kiowas with a small number of Comanches, Apaches, and Arapahoes"—broke off the engagement, which had lasted from 8:30 in the morning until sundown. Because of the poor condition of the mounts and nearly exhausted ammunition, Carson gave no chase to the retreating Indians and made no

---

[46]Carleton to Carson, October 23, 1864, ibid., p. 214. Carleton reminds Carson that no wanton, willful killing of women and children is to be permitted.

effort to capture their stock or destroy the large village below Fort Adobe. Instead, the colonel returned to his wagon train, which had been left some ten miles west of the old fort and which had not been molested. On the morning of November 27 camp was broken and the return to Fort Bascom begun.

Carson was generous in praise of his troops, both Indian and white, and noted of the enemy "that they acted with more daring and bravery than I have ever before witnessed." The colonel's casualties amounted to two soldiers and one Indian Killed and ten soldiers and five Indians wounded. Of the enemy Carson estimated at least sixty either killed or wounded. "I flatter myself that I have taught these Indians a severe lesson," wrote Carson, "and hereafter they will be more cautious about how they engage a force of civilized troops."[47]

General Carleton was laudatory in his response to the campaign. He wrote to Carson: "I beg to express to you and the gallant officers and soldiers whom you commanded . . . as well as to our good auxiliaries, the Utes and Apaches, my thanks for the handsome manner in which you all met so formidable an enemy and defeated him. . . . This brilliant affair adds another green leaf to the laurel wreath which you have so nobly won in the service of your country."[48]

Upon reconsideration, Carson apparently felt that the Plains Indians had not been taught such a "severe lesson" after all, for he recommended that after adequate rest his command take the field again—but supported by more artillery and increased to about one thousand men. Noting that the Indians were well supplied with arms and ammunition, Carson staunchly urged that trade between Mexicans, obviously Comancheros, and the Plains Indians be stopped.[49]

General Carleton considered further campaigning upon the Plains beyond his resources, and dispatched the units attached to Carson's command to other duties.[50] Well aware, however, that the Plains tribes were far from defeated, the general sought aid in subjugating the Plains warriors from his fellow officer, Major General Samuel Curtis at Fort Leavenworth, Kansas.[51] Also aware of the justice of Carson's complaint that the Kiowas

[47] The foregoing account is taken from Carson's official report. See Carson to Captain Benjamin C. Cutler, December 4, 1864, ibid., Part I, pp. 939-942.

[48] Carleton to Carson, December 15, 1864, ibid., p. 944.

[49] Carson to Carleton, December 16, 1864, ibid., p. 943.

[50] Ben C. Cutler to Carson, December 26, 1864, ibid., Part IV, pp. 939-940.

[51] Carleton to Samuel R. Curtis, January 24, 1865, ibid., Series I, Vol. XLVIII, Part I, pp. 635-636.

and Comanches were not only armed by New Mexican traders but were indeed forewarned of the Carson expedition, Carleton issued stern orders intended to halt the Comanchero trade.[52]

In terms of its original objectives the Carson expedition succeeded, in that the Utes and Jicarilla Apaches were pitted against the Kiowas and Comanches. In a strict military sense, however, the first battle of Adobe Walls was hardly a victory for Kit Carson or the "brilliant affair" that Carleton credited it with being. Later, in fact, Carson "admitted that he was beaten on that day and was fortunate to escape with any of his men at all."[53] On the other hand, the battle may well have paid some subtle but significant dividends. Doubtless the casualties inflicted upon the Indians and the loss of an entire village hurt them substantially. Moreover, the fact that they were attacked by a strong force so late in the year and while presumably safe in the depths of the Llano Estacado must have shaken thoroughly the Indians' confidence in their traditional security. Finally, if Carson may not be credited with a victory, he certainly may be commended for cool judgment that enabled his command to retreat from a rapidly deteriorating military situation with remarkably small losses.[54]

The first battle of Adobe Walls is best placed in historical context when viewed as a part of the long-term efforts of Anglo-Americans to subdue the Plains Indians. Although fought during the Civil War, first Adobe Walls is only incidentally related to that conflict. It has been charged that Comanche and Kiowa atrocities in New Mexico were incited by Confederate authorities.[55] Conversely, federal agents have been blamed for Texas' Indian troubles.[56] Supposing that both allegations are true, the real point is that the Indians of the southern Plains needed neither encouragement nor instruction in marauding the frontiers of either Texas or New Mexico. Though the precise character of the battle and its surrounding circumstances were conditioned by the Civil War, the basic and significant causes of first battle of Adobe Walls lie in the tragic conflict between the red aborigine and the white invader.[57]

[52] General Orders No. 2, January 31, 1865, ibid., pp. 699-700. See also Kenner, *New Mexican-Plains Indian Relations,* pp. 147-149.

[53] McClure, ed., "The Battle of Adobe Walls, 1864," pp. 64-65.

[54] Lowell H. Harrison, "The Two Battles of Adobe Walls," *Texas Military History* 5 (Spring 1965):6.

[55] McClure, ed., "The Battle of Adobe Walls, 1864," p. 21. See footnote 7.

[56] Kenner, *New Mexican-Plains Indian Relations,* p. 156.

[57] See ibid., pp. 138-154. For more extended accounts of first Adobe Walls see McClure, ed., "The Battle of Adobe Walls, 1864," pp. 18-65, and Harrison, "The

On the eve of permanent Anglo-American occupation a group of New Mexican sheepmen occupied the western Panhandle along the Canadian River. Early Anglo-American residents of Tascosa apparently believed that these herdsmen had occupied the banks of the Canadian for some time before their own arrival.[58] Some seem to have thought that the New Mexicans first came to the Panhandle as Comancheros.[59] The surveyor, W. S. Mabry, believed this possibility, which is far from incredible. From the appearance of the old adobe buildings, which he first saw in 1882, Mabry judged that the settlements might have been established as early as the Civil War.[60]

Long before any permanent settlers arrived, New Mexican sheep may have been seasonally herded as far eastward along the Canadian as present Oldham County. If so, crude buildings probably were erected by the *pastores*. Documentary evidence supports the view, however, that New Mexicans were actually domiciled along the Canadian no earlier than the late fall of 1876. In November 1876, Casimero Romero, long a resident of Mora County, New Mexico, led the first group of sheepmen eastward into the Panhandle and settled on the Canadian at the site where Tascosa developed.

Following an old but dimly marked trail—doubtlessly a Comanchero trail—the Romero family traveled in a substantial carriage similar to a Concord coach. These first arrivals on the Canadian found no evidence of prior occupancy. A man of substance, Romero brought about a dozen hired hands, some of whom had families with them; about three thousand sheep, a number of horses, and enough cows to provide milk and beef. Accompanying the Romeros were Agapito Sandoval, who owned about fifteen hundred sheep, and his large family, plus the blacksmith, Henry Kimball, and his family.[61] Although kept busy tending stock, Romero's

---

Two Battles of Adobe Walls," pp. 1-6. See also Mooney, "Calendar History of the Kiowa Indians," Part I, pp. 314-317, and Mayhall, *The Kiowas*, pp. 200-204.

[58] John Arnot, "A History of Tascosa" (MS, Earl Vandale Collection, Archives, University of Texas at Austin), p. 6.

[59] Interview, James East to J. Evetts Haley, September 27, 1927, Earl Vandale Collection, Archives, University of Texas at Austin, p. 55.

[60] W. S. Mabry, "Some Memories of W. S. Mabry," *Panhandle-Plains Historical Review* 11 (1938): 50.

[61] José Ynocencio Romero, "Spanish Sheepmen on the Canadian at Old Tascosa," ed. Ernest R. Archambeau, *Panhandle-Plains Historical Review* 19 (1946): 46-48. Romero, the foster son of Casimero Romero, came to the Canadian with his family at the age of five. His boyhood was spent in the vicinity of Tascosa, and he was the last survivor of the sheepmen who came from New Mexico. Romero's account of the

men gradually manufactured and stockpiled adobe brick. In 1877 they completed a commodious and very substantial house comfortably equipped with good furniture brought from Las Vegas. An irrigation ditch watered a large truck patch and cottonwoods planted along the ditch shaded the Romero home.

Sandoval settled his wife and seven children on Corsiño Creek about eight miles below the Romeros. Kimball, a former United States soldier who married a Mexican wife while stationed in New Mexico, settled a short distance downstream from the Romeros. Each homesite was located near good spring water.[62]

In 1877 additional New Mexican sheepmen arrived on the Canadian, having been attracted by the lush grazing found by Romero. Juan Trujillo led his own and several other families from Mora and settled opposite the mouth of Cheyenne Creek. A year later Mariano Montoya, José Tafoya, and Miguel Tafoya established their families on the Puenta de Agua near its confluence with the Rita Blanca. In the winter of 1878-1879 Ventura Barrego established a tiny village about a mile southeast of the Romero settlement. By 1880 the Spanish-Mexican population along the Canadian in the Tascosa vicinity numbered almost three hundred persons.[63]

Under the watchful eyes of herders, flocks of sheep scattered along the Canadian and its tributaries, and the New Mexicans prospered. Cattlemen soon arrived, however, acquired title to and fenced the land. The sheepmen did not dispute them. Rather, as free range disappeared, most of the sheepmen drifted back to New Mexico where free range was still to be had.[64] A few of the New Mexicans remained in the Panhandle and turned

---

Spanish sheepmen, taken in January and February, 1946, is that of an "eye witness." It was taken by a highly competent investigator and is regarded as the most authoritative source on this phase of Panhandle history. It is possible, of course, that New Mexicans lived in the Panhandle earlier than 1876. Romero believed that Trujillo Creek in western Oldham County was named for a trader who maintained a post there for hunters and Indians. If so, the trader was gone when the sheepmen arrived. See ibid., p. 52. See also Kenner, *New Mexican-Plains Indian Relations*, p. 116.

[62] Romero, "Spanish Sheepmen on the Canadian," ed. Archambeau, pp. 48-50.

[63] Ibid., pp. 52-54, 96; Ernest R. Archambeau, "The First Federal Census in the Panhandle, 1880," *Panhandle-Plains Historical Review* 23 (1950): 25-26. These little communities were known to the Anglo-Americans as "plazas." John Arnot, who makes frequent references to the Ortega, Charves, Salinas, and Trojillo [sic] plazas, believed that several of these existed before anyone lived at the site of Tascosa and that the first persons to occupy the site came from the various plazas scattered along the river. See John Arnot, "A History of Tascosa" (MS, Earl Vandale Collection, Archives, University of Texas at Austin), p. 5.

[64] Romero, "Spanish Sheepmen on the Canadian," ed. Archambeau, pp. 60-62, 68-69.

successfully to other enterprises. Casimero Romero, who had pioneered the movement of sheep into the Panhandle, sold out in 1882 and established a freighting business between Tascosa and Dodge City. He owned a hotel and restaurant in Dodge City for a time, freighted locally for ranchers after the railroad came to the Panhandle, and ran a butcher shop in Tascosa. Romero finally bought a ranch in 1893 near present Endee, New Mexico, and moved his family there in 1896.[65]

While the tenure of the Spanish sheepmen along the Canadian river was short, their presence provides an engaging historical vignette. They left permanent marks upon the region in conferring place names[66] and in founding Tascosa, one of the original Panhandle towns. While it is reasonable to suppose that some were not overly desirable people, as some of their Anglo-American neighbors believed,[67] it is hard to imagine a more solid pioneer citizen than the enterprising Casimero Romero, whose freighting business alone must have been significant in the development of Tascosa and vicinity. Others who remained in the Panhandle contributed to regional development in other ways. Juan Ortega, "who could not tell time," nevertheless was a leader in the organization of Oldham County, and Aliseo Barrego served as the first county clerk.[68]

---

[65] Ibid., pp. 62-68, 71.
[66] Ibid., p. 71.
[67] East to Haley, September 27, 1927, p. 55.
[68] Ibid., pp. 53-54.

# 5. Anglo-American Exploration

The redirection of the Texas Panhandle toward the Anglo-American part of North America, and indirectly toward Anglo-American Texas, was largely initiated by persons who entered the region for the express purpose of scientific exploration.

Major Stephen Harriman Long, the first explorer to enter the Panhandle, was born December 30, 1784, at Hopkinton, New Hampshire. Graduating from Dartmouth College in 1809, Long taught for a time and was then commissioned a lieutenant of engineers in 1814. After two years of teaching mathematics at the Military Academy, Long was breveted a major in the Corps of Topographical Engineers, thus becoming one of the first officers and one of the few non-West Pointers to serve in that distinguished corps.[1]

The Long expedition originated as the Yellowstone expedition, which

---

[1] Reuben Gold Thwaites, ed., *Early Western Travels, 1748-1846*, XIV, p. 11; William H. Goetzmann, *Army Exploration in the American West, 1803-1863*, pp. 12-13; William H. Goetzmann, *Exploration and Empire*, pp. 59-60; Dumas Malone, ed., *Dictionary of American Biography*, VI, p. 380.

"had military, commercial, diplomatic, and scientific aspects and was a grandly conceived, far-flung project." Largely a concept of John C. Calhoun, secretary of war in President James Monroe's cabinet, the Yellowstone expedition was stalked by discouraging setbacks, while a cost-conscious Congress, greatly restricting its scientific and military scope, redirected its path "across the prairies toward the headwaters of the Platte, Arkansas, and Red Rivers."[2] Notwithstanding congressionally imposed restrictions, Long's scientific contingent was impressive, most of its personnel being "representative of a school of naturalists that centered at Philadelphia, then the scientific capital of the country."[3]

In the spring of 1820 Long set out to execute his amended orders to explore the Platte River to the Rocky Mountains and to descend the Arkansas and Red rivers. Ascending the north bank of the main Platte to the confluence of its forks, Long crossed to the South Fork and followed it to the mountains, first sighted on June 30. Long's Peak was discovered, and Dr. James and two others achieved the first ascent of Pike's Peak. Moving southward along the wall of the mountains, Long reached the Arkansas River, and on July 24 the party divided into two groups. Captain J. R. Bell led one down the Arkansas and the other under Long, including James and Peale, continued southward to find the Red River. After eleven days' march, the party encountered the Canadian River, which was mistaken for the Red. Instead of searching for its headwaters, however, Long turned downstream. When the course of the stream deviated from the direction he supposed the Red would take, Long suspected he was on another stream. The suspicion was confirmed when the confluence of the Canadian and the Arkansas was reached.[4]

---

[2] Goetzmann, *Army Exploration*, pp. 39-42. See also Thwaites, ed., *Early Western Travels*, XIV, p. 12.

[3] Goetzmann, *Exploration and Empire*, pp. 182-184. Brief biographical data on Long's scientific associates are to be found in *Early Western Travels*, ed. Thwaites, XIV, pp. 11, 13, and editor's footnote 1, pp. 39ff. Titian Ramsey Peale, naturalist, and Dr. Edwin James, physician, geologist, and botanist, accompanied Long on the Canadian River phase of the exploration.

[4] Ibid., pp. 14-16. Goetzmann, *Army Exploration*, pp. 41-43. The basic document of the Long Expedition is the four volumes of Edwin James, *Account of an Expedition from Pittsburgh to the Rocky Mountains, Performed in the Years 1819, 1820*, in *Early Western Travels, 1748-1846*, ed. Thwaites, vols. XIV-XVII, of which vol. XVI, pp. 81-133, contains that portion of the account pertaining to the crossing of the Panhandle. The work will be cited hereafter as James, *Expedition from Pittsburgh to the Rocky Mountains*, in *Early Western Travels*, ed. Thwaites.

Long's party ascended the High Plains, or an arm of them, on July 29, and for two days their march was severely inhibited by thunderstorms that occasioned much inconvenience and some suffering.[5] On July 30, at noon, Long and his men arrived "in the sight of a creek, which, like all the watercourses of this region, is situated at the bottom of a deep and almost inaccessible valley."[6] Operating under the common misconception that the headstreams of the Red River lay in the same vicinity as those of the Canadian, Long assumed he had found one of the source streams of the Red and descended the stream. On his map Long designates this stream as the Rio Mora.[7]

Without doubt, the stream in question was Ute Creek, because James' description exactly fits the characteristics of Ute Creek[8] which rises in southwestern Union County, New Mexico, flows south and a little east across eastern Harding County, and into the Canadian near the town of Logan, New Mexico.[9] The march down Ute Creek was embittered by thirst and hunger, but after a sixteen-mile march on August 4, 1820, Long reached the confluence of the Ute and the Canadian. James comments upon the Canadian thus:

> The stream is still very inconsiderable in magnitude; the water brack-ish, and holds suspended so large a quantity of red earth as to give it the colour of florid blood. The general direction of its course inclining still towards the south-east, we were now induced to believe it must be one of the most considerable of the upper tributaries of Red River.[10]

[5] James, *Expedition from Pittsburgh to the Rocky Mountains* in *Early Western Travels*, ed. Thwaites, XVI, pp. 81-82.

[6] Ibid., pp. 83-84.

[7] Ibid., pp. 84-85. See editor's footnote, p. 85. Actually, Long was too far east to be on the real Rio Mora, which is a western tributary, not the main stream, of the Canadian River.

[8] Interview, H. Bailey Carroll to Frederick W. Rathjen, September 24, 1959, in possession of the writer.

[9] Moreover, Long was not on the stream that came to be called Major Long's Creek. The terrain does not fit the description contained in James' account, and apparently Long was on the Canadian before he entered the Panhandle. This would not have been possible had Major Long's Creek been followed, since that stream, rising in southeastern Union County, flows southeastward into the Texas Panhandle just below the thirty-sixth parallel and therefore many miles north of the Canadian. Since no trail study on the Long expedition has been done, it is difficult to fix its exact path across the Panhandle.

[10] James, *Expedition from Pittsburgh to the Rocky Mountains*, in *Early Western Travels*, ed. Thwaites, XVI, pp. 94-95.

Also tending to confirm the erroneous opinion of the party was the fact that they fell in with "a large and much frequented Indian trace," which they felt must connect the "Pawnee Piqua" villages on the Red River with Santa Fe.[11] On Sunday, August 6, Long camped near good grass to rest his jaded horses and to make astronomical observations. Of the Canadian, James writes:

> The river bed in front of our camp was . . . sixty yards in width, twenty of which were naked sandbar, the remaining forty covered with water, having an average depth of about ten inches. The current is moderate, the water intensely red . . . it is more grateful to the taste than any we had met with since leaving the mountains, and though drank in large quantities, produces no unpleasant effect.[12]

On August 7 and 8 Long continued his march down the Canadian, and James describes in some detail the flora and fauna observed in the two days' march. He indicates that the party suffered considerably because of the lack of game.[13] So great, in fact, was the need for meat that on August 5 a hunter had killed a beautiful wild horse that had affectionately attached himself to Long's command. Breakfast was made on the last of the horse meat on August 9. On the tenth, à buffalo was killed. Though obviously diseased, it was eaten.[14]

On August 11, the Long party met a band of Kaskaias Indians. Known in English as Bad Hearts, the Kaskaias were Kiowa Apaches[15] who in complete honesty assured Long that he was on the Red River. Among the Kiowas, the South Fork of the Canadian was called Gúadal P'a,–Red River![16] At their somewhat belligerent invitation, Long and his men encamped with the Indians. James expresses amazement at the speed with which his hosts could turn a barren spot on the prairie into a bustling village.[17] Though

[11] Ibid. The "Indian trace" was quite likely exactly that; James just did not recognize it as belonging to the right Indians. Also, it is possible that that trail was used by Comancheros.
[12] Ibid., p. 97.
[13] Ibid., pp. 97-102.
[14] Ibid., p. 102.
[15] Frederick Webb Hodge, ed., *Handbook of American Indians North of Mexico*, Part I, p. 702; Mildred P. Mayhall, *The Kiowas*, pp. 51-52.
[16] H. Bailey Carroll, ed., *Gúadal P'a: The Journal of Lieutenant J. W. Abert, from Bent's Fort to St. Louis in 1845*, p. 7. Moreover, as shown in chapter 3, the Canadian was known in New Mexico as the Red–Rio Colorado–until Anglo-Americans renamed it.
[17] James, *Expedition from Pittsburgh to the Rocky Mountains*, in *Early Western Travels*, ed. Thwaites, XVI, pp. 104-106.

the Bad Hearts gave no serious trouble, their rather surly disposition was a constant source of inconvenience, and on one occasion the Indians attempted to break camp and move on. This in itself would have been welcomed by the whites, but since several horses and other property belonging to the expedition were about to leave also, Long protested against this sudden decision to move. A show of force by Long and his men resulted in the return of the straying property.[18]

Long's contact with the Bad Hearts is, so far as it is known, the first recorded Anglo-American observation of Kiowa Apaches in the Texas Panhandle, so that James' description and estimate of these aboriginal residents is significant:

> Though we saw much to admire among this people, we cannot but think they are among some of the most degraded and miserable of the uncivilized Indians on this side of the Rocky Mountains. Their wandering and precarious manner of life, as well as the inhospitable character of the country they inhabit, precludes the possibility of advancement from the profoundest barbarism. As is common among other of the western tribes, they were persevering in offering us their women, but this appeared to be done from mere beastliness and the hope of reward, rather than from any motive of hospitality or a desire to show us respect. We saw among them no article of food except the flesh of the bison; their horses, their arms, lodges, and dogs, are their only wealth.[19]

On August 12, when leave was taken of the Bad Hearts, the party traveled twenty-eight miles. Camp was made that evening just beyond a large, completely dry streambed. On August 13 the party found the course of the Canadian "considerable serpentine, so that our route along its valley was of necessity somewhat circuitous." In an effort to avoid the winding course of the river, Long led his men into the breaks adjacent to the Canadian seeking an "Indian trace leading across the country by the most direct route." The effort was unavailing, however, for Long encountered only "irregular hills, abrupt ravines, and deep valleys." The party stopped at noon among some trees where there were "grape vines, loaded with ripe and delicious fruit." From noon until 3 P.M., a temperature of 105°F. was recorded. During the afternoon march, the explorers sighted a grove of

---

[18] Ibid., pp. 114-115.
[19] Ibid., pp. 118-119.

timber, and James' comment well exemplifies a reaction that characterized succeeding generations of Plains travelers. He says: "This cheering sight was like a discovery of land to the mariner, reminding us of the comparative comfort and plenty which we had learned to consider inseparable from a forest country."[20]

The grove of timber was an omen of more hospitable country, for on the afternoon of August 15 several buffalo were sighted far ahead and hunters promptly sent forth. They hunted successfully, and buffalo meat was made into jerky, thus solving Long's food problem for several days. On the next day, August 16, the party moved well into the eastern Panhandle, and just below the campsite occupied on the night of the sixteenth another great dry tributary stream was found. That a less demanding area lay ahead, however, is indicated by James' observation that wild horses and buffalo were becoming more numerous. More memorable, however, was a violent hailstorm that overtook the explorers in the afternoon and pummeled them with hailstones nearly an inch in diameter. The horses refused to move except before the wind, and the men found protection only by wrapping themselves loosely with blankets. Moved by the violence of the storm and the vast quantities of water that fell, James quaintly predicted of the region's future: "If the wide Plains of the Platte, the Upper Arkansa, [*sic*] and the Red River of Louisiana should ever become the seat of a permanent civilized population, the diseases most incident to such a population will probably be fevers, attended with pulmonary and pleuritic inflammations, rheumatism, scrofula, and consumption." After the storm had passed, however, the bed of the Canadian was found to be "smooth and unobstructed," and the expedition followed the river's bed for several days.[21]

Long halted in the middle of the day on August 17 so that buffalo could be killed. Camp was pitched "on the south-west side of the river, under a low bluff, which separates the half-wooded valley from the open and elevated plains." Also, on the same day, according to Thwaites, the party passed the one hundredth meridian and out of the Panhandle.[22] In any case, Long's map places the expedition well east of the Texas-Oklahoma boundary on August 18.[23]

[20] Ibid., pp. 119-123.
[21] Ibid., pp. 128-132.
[22] Ibid., p. 133. See editor's footnote 63.
[23] Ibid., XIV, p. 29.

The historic reputation of the Long expedition was not very good,[24] and its effect mainly was to brand the Plains of the United States as the Great American Desert. On this point James observes:

> In regard to this extensive section of country, I do not hesitate in giving the opinion, that it is almost wholly unfit for civilization, and of course uninhabitable by a people depending upon agriculture for their subsistence. Although tracts of fertile land considerably extensive are occasionally to be met with, yet the scarcity of wood and water, almost uniformly prevalent, will prove an insuperable obstacle in the way of settling the country.[25]

Although the concept of a Great American Desert has been denounced as a myth by westerners, it is apparently the word rather than the reality that evokes their wrath. Doubtless many who have sworn at the desert "myth" have expressed themselves even more fervently at the failure of rain. Further, the whole experience of Anglo-Americans in the Great Plains substantiates James' prediction, as the work of Walter Prescott Webb has shown. That an agricultural people were ultimately able to occupy the region was made possible by a technology that did not exist in James's time.

James' account of the Panhandle segment of the Long trail[26] is replete with references to the ubiety of game such as buffalo, turkey, deer, antelope, black bear, and partridges (quail) and of wild fruits, notably grapes and plums. Though found more abundantly in the eastern Panhandle than in the western portion of the region, these were present even while the personnel were suffering from want of food. James attributes the lack of hunter success to the constant roaming of Indians, which caused the game to be unusually wary. The absence of trees, James suggests, made stalking difficult.

Ample and repeated evidence of recent Indian occupancy was found, but again, more abundantly in the eastern than in the western part of the region. Except for the Kaskaias, however, no Indians were met. Possibly the Indians surreptitiously watched the white men while deliberately avoiding personal contact.

Finding fresh water was a constant problem; often only stagnant, foul

---

[24] Hiram M. Chittenden, *The American Fur Trade of the Far West*, II, pp. 574-575.
[25] James, *Expedition from Pittsburgh to the Rocky Mountains*, in *Early Western Travels*, ed. Thwaites, XVII, p. 147.
[26] Ibid., XVI, pp. 81-133.

ponds were found. The timing of the exploration—August—may have had something to do with this, and it may be that 1820 was just a generally dry year. In the eastern Panhandle, at least, the water problem could sometimes be remedied by digging a few feet into the sands of the river bed. The failure to find the Tertiary springs that feed the Canadian's tributaries may indicate that Long kept very close to the main bed. James' comments on the Canadian River itself picture a wide, sand-choked river in 1820 that was not essentially different from its present appearance.

The scientific value of the Long expedition was seriously compromised by the theft of many data and specimens by three deserters from the Bell party, which returned along the Arkansas. The lack of techniques and instruments also hampered the work of scientific investigation, although perhaps, as Goetzmann suggests, men like "Long, Graham, and, especially, Edwin James, who had been trained by Amos Eaton and John Torrey, should have been expected to produce better results."[27] Actually, the Long expedition was of considerable import. Consider the following:

> For the first time a team of scientists had surveyed the immense plains region in realistic terms, and taken some measure of the possibilities for settlement in that treeless area. They had revealed the complexity of the river systems in the Southwest, and had visited tribes seldom seen by the white man. But for the misfortune of losing the scientific notebooks to deserters, and the parsimony of the government, they might have produced a monumental scientific report even though they were without the highly developed instruments that explorers would carry as standard equipment a decade later.[28]

Although the journey of Long, James, and their companions across the

---

[27] Goetzmann, *Army Exploration*, pp. 41-44 summarizes the deficiencies and achievements of the Long expedition.

[28] Goetzmann, *Exploration and Empire*, p. 62. Goetzmann goes on to absolve Long of responsibility for the "myth" of the Great American Desert and attributes it to Zebulon M. Pike. Interestingly, if the term is given only moderately flexible definition, the concept of a Great American Desert is not new with Pike and may be traced back to Coronado—who obviously had little to do with American public opinion in the nineteenth century. Moreover, as Goetzmann properly points out, the essential observations of both Pike and Long were borne out by subsequent history. As noted above, the same westerner who was outraged by the term "desert" was also outraged by the lack of rain, and it would seem that the use of the term, not acknowledgment of the reality, was the basis of western defensiveness. The lapse of many years apparently did not change this phenomenon, as Walter Prescott Webb discovered when in 1957 he interpreted the American West as dominated by desert influences. See Webb, "The American West: Perpetual Mirage," *Harper's Magazine* 124 (May

Panhandle was but a small segment of their whole enterprise, it is a significant segment. Their contact with Kiowa Apaches is of anthropological importance and James' journal constitutes the first recorded observation of the region by scientifically trained men. For whatever scientific defects the reports may have—and they are rather limited to reporting the obvious—they are nevertheless significant simply because they are the first such observations extant.

Long of course failed to discover the Red River and to locate the whereabouts of its headstreams. Instead of dispelling the mysteries surrounding Red River, perhaps Long only thickened them. On the other hand, he located fairly closely the source and course of the upper Canadian. From these data careful geographers should have been able to infer reasonably accurate generalizations relative to the upper Red.

Three months after Long and his party left the Texas Panhandle, James William Abert, the next scientific explorer of the region, was born at Mount Holly, New Jersey, on November 18, 1820. Consigned by historians to a totally unmerited oblivion for almost a century after his Canadian River reconnaissance, Abert was finally rescued and properly recognized by H. Bailey Carroll[29] and, twenty years later, related to the broader picture of western exploration by William H. Goetzmann.[30]

The American branch of the Abert family was established by John Abert, who came from France as a member of the army led by Comte de Rochambeau. Participating in the Revolutionary War, and especially in the Yorktown campaign that led directly to American independence, the original Abert established a family military tradition and a precedent for being

---

1957): 25-31. For Webb's account of the stormy aftermath of this publication see, "The West and the Desert," in Webb, *An Honest Preface and Other Essays*, ed. Joe B. Frantz, pp. 175-193. Perhaps in its outburst against Webb the West lost its stinger, for about ten years later another historian entitled a book with the very words that Long placed on his famous map and hardly caused a ripple. See W. Eugene Hollon, *The Great American Desert: Then and Now*.

[29] Abert's journal was published originally as James W. Abert, *Journal of Lieutenant James W. Abert, from Bent's Fort to St. Louis in 1845*, 29th Cong., 1st sess., Sen. Exec. Doc. 438 (1846). Abert's original text was republished and extensively elaborated with editorial notes as H. Bailey Carroll, ed., "The Journal of Lieutenant J. W. Abert from Bent's Fort to St. Louis in 1845," *Panhandle-Plains Historical Review* 14 (1941): 2-113. This publication appeared also in book form as Carroll, ed., *Gúadal P'a, The Journal of Lieutenant J. W. Abert from Bent's Fort to St. Louis in 1845*, which is used for this study and is cited hereafter as Carroll, ed., *Abert's Journal*. Carroll traces Abert's trail precisely from campsite to campsite.

[30] Goetzmann, *Army Exploration*, pp. 123-127.

present at moments of historic import. John Abert's son, John James Abert, following in the soldierly tradition, was graduated from the United States Military Academy in 1811 just in time to serve in the War of 1812. Except for a brief return to civilian life in 1815 and 1816, John James Abert served in the Topographical Corps until September 9, 1861, when he retired with the rank of colonel.

James William Abert attended Princeton for a time and entered the Military Academy in 1838, thus following in the footsteps of his father and grandfather. As a cadet Abert excelled in drawing. Otherwise, his academic and discipline records were very poor, and upon graduation in June 1842, as fifty-fifth man in a class of fifty-six, Abert was assigned to the infantry—an assignment doubtless consistent with his indifferent record as a cadet. Soon, however, this apparently unpromising young officer was transferred to the Corps of Topographical Engineers, an elite and coveted branch. Perhaps Abert's excellence in drawing was the basis of the transfer, but whatever the reason, the arrangement was nice from a filial point of view, since the young Abert's father was also a topographical engineer—chief of the corps in fact.[31]

August 1845 found the twenty-five-year-old Abert at Bent's Fort on the Arkansas with the great western pathfinder, John Charles Frémont. Frémont's orders directed him "to make a reconnaissance southward and eastward along the Canadian River through the country of the Kiowa and Comanche." Instead of executing these orders, however, Frémont chose to strike out on his own initiative toward California and gave Abert a detached command with orders to execute the Canadian River reconnaissance. Lieutenant William G. Peck, an outstanding mathematician who was graduated first in his class at the Military Academy, was assigned as assistant topographical officer. The famed Tom Fitzpatrick was Abert's guide, while Caleb Greenwood and the noted mountain man John Hatcher were hired as hunters. The rest of the command were, like Fitzpatrick, Greenwood, and Hatcher, civilians, so that of thirty-three men, only the two lieutenants were military personnel.[32]

[31] Carroll, ed., *Abert's Journal*, pp. 3-5.
[32] Goetzmann, *Army Exploration*, p. 123; Carroll, ed., *Abert's Journal*, p. 18. Interestingly, as Carroll points out, at least eleven of the names appearing on the roster suggest French ancestry, and two members, Raphael Harrison and Silas Sublett, were Negroes. John Hatcher was doubtless the most valuable man, since he had been in the Canadian River country as an agent of the Bent brothers. Moreover, Hatcher was an adopted Kiowa and thus constituted protection for the expedition while in the country of often temperamental and perhaps hostile Indians.

Poor West Point cadet though he may have been, Abert certainly is to be reckoned among the great explorers of the southwest. Consider the magnitude of his exploration:

> This expedition started at Bent's Fort on the Arkansas and proceeded over Raton Pass on the Mountain branch of the Santa Fe trail. From there it went down the headwaters of the Canadian to its Grand Canyon, across the Mosquero Flats and down Ute Creek again to the Canadian which was followed through the present eastern New Mexico and across a large portion of the Texas Panhandle; thence it filed off southward to the headwaters of the North Fork of Red River and back once more to the Canadian, which was followed for almost its total course through the present state of Oklahoma.[33]

Not only did Abert explore a vast territory, but he managed to maintain exceptional qualitative standards in his reporting.

> As an early recorder of the Texas and Southwestern scene Abert displays the insatiable thirst for information which must characterize the true naturalist and scholar. He had a great eye for detail. Traveling rapidly he observed the country with remarkable clarity and fidelity; with graphic touches he describes birds, plants, animals; at the same time he made a map of the area traversed which was so accurate that it could be used successfully today as a guide over the same route.[34]

Abert, finally, was a sensitive, perceptive man relative to his environment and other human beings; unlike technologists of a later time, he was literate in English and produced a written account characterized by literary quality, force, and in spots, downright beauty.

Upon approaching the western Panhandle, Abert took extra precautions to guard against surprise attack by Comanches whose presence was amply attested to by volumes of smoke from their signal fires. On September 5 the party entered the Panhandle and camped on Minneosa Creek, which Abert described as "a little stream of clear water, in which I had a delightful bath where it made a very abrupt bend back on itself, and seemed enclosed by a coliseum of rocks." Some of Abert's men caught a skunk among the rocks near the camp and the "French people" dined upon the

---

[33] Carroll, ed., *Abert's Journal*, p. 3.
[34] Ibid., p. 6.

animal. "The odor, however," observes Abert, "was too pungent to suit every one's olfactories."[35]

On September 6 the Abert command traveled about twelve hard, rough miles and reached the Canadian, where camp was made, by way of a "tributary ravine." Some uneasiness was caused "by the discovery of an Indian trail, the breadth and freshness of which showed that Indians were near and in great numbers." Nevertheless, Abert was able to write of a memorable night: "To-night we made our beds under the canopy of the starry heavens, which shone so luminously that there was more pleasure in tracing the various constellations than in endeavoring to sleep. Every one must be struck with the extraordinary brightness of a prairie sky, due to the singular purity of the atmosphere."[36]

On September 7 Abert again found fresh Indian signs and admired both the skill with which Indians' trails found the path of least resistance and the efficient manner in which Indians, unencumbered by wagons, moved over the Plains. Continuing their precautions against surprise attack, the command encamped after a nineteen-mile march, "but no sooner were our tents pitched," says Abert, "than we were attacked by myriads of mus-ketoes [*sic*], which not only drove sleep from our eyes, but the idea of it from our heads."[37]

On September 8 Abert's group was shadowed by an Indian scout who exposed himself but who could not be induced to contact even a lone horseman. Atascosa Creek, which carried marvelously sweet water, was headed because its ravine could not be crossed. When the first buffalo were encountered on the Canadian, John Hatcher hunted with great success. Though the evening camp was sopped by a drizzling rain that began at nightfall, good cheer prevailed because of the generous supply of good meat.[38] When the rain continued spasmodically through the ninth, camp was maintained through the day, the time being utilized to jerk meat, doubtless from the buffaloes killed the previous day. The day turned out to be an eventful one, however, for Indians—identified by Fitzpatrick as Buffalo Eater Comanches—were finally induced to enter the camp. Cordial

[35] Ibid., pp. 53-54, footnote 63. See figure 4. The representations of the trails of Abert, Gregg, and Marcy along the Canadian River, and of Marcy along the Red River in figure 4, are taken from sources cited relative to each.

[36] Ibid., p. 55, footnote 176.

[37] Ibid., pp. 56-57, footnote 178.

[38] Ibid., pp. 57-60, footnote 179; pp. 58-59 contain Abert's interesting observations of the buffalo.

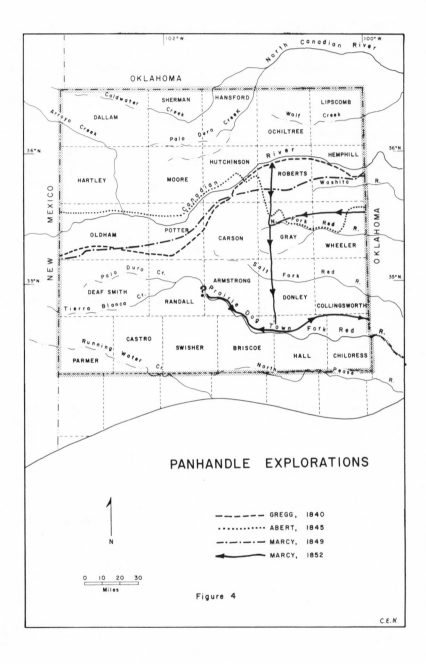

PANHANDLE EXPLORATIONS

— — — — — GREGG, 1840
• • • • • • • • • • • • ABERT, 1845
— • — • — • — MARCY, 1849
◄——————— MARCY, 1852

N

0   10   20   30
Miles

Figure 4

C.E.N.

relations were established and maintained, although it would appear that it was difficult to convince the Indians of the peaceful intent of the expedition. The food supply was enriched by abundant wild turkeys. "As they persisted in retaining possession of their accustomed roosts," observes Abert, "our men had a fine opportunity of trying their skill in shooting them."[39]

The trail of September 10, 11, and 12 took the expedition through the northern part of present Potter County. Maximum exertion was required to pull the wagons through extensive stretches of sand, and the ravines and creek beds tributary to the Canadian caused extensive detours away from the course Abert would like to have followed.[40] Despite an unusually frustrating day on the eleventh, Abert notes that the afternoon's march "led us over a plain strewed with agates, colored with stripes of rose and blue, and with colors resulting from their admixture. They were coarse and of little value, but so numerous that we gave the place the name of Agate bluffs."[41] These agates, of course, were from the deposits that were to become known as Alibates Flint Quarries. Perceptive as he was, little did Abert realize that he had stumbled upon a nerve center of native industry.

During the night of September 11 a few Kiowas crept into the camp and very nearly attacked the whites, who were mistaken for Texans. Next morning, the Indians, who had quietly withdrawn after their nighttime foray, approached openly, and friendly contact was established. Abert had thereupon a remarkable opportunity to observe the Kiowas, who left a very favorable impression upon the explorers. "The Kioways [*sic*] are a people excelling the Camanches [*sic*] in every respect," wrote Abert, "and, though far inferior to them in numbers . . . exercise almost complete control over them."[42]

Travel on September 12 and 13 was difficult and vexatious because of the rugged terrain. When the wagons proved especially hard to maneuver, the idea of abandoning them was considered seriously although not carried out. On the thirteenth, two Kiowa braves and a squaw voluntarily joined the command. Amiable and helpful, the three Kiowas wished to protect

[39] Ibid., pp. 60-61.    [40] Ibid., pp. 61-64, footnotes 186, 187, 190, and 191.
[41] Ibid., p. 64, footnote 191.
[42] Ibid., p. 66; pp. 64-68 contain Abert's fascinating account of the Kiowas. Abert's command was regarded with fear and hostility by the Indians until they were satisfied that the expedition was not Texan. This state of affairs derived from the distrust that existed between the Plains Indians and the Republic of Texas, and, more specifically, from the ill will that followed the Council House Fight that occurred in San Antonio on March 19, 1840.

the Americans from other Indians who might mistake them for Texans. Communication was largely by sign language, but one of the braves had picked up a little English around Bent's Fort. His vocabulary was limited to such expressions as "how d'ye do" and "yes" and "a few profane oaths, a severe satire," in the view of the conscientious Abert, "on the moral influence exercised by the white people."[43]

Travel on the fourteenth was brightened by the sighting of many green-winged teal, brant, Canadian geese (which Abert thought were easily domesticated), wild turkeys, of which "great numbers" were killed, and an unusual number of rattlesnakes, one of which, to Abert's dismay, "never gave the usual warning signal."[44] On September 15 Abert's Kiowa friends brought a group of Comancheros to the camp. Regarding his new visitors as sorry, Abert described them as "a good specimen of the class to which they belong."[45]

Since by the terms of his agreement John Hatcher was obligated to go no farther than Bent's trading house on the Canadian, both he and Caleb Greenwood departed the expedition on September 15 to return to the Arkansas. At the same time the Kiowas chose also to leave, bearing away gifts that the command could ill afford to lose. September 16 found Abert's party leaving the Canadian and heading southeastward in order to locate the Washita River, as instructions required, and to follow it as far as the "Sand hills"—apparently Antelope Hills—before returning to the Canadian.[46]

Abert's diary denotes September 17 as "the day of anxiety." The description was indeed apt, for on that day the explorers crossed the Llano Estacado. Since both John Hatcher and the Kiowas had left, this perilous segment of the exploration had to be executed without a guide and, though he followed directions given by his Kiowa friend, Tiah-na-zi, Abert found no water. So, cooked by the sun, confused by mirages, and tor-

---

[43] Ibid., p. 69.

[44] Ibid., pp. 69-70.

[45] Ibid., p. 71.

[46] Ibid., pp. 72-73. Abert records nothing to indicate the presence of any sort of building in the vicinity of Bent's Creek on the Canadian and hence reinforces the likelihood that no permanent building was erected before 1846. Abert's orders instructed him to explore the waters of the Canadian and the "False Washita." Carroll identifies this stream as that known in modern times as the Washita, which rises in the Llano Estacado near the present Miami and empties into the Red River above Denison, Texas. Ibid., p. 9, footnote 5.

mented by thirst, the Americans found the Llano Estacado to be a terrifying place.

> Our tongues seemed to cleave to the roofs of our mouths, and our throats were parched with dryness. The rude joke and boisterous laugh had long since died away, and the "hep" of the driver, as he urged his panting team, under the scorching sun, grew fainter and fainter, until we moved on in dead silence. The idea of having been misled evidently began to steal into our minds, though not a word was spoken; but the tales we had heard by the camp-fires, of treachery, surprise, and massacre, were evidently revolving in our minds. This sort of depression, akin to fear, is contagious; and as we pursued our way each one examined his rifle, and closed in with the main body. An Indian, mounted, now appeared, and, as he swept along the horizon, looked a very giant; another and another burst upon our view, on every side, which led us to believe that we were surrounded. . . . These were moments of fearful forebodings. Could it be possible that the wily savage had laid a plan to decoy us upon this broad desert, rich in the bloody legends of travellers, but to make us an easy prey? Many bore up against this conclusion, while others were by no means so sanguine.
>
> In this state of suspense we travelled for some hours, when we observed some slight irregularities in the horizon. Soon the falling of the ground became evident, bringing back hope to our hearts. . . . The camp was completely metamorphosed from gloomy despair to glad delight.[47]

Through the night of September 17 the Indians seen during the day—again, Kiowas who mistook the Americans for Texans—harrassed the camp, but on the eighteenth were induced to enter. Having ascertained that they were not dealing with Texans, the Kiowas became quite friendly. They were from a nearby village that turned out en masse to meet the whites; among the guests was the famed Kiowa chief Dohasan, or Little Mountain. Indeed few white men visited with so distinguished a chieftain under such congenial circumstances. Abert now determined to utilize this aggregation of local authority to verify his geographical position. Though

[47] Ibid., pp. 75-76. The Llano Estacado was crossed from a point on Red Deer Creek near present Hoover (p. 73, footnote 207) to the North Fork of the Red River near the present town of Lefors (p. 76, footnote 211). The march lay entirely within the present Gray County.

the effort was doubtless a massive frustration, the lieutenant's sense of humor did not fail him.

> We now placed before them a map of the country, which had been made out at Bent's Fort. . . . Quite a council was called to decide whether or not Buffalo creek runs into Red river or into the "Goo-al-pa," as represented on the map. A clean sheet of paper was produced, and the map drawn according to their directions. But the council being composed of old men, to whom great deference was paid, and a great discrepancy of opinion existing among them, like most celebrated politicians, they at length agreed to compromise, and represented all the rivers as running parallel, ad infinitum.[48]

On September 18 Abert traveled fourteen miles downstream and camped on the North Fork at a point directly south of the present town of Laketon, Gray County. The march was in delightful contrast to that of the previous day. Abert says: "The travelling now became more favorable, and the country, too, looked smilingly, for it was evident that we had passed the great desert; and we hailed with delight the signs of fertility."[49]

Continuing downstream under the illusion of being on the Washita, Abert apparently late on the nineteenth decided to return to the Canadian. He had taken astronomical observations at three separate points to establish the location of the stream and, moreover, had sighted sand bluffs that he took to be Antelope Hills. By the morning of the twentieth, however, Abert had changed his mind and decided to stay a bit longer on the North Fork. In the afternoon, the stream abruptly turned southward and Abert struck for the Canadian, the change in the river's course seemingly to have decided the direction the explorer would take. After fourteen miles' journey, camp was set up "in a little bowl-shaped valley, surrounded by sand-buttes and cottonwoods." The campsite was a fortunate one, for the night of the twentieth, as is not uncommon on the Plains, was "exceeding chill, and," records Abert, "had we not selected this position, we should have suffered much from cold." Although Abert was a confident, poised leader,

----

[48] Ibid., p. 78. Buffalo creek, referred to above, was the name by which Kiowas knew the North Fork. Abert, thinking he was on the Washita, presumably thought the Indians referred to that stream. Perhaps poor communications contributed to Abert's failure to get more satisfactory aid. Possibly, however, the Kiowas, indisputably able to take care of themselves in their own country, understood little of its broader geographic features.

[49] Ibid., p. 79, footnote 215. Notice how casually Abert applies the term "desert" as he does elsewhere in his journal.

he was far from indifferent to potential danger. Of the night of the twentieth, the lieutenant continues: "We could not help contrasting our preparations for sleep in this country with those of our comfortable homes. Each one now lies with his gun in hand, the muzzle towards his feet, and knows not that he will ever again see the light of day."[50]

Following the compass slightly north of east, Abert led his men toward the Canadian on the twenty-first. A sixteen-mile march led the expedition to a point northeast of the present town of Wheeler, near Sweetwater Creek. The thirty-eighth camp since leaving the Arkansas was pitched in a grove of oak trees, which was also obligingly occupied by a drove of wild turkeys—a "great number" of which were killed for a welcome change in diet.[51] On the twenty-second the explorers bore somewhat more to the north than they had on the previous day and in midmorning hit a tributary of Sweetwater Creek, well timbered and rich in delicious wild grapes. After a two-hour rest the command moved on, passed through an abandoned Comanche village, and sometime during the afternoon's march passed out of the Panhandle.[52]

Abert's contributions to the knowledge of American geography were significant. His map of the Canadian River region was the "first trustworthy representation" of that vast territory, and his written account elaborated upon what a map could not show. Abert's landscapes, drawn to illustrate strategic points along the trail, are beautiful and remarkably accurate.

Because of Abert's encounters with the Comanches and Kiowas and his descriptions of them, the national government had its first data on these tribes from an observer of its own. If there should be any doubt that the Texas Panhandle, in the middle nineteenth century, was the domain of the Comanches and Kiowas, Abert's testimony should surely quiet such doubt forever. As a scientific investigator Abert was a collector rather than an interpreter of data. Well read in the works of John James Audubon and Alexander Wilson, ornithologists, and in the travel accounts of Josiah Gregg and George Wilkins Kendall, Abert "noted regional geography with an eye to everything that would contribute toward the possible solution of the problem of settlement and national development in the particular area."[53]

[50] Ibid., pp. 85-87, footnotes 246 and 247.
[51] Ibid., p. 87, footnote 252.
[52] Ibid., p. 88, footnotes 255, 256, and 260.
[53] Goetzmann, *Army Exploration*, pp. 126-127.

From the point of view of regional history, Abert's report is unique. The best description of the primeval Panhandle, it is replete with observations of the land and its native human, animal, and vegetable occupants. Like the descriptions by Edwin James, Abert's suggest that the Canadian River in 1845 was much as it is today, at least in basic character. The lieutenant's frequent reference to "musquit" prove the presence of that woody species, at least in the breaks, long before the arrival of domestic herds and plows. Abert's records of animal life include the obscure creatures as well as those which would more nearly benefit man for sustenance or economic exploitation, and he exhibits an appreciation for birds that would have delighted Roy Bedichek.

As compared to the Long expedition of twenty-five years earlier, Abert certainly produced better results from a scientific point of view. Moreover, Abert's party, while not exactly on a Sunday picnic complete with charcoal grill, seems to have suffered little of the privation that bedeviled Long. Although game was, as in Long's case, more plentiful in the eastern than in the western Panhandle, it was everywhere available and often abundant. Abert always found sweet water, doubtless from the Tertiary springs feeding the Canadian's tributaries, which Long seems not to have found. Several possibilities may explain this difference in experience. Although less than a month separated the time of year in which the two expeditions explored the Panhandle, Abert may have found a generally more seasonable year or perhaps came during a "wet cycle" of several years that would have doubtlessly affected nature's prosperity. It may be that by background and experience Abert's men were better able to take care of themselves in the wilderness. As frontiersmen, perhaps they were simply better finders of game and water. It may be also that Abert was a better leader than Long was.

Since Abert's orders were to explore the Canadian River, the Red River was therefore of no official concern to him as it had been to Long. Interestingly, however, by seeking what he knew of as the False Washita, Abert hit and followed the North Fork of the Red River. Had he continued on that stream—which would have required violation of his instructions, of course—the lieutenant would have found the main Red and contributed materially to geographic knowledge of the upper Red River. Abert observed his orders, however, and the sources of the Red remained mysterious for seven years more.

Despite their excellence, Abert's map and journal, which would have been superlative guides for almost any undertaking, were destined to play a limited role in the subsequent development of the Panhandle and served mainly as guides for explorers who came later and as source materials for evaluating the Canadian River Valley as a possible route for a Pacific railroad. Settlement, clearly out of the question in the 1840's for a variety of substantial reasons, was delayed until Abert was forgotten. In fact, any sort of Anglo-American civilian activity, even the enterprises of such established and knowledgeable frontier entrepreneurs as the Bent brothers, could not succeed in the Panhandle in the 1840's. To what use government might have put Abert's report is purely speculative. But the important point is that whatever plans the government might have developed, they were or would have been overwhelmed by infinitely greater enterprises.

In the 1840's the spirit of Manifest Destiny was abroad in the land—in fact, it could be cogently argued that Manifest Destiny brought Abert to the Panhandle—and expressed itself politically in 1844 when President James K. Polk was elected to reoccupy Oregon and reannex Texas. Disposing quickly of the Oregon and Texas questions, Polk and the nation turned to the Mexican War and added vast acreage to the national domain. Hardly had the smoke of battle cleared when the discovery of gold in newly acquired California demonstrated that more than west coast ports, separated by awful desolation from the humid region, had been acquired. So it was then that a new Quivira brought latter-day Coronados through the Panhandle. As with the original Coronado they found nothing in the region—and for that matter sought nothing—to cause them to remain and appropriate the land. They passed through to the other side.

As the gold mania swept the easterly states, western towns such as Fort Smith and Van Buren, Arkansas, became points of departure for California-bound immigrants.[54] Though many wagon parties followed the well known Santa Fe Trail from Independence, Missouri, many others sought passage westward by the south bank of the Canadian River—the Fort Smith-Santa Fe Trail—which carried perhaps as many as two thousand travelers in the summer of 1849. Josiah Gregg's *Commerce of the Prairies* popularized the Canadian River route and apparently served to some extent as a guidebook. Abert's journal, now beautifully embalmed in a government document, would have served far better.

Gregg's trail, running well south of the Canadian proper, intersected tributary streams where wood and sweet water were consistently found.

---

[54] For an account of the relationship of these towns to the gold rush, see *Marcy and the Gold Seekers*, ed. Grant Foreman, pp. 3-65; Goetzmann, *Army Exploration*, pp. 212-213.

Proceeding eastward Gregg crept increasingly nearer the Canadian and followed the river very closely from about the center of Hutchinson County on across the Panhandle.[55] The Fort Smith-Santa Fe Trail enjoyed a fine reputation and Fort Smith businessmen seized quickly upon its potential. The popularity of the route appears to have been promoted by four basic features: (1) much of the trail passed through country already settled; (2) it was about two hundred miles shorter than the Missouri River route; (3) wood, water, forage, and pleasant campsites were ample; and (4) travel at least one month earlier in the spring was possible because warmer latitude brought earlier forage. The latter factor had encouraged Gregg to seek a trail south of the Canadian in the first place.[56]

Most emigrant parties contained upward of twenty persons; one was composed of only four; while another, of primary interest to this study, comprised nearly five hundred civilians and a military escort of about eighty men. This large party was recruited by Captain John Dillard at Fort Smith and Van Buren, and political influence of some members obtained a military escort that the army charged to appropriations for a preliminary railroad survey. The highly competent, hard working, ubiquitous frontier infantryman, Captain Randolph B. Marcy, commanded the escort,[57] while Lieutenant J. H. Simpson, of the Corps of Topographical Engineers, accompanied the expedition to prepare "a report and plan in reference to the road from Fort Smith to Santa Fe, in which you will include all circumstances bearing upon this route as a good route, military and commercial, particularly reporting upon its facilities in grass, wood, and water."[58]

[55] Ernest R. Archambeau, "The Fort Smith-Santa Fe Trail Along the Canadian River in Texas," *Panhandle-Plains Historical Review* 27 (1954): 3-9, works out Gregg's trail in detail. See also Archambeau's excellent map following page 26.

[56] See the letters of B. L. E. Bonneville and Brigadier General M. Arbuckle to the editor of the *Fort Smith Herald*, November 22, 1848. Bonneville considered only one thing essential "to make this route perfect. It is a Post where the Texas boundary crosses the Canadian River . . . [which] would be as it were a half way house, where parties might refresh and rest if necessary. It would draw around it numerous traders desirous to participate in the trade of the prairies. . . . Creeks and Texans, would advance under its protection, and it is the very spot to control the wild spirits of the prairies."

[57] Archambeau, "The Fort Smith-Santa Fe Trail," pp. 10-11. Randolph B. Marcy, "The Report of Capt. R. B. Marcy's Route from Fort Smith to Santa Fe," in *Reports of the Secretary of War*, 31st Cong., 1st sess., Sen. Exec. Doc. No. 64 (1850), p. 169, hereafter cited as Marcy, "From Fort Smith to Santa Fe."

[58] James H. Simpson,". . . the Report and Map of the Route from Fort Smith, Arkansas, to Santa Fe, New Mexico, made by Lieutenant Simpson," in *Report from the Secretary of War*, 31st Cong., 1st sess., Sen. Exec. Doc. No. 12 (1850), p. 2, hereafter cited as Simpson, "Report."

Marcy's instructions, somewhat broader than those given Simpson, resolve themselves into these basic objectives: (1) to find, measure, map, and describe the best route to Santa Fe wholly along the south side of the Canadian River; (2) to give aid and protection to the civilian company; and (3) to establish friendly relations with potentially hostile Indians, mainly the Comanches, and to remind them of their treaty obligations to permit unmolested passage of Americans through their domain. Complying with his orders, Marcy hired Dr. Julian Rogers of Wilmington, Delaware, to serve as physician to the expedition, which also included Lieutenant J. Buford and twenty-six men of the First Dragoons, and Lieutenants M. P. Harrison and J. Updegraff and fifty men of the Fifth Infantry.[59]

Marcy led his "train," consisting of "eighteen wagons, one six pounder iron gun and a travelling forge, each drawn by six mules," from Fort Smith on the evening of April 4, 1849. At Edwards' trading houses, about 130 miles from Fort Smith, the captain hired an experienced Delaware Indian named "Black Beaver" as guide and interpreter.[60]

In the early days of May the timbered country gradually faded behind, but heavy rains delayed the march. Marcy's journal entry of May 6 shows something of the character of this frontier soldier and suggests that beneath his tunic there beat a poetic, reverent heart. He writes:

> This evening we have another thunder storm, accompanied by the most intensely vivid lightening I have ever seen. The whole artillery of heaven appears to be playing; and as the sound reverberates in the distance over the vast expanse of prairie, the effect is indeed most awfully sublime. Upon such an occasion one realizes truly the wonderful power and majesty of the Deity, and the total insignificance of man.[61]

What kind of a man, with his equipment so waterlogged and the earth so saturated that his column could move only with excruciating effort, would have contemplated the majesty of Deity and thought of a line like "the whole artillery of heaven?"

Contact with the civilian train was not established until May 16, well along the trail,[62] but the night of May 31 found the united caravan

[59] Marcy, "From Fort Smith to Santa Fe," pp. 169-171.
[60] Ibid., pp. 173-174.
[61] Ibid., p. 175.
[62] Ibid., p. 177.

camped at Antelope Hills, easily recognized by Simpson from Abert's "faithful drawing of them."[63] Water was found, but not wood, and the party therefore resorted to what would later be known commonly as "prairie coal"—buffalo chips. A march of "fourteen miles over a very direct and firm road" on June 1 brought Marcy into the Panhandle.[64] On his first evening in the Panhandle, the officer was visited by four Kiowa braves, who, armed to the teeth, assured the Captain that they were on their way to steal mules in Chihuahua, Mexico, and expected to be gone a year or more. A gracious host, Marcy invited his guests to dine with him, gave them pipes and tobacco—and apparently tactfully made it plain that their "great father" (the U.S. president) wanted peace with all his "red children." The conference was conducted through Black Beaver and the sign language. Utterly astonished at the grace, speed, accuracy, and detail of the Indians' communication through this medium, Marcy observed, "I had no idea before that the Indians were such adepts at pantomime; and I have no hesitation in saying that they would compare with the most accomplished performers of our operas."[65]

Marcy continued along the divide between the Washita and the Canadian on June 2, finding a "very good road." "The wife of one of the emigrants . . . has been sick for several days," Marcy observes in his journal on June 2 with a sense of impending tragedy, "and reported tonight as very low. The fatigue and inconveniences . . . has, no doubt," opined Marcy, "had a tendency to aggravate her disease."[66]

On June 4 the caravan approached Dry River (Red Deer Creek in eastern Hemphill County).[67] While at this location, Marcy records an interesting and possibly highly important bit of information he got from Black Beaver.

[63] Simpson, "Report," p. 9.
[64] Marcy, "From Fort Smith to Santa Fe," p. 180. For Marcy's exact route through the Panhandle, see Archambeau, "The Fort Smith-Santa Fe Trail," pp. 11-21, and map following page 26. Notice that Marcy, unlike Gregg, stayed well south of the main bed of the Canadian, intersecting the hospitable tributaries, until the two trails more or less coincided in Hutchinson County and remained closely parallel across northwestern Carson County. Marcy veered to the west while in western Carson County and, while remaining well away from the main bed of the Canadian, was closer to it than Gregg had been. At a point just northwest of Vega, in Oldham County, the two trails merge and remain closely parallel to the New Mexico line.
[65] Marcy, "From Fort Smith to Santa Fe," pp. 180-181. Doubtless this comparison of Indians to opera singers would have delighted the prima donnas of Marcy's day.
[66] Ibid., p. 181.
[67] Ibid. Archambeau, "The Fort Smith-Santa Fe Trail," p. 14, places the camp site of June 4 at present Mendota and notes that the ruts of the old wagon road are still

I am informed by Black Beaver, who is well acquainted with this part of the country, that this stream has its source in an extensive salt plain southwest of here, and that "Red river," which has never been explored to its head, rises in the same plain, and near the same place. It has generally been supposed that Red river extended far west of here, near the Pecos, and passed through a portion of the "Llano Estacado," but Beaver says it rises east of that plain.[68]

While Marcy and Beaver speculated on geographic matters, Simpson, the topographer, speculated upon the origins of the caprocked, mesa-like, cone-shaped hills so common along the Canadian Valley. The lieutenant's speculations seem quaint by modern standards:

Have they arisen on account of upheaving causes, or have they resulted from the abrasion and consequent degradation of the soil and rocks around them? To my mind, they are attributable to the same causes which have been operating to produce the changes which have been going on about Dry river, [i.e., degrading forces] but on a scale sufficiently great to produce them. That scale, I conceive, was afforded during the period of the *Noachic* deluge, and to this period do I date their origin and formation.[69]

Simpson's "acceptance of biblical-catastrophic geology . . . illustrates," observes Goetzmann appropriately, "that the advanced scientific theories had by no means been universally accepted."[70]

Reaching White Deer Creek on June 6—Marcy called it Timbered Creek—the travelers found an exceptionally beautiful, inviting camp ground. Since "some of our wagon tires are loose and need resetting," the Captain decided to "lie over" at this especially delightful place on June 7.[71] On June 8 Marcy left the emigrant company on "Timbered Creek" and pushed on, apparently feeling that his function as an escort

---

visible just south of State Highway 33 and one mile east of its juncture with U.S. Highway 60.

[68] Marcy, "From Fort Smith to Santa Fe," pp. 181-182. This seemingly incidental bit of Marcy's report may be anything but that. Did it influence Marcy three years later to seek the headwaters of the Red or tip him off as to where to find them? One wonders.

[69] Simpson, "Report," pp. 11-12.

[70] Goetzmann, *Army Exploration*, p. 216.

[71] Marcy, "From Fort Smith to Santa Fe," p. 182; Archambeau, "The Fort Smith-Santa Fe Trail," p. 15.

was unnecessary. The circumstances that caused the emigrants to be left behind are of unique interest in regional history, however.

> They were detained in consequence of the illness of the wife of an emigrant [presumably the same woman whose "disease" had been aggravated by the rigors of the trail] ; and we have learned this evening that the result of the detention has been an addition to the company of two promising boys, (twins) which the happy father has done Captain Dillard and myself the honor of calling 'Dillard' and 'Marcy.' For my part I feel highly complimented; and if I never see the gold regions myself, I shall have the satisfaction of knowing that my name is represented there. I wish the young gentleman a safe journey to California, and much happiness and gold after he gets there.

These twin boys were, certainly beyond all reasonable doubt, the first Anglo-American children born in the Texas Panhandle—but Marcy, apparently deliriously happy, failed to record their last name![72]

Through June 9, when he located Antelope Peak, June 10, 11, 12, and 13, Marcy traveled through Carson, Potter, and into Oldham counties, crossing or camping upon Dixon, Antelope, Bonita, East Amarillo, and West Amarillo creeks, consistently finding wood, water, and forage. Although pleased with the abundance of water, wood, grass, wild grapes, and wild gooseberries, Marcy found game scarce and wary and the hunting mediocre and disappointing. On the thirteenth, the trail led "through a continuous [prairie] dog town." Examining a live specimen, Marcy, with a naturalist's discernment, noted the little creature's similarity to the gray squirrel, and concluded, "a more appropriate name . . . would be 'prairie squirrel.' " The Captain quickly perceived further that the alleged friendly relationship of prairie dogs, burrowing owls, and rattlesnakes was pure myth; not in the least friendly, but entirely predatory![73]

A two-mile march on June 14 brought the expedition to "a spur of the plain," which Marcy felt obliged to cross since there was an easy ascent and the distance around the spur prohibitive. Ascending the escarpment, the company beheld the awesome sight of the Llano Estacado. Marcy reacted thus:

> When we were upon the high table-land, a view presented itself as

---

[72] Marcy, "From Fort Smith to Santa Fe," p. 182.
[73] Ibid., pp. 183-185; Archambeau, "The Fort Smith-Santa Fe Trail," pp. 15-18.

Scene in Palo Duro Canyon State Park showing an outcrop of the caprock and its influence on erosion. (Photo by the author.)

Model of an Antelope Creek Focus village. (Courtesy Panhandle-Plains Historical Museum.)

Tecovas Springs in southwestern Potter County. Typical of the headsprings of Canadian River tributaries, Las Tecovas was a Comanchero trading point, a campsite on the Fort Smith-Santa Fe Trail, and headquarters of the Frying Pan Ranch. The building is the Frying Pan springhouse. (Photo by the author.)

Wagon-wheel ruts on the Fort Smith-Santa Fe Trail, southwest of highway 136 near Fritch. (Photo by the author.)

James W. Abert some years after his Canadian River reconnaissance, from a drawing by Harold Bugbee. (Courtesy Panhandle-Plains Historical Museum.)

Frank D. Baldwin, head of scouts for Colonel Nelson A. Miles during the Red River War. (Courtesy Panhandle-Plains Historical Museum.)

Buffalo herd on the Goodnight Ranch. The dark area in the foreground is a developing buffalo wallow. (Courtesy Panhandle-Plains Historical Museum.)

Wheeler County courthouse and jail, 1879-1907. (Courtesy Panhandle-Plains Historical Museum.)

boundless as the ocean. Not a tree, shrub, or any other object, either animate or inanimate, relieved the dreary monotony of the prospect; it was a vast, illimitable expense of desert prairie—the dreaded "Llano Estacado" . . . or, in other words, the Great Zahara [*sic*] of North America. It is a region almost as vast and trackless as the ocean—a land where no man, either savage or civilized, permanently abides; it spreads forth into a treeless, desolate waste of uninhabited solitude, which always has been, and must continue, uninhabited forever; even the savages dare not venture to cross it except at two or three places, where they know water can be found. The only herbage upon these barren plains is a very short buffalo grass, and, on account of the scarcity of water, all animals appear to shun it.[74]

Simpson reacted to the Llano Estacado with equal fervor:

Whilst upon the staked plains, he [the traveler] *sees what he has not before seen during his whole route*—an uninterrupted expanse of *dead level prairie*, with not a tree anywhere upon it to vary the scene. Here the tantalizing and shifting *mirage*—the well-known characteristic of the arid plains of Mexico—he will see in perfection. Sheets of water will appear to him, reflecting . . . the objects beyond them. Antelopes will appear bounding over the plain like buffalo, and men in the distance will look like elongated spectres. Sometimes the mirage will present the appearance of smoke, and sometimes that of distant woods, with an outline of retreating steps.[75]

Notwithstanding its forbidding character, the Llano Estacado provided easy traveling over a "road . . . perfectly hard and smooth, and our animals did not suffer much from the effect of the long drive of twenty-eight miles which we made." Late in the day the spur of the Llano was descended and camp pitched two miles beyond on "a creek with fine water, but little wood."[76]

June 15 found Marcy stopping on "a stream where water was standing in large pools, with sufficient wood and grass." The officer recognized the place as one often used "as the trees in the vicinity are well stripped of

[74] Marcy, "From Fort Smith to Santa Fe," p. 185.

[75] Simpson, "Report," p. 12.

[76] Marcy, "From Fort Smith to Santa Fe," p. 185. Archambeau, "The Fort Smith-Santa Fe Trail," p. 19 places the march across the Llano Estacado along the route of present Interstate 40 and approximately through the sites of the present towns of Vega and Adrian in Oldham County.

their branches, and show marks of the axe; moreover, we are now upon the old Mexican cart-road." Whether Marcy realized he was on a Comanchero campground is not indicated, but that doubtless was the case.

The morale of the emigrant company had held up well, especially considering their long absence from civilization. With apparent admiration, Marcy describes their evenings' activities: "Our friends in the emigrants' camp are enjoying themselves much this evening; they have managed to raise some music, and are dancing around their camp fires most merrily. It certainly looks as if they were determined to keep up their spirits as they go along."[77] Although delayed by an early morning shower on June 16, the company covered twenty-two miles, which took them well beyond the western boundary of the Panhandle and within sight of Cerro Tucumcari.[78]

In comparing the influence of Gregg and Marcy in establishing the Fort Smith-Santa Fe Trail through the Texas Panhandle, it would seem fair to say that Gregg's function, carried out through *Commerce of the Prairies*, was to call attention to the area south of the Canadian as a desirable location for a route across the plains. Marcy's function was actually to blaze a specific route and to describe it with such clarity and detail that anyone capable of comprehending and applying what he read could follow it. Marcy writes interestingly and clearly and, like Abert, presents an absorbing account of the journey along the Canadian River Valley in the middle nineteenth century.

Simpson's report is brief and far from the thorough job turned in by Abert. Moreover, from a literary point of view, Simpson's report, as compared to Abert's, is an assault upon virtue. On the other hand, and in fairness to Simpson, it may be that since he could compare Abert's report with the terrain, Simpson saw little point in plowing the same ground again, especially since Abert's function was general reconnaissance and Simpson's was specifically to evaluate the terrain as a possible railroad route. In contrast to Marcy's version of the journey, Simpson had the thoughtfulness to conclude his report with practical advice and observations for prospective emigrants. Since the party had found game scarce,

[77] Marcy, "From Fort Smith to Santa Fe," p. 185. Archambeau, "The Fort Smith-Santa Fe Trail," p. 20, identifies the campsite of June 15 as on a branch of Trujillo Creek in Oldham County near the place where Gregg was attacked by Indians on the night of March 10, 1840.
[78] Marcy, "From Fort Smith to Santa Fe," pp. 185-186; Simpson, "Report," pp. 13-14.

Simpson advised future travelers not to rely upon the land to support them, but to provision themselves upon the premise that game would not be found; west of the Cross Timbers, advised Simpson, the divide between the Washita and Canadian rivers provided the easiest and most pleasant route except, perhaps, in time of drouth, while "in respect to *safety* with which the emigrants traversed the route, so far as *molestation by the Indians is concerned*, party after party, unescorted, some of them very small—one of them composed of but four Germans—travelled the whole distance from Fort Smith to Santa Fe without meeting, so far as I can learn, with the least obstruction from this quarter." Finally Simpson recommended establishment of a series of military posts at strategic points along the route to provide way stations for the convenience of emigrants and from which the government might more effectively deal with the prairie Indians.[79]

As to the Fort Smith-Santa Fe Trail as a railroad route, Marcy and Simpson sharply disagreed. Marcy, having described the route in general terms, concludes his report:

> I am, therefore, of the opinion, that but few localities could be found upon the continent which (for as great a distance) would present as few obstacles to the construction of a railway as upon this route. . . . The surface of the ground is generally so perfectly even and level that but little labor would be required to grade the road; and, as there are but few hills or ravines, there would not be much excavation or embankment.[80]

Simpson accepted Marcy's view of the land, but evaluated it as a railroad route with a more discerning eye—an engineer's discerning eye—and emphasized: "*But to my mind the time has not yet come when this or any other railroad can be built over this continent.*" Conscious of his military status and eschewing political meddling, Simpson invoked his status as an

[79] Simpson, "Report," pp. 20-21. Randolph B. Marcy, *The Prairie Traveler: A Handbook for Overland Expeditions*, was published in 1859 as a guide for those traveling the overland trails. In concise form Marcy discusses varied topics, including organization of parties, packsaddles, hunting methods, use of firearms, firearms safety, camp furniture, and the like. A long appendix contains itineraries of twenty-eight western trails. *The Prairie Traveler* may well have been the first "camping manual" published in the United States and in terms of basic techniques and skills described is little different from the "how to" camping books of current publication. Equipment is a different matter; an outdoorsman like Marcy would have been delighted with the equipment modern technology has made available.

[80] Marcy, "From Fort Smith to Santa Fe," p. 192.

engineering officer to argue that a transcontinental railroad simply was not a feasible undertaking. "That this work will some day be accomplished, I would not be so presumptuous as to say that it will not; but that it can be commenced now, and be brought to a successful period [*sic*] within ten or twenty years, I do not believe." On this point Simpson was amazingly foresighted, for it was exactly twenty years before the first transcontinental railroad was completed. Finally, Simpson pointed out the difficulties of building a railroad over such a vast expanse of territory uninhabited by "a good, producing population . . . and the resources which such a population naturally develops." As an alternative to railroads, Simpson advocated "military roads"—wagon roads—and the construction of posts along their routes to support migration and around which centers of population could develop. "In a word, to my mind the order of means in respect to the establishment of this railroad is, first, the creation of centres of population wherever along the route they can be created; second, the development of the resources of these several points by this population; and, third, the taking advantage of these resources to aid in the prosecution of the road."[81]

Simpson's more critical estimate of trans-Mississippi railroading, as compared to that of Marcy, is broadly significant. Goetzmann makes the point beautifully when he says, "It was the Topographical Engineer's job to render a considered judgment in these matters, and a comparison of the engineer's report with that of the enthusiastic infantryman Marcy reveals something of the unique value of the trained army topographers in the work of western development."[82]

By 1850 the Canadian River Valley had been thoroughly explored by Anglo-Americans and practicable trails clearly established. Through the wide dissemination of George Wilkins Kendall's *Narrative of the Texan Santa Fe Expedition* the public presumably gained some insight into the area of upper Tierra Blanca Creek. There remained, then, two unknowns: what lay in the interior of the Staked Plains, and where were the headwaters of the Red River? As to the interior of the Staked Plains, evidently men such as Long, Abert, Marcy, Simpson, and the Texan Santa Fe pioneers, having concluded that the Llano was uninhabitable, felt that exploration would not be worth the danger and suffering that would inevitably attend such an undertaking.

[81] Simpson, "Report," pp. 22-23. The experience of the post-Civil War transcontinental railroads would certainly seem to support Simpson's views.
[82] Goetzmann, *Army Exploration*, p. 217.

Locating the sources of the Red River, however, was a matter of importance, though until 1852 their location remained a mystery. Also some mystery exists as to what was commonly believed about the location of these headwaters. After Long's error of mistaking the Canadian for the Red, it would appear to have required no great genius to realize that the Red River rose somewhere to the south. More specifically, Abert recognized in 1845 that the Staked Plains gave rise "not only to the Washita, but to all the main branches of the Red River, as well as the rivers of upper Texas, or their affluents."[83] Abert's rather casual comment indicates that the lieutenant had no notion of announcing newly discovered truth. Inferentially, therefore, other persons with current knowledge of southwestern geography realized that the Red rose in the Staked Plains. Nonetheless, even informed opinion was vague because Abert, accidentally getting on the North Fork, failed to associate the stream with the Red River.

Outside more or less scientific circles, there may well have been far-reaching confusion relative to the sources of the Red. Considering the great size of the lower Red, an assumption that it arose in the western mountains would not have been unreasonable. Or, given the mineral content of its waters, an apparently common assumption that the Red rose in "salt plains" was not unwarranted.[84]

After Long's failure to find the Red from the west, no further efforts were made, perhaps because of the necessity to invade the Staked Plains. In view of the impression that forbidding land had made on Long, Abert, and Marcy, it is not surprising that no one cared to seek the Red by crossing the Staked Plains. The Texan Santa Fe pioneers, who crossed the Staked Plains from the east by way of Tierra Blanca Creek, and Abert, who found the North Fork, failed to relate these streams to the Red, so that it remained for the indefatigable Randolph B. Marcy to come up with the right and obvious approach of merely following the Red from the east until its headwaters were found. Pointing out that the Red had not been fully explored and that available knowledge was of dubious accuracy, and calling attention to his own experience in southwestern exploration, Marcy requested the adjutant general of the army to send him on a mission into the unknown region.[85] On March 5,

---

[83] Carroll, ed., *Abert's Journal*, pp. 74-75.

[84] Randolph B. Marcy, *Exploration of the Red River of Louisiana, in the Year 1852*, pp. 1-4, gives a brief account of previous efforts to explore the Red and provides some insight into the theories of its origin.

[85] Randolph B. Marcy, *Adventure on Red River*, ed. Grant Foreman, pp. xii-xiii. This edited version of Marcy's official report contains background information and some effort to locate the expedition's whereabouts at given times, although it is not

1852, the adjutant general ordered Marcy "to make an examination of the Red River and the country bordering upon it, from the mouth of Cache creek to its sources." Brevet Captain George B. McClellan of the engineers was designated to accompany the expedition.[86]

Arriving on Cache Creek on the evening of May 13, 1852, Marcy began the long trek to the headwaters of the Red. By May 28 the expedition had arrived at a point McClellan computed to be almost on the one hundredth meridian.[87] Actually McClellan located the position about fifty miles to the east of the true position of one hundred degrees. From the position of May 28, Marcy proceeded up the Red to its confluence with the North Fork, and up the North Fork toward the eastern boundary of the Panhandle—the true one hundredth meridian—which he approached, according to Grant Foreman's reasonable placement, on June 9.[88] Following a stream he called "Sweetwater Creek," a tributary of the North Fork, Marcy entered eastern Wheeler County on June 10.[89] Underway at three o'clock on the morning of the eleventh, Marcy took to the high prairie adjacent to the valley of the Sweetwater. An eight-mile march brought the expedition to two fresh Indian trails that Marcy judged to be those of war parties, since they revealed no sign of lodge poles having been dragged. Continuing toward the head of North Fork on June 13, 14, and 15, Marcy found the Panhandle abundant in beauty, fresh water (although the mineralized kind was common, too), game, wild fruits and onions, and widespread signs of Indians.[90]

On June 16 Marcy's party reached the head of the North Fork and apparently ascended the Llano Estacado. In a grove of cottonwoods near the camp of June 16, Marcy "buried a bottle containing the following memorandum: On the 16th day of June, 1852, an exploring expedition, composed of Captain R. B. Marcy, Captain G. B. McClellan, Lieutenant

---

intended to be a thorough trail study. This version will be cited where helpful. Randolph B. Marcy, *Exploration of the Red River of Louisiana, in the Year of 1852* is Marcy's official report and will be cited hereafter as Marcy, *Exploration of the Red River*, to convey what Marcy and his associates found.

[86] Marcy, *Exploration of the Red River*, p. 1. Cache Creek flows into the Red from the North opposite northern Clay County, Texas.

[87] Ibid., p. 19.

[88] Ibid., pp. 19-33; Marcy, *Adventure on Red River*, ed. Foreman, pp. 32-49.

[89] Marcy, *Adventure on Red River*, ed. Foreman, pp. 49-51, footnotes 2, 3, and 4.

[90] Marcy, *Exploration of the Red River*, pp. 35-41. Foreman places the camp of June 12 near the site where Fort Elliot was later located and places the explorers in eastern Gray County on the fourteenth. See Marcy, *Adventure on Red River*, ed. Foreman, pp. 59-60, footnotes 6 and 7.

J. Updegraff, and Doctor G. C. Shumard, with fifty-five men of company D fifth infantry, encamped here, having this day traced the north branch of Red River to its sources. Accompanying the expedition were Captain J. H. Strain, of Fort Washita, and Mr. J. R. Suydam, of New York City."[91]

Realizing that he was near the Canadian River, which he had traveled three years earlier, and anxious to establish the relationship between it and the North Fork, Marcy spent June 16 through 19 visiting the Canadian. With a selected party the Captain struck northward across the Staked Plains "where the eye rests upon no object of relief within the scope of vision." A march of twenty-five miles led to a point on the Canadian that Marcy immediately recognized. Having thus established his position, he then decided to march his whole command due south over the Staked Plains to the Salt Fork, which he had passed near the Wichita Mountains. Although he expresses concern for his water supply on the southward journey, Marcy was surprised and well pleased with the way the Panhandle had treated him thus far. "I have never travelled over a route on the plains west of the Cross Timbers, where the water, grass, and wood were as good and abundant as upon the one over which our explorations have led us."[92]

On June 20 the entire command moved southward toward the Salt Fork for twelve miles and found a small stream of sweet water that Marcy named McClellan's Creek, because he believed McClellan "to be the first white man that ever set eyes upon it." Quite probably the explorers were on the stream in southern Gray County known presently as McClellan Creek.[93] Continuing southward, the party crossed the divide between the North and Salt forks in northern Donley County on June 21 and explored a tributary of the Salt Fork. Having consistently found sweet water in the upper tributaries of the Red near the Staked Plains, Marcy concluded, "This settles the question that these branches of the river do not take their rise in salt plains, as has heretofore been very generally supposed."[94]

By the day's end on the twenty-third, Marcy, having explored the

[91] Marcy, *Exploration of the Red River*, pp. 41-42. Marcy, *Adventure on Red River*, ed. Foreman, p. 65, footnote 2, places the camp of June 16 "near Lefors in Gray County, Texas."

[92] Marcy, *Exploration of the Red River*, pp. 42-43. Marcy's trail between the North Fork and the Canadian must have roughly paralleled that followed by Abert seven years earlier.

[93] Ibid., p. 44 and Marcy, *Adventure on Red River*, ed. Foreman, p. 68, footnote 5.

[94] Marcy, *Exploration of the Red River*, p. 45. See also Marcy, *Adventure on Red River*, ed. Foreman, p. 70, footnotes 8 and 9. Foreman reasonably places Marcy in Armstrong County by the end of the march on the twenty-second.

environs of Salt Fork to his satisfaction, determined to go as directly as possible to the "south branch" of the Red River and complete his mission. For the next four days the trail southward passed over rugged, sandy, broken country, as was to be expected since Marcy was getting closer to the main branch of the Red River. The trail was necessarily circuitous, but game was plentiful and fresh water continued to be found. On June 27 the explorers approached the Staked Plains, and later in the day reached the main branch of the Red River. Marcy describes the day's incidents thus:

> Directly in front of us lay the high table-lands of the "Llano Esta-cado," towering up some eight hundred feet above the surrounding country, and bordered by precipitous escarpments capped with a stratum of white gypsum, which glistened in the sun like burnished silver. After travelling fourteen miles, we reached the valley of the principal branch of the river.
>
> It was here nine hundred yards wide, flowing over a very sandy bed, with but little water in the channel, and is fortified upon each side by rugged hills and deep gullies, over which I think it will be impossible to take our train.[95]

The march of June 28 led directly to the base of the High Plains Escarpment. Marcy describes the experience: "After marching eight miles . . . we reached the base of those towering and majestic cliffs, which rise almost perpendicularly from the undulating swells of prairie at the base, to the height of eight hundred feet, and terminate at the summit in a plateau almost as level as the sea, which spreads out to the south and west like the steppes of Central Asia, in an apparently illimitable desert."[96] Marcy apparently hoped to find a trail up the escarpment that would accommodate his wagons. Investigation proved that not even the horses could ascend the precipice so that the easier trail along the rim of the Staked Plains could be followed. So, like another Plains explorer of three centuries earlier, the Captain resolved to pursue his objective with a picked force. Leaving Lieutenant Updegraff in command of the main body, Marcy, with McClellan and ten men, pushed on.[97]

Packing six days' provisions on mules, Marcy's advance party moved upstream on the morning of June 29. Almost immediately the rough ter-

---

[95] Marcy, *Exploration of the Red River*, pp. 47-53.
[96] Ibid., p. 54. Note Marcy's use of the term "desert" in connection with the Staked Plains.
[97] Ibid., pp. 54-55.

rain slowed progress, and, before the day ended, only highly mineralized water was to be had. Its consumption only increased thirsts already made intense by the heat of the day. Trying to follow the river on the thirtieth, the tiny party wound its way between escarpments that "rose precipitously from the banks of the river. . . . In many places there was not room for a man to pass between the foot of the acclivities and the river." Although small tributary rivulets were often found, no sweet water was to be had. By noon, fifteen grueling, tortuous miles had been covered. After resting until four o'clock, Marcy pushed on, desperately seeking fresh water, for several men had become violently ill from the "nauseating and repulsive water" they had been forced to drink. None was found, and of that night Marcy says "my slumbers were continually disturbed by dreams, in which I fancied myself swallowing huge draughts of ice water."[98]

The width of the stream diminished gradually as it was ascended on July 1, but again none of several tributaries carried good water. Later in the day, however, a point was reached at which the river bed "suddenly changed to rock, with the water . . . much to our delight . . . entirely free from salts." From this point Marcy soon reached what he considered to be the main head spring of the Red River. He describes the approach as follows:

> And following up for two miles the tortuous course of the gorge, we reached a point where it became so much obstructed with huge piles of rock, that we were obliged to leave our animals and clamber up the remainder of the distance on foot.
>
> The gigantic escarpments of sandstone, rising to the giddy height of eight hundred feet upon each side, gradually closed in until they were only a few yards apart and finally united over head, leaving a long, narrow corridor beneath, at the base of which the head spring of the principal or main branch of Red River takes its rise.[99]

Climbing up onto the surface of the Llano Estacado, McClellan computed his geographical position as "latitude 34° 42' north, and longitude 103° 7' 11" west" and computed the altitude above sea level at 2,450 feet.[100] Although not far wrong in his latitudinal position,

---

[98] Ibid., pp. 55-59.

[99] Ibid., pp. 59-60. Despite the dreadful character of the country surrounding the headwaters of the Red, Marcy reports the presence of much wildlife, and especially notes numerous black bear inhabiting the area.

[100] Ibid., p. 61.

McClellan was glaringly in error in his longitudinal computations, for any canyon even remotely resembling Marcy's description is well east of the 102nd meridian. Foreman is certain that the great spring was found in Palo Duro Canyon, for he says, "The Mexicans called this canyon Arroyo Palo Duro and Arroyo Tierra Blanca."[101] Marcy's descriptions of where he was, although seemingly somewhat dramatic, rather clearly supports the view that he was in Palo Duro Canyon or one of its main tributaries. More precise location of Marcy's whereabouts is difficult, however, because as Foreman also points out, it is difficult to reconcile Marcy's text with his map or to reconcile either with modern nomenclature.[102] The important point is, of course, that Marcy settled the basic question of where the Red River of Louisiana came from, the whole purpose of his exploration.

Marcy makes no entry in his journal for July 2, and merely notes that he arrived at his base camp on July 3, having journeyed sixty-five miles from the head of the river.[103] The command celebrated Independence Day, 1852, by turning toward the east and home. An effort to stay near the Red—or Prairie Dog Town Fork of the Red—was frustrated by the highly eroded surface, and on the sixth Marcy was forced almost to the crest of the divide between Salt Fork and Prairie Dog Town Fork to get easier passage. Clear, cold streams continued to be found along a trail that led doubtlessly through Hall and Childress counties, but the taste of gypsum continued to be present.[104] Maintaining the habit of starting very early, the party continued without particular incident until on the ninth, from the crest of the divide, "some of the most lofty peaks at the western extremity of the Wichita chain of mountains showed themselves in the distance."[105] Surely no sight could have been more welcome to Marcy and his men; probably by this time—and if not, quite shortly thereafter—they had passed out of the Texas Panhandle.

Although the exact terminal point of Marcy's exploration may not be fixed as precisely as one would like, the completion of his examination of the Red River was certainly more than adequate to dissipate the aura of mystery that had surrounded the location of the headwaters of the Red River. Moreover, from the point of view of regional history Marcy accomplished a thorough examination of the Eroded Plains lying within the

[101] Marcy, *Adventure on Red River*, ed. Foreman, p. 90, footnote 2.
[102] Ibid., p. 94, footnote 4.
[103] Marcy, *Exploration of the Red River*, pp. 62-63.
[104] Ibid., pp. 63-66.
[105] Ibid., pp. 67-68.

Panhandle and provided remarkably detailed descriptions of what was to be found. Seeming to have found almost a boyish delight in the outdoors, the Captain assiduously collected and preserved specimens for scientific study. Thus, the Red River expedition would seem also to have had significant value to several scientific fields, in addition to its contributions to knowledge of southwestern geography.[106]

Notwithstanding the soundness of James H. Simpson's conservative regard for the feasibility of a Pacific railroad, he may as well not have spoken, for public and political clamor for such a road increased after 1849. To locate an appropriate route, the government turned to the topographical engineers to resolve scientifically the issue of where to lay the first rails. The Pacific Railroad Survey bill, passed on March 2, 1853, provided that the Secretary of War should

> employ such portion of the Corps of Topographical Engineers, and other persons as he may deem necessary, to make such explorations and surveys as he may deem advisable, to ascertain the most practicable and economical route for a railroad from the Mississippi river to the Pacific ocean . . . [and] that the engineers and other persons employed in said explorations and surveys shall be organized in as many distinct corps as there are routes to be surveyed, and their several reports shall be laid before Congress on or before the first Monday in February, 1854.[107]

Compliance with this gargantuan congressional directive could be achieved only because reconnaissances, not literal surveys, were required. "The operation," explains Goetzmann, "was to be a general topographical survey aimed at determining the relative merits of the competing routes rather than minute projections of actual rights-of-way."

Information in any way relevant to railroad construction was to be gathered. "Here, as never before," says Goetzmann, "was a chance to compile a great scientific inventory on all levels and at the same time to make that data relevant to the national problem at hand."[108] Consequently, teams of scientific specialists were attached to the four main parties originally ordered into the field. One of these was directed "to operate along the 35th parallel from Fort Smith via Albuquerque and Zuñi to California."[109] The proposed

---

[106] See ibid., pp. ii-v and the appendixes, pp. 125-300, which contain the scientific reports.

[107] *Congressional Globe*, 32nd Cong., 2nd sess., XXVI (1853), p. 841.

[108] Goetzmann, *Army Exploration*, p. 275.

[109] Ibid. Scientific evaluation of competing railroad routes did not quiet the politics involved, for there was indeed an horrendous clash of sectional, economic, poli-

thirty-fifth parallel route had especial significance because it compromised in some measure the conflicting interests of southern and north-central railroad advocates. First Lieutenant Amiel Weeks Whipple, having served ably as a member of the Mexican Boundary Survey, was placed in charge of the thirty-fifth parallel railroad survey.[110]

Whipple, thirty-seven years old when he led the survey that crossed the Panhandle, was a native of Greenwich, Massachusetts, had attended Amherst College, and was graduated from the Military Academy in 1841. With the coming of the Civil War, Whipple distinguished himself in combat, became a personal friend of President Lincoln, and in September 1862 was promoted to the rank of brigadier general. While in the thick of the fighting at Chancellorsville, Whipple was hit in the stomach by a Confederate sniper and died without ever regaining consciousness.[111]

In the sense of blazing a new trail through the Panhandle, the Whipple expedition was superfluous. Since Gregg, Abert, Simpson, and Marcy had already reported the region thoroughly, the government doubtless had the information required by the Pacific Railroad Survey bill. Archambeau's excellent study shows that Whipple followed closely the trails of Gregg and Marcy, deviating only where topographical considerations required it.[112] Indeed, the main objective of the thirty-fifth parallel survey was "to examine more carefully than ever before the country between the Zuñi villages and the Colorado River."[113] Clearly bearing out Goetzmann's observation are Whipple's instructions from Secretary of War Jefferson Davis and the plain emphasis of the report itself.[114]

That the scientific investigations of the survey were taken seriously is

---

tical, financial, and municipal interests as Goetzmann clearly shows. See ibid., pp. 262ff. It is significant that no railroad bill was passed until 1862, when there was no effective Southern representation in Congress.

[110] Ibid., p. 287.

[111] Malone, ed., *Dictionary of American Biography*, X, pp. 62-63; David E. Conrad, "The Whipple Expedition on the Great Plains," *Great Plains Journal* 2 (spring 1963): 44-45. This article is a thorough summary of the Great Plains segment of the Whipple survey.

[112] Archambeau, "The Fort Smith-Santa Fe Trail," pp. 21-24.

[113] Goetzmann, *Army Exploration*, p. 288.

[114] Lieutenant A. W. Whipple, "Report of Explorations of a Railroud Route, Near the Thirty-Fifth Parallel," Part I, pp. 1-2 in *Reports of Explorations and Surveys, to Ascertain the Most Practical and Economical Route for a Railroad from the Mississippi River to the Pacific Ocean*, III, 33d Cong. 1st sess., House of Representatives, Exec. Doc. No. 91 (1856). Hereafter cited as Whipple, "Report." This document is more conveniently available in "Lieutenant A. W. Whipple's Railroad Reconnaissance across the Panhandle of Texas in 1853," ed. Ernest R. Archambeau, *Panhandle-Plains Historical Review* 44 (1971): 1-128.

reflected in the accompanying civilian personnel. Among eleven specialists hired by Whipple were J. M. Bigelow, M. D., surgeon and naturalist; Jules Marcou, geologist, mining engineer, and protégé of Louis Agassiz; C. B. R. Kennerly, M. D., physician and naturalist; and Heinrich Baldwin Möllhausen, "an artist-naturalist who had been sent to America by the great Humboldt himself."[115]

Commencing the survey at Fort Smith with "chain, compass, and level" on July 14, 1853,[116] Whipple reached the now routine landmark, Antelope Hills, on September 6, with an early mild norther relieving what had been an uncomfortably warm march.[117]

While Whipple's exploration of the Panhandle contributed nothing new in terms of a trail, his journey through the region was eventful enough.[118] In the first place Whipple experienced more than usual contact with the Plains Indians, both Comanches and Kiowas, who seem almost to have overrun the Canadian Valley in the early fall of 1853. The Indians were typically unpredictable—either friendly, aloof, surly, or occasionally bellicose—adopting whatever posture seemed best to serve the expediency of moment and circumstance. Adopting an attitude of friendly firmness, Whipple, despite some tense moments, avoided serious trouble with the red men. Fortunately the expedition was sufficiently large, strong, and well armed that challenges to the lieutenant's attitude were not pushed very far, nor was the whole expedition in danger of attack. Smaller parties were another matter, however, and caused Whipple constant concern for the safety of surveying or scientific parties who necessarily separated themselves from the main body. Bigelow appears to have created a special problem because in his devotion to scientific investigation and collection of specimens he showed a notable indifference to his own safety and must have strained Whipple's sense of humor on more than one occasion.

Mexican captives were found among the Indians, including a woman of about twenty-seven who was the favorite wife of a chief and the mother of his blue-eyed son. Although anxious to secure the release of the captives, Whipple decided against taking them by force (since that might jeopardize his mission) and was unable to negotiate their release. The situation of the captives illustrates one side of the peculiar relationship of the Plains Indians to New Mexico. The other side is illustrated by other New Mexi-

---

[115] Ibid., p. 3; Goetzmann, *Army Exploration*, p. 287.
[116] Whipple, "Report," p. 5.
[117] Ibid., p. 29.
[118] The following summary is based on ibid., pp. 29-38.

cans who moved and traded freely among the Comanches and Kiowas. Several Comancheros were encountered, traveled with Whipple, advised the soldier on regional topography, and even encamped with the expedition. From one, José Garcia, Whipple learned "that both by Mexicans and Indians Red River is called 'Rio Palo Duro'; Washita, 'Rio Negro'; and the Canadian, 'Rio Colorado.' "[119]

In general, the Whipple expedition found the Panhandle hospitable, with wood and water usually available. Game was abundant, apparently more so in the eastern portion of the region. The Staked Plains made their accustomed impression, but evidently took Whipple and his party by no particular surprise, as they doubtless knew what to expect from the journals of their predecessors.

The examination of the Panhandle conducted by the thirty-fifth parallel survey team is by far the most thorough and elaborate. Of course, it should have been, given its more numerous scientific personnel and more elaborate equipment and instrumentation, although little, if anything, really new was found. This is not to disparage the expedition's work, however, for it did reinforce and elaborate the findings of earlier investigators. The final report on the thirty-fifth parallel survey was compiled by a number of specialists who utilized the data collected by Whipple's personnel, but in several instances relied heavily on the previous reports of Abert, Marcy, and Simpson.[120] Perhaps the use of these earlier documents reflects that the Panhandle was relatively well known to the government and that it was the area west of Albuquerque that Whipple was most concerned about. In any case, the real high point of the report is Möllhausen's magnificent lithographs.

The passage of the Whipple expedition through the Canadian River Valley marks the end of the formal exploration of the Panhandle and the end of the first phase of the region's reorientation toward the east—toward the United States, in fact, and not yet especially toward Texas. Through

[119] Ibid., p. 33. On September 11 the ruins of Bent's Fort were sighted. The condition of the ruins indicated clearly that the old post had long been out of use. Whipple believed that the white occupants had been murdered and the fort burned by Indians who were thoroughly drunk on trade whiskey.

[120] The final official version of the thirty-fifth parallel survey as cited in footnote 114 is composed of six parts including Part I, "Itinerary"; Part II, "Report on the Topographical Features and Character of the Country"; Part III, "Report upon the Indian Tribes"; Part IV, "Report on the Geology of the Route"; Part V, "Report on the Botany of the Expedition"; and Part VI, "Report on the Zoology of the Expedition."

the explorations of Long, Abert, Marcy, Simpson, Whipple, and their associates, a great store of scientific information regarding the region had been accumulated, trails through the region clearly established, and the major water courses explored. Indeed, much of the Panhandle, especially the Staked Plains, remained to be examined by an Anglo-American eye; this was to be done by other men—soldiers, hunters, surveyors, and cattle-men—who entered the region after the nation had taken time from its positive development to engage in the tragedy of the Civil War. Unlike the pre-Civil War explorers, these relative latecomers entered the Panhandle for reasons other than to find out what was there. Like Josiah Gregg, they sought other things, usually of a commercial character, and exploration, if it may be called that, was purely incidental.

Significantly the scientific exploration of the Texas Panhandle was exclusively financed and directed by the federal government and executed by its agents, and was in no way a function of state or private enterprise. Having occurred in a state that owned its public lands, this fact, in turn, suggests that the federal government was far more of a factor in the development of the American West than has generally been supposed. The agency that the government used for this function was, obviously, the U.S. army, or, more specifically, in all instances except the case of Captain Marcy, the Corps of Topographical Engineers.

The reports of the explorers establish clearly the domination of the region by the southern Plains Indians, especially the Comanches and the Kiowas. None contain anything to suggest any kind of permanent civilized settlements in the Canadian River valley and specifically contain no shred of evidence to support the supposed residence of the New Mexican sheep-men before the Civil War.

The constant reference of the reports to wood, water, and grass gives ample evidence of the importance of these products of nature to Anglo-American pioneer culture as it developed in the humid east and lends support to the Webb thesis that the changed environment of the Great Plains required drastic adjustments on the part of frontiersmen who had learned their pioneering in a humid land. The necessity for these commod-ities kept explorers rather well confined to the Canadian River valley, where they were found in relative abundance. Although the Staked Plains were crossed at narrow extensions, they were usually studiously avoided. Devoid especially of water, the Staked Plains consistently evoked a respect bordering on dread of a region where fearful things would befall anyone foolhardy enough to enter. Obviously Marcy's Red River exploration was not confined to the Canadian Valley, and Marcy did cross the edges of the Staked Plains, but, unable to find sweet water, suffered considerably as he penetrated the upper reaches of Prairie Dog Town Fork.

The most complete expedition to examine the Panhandle was that led by Whipple to survey the thirty-fifth parallel railroad route. The scientific contingent surpassed that of any other Panhandle expedition, and the report excelled in thoroughness and depth. As an individual performance, however, that of Abert far exceeds any other. Although in matters of scientific examination, he had only the aid of his assistant topographer, Lieutenant William G. Peck, Abert's journal is superlative. In consideration for Peck it should be said that he may deserve more credit for the expedition's success than is apparent from the documents.

The soldiers who led the scientific exploration of the Panhandle were all relatively young men who ranged in age from Abert, who explored the Canadian River at twenty-five, to Marcy, who found the headsprings of the Red River when he was forty. As professional soldiers, all seem to have had a strong sense of duty and of the responsibilities of command. But their fascination with exploration of the unknown seems to have been motivated by something akin to George Leigh Mallory's "because it's there." All the explorers but Long, a Dartmouth graduate, were products of the Military Academy, and all were born and reared in the east— Whipple and Marcy in Massachusetts; Long in New Hampshire; and Simpson and Abert in New Jersey. In other words, the first men really to examine scientifically the Panhandle region were products of fine educational systems and of the urban part of the nation. Although writing styles and modes of expression differ substantially, there is found consistently among the reports at least an implied love for wilderness and the thrill of wilderness exploration and adventure. This suggests that an appreciation for nature in her primeval state is a characteristic of a cultured, cultivated mind and not necessarily of one who is a product of the wilderness.[121] In any case, the explorers are a privileged few in regional history for they, from the viewpoint of cultivated and civilized minds, were permitted to see the primordial Panhandle.

[121] In this connection see Roderick Nash, *Wilderness and the American Mind*, p. 201.

# 6. The Buffalo Hunters

"The time of great dying," as C. Stuart Johnston characterized the close of the Pleistocene epoch,[1] robbed the South Plains of the incomparably great and diverse wildlife herds of prehistoric times. More adaptable than the Columbian mammoth and *Bison antiquus*, one of the later arrivals upon the Pleistocene landscape, *Bison occidentalis*, more effectively coped with the environmental changes that accompanied the close of the epoch and from *Bison occidentalis* the historic form, *Bison bison*, appears to have developed.[2] Though *Bison occidentalis* eventually followed his prehistoric predecessors and contemporaries into extinction, his descendant, *Bison bison*, remained to suggest to historic man something of the unimaginable richness of the Pleistocene wildlife complex. Indeed, *Bison bison* was an incredible phenomenon of nature in his own right and his impact upon man greater than that of any other native Plains animal.

[1] C. Stuart Johnston, "Prehistory in the Texas Panhandle," *Panhandle-Plains Historical Review* 10 (1937): 82-83.
[2] Morris F. Skinner and Ove C. Kaison, "The Fossil *Bison* of Alaska and Preliminary Revision of the Genus," *Bulletin of the American Museum of Natural History* 89 (1947): 149, 162-163, 171.

As usual with Plains creatures, the bison was misnamed and commonly called "buffalo." "In Canada and elsewhere the early French *voyageurs* called the strange animals *les boeufs*, meaning oxen or beeves. Hence came the English *buffle*, *buffelo*, and finally *buffalo*."[3] So entrenched in the public mind did the name "buffalo" become that William T. Hornaday, writing in 1887, could say that the custom "has now become so universal that all the naturalists in the world could not change it if they would."[4] To be sure, changing a long-standing folkway would serve no useful purpose. The buffalos' story, not technicalities of nomenclature, is important.

By 1607 when about one hundred souls planted themselves near the mouth of the James River to establish the first permanent English colony in America, the buffalo had extended its range over most of the present area of the United States, over much of Canada, and had occupied eastern woodland areas in quite substantial numbers.[5] In relatively few years, however, advancing civilization drove the buffalo out of the woodland, and they retreated to their natural habitat, the Great Plains. Truly at home in the Great Plains, the buffalo there multiplied into incomputably great numbers and made their last stand against the overwhelming onslaught of an advancing frontier that was backed by a rapidly developing technology. It was an uneven contest.

That the Great Plains was the natural home of the buffalo has been well established and need not be belabored.[6] Estimating accurately the total number of buffalo that once roamed the Plains would be impossible; even a rough guess is risky. Some insight into their numbers may be gained by Hornaday's estimate that a single herd, sighted by Richard I. Dodge near the Arkansas River in 1871, contained not less than four million head![7] The buffalo would have been impressive by the sheer weight of their numbers, but their individual appearance was little less imposing. "With an

[3] Wayne Gard, *The Great Buffalo Hunt*, p. 7. This work is the best historical study of the buffalo hunt, despite an emphasis on the South Plains; it leaves little to be said, except for elaboration of detail, on that phase of the subject. More concerned with technical matters relating to the buffalo is the exhaustive study of Frank Gilbert Roe, *The North American Buffalo: A Critical Study of the Species in Its Wild State*.

[4] William T. Hornaday, "The Extermination of the American Bison," *Annual Report of the United States National Museum* (Smithsonian Institution, 1887), Part II, p. 371. Hornaday's work is decidedly the best of the early studies of the buffalo from both scientific and historical points of view. *Bison americanus* is the technical name applied by Hornaday to the buffalo.

[5] Ibid., pp. 376-386.

[6] Walter Prescott Webb, *The Great Plains*, pp. 42-44.

[7] Hornaday, "The Extermination of the American Bison," Part II, pp. 389-391.

acquaintance which includes fine living examples of all the larger ruminants of the world except the musk-ox and the European bison," writes Hornaday, "I am sure that the American bison is the grandest of them all."[8] Hornaday considers only the gaur of southern India and the aurochs (European bison) as worthy competitors for the American buffalo. For various reasons Hornaday dismisses the aurochs and concludes "that *Bison americanus* will easily rank his European rival." The naturalist then compares the buffalo with the gaur, and in the process strikingly describes the buffalo:

> The magnificent dark brown frontlet and beard of the buffalo, the shaggy coat of hair upon the neck, hump, and shoulders, terminating at the knees in a thick mass of luxuriant black locks, to say nothing of the dense coat of finer fur on the body and hindquarters, give to our species not only an apparent height equal to that of the gaur, but a grandeur and nobility of presence which are beyond all comparison amongst ruminants.[9]

Taking into account Hornaday's naturalist's appreciation for the beauty of wild creatures, he understandably considered the buffalos' appearance as nothing less than regal. Dodge, observing the same characteristics that Hornaday noted, felt that the buffalo appeared to be ferocious, though the appearance was wholly misleading. "Dangerous as he looks," says Dodge of the buffalo, "he is in truth a very mild, inoffensive beast, timid and fearful, and rarely attacking but in the last hopeless effort of self-defense."[10]

Their great mobility was one of the most striking characteristics of wild buffalo and one of the most significant from the point of view of man. Hornaday believed that buffalo were migratory in a scientific sense of that term.[11] The naturalist's view is disputed by Roe, however.[12] If not made

---

[8] Ibid., p. 393.

[9] Ibid., pp. 393-394.

[10] Richard Irving Dodge, *The Hunting Grounds of the Great West*, p. 110.

[11] Hornaday, "The Extermination of the American Bison," *Annual Report of the United States National Museum,* 1887, Part II, pp. 420-424.

[12] Roe, *The North American Buffalo*, pp. 521-542. A resolution of the question is not material to this study if the mobility of buffalo is recognized. The writer's own view is that buffalo were not migratory in the same sense that waterfowl, for example, are migratory and that the presence of buffalo trails proves little except that large numbers of large animals leave large numbers of large trails. However, see James M. Day, "A Preliminary Guide to the Study of Buffalo Trails in Texas," *West Texas Historical Association Yearbook* 36 (1960): 137-155.

in haste, the movement of a herd was methodical and without excitement, the buffalo scattering into small bunches and spreading out over substantial areas. If, on the other hand, there was reason to hurry, movement was in a tightly packed mass of animals that simultaneously followed its leaders blindly and prodded them into whatever peril might lie in the path ahead.[13] The results of such pell-mell travel could be both horrifying and disastrous.

Late in the summer of 1867 a herd of probably 4,000 buffalo attempted to cross the South Platte, near Plum Creek. The water was rapidly subsiding, being nowhere over a foot or two in depth, and the channels in the bed were filled or filling with loose quicksands. The buffalo in front were soon hopelessly stuck. Those immediately behind, urged on by the horns and pressure of those yet farther in the rear, trampled over their struggling companions, to be themselves engulfed in the devouring sand. This was continued until the bed of the river, nearly half-a-mile broad, was covered with dead or dying buffalo. Only a comparatively few actually crossed the river. . . . It was estimated that considerably over half the herd, or more than 2,000 buffalo, paid for this attempt with their lives.[14]

Buffalo normally watered once daily in late afternoon and might travel a score or more miles to water,[15] but if necessity demanded they might water no more than once in seven days.[16] The pock-marked appearance characteristic of an occasional Plains pasture derives from the buffalos' habit of rolling or wallowing. Bulls especially liked to cover themselves with dust by wallowing and with a bit of pawing, rolling, and plowing with their horns as they rolled, broke the crust of the earth. Continued use of the same "buffalo wallow," coupled with wind erosion, produced sizeable depressions.[17]

The buffalos' mating, or "running," season occurred in August and September, while the summer ranges were still occupied. Having stuffed

[13]Hornaday, "The Extermination of the American Bison," Part II, pp. 420-422. Hornaday describes buffalo movements in connection with what he considers to be their migrations.
[14]Dodge, *Hunting Grounds of the Great West*, p. 122.
[15]W. C. Holden, "The Buffalo of the Plains Area," West Texas Historical Association *Yearbook* 2 (1926): 10.
[16]W. C. Holden, "Robert Cypret Parrack, Buffalo Hunter and Fence Cutter," West Texas Historical Association *Yearbook* 21 (1945): 33.
[17]Hornaday, "The Extermination of the American Bison," Part II, p. 418; Holden, "The Buffalo of the Plains Area," p. 10.

themselves all summer with nutritious grasses, the animals were in top condition when running season came. The easygoing attitude toward life that ordinarily characterized the buffalo disappeared completely and was replaced by frenzied excitement. They packed themselves together so tightly "as to actually blacken the face of the landscape." "As usual under such conditions," says Hornaday, "the bulls were half the time chasing the cows, and fighting each other during the other half." Furious but brief, the fights seldom resulted in serious injury to the contestants; and, having thus nominally settled their *affaires d'honneur*, the disputants resumed their *affaires d'amour*.

The literature of the buffalo is replete with references to their alleged stupidity. Despite his unabashed admiration for them, Hornaday felt that in seeking food "the buffalo displayed but little intelligence or power of original thought."[18] Their "rather low order of intelligence," contributed substantially, in Hornaday's view, to the buffalo's rapid destruction.

> He was provokingly slow in comprehending the existence and nature of the dangers that threatened his life, and, like the stupid brute that he was, would very often stand quietly and see two or three score, or even a hundred, of his relatives and companions shot down before his eyes, with no other feeling than one of stupid wonder and curiosity. Neither the noise nor smoke of the still-hunter's rifle, the falling, struggling, nor the final death of his companions conveyed to his mind the idea of a danger to be fled from, and so the herd stood still and allowed the still-hunter to slaughter its members at will.[19]

Dissenting from the multitude of the buffalos' detractors, Charles Goodnight defended the buffalo. The cowman's biographer presents his views:

> The buffalo is not stupid; it is smarter than the Plains horse or the antelope. It does not resort to fraud to protect its young, but will fight at once and will fight anything. It can go without drinking as long again as a cow, and possibly can smell water eight or ten miles away "if the wind is right." He believed it to be the hardiest and thriftiest of the bovine world. With two more incisors than the cow, it gets more food, and out of more difficult places.[20]

Whether the buffalo were stupid or smart depends largely on definition of

---

[18] Hornaday, "The Extermination of the American Bison," Part II, pp. 415-416.
[19] Ibid., pp. 429-430.
[20] J. Evetts Haley, *Charles Goodnight: Cowman and Plainsman*, pp. 442-443.

terms—obviously Hornaday and Goodnight applied different standards of evaluation. The point is somewhat academic anyway because it is the buffalos' relationship to man upon which their historic significance rests. Inquiry into this relationship begins with a consideration of the buffalo and the Plains Indians.

Seldom in the history of humankind has a civilization adapted itself so exactly and so completely to its environment as the Plains Indians adapted to the vast prairies of North America. Nothing in the culture of the Plains Indians is illogical, out of place, or inconsistent with their environment. The Plains environment offered various cultural options to aboriginal man, and there was nothing particularly inevitable about the cultural patterns displayed by the historic Plains Indians. The historic Indians are remarkable, however, in that they developed (regardless of the basic reasons) a culture completely compatible with the Plains environment—an environment dreadfully deficient, in the view of white men, in the things necessary to support life. The primitive Plains mind accepted nature as nature was, adjusted and adapted to the conditions nature imposed, and made the most of what nature did provide. A society more joyously satisfied with its circumstances than were the historic Plains Indians is hard to imagine. Modern man would do well to profit from their example!

"Historically the buffalo had more influence on man," says Walter Prescott Webb, "than all other Plains animals combined."[21] Webb's generalization is thoroughly substantiated by the importance of the buffalo to the Comanches. "The buffalo was as indispensable to the Comanche as the horse. No part of the slaughtered animal was wasted except the rump, spine, and skull. Hair, skin, flesh, blood, bones, entrails, horns, sinew, kidneys, liver, paunch, and the dried excrement were all utilized."[22]

The buffalos' blood quenched the Comanches' thirst when water was not at hand; the paunch served as a canteen or cooking utensil; buffalo chips provided fuel for both cooking and comfort and served ceremonial purposes. The bones, hoofs, and horns were turned into eating utensils or ornaments, and bows and ceremonial headdresses were made of horns. The buffalos' back sinews provided bow strings and thread; ropes were made of twisted hair and rawhide; the buffalos' hide was turned into tepees,

[21] Webb, *The Great Plains*, p. 44.
[22] Ernest Wallace and E. Adamson Hoebel, *The Comanches: Lords of the South Plains*, p. 50. Since the concern of this study is with the Texas Panhandle the following discussion of the Indians' use of the buffalo will be confined to the Comanches, the dominant South Plains tribe.

clothing, saddles, and other objects. Properly finished with the hair left on, the hide provided a warm robe for protection against cold; with the hair removed it became a blanket; and a green hide was the Comanches' kettle.[23]

The Comanches embarked upon major buffalo hunts twice yearly—in the summer and in late fall. Community affairs, these hunts involved elaborate preparation by all members. Preparation for the fall hunt, for example, began in October when the exact time and place for the hunt was set at a tribal gathering. Braves learned in such matters were dispatched to find a site for the hunting camp, and when all was prepared, the able-bodied, traveling light, left the main camp and headed for the hunting camp. The hunting party got a rousing psychological send off, for on at least one and usually several nights prior to its departure, the entire Indian band assembled for the Hunting Dance. Lasting from dusk until about midnight, the Hunting Dance vividly expressed lusty anticipation. Having no spiritual significance, the Hunting Dance merely reflected the joy of "the People," as the Comanches called themselves, at the prospect of a hunt.

Though highly individualistic, the Comanches voluntarily submitted to the discipline necessary to a successful hunt and did not police their communal hunts as did other Plains tribes. Scouts first determined the location of a buffalo herd, which was then approached against the wind. Gradually, the hunters encircled the buffalo except on the windward side where a gap was carefully left to avoid alarming the prey. When all was ready, the hunt leader signaled for the gap to close and the entire circle contracted forcing the buffalo into a diminishing area. Soon, the animals were broadside to the hunters, who, mounted on well-trained ponies, drove their arrows, and in some cases lances, into the soft area between the buffalos' right hip and last rib. Since the projectile came from above, behind, and to the side of the target, it passed through the animal and reached the vital organs in the forepart of the body.

At times it was not possible to work the surround method, and on these occasions the hunters stalked the herd against the wind. When in position, a straight line was formed and, at a signal from the hunt director, the hunters charged simultaneously. A coordinated, quickly executed charge was essential to avoid scattering the herd and to insure quick kills, for if the buffalo ran too long and became overheated before being killed the meat was apt to spoil before it could be cured.

[23] Ibid., pp. 50-51.

Subterfuge and somewhat fortuitous conditions were necessary to a third method of taking buffalo. A fleet young brave disguised in a buffalo skin placed himself between a herd and a precipice. As his fellows spooked the buffalo from the flanks and rear, the disguised Indian led the game to the edge of the cliff. When buffalos approached the edge, the man secured himself in a previously selected hideaway, but the confused animals, unable to turn or retreat and pushed forward by those behind, plunged over.

A fourth method of hunting buffalo involved only an individual hunter who disguised himself as an animal and crept on hands and knees to within bow-and-arrow range of the game. By careful stalking and with strict attention to wind direction, the hunter could do his deadly work before the buffalos suspected the source of their danger.

Customarily among many Plains tribes the women took over as soon as the killing was completed, but among the Comanches the braves skinned the dead buffalo and accomplished the rough butchering in the field. The hides and bulk meat were then packed to the camp for processing by the women, who prepared the meat for sun drying and pegged out the hides on the ground for the initial steps of tanning. While the women worked, the braves took their ease, feasted, and swapped hunting yarns—after the fashion of any hunters, anywhere, anytime. As quickly as the women were caught up with their work, another kill was made, and the sequence repeated until either an adequate supply of skins and meat was obtained, until cold weather drove the Indians into winter camp, or until the buffalo were no longer to be found.[24]

In view of the extensive use made of the buffalo and the social importance of their buffalo hunts, the animals not surprisingly had considerable spiritual significance to the Comanches. Buffalo skulls were frequently placed before the entrances of sweat lodges, and on the prairie buffalo skulls were placed so as to face the main Comanche camp in the hope that supernatural powers would cause the living buffalo to travel in the direction that the dead were facing. In ceremonial smoking, the Comanches sometimes blew a puff of smoke to a buffalo skull and prayed that it would provide them with meat and skins. In Comanche mythology buffalo sometimes spoke to humans or turned themselves into men and brought great blessing to the People.[25]

Since the Plains Indians relied so extensively upon the buffalo they

[24] Ibid., pp. 54-61.
[25] Ibid., pp. 199-200.

necessarily killed large numbers and perhaps were gradually exterminating the herds.[26] If so, a contributing factor was the importance of buffalo robes (not hides) in the western fur trade. Buffalo robes were widely used among Americans to shield against the chill of winter travel, and through trade in buffalo robes the northern Plains Indians had their major access to trade goods.[27] Even if the Indians were taking the buffalo faster than they could reproduce, the depletion was gradual and the life of the Plains, as it existed prior to 1870, might have gone on for decades had no extraneous element entered to alter it. Obviously, however, several extraneous elements did enter. One of the most significant was the white hide hunter who drove the buffalo from their favored grazing grounds and then dug them out of every secluded hiding place offered by the illimitable Plains.

Hide hunters operating in western Kansas faced grim prospects after the hunt of 1872 and 1873. The slaughter of the buffalo in the area adjacent to Fort Dodge had been prodigious and it had been swift. Only three years before, in the winter of 1870-1871, W. C. Lobenstine, a Fort Leavenworth fur trader, appraised his western Kansas agents, Charles Rath and A. C. Myers, that an English tannery was interested in acquiring five hundred buffalo hides for experiments in making leather. If successful, said Lobenstine, an unlimited number of buffalo hides could be sold. Responding quickly to this new opportunity Rath and Myers forthwith began to hunt from Fort Hayes. The project attracted other hunters, including a young easterner, J. Wright Mooar, who agreed to supply some of the five hundred hides.

After filling his quota, Mooar had fifty-seven hides left, which he consigned to his brother John W. Mooar and brother-in-law J. W. Combs in New York City, suggesting that American tanners be induced to experiment with buffalo hides. A tanning firm, having been persuaded to buy the hides, reported highly successful experiments and ordered as many hides as

---

[26] This observation is based on Hornaday's account of Indian inroads on the buffalo. See Hornaday, "The Extermination of the American Bison," Part II, pp. 486-490.

[27] The robe trade was enormously important along the upper Missouri River—an area convenient to markets because of water transportation. In the Southwest the Santa Fe Trail carried robes eastward and Bent, St. Vrain, and Company were the most successful southwestern robe merchants. Probably some, maybe many, robes came from the Panhandle region, but, given the failure of the Bents' Canadian River trading post, the likelihood of a really voluminous robe trade between the Panhandle and the Anglo-American market is dubious. See Gard, *The Great Buffalo Hunt*, pp. 43-58, especially pp. 53-57. As shown in chapter 4, robes were significant in Plains-pueblo commerce and later in the Comanchero trade.

could be delivered. Thus a market for buffalo hides opened with the shock of a Plains thunderclap, and the rush of hunters to the buffalo range was on. When Rath and Myers, seeking to tap the hunting trade, established trading posts at Fort Dodge and in the area south of the Fort,[28] hunters were provided with both a market for hides and a convenient source of supplies. Maybe Myers and Rath made the enterprise too convenient, because in three seasons the hunters made such inroads that buffalo hunting was no longer profitable in western Kansas.

For hide hunting to continue, new hunting grounds had to be tapped. The Texas Panhandle was known to be rich in buffalo, but hunting there was more easily talked about than done, for there were both real and imaginary obstacles. Three basic obstacles were (1) the Comanches and Kiowas in the Panhandle, whose presence would cause even the most daring frontiersmen to hesitate, (2) the remoteness of the Panhandle from sources of supply and markets, and (3) the widely held notion that hunting south of the Arkansas River and crossing the "Neutral Strip" were somehow illegal.

As far as the Indian problem was concerned, little could be done but to accept the risks. Aid from Fort Dodge or Fort Hayes could not be expected, and the Panhandle provided no place to run. Experienced frontiersmen, who knew what the risks were, simply had to weigh them against the possibilities of economic reward. If there were courageous hunters, however, there were also courageous, ambitious merchants who would solve the supply problem. A. C. Myers, seeing business opportunities, agreed to establish a trading post at an appropriate location in the Panhandle. The hunters agreed to transport Myers' merchandise in their wagons and then to buy from Myers at Dodge City prices.[29]

Though entirely mythical, the third obstacle to buffalo hunting in the Panhandle seems to have been taken most seriously. The hunters believed that the Medicine Lodge treaties of 1867 had reserved the Panhandle as an Indian hunting ground and that the U. S. army was bound to protect the region against white intrusion. The "Neutral Strip" or Oklahoma Panhandle was believed to be patrolled by the army, and buffalo hunters who attempted to cross presumably stood to have their property confiscated.

[28] Interview, J. Wright Mooar to Frank P. Hill, J. B. Slaughter, and Jim Weatherford, May 15, 1936, Panhandle-Plains Historical Museum; J. Wright Mooar, "The First Buffalo Hunting in the Panhandle," West Texas Historical Association *Yearbook* 6 (1930): 109; Holden, "The Buffalo of the Plains Area," p. 12.
[29] Olive K. Dixon, *Life of "Billy" Dixon*, p. 111.

Actually, the Medicine Lodge treaties merely recognized the right of the tribes to hunt on lands south of the Arkansas River "so long as the buffalo may range thereon in such numbers as to justify the chase."[30] In no sense does the terminology of the treaties exempt the area south of the Arkansas from white hunting nor do they charge the United States with policing the area against white intrusion.

The Indians' confusion relative to the provisions of the Medicine Lodge treaties is understandable. In the first place, it seems doubtful that the Indians even slightly comprehended the legalistic terminology. Second, they desperately wanted their hunting grounds protected and perhaps assumed that their right to hunt south of the Arkansas automatically excluded the whites. Third, the Indians may have been given verbal assurances that no whites would be permitted to hunt south of the Arkansas.[31] Such verbal promises could hardly be kept, of course, and probably neither written nor oral agreements could be legally applied to the Texas Panhandle without the consent of Texas, since the state retained its public lands—a technicality doubtlessly lost on the Indians.

The confusion among the buffalo hunters as to the terms of the Medicine Lodge treaties is not so easily explained, but they gravely doubted their legal right to hunt in the Panhandle. "Hunters were all under the impression," recalls J. Wright Mooar, "if we crossed the Cimarron the U.S. Army . . . would confiscate our teams."[32] Recognizing that the way to settle the question was to go straight to the source of authority, the hunters appointed J. Wright Mooar and Steel Frazier to address their question to Major Richard I. Dodge, commanding officer of Fort Dodge. The officer put many questions to the hunters that Mooar and Frazier answered patiently. Eventually they had to remind the soldier of the purpose of their visit. "Boys," Mooar reports Dodge as having replied, "if I were a buffalo hunter I would hunt buffalo where buffalo are."[33] Rather than constituting tacit consent to illegal activity, Dodge's reply is an unnecessarily oblique way of telling the hunters that he had no authority to prevent their entry into the Texas Panhandle.

---

[30] Charles J. Kappler, comp., *Indian Affairs: Laws and Treaties*, II, pp. 980, 988. Three treaties were developed at Medicine Lodge Creek in October 1867. These were with the Kiowas and Comanches (ibid., pp. 977-982); the Kiowas, Comanches, and Apaches (ibid., pp. 982-984); and the Cheyennes and Arapahos (ibid., pp. 984-989).
[31] Gard, *The Great Buffalo Hunt*, p. 41.
[32] Mooar, "The First Buffalo Hunting in the Panhandle," p. 109.
[33] Ibid., p. 110; interview, J. Wright Mooar to J. Evetts Haley, November 28, 1927, Panhandle-Plains Historical Museum; Gard, *The Great Buffalo Hunt*, pp. 130-132.

Doubtless Mooar regarded the soldier's attitude enthusiastically, for in July 1873 he and John Webb had scouted the Panhandle. Dropping southward from a permanent camp on the Cimarron River, Mooar and Webb crossed the Cimarron and Beaver Creek to Wolf Creek in the northeastern Panhandle, turned westward from the head of Wolf Creek, and, following the divide between Palo Duro Creek and the Canadian River, passed through "a solid herd as far as we could see, all day they opened up before us and came together again behind us." Turning northward across Palo Duro Creek, Mooar and Webb crossed Coldwater and Beaver creeks and hit the Cimarron about one hundred miles west of the point from whence their journey had originated.[34]

Knowing that the Panhandle had buffalo to spare and now armed with official sanction to cross the Cimarron, Mooar and his brother and partner, John W. Mooar, hired eight men and organized a hunting outfit. Late in September 1873 the Mooars led their party into the Texas Panhandle and set up camp on the Canadian about eighteen miles above old Bent's Fort. They hunted successfully, but encountered Comancheros who resented the intrusion and apparent competition of the Anglo-American hunters. "We had two or three set-to's with them and killed a number. Twenty-five of them came into our camp one day to kill us," says Mooar, "but they got it pretty bad." But since their interest was not open season on Comancheros but on buffalo, the Mooar brothers retreated northward to Palo Duro Creek in present Hensford County and wintered, remaining there from November until the following spring. Here the party "made a good hunt."

Toward the end of November 1873 two hunters known only as "Lane and Wheeler" encamped with an outfit of ten men about six miles upstream from the Mooars. From their permanent camps on the Palo Duro, both the Mooar and Lane and Wheeler outfits hunted on the divide between the Canadian and Palo Duro, intercepting the buffalo as they moved east and west between Wolf and Coldwater creeks. Contact between the two outfits was maintained by the sound of gunfire—the roar of heavy buffalo rifles meant that only buffalo were being fired upon, but the sharper reports of smaller arms was understood to mean an attack.

Toward the end of February 1874 Wheeler was bushwhacked by an Indian whom he had previously lashed with a blacksnake when the Indian,

---

[34] Mooar, "The First Buffalo Hunting in the Panhandle," pp. 109-110. See also Mooar to Haley, November 28, 1927. While in essential agreement, these accounts vary in detail. Presumably the published version had the benefit of editorial verification, and it is therefore followed.

visiting Wheeler's camp, tampered with some object. The Lane and Wheeler party then left the Panhandle in a vain effort to get the critically, and as it turned out, fatally wounded Wheeler to medical aid. During the winter, apparently in 1874, other Dodge City hunters visited the Mooar camp and pushed on to the Canadian, but made no permanent camps since their interest was, at this point, more in prospecting than in buffalo hunting. That the hunting phase of Panhandle history entered from Dodge City is more than mere coincidence. Dodge City had the Santa Fe Railroad and therefore became the gateway to the Panhandle because it provided the isolated region with its sole access to the outside world.[35] During the hunting phase, hence, the Panhandle was a commercial satellite of the Kansas frontier town.

In December 1873 Palo Duro Creek was occupied also by James H. and Robert Cator, immigrant descendants of a long line of seafaring Englishmen, who had arrived at Fort Dodge in the summer of 1871. Finding an ample supply of wood and water on Palo Duro Creek, the Cators built a dugout about twenty-five miles below the northern Panhandle line in present Hansford County and began hunting buffalo.[36]

The success of the Mooars, the Cators, and Lane and Wheeler pointed the way to the Texas Panhandle for a horde of hunters, and, according to Mooar, it was this success that encouraged A. C. Myers to establish a trading post, Adobe Walls, in the Panhandle. In March 1874 Myers located on the Canadian in Hutchinson County about four miles east of old Bent's Fort. The merchant built a stockade, corral, and storehouse. He was followed quickly by a competitor, Charles Rath, who set up business in a sod

[35] Deposition of R. M. Wright, undated, Indian Depredation Case No. 4593, photocopy, Panhandle-Plains Historical Museum.
[36] The foregoing account is synthesized from J. Wright Mooar, "Frontier Experiences of J. Wright Mooar," *West Texas Historical Association Yearbook* 4 (1928): 89; Mooar, "The First Buffalo Hunting in the Panhandle," p. 110; and Mooar to Haley, November 28, 1927, which gives the account of Mooar's clash with the Comancheros and supplies details of the location of the buffalo and of the shooting of Wheeler not contained in the published versions. Among those who visited the Mooar camp during the winter of 1873-1874 was Billy Dixon, who claims that he sought a good buffalo range to hunt the following summer. In Dixon's view, reconnoitering the buffalo range during the winter involved less risk of Indian trouble. See Dixon, *"Billy" Dixon*, p. 109. For the activities of the Cator brothers, see Deposition of James H. Cator, October 11, 1892, Indian Depredation Case No. 4593, photocopy, Panhandle-Plains Historical Museum; and Ernest Cabe, Jr., "A Sketch of the Life of James Hamilton Cator," *Panhandle-Plains Historical Review* 6 (1933): 18. Cabe reports the Cators as arriving in the Panhandle in September 1872. Cator's deposition places his arrival in December 1873.

house; Tom O'Keafe, a blacksmith; and James Harrahan, who opened the inevitable–and doubtless necessary–saloon. Business was good from the beginning and when about May 1 more hunters arrived, business at Adobe Walls was even better.[37] The business firms at Adobe Walls involved a fair investment, with Myers bringing about $50,000 and Rath about $20,000 in goods to the isolated outpost.[38]

As spring came late in 1874, the hunters gathered at Adobe Walls had time on their hands waiting for the buffalo to move northward. "Our amusements," says Billy Dixon, "were mostly card-playing, running horse-races, drinking whisky and shooting at targets, the latter to improve our marksmanship." But idleness weighed heavily on men anxious to be about business, and toward the end of May Dixon pulled out of Adobe Walls to intercept the buffalo. The young hunter found an ideal campsite on Dixon Creek (probably in present Carson County) and was soon greeted by a brown sea of buffalos. Idle days were gone; Dixon and his skinners were in business.[39] Similarly, other hunting outfits spread out from Adobe Walls and the hunt proceeded apace. J. Wright Mooar hunted south of the Canadian, while his brother, John Mooar, freighted hides to Dodge City.[40] Besides the Mooars and Cators the "larger outfits" in the Panhandle in 1874 included Lane and Wheeler (who left in February), Cox and Frazier, and Galloway and Sisk. Altogether, Mooar estimates, there were about fifty hunting outfits in the Panhandle before the Indian attack on Adobe Walls. Among the individuals present were Red Lummis, Brick Bond, and Fred Singer. John Webb and Tobe Robinson, who later became Oldham County sheriff, were members of the Mooar party.[41] The range must have been well covered, because after the attack on Adobe Walls "between two and three hundred hunters" gathered at the little post.[42]

The portion of the Panhandle covered by the buffalo hunters in 1874 would seem to include that part lying east and south of Adobe Walls and to some extent to the northeast. Buffalo normally did not range much

[37] Mooar, "Frontier Experiences," p. 89; Mooar, "The First Buffalo Hunting in the Panhandle," p. 111.

[38] Mooar to Haley, November 28, 1927.

[39] Dixon, *"Billy" Dixon*, pp. 139-141.

[40] Mooar, "Frontier Experiences," p. 89.

[41] Interview, J. Wright Mooar to J. Evetts Haley, January 4, 1928, Panhandle-Plains Historical Museum.

[42] Deposition of James Langton, January 28, 1896, Indian Depredation Case No. 4593, photocopy, Panhandle-Plains Historical Museum.

upon the Staked Plains except seasonally in the summer months when the playa lakes held water. Therefore one may infer that the buffalo hunters in the Panhandle in 1874 hunted along the breaks of the Wolf and Palo Duro creeks, the Canadian River and its tributaries, and along the North and Salt forks of the Red River. Hunting in these areas was feasibly near Adobe Walls. It is unlikely that hunters from Adobe Walls got as far south as Prairie Dog Town Fork although it is, of course, possible.[43]

The sudden swarm of white hunters onto the Panhandle buffalo range could hardly have had any other effect than to infuriate the Indians, whose objections were made known forthwith. Two hunters, Dave Dudley and Tommy Wallace, apparently were caught asleep in a camp on Chicken Creek. Their companion, Joe Plummer, away at the time of the attack, returned to find his associates killed, scalped, otherwise mutilated, and Dudley's corpse pinned to the ground by a wooden stake driven through the abdomen. In the camp of Anderson Moore on the Salt Fork north of present Clarendon, an Englishman, John Jones, nicknamed "Cheyenne Jack," and a German known as "Blue Billy" were killed. Both Plummer and Moore got away to bring word of these tragedies to Adobe Walls.[44]

News of the Indian attacks spread rapidly among the hunting camps, and the hunters concentrated at Adobe Walls to take refuge and to size up the situation. Although among those who gathered at Adobe Walls none had actually seen an Indian, their ghastly calling cards left at the Moore and Plummer camps indicated clearly that Indians of ugly disposition infested the country. Attacks on isolated parties, the hunters figured, were intended as warning to all hunters to get out of the Texas Panhandle. Yet, buffalo were in the region and it was clear that the days of profitable hide hunting were numbered. If one wanted to make money off the buffalo, it had to be made quickly. Resolving to continue hunting, the men combined

---

[43] Data on the location of the buffalo range are in essential agreement. See the following: Interview, George A. Simpson to L. F. Sheffy, November 30, 1929, Panhandle-Plains Historical Museum, which says, "In the early days the buffalo stayed mainly under the Plains as they would have to come to the streams for water. But in summer they did graze out on the plains . . . when the lakes were full of water." Rex W. Strickland, ed., "The Recollections of W. S. Glenn, Buffalo Hunter," *Panhandle-Plains Historical Review* 22 (1949): 34, observes "Toward the *latter part* of the hunt, when the buffalo had all been *driven back* and killed, *at the foot of the plains*. . . ." (emphasis added). Haley, *Goodnight*, p. 437, quotes Goodnight as saying, "The animals [buffalo] rarely got out on the High Plains, though finally they were driven there by the hunters, and they were unknown beyond the Pecos."

[44] Mooar to Haley, January 4, 1928; Dixon, *"Billy" Dixon*, pp. 146-147.

into larger parties for better defense and returned to the range, going mostly north and west of Adobe Walls so as to get away from the Indians thought to be encamped along the headwaters of the Washita and Sweetwater.[45]

Toward the end of June the buffalo hunt had normalized. Little thought was given to the recent tragedies—after all, what was really unusual about a few scalpings on the southwestern frontier?—and activities around Adobe Walls resumed their routine. On the evening of June 26, twenty-nine persons including one woman, Mrs. William Olds, occupied the buffalo hunter's oasis. About twenty hunters gingerly anticipated returning to the buffalo range on the morrow. Since it was an occasion for levity, the hunters indulged themselves with little concern for impending danger. "Hanrahan did a thriving trade." As the celebrants grew tired, and, no doubt, as Hanrahan's wares took effect, they turned in, one by one, most taking their rest on the ground outside the buildings. Soon, all was quiet around Adobe Walls.[46]

As a matter of fact, the Adobe Walls hunters were almost unbelievably casual about the chances of Indian troubles. Bat Masterson regarded the events of June 27, 1874, as marking the *beginning* of a general Indian uprising. James Langton, a partner in Charles Rath and Company and manager of the Adobe Walls store, seemed downright astounded at the suggestion of Indian hostilities in the Panhandle. "I would not have been there," he deposed, "if there had been a declaration of war and I had known it."[47] If these statements reflect the beliefs of the deponents (and one must remember they were trying to win a lawsuit) as of 1874, one wonders how experienced frontiersmen could have been so naive. Perhaps an explanation lies in insufficient communication and therefore an absence among the buffalo hunters of broader knowledge of the Texas frontier picture.

As early as January 1874 it had become apparent at Fort Sill that the forthcoming year would be troublesome. Various Indian parties raiding into Texas had suffered casualties and the desire for revenge, coupled with anxiety of warriors to distinguish themselves in battle, pointed toward

[45] Dixon, *"Billy" Dixon*, pp. 142-150.

[46] Ibid., pp. 153-155. The saloon keeper's name is spelled variously "Hanrahan," "Hanahan," and "Harrahan," while the name of Adobe Walls' blacksmith is spelled "O'Keefe" and "O'Keafe."

[47] Depositions of William B. Masterson, June 24, 1893, and James Langton, January 28, 1896, Indian Depredation Case No. 4593, photocopies, Panhandle-Plains Historical Museum.

increased Indian raiding. Combined with these traditional motivations to raid were relatively new ones which intensified Indian restiveness. Not the least was the destruction of the buffalo, disastrous from the Indians' point of view and an incomprehensible injustice. Moreover, the whole policy of the United States government was directed toward confinement of the Plains tribes upon reservations—an indignity to which a proud and independent race could hardly have been expected to submit willingly. In early 1874, therefore, the Comanches, Kiowas, Cheyennes, and Arapahos seethed with resentment and outrage that their sacred ancestral soil was being usurped and defiled by a patently inferior order of people.[48]

The prevailing restiveness among the Indians opened opportunities for potential leaders, and two ambitious young Comanches, the medicine man Isa-tai and Quanah, the son of the white captive Cynthia Ann Parker, quickly asserted themselves. Isa-tai (which translates variously as Little Wolf, and, politely rendered, Coyote Droppings or Rear-End-of-a-Wolf) won the support of Comanche, Cheyenne, and probably some Kiowa warriors with feats of magic that seemed to prove the efficacy of his medicine, namely a paint that allegedly would deflect the white man's bullets. Doubtless influenced by their knowledge of the outpost's inadequate fortifications and its occupants' tendency toward laziness, Isa-tai and Quanah chose Adobe Walls as the target of their opening shot. Protected from bullets by Isa-tai's medicine, the braves could sweep with the dawn into the sleeping community and relieve the whites of their lives and scalps. Other hunters could be waylaid later as they unsuspectingly approached in small parties. It all seemed so easy. In any case, once the war party reached the vicinity, probably every move made at Adobe Walls was carefully observed by Indian scouts.[49]

About two o'clock in the morning of June 27, Oscar Shepherd, Hanrahan's bartender, and Mike Welch, who were sleeping in the saloon, "were awakened by a report that sounded like the crack of a rifle." Investigating, the two frontiersmen found that the cottonwood ridgepole of the saloon had cracked—or so they claimed.[50] Fearing that the roof might collapse,

---

[48] W. S. Nye, *Carbine and Lance: The Story of Old Fort Sill*, pp. 187-188; Rupert N. Richardson, "The Comanche Indians and the Fight at Adobe Walls," *Panhandle-Plains Historical Review* 4 (1931): 33.

[49] Nye, *Carbine and Lance*, pp. 189-191; G. Derek West, "The Battle of Adobe Walls (1874)," *Panhandle-Plains Historical Review* 36 (1963): 9-12; Richardson, "The Comanche Indians," pp. 25-28. The Indians were not so confident of Isa-tai's medicine that they were willing to forego any tactical advantages.

[50] Except as otherwise noted, the following account of second Adobe Walls is based on Dixon, *"Billy" Dixon*, pp. 155-183, the most extended account by a participant.

Shepherd and Welch awakened several others to assist in effecting repairs. The story of the ridgepole cracking is implausible. Two days before the attack, Amos Chapman, a squaw man employed as a government scout, and J. E. McAllister, a freighter for the Lee and Reynolds firm of Camp Supply, Indian Territory, visited Adobe Walls. According to McAllister, Indians around Camp Supply had bragged of the impending attack upon Adobe Walls and that they would kill the hunters. "We . . . told the hunters what the Indians had said . . . but they wouldn't believe us."[51] Harrison believes that only the businessmen knew of the impending attack and purposely kept quiet lest the hunters flee Adobe Walls and leave the stores unprotected. Gard claims that Hanrahan fired a six-shooter to awaken the men, and J. Wright Mooar, who was not present, declares flatly "the ridgepole did not break that night."[52] In any case, a number of men turned to and propped up the ridgepole. Doubtless in gratitude, Hanrahan offered them drinks on the house. They accepted.[53]

By this time the reddening eastern sky suggested that there was little

---

See also "J. W. McKinley's Narrative," *Panhandle-Plains Historical Review* 36 (1963): 61-64, and Lowell H. Harrison, "Damage Suits for Indian Depredations in the Adobe Walls Area, 1874," ibid., pp. 37-60, which contains summaries of the depositions of witnesses in the Indian Depredations Claims cases of the Cator brothers (Case No. 4601) and Rath and Company (Case No. 4593). Photocopies of the original depositions are in the Panhandle-Plains Historical Museum. Understandably there was much confusion as to exactly what had happened at Adobe Walls; accordingly there is much variation in the details contained in contemporary accounts, although there seems to be little controversy as to the main events. The best secondary account is West, "The Battle of Adobe Walls (1874)," pp. 1-36, which does as well as can be done in disentangling the contradictions. Shorter but thoroughly competent accounts are Gard, *The Great Buffalo Hunt*, pp. 166-181, and Lowell H. Harrison, "The Two Battles of Adobe Walls," *Texas Military History* 5 (Spring 1965): 6-11. For the Indians' side of the story, see Donald J. Berthrong, *The Southern Cheyennes*, pp. 385-386; Mildred P. Mayhall, *The Kiowas*, pp. 244-247; Richardson, "The Comanche Indians," pp. 24-38; and Wallace and Hoebel, *The Comanches*, pp. 325-326. Some accounts of the battle are outlandish. See one by J. Marvin Hunter in the *Clarendon News*, September 18, 1924, which confuses other events with Adobe Walls and, in general, describes an incident approaching an Alamo siege with a San Jacinto ending.

[51] Interview, J. E. McAllister to J. Evetts Haley, July 1, 1926, Panhandle-Plains Historical Museum.

[52] Mooar to Haley, November 28, 1927; Gard, *The Great Buffalo Hunt*, pp. 166-167; Harrison, "The Two Battles of Adobe Walls," p. 8. The story of the cracking ridgepole constrains the writer to point out that somewhere around the site of Adobe Walls must lurk the ghost of the Panhandle's own Baron von Muenchhausen.

[53] Gard, *The Great Buffalo Hunt*, p. 167; West, "The Battle of Adobe Walls (1874)," p. 16.

point in going back to bed, and Dixon and Hanrahan, partners for the forthcoming hunt, decided that their party might as well get an early start to the buffalo range. Accordingly, Dixon packed his bedding. Turning to get his horses, he noticed strange shapes advancing toward the buildings through the early morning dimness. Presently the young hunter realized that the objects were Indians apparently intent on stealing stock. As soon as he had secured his saddle horse, staked close-by to his wagon, Dixon realized that the charging warriors sought not stock, but scalps. Running desperately, Dixon headed for the saloon, the nearest building. Billy Ogg, whom Dixon had sent to the creek bottom to get horses staked there, won an even more dramatic race with fate and reached the saloon just behind Dixon "and fell inside, so exhausted that he could no longer stand." Like Dixon and Ogg, other hunters, in various stages of dress and undress, got inside the nearest building as quickly as they realized what was happening. Scarcely had the last man taken refuge when the settlement was overrun by howling Indians.

Since there had been no time to prepare a defense (indeed, no system of defense had even been considered), the defenders of Adobe Walls found themselves split into three groups. Nine, including Dixon and Bat Masterson, were in Hanrahan's saloon; eleven were in Myers' store; and six, including Mrs. Olds, found protection in Rath's store. Doors were quickly barricaded and though it must have seemed an eternity, the defenders were in action in very short order. Jabbing loopholes through the chinking of the buildings, the besieged men found targets for their powerful, large-caliber buffalo rifles.

The Indian attackers, numbering in Dixon's understandable overestimation about seven hundred warriors, were mostly Comanches and Cheyennes but included a few Kiowas. A more conservative estimate puts the number at from 250 to 300.[54] On balance, the lower figure seems more reasonable.

In their first wild charge the warriors rode audaciously up to the buildings. Beating against the doors with rifle butts, they clearly expected to overwhelm the whites through the element of surprise. Perhaps through desperation, the hunters went in for fewer dramatics, so that the accurate fire of buffalo rifles quickly cooled any Indian taste for the dramatic. As a matter of fact, as Indian saddles were emptied, confidence in Isa-tai's medicine declined sharply. Moreover, as the hunters' fire became more

[54] Berthrong, *The Southern Cheyennes*, p. 385.

effective, the Indians fell back and noted that for all their casualties they had only two scalps, those of the Shadler brothers, caught asleep in their wagon. Clearly, the tide of battle was not running as expected.

By ten o'clock the long-range weapons and fine marksmanship of the hunters had made the Indians considerably more cautious; by two o'clock in the afternoon they had substantially withdrawn and were firing sporadically. By four o'clock the whites found it safe to venture outside. Indians appeared on June 28 and again the next day, but made no serious attempt to resume the attack. For all their effort and all their losses, the Indians had killed only three persons; the Shadlers and Billy Tyler, who fell at the door of Myers' store after a vain—and probably foolish—attempt to protect the hunters' livestock. A fourth fatality, that of William Olds, occurred after the battle by accidental discharge of a rifle. Other than the deaths, the worst loss of the buffalo hunters was their livestock, all of which was either captured or killed.

The best evaluation of the historic import of the fight is that of G. Derek West, who observes:

> Neither side gained much advantage from the Battle of Adobe Walls. Because of their spirited resistance the whites survived, but buffalo hunting in the area was restricted for the season of 1874. . . . Some of the defenders . . . never hunted again, and the merchants suffered severe financial loss.
>
> For their part, the only success achieved by the Indians was the temporary prevention of extensive buffalo hunting by the whites. On the debit side was their failure to overrun and exterminate a numerically inferior enemy—a failure which cost them casualties. Smarting under this humiliation, the hostile tribes spread out across the plains. Their actions caused the intervention of the army, and the campaigns of 1874 and 1875. The inevitable result was defeat for the Indians, followed by what many of them had dreaded: life on the reservations.[55]

Despite not counting for much in the broad view of regional history, Adobe Walls, as such incidents usually do, had its heroes, its pathos, and its brutality. Consider, for example, twenty-year-old Bat Masterson holding his dying friend, Billy Tyler, in his arms. Tyler begged for water and young Masterson, taking a bucket, started outside for a well. Grabbing the bucket away from Masterson, who still had a lifetime before him, "Old

[55] West, "The Battle of Adobe Walls (1874)," p. 31.

Man" Keeler declared that since he was known to the Cheyennes, they might not hurt him and dashed outside. The gruff old gentleman, by nothing less than providential protection, escaped the hail of lead and arrows that followed him to the well and back again to the store. Billy Tyler had his drink of water and shortly died, while the salty old saint who fetched it roundly cursed the Indians for having killed his dog, which had followed him to the well.[56]

Or consider the courage—and tragedy—of Mrs. William Olds. By all accounts she conducted herself in the finest traditions of pioneer womanhood. Knowing full well what capture would mean for her, she remained cool throughout the battle, only to have her husband accidentally shoot himself in the head and fall bloodily at her feet after the fight was over.

The Indians were not without their glory and had some of their number been less loquacious around Camp Supply, their plan of attack might have worked and the outcome been entirely different. Even so, the attack did not fail because of a lack of daring and audacity. Again and again warriors braved the fire of the defenders to remove their dead and wounded from the battlefield. And, displaying a quaint sense of respect, the Indians "scalped" the St. Bernard dog of the Shadler brothers, who evidently defended his masters bravely and was accorded the honor due a fallen enemy. What the Indians might have done with white prisoners, had they taken any, is conjectural, but there are several indications that the hunters adorned corral posts with the severed heads of fallen Indians whose bodies could not be rescued. At least one white defender, Fred Leonard, took a scalp.[57]

Had the Indians been willing to pay the price, they might have stormed Adobe Walls successfully, but their obvious discouragement over the failure of Isa-tai's medicine (which the medicine man attributed to the killing of a skunk by one of his followers) and the more concrete weighing of the price of total victory against its cost dissuaded them. Obviously their tactical purpose in attacking Adobe Walls was to kill the occupants and to destroy individually smaller parties of hunters coming later into the settlement. The broader purpose of the attack was, hopefully, to halt the

[56] Ibid., pp. 22-23. Keeler's first name is unknown.
[57] Fred Leonard to A. C. Myers, July 1, 1874, quoted in letter of E. R. Archambeau to Lester Wood, August 10, 1963, copy, Archambeau Papers, Panhandle-Plains Historical Museum. Leonard's communication was the first word out of Adobe Walls after the battle and is the first written account of the incident. Leonard says, "About 25 or 30 Indians were killed; we found 11."

slaughter of their buffalo herds. The Indians failed on both counts because in retrospect all they did (besides throwing the fear of God into the hunters for a time) was temporarily to interrupt an inexorable process.

Word of the attack flashed quickly over the Panhandle buffalo range and, according to James Langton, from two to three hundred hunters congregated around Adobe Walls. The merchants boarded them, pending arrival of wagons from Dodge City to evacuate the merchandise.[58] Substantial amounts of buffalo hides and merchandise had to be abandoned because of transportation inadequate to get it all to Dodge City,[59] and the outpost was entirely deserted by the middle of August, according to Bat Masterson, who visited the place in that month and again encountered hostile Indians. In September or October of 1874, when Masterson visited Adobe Walls for the last time, he found the buildings burned, apparently by the Indians.[60]

Although the fight at Adobe Walls scared white hunters from the Panhandle momentarily, their fright did not last long. Jim and Bob Cator, who travelled to Dodge City with the Rath and Wright wagon train on July 29, returned to the Panhandle to hunt in the Adobe Walls area the following September and perhaps earlier. The Cator brothers resumed residence on Palo Duro Creek and hunted north of the Canadian as long as it paid.[61] Though evidence is fragmentary, little doubt exists that the Adobe Walls incident interrupted hunting in the Panhandle for no more than a few months. In 1875 John Woods and George Simpson, who had hunted southward from Colorado, hunted on Gageby Creek north of Mobeetie and from a later camp located ten miles south of the town killed 106 buffalo in one morning.[62] Richard Bussell, who claimed that buffalo did not move north of the Canadian in 1875, killed eight hundred near the site of present Canadian and in November got two hundred more on the Quitaque, "one of the best little streams in this country." According to Bussell, twenty-five outfits of about six men each operated in the eastern Panhandle (apparently in 1875), camping "as close together as we could."[63] Earlier in

[58] Deposition of James Langton, January 28, 1896.

[59] Deposition of Charles Rath, October 10, 1892, Indian Depredation Case No. 4593, photocopy, Panhandle-Plains Historical Museum.

[60] Deposition of William B. Masterson, June 24, 1893.

[61] Deposition of James H. Cator, October 11, 1892, Indian Depredation Case No. 4601, photocopy, Panhandle-Plains Historical Museum.

[62] Interview, John Woods to L. F. Sheffy, December 28, 1929, Panhandle-Plains Historical Museum.

[63] Interview, Richard Bussell to L. F. Sheffy, December 27, 1929, Panhandle-Plains Historical Museum. Bussell claims to have hunted buffalo "from 1874-77 in the

the year Bussell had travelled north to the Red River from Fort Griffin and about May 1 had made camp south of the site of present Clarendon near the mouth of Mulberry Creek. Here he "made [a] pretty good hunt, got [a] bunch of hides, [and] stayed until about the first of June, [when the] buffalo drifted north." In the spring of 1876, Bussell established his camp on the Quitaque and remained there for about three years.[64]

The concentration of hunters in the eastern Panhandle soon produced a new trade center known by the unoriginal and unglamorous name of "Hidetown." About a mile east of present Mobeetie, Hidetown received thousands of hides for freighting to the railroad at Dodge City by way of the Jones-Plummer trail connecting the eastern Panhandle with Dodge.[65] Ed Jones and Joe Plummer were merchants who followed the buffalo hunters south and sold guns, ammunition, and whiskey, while buying dried buffalo meat, buffalo tongues, and hides.[66] As the hide trade developed around Mobeetie, the usual supplementary enterprises followed: "Henry Fleming built a stone building at Old Mobeetie and it was a saloon. Mobeetie was a tough place. As saloons and gambling houses got started in Mobeetie bad women came. They all go together."[67] Doubtless "they all" came despite the moral outrage of the hunting community.

In 1875 Fort Elliott was established northwest of Mobeetie to keep the presumably pacified Plains Indians in Indian Territory.[68] Lee and Reynolds, the post traders, supplied the men who hunted along the Canadian and the upper tributaries of the Red River.[69] Thus Fort Elliott served the unofficial but very real purpose of protecting the buffalo slaughter against Indian reprisal.

---

Panhandle." He notes that the government "did not try to keep us from hunting, but they would not let us hunt in the Indian Territory." Perhaps Bussell here suggests a clue to why the buffalo hunters feared government intervention in their hunting in the Panhandle in 1874.

   [64] Interviews, R. "Dick" Bussell to J. Evetts Haley, July 19, 1926 and R. Bussell to L. F. Sheffy, undated, Panhandle-Plains Historical Museum.

   [65] Interview, George A. Simpson to L. F. Sheffy, November 30, 1929, Panhandle-Plains Historical Museum. Simpson arrived in the Panhandle in the fall of 1875. See also L. F. Sheffy, "Old Mobeetie–The Capital of the Panhandle," West Texas Historical Association *Yearbook* 6 (1930): 9.

   [66] Interview, Mose Hayes to J. Evetts Haley, June 10, 1930, Earl Vandale Collection, Archives, University of Texas at Austin. The 135-mile-long Jones-Plummer trail later carried cattle drives to Dodge City.

   [67] Woods to Sheffy, December 28, 1929.

   [68] James M. Oswald, "History of Fort Elliott," *Panhandle-Plains Historical Review* 32 (1959): 1.

   [69] L. F. Sheffy, *The Life and Times of Timothy Dwight Hobart*, pp. 137, 139.

The buffalo hunting that continued in the Panhandle after the attack upon Adobe Walls was a relatively small part of a much larger picture, for the region no longer monopolized hide hunting as it had before June 1874. Fort Griffin became the major center of the Texas hide industry, as the bulk of the hunters approached from the eastern flank of the buffalo range. Although the Adobe Walls incident probably hastened this shift, it certainly would have come anyway, since an approach from the east could be made with readier access to market towns, railroads, and supply sources. Moreover, the attack upon the herds could be delivered over a much longer front.

When the emphasis of the buffalo hunt shifted to the south, other towns, especially Fort Griffin, replaced Adobe Walls and overshadowed Mobeetie as centers of the buffalo hunting trade. As a part of the program of frontier defense for post-bellum Texas, Fort Griffin was established on the Clear Fork of the Brazos in present Shackelford County. Though its original purpose was purely military, the post became the center of the hide industry and later figured in the cattle drives.[70] Fort Griffin attracted the usual frontier characters, both good and bad, and soon acquired a vile reputation.[71] Open daylight robbery was not uncommon,[72] and during the twelve-year life of Fort Griffin, "thirty-four men were publicly killed and eight found dead. Eleven of these were killed either by the officers or the Vigilance Committee."[73] Despite its sins, Fort Griffin boasted at least one redeeming feature: a well-organized and well-attended school that gave instruction in reading, writing, Greek, Latin, mathematics, and grammar.[74]

On Christmas Day, 1874, twenty-year-old Joe S. McCombs led the first hide-hunting expedition out of Fort Griffin.[75] Moving out the Mackenzie Trail, McCombs and his skinners, John Jacobs and Joe Poe, camped about six miles northeast of present Haskell; in two months McCombs had killed seven hundred buffalo. Moving then to the Clear Fork of the Brazos, the

---

[70] Ben O. Grant, "Life in Old Fort Griffin," *West Texas Historical Association Yearbook* 10 (1934): 32. The definitive history of Fort Griffin is Carl Coke Rister, *Fort Griffin on the Texas Frontier*.

[71] Grant, "Life in Old Fort Griffin," p. 34.

[72] C. C. Rister, "Fort Griffin," *West Texas Historical Association Yearbook* 1 (1925): 21; Rister, *Fort Griffin*, pp. 125-140.

[73] Grant, "Life in Old Fort Griffin," p. 36.

[74] Ibid., p. 39.

[75] Ben O. Grant and J. R. Webb, contribs., "On the Cattle Trail and Buffalo Range, Joe S. McCombs," *West Texas Historical Association Yearbook* 11 (1935): 93, 97.

McCombs party took thirteen hundred more hides, making a total of two thousand for the 1874-1875 season. During the entire season on the buffalo range, McCombs and his partners were unmolested and saw no one save each other.[76] Less than five years later, in the fall of 1878, McCombs went to the buffalo range for the last time. Camping near present Midland, he could take only eight hundred hides from September until the middle of March. "I do not recollect having seen a buffalo on the range after my return from my last hunt," says McCombs. "There was no hunting after that."[77]

Several factors combined to bring about this rapid extinction of the Texas buffalo herds: the systematization of hunting; the development of adequate weapons; the convenience of supply and markets; and the basic character of the buffalo, which contributed enormously to their destruction. Richard I. Dodge, who observed the beginnings of hide hunting in Kansas, felt that the first hunting expeditions were poorly organized and produced little profit and much waste. When merchants began to sponsor hunting parties, however, they brought organizational know-how to the hunt and replaced chaos with at least some order.[78] A well-organized hunting party was led by a hunter of proven marksmanship and knowledge of buffalo lore. A glamourless but essential member was the camp rustler, whose main job was cooking and general maintenance of the camp. The hardest and meanest chore of the hunt was performed by the skinners.[79] Occasionally, parties were quite large. Robert Cypret Parrack was once a member of a sixteen-man outfit that included two hunters, one rustler, and ten skinners, while two men hauled hides and one loaded ammunition.[80] In summary then, the division and specialization of labor, coupled with good management, simply made for more efficient production, which in this case was killing buffalo for their hides. With experience came improvement in the techniques of hunting and especially of skinning the dead buffalo.[81]

Just as the Industrial Revolution had come to the aid of the Texas Rangers by producing the Colt revolver about forty years earlier, the needs of western buffalo hunters were similarly filled by technological advances.

[76] Ibid., pp. 97-98.
[77] Ibid., pp. 100-101.
[78] Dodge, *Hunting Grounds of the Great West*, p. 134.
[79] Ibid., p. 135; Strickland, ed., "Recollections of W. S. Glenn," pp. 25-27.
[80] Holden, "Robert Cypret Parrack," p. 32.
[81] See John R. Cook, *The Border and the Buffalo*, pp. 116-117, and Strickland, ed., "Recollections of W. S. Glenn," pp. 29-31, for descriptions of skinning techniques.

As commercial hide hunting began, hunters used whatever firearms they could get, including Enfields, Winchesters, and Springfields.[82] Heavy-bodied, big boned animals like buffalo were hard to kill, however, and the firearms available lacked the power to immobilize and kill quickly. Early in the 1870's the Sharpes Rifle Company began production of large-bore rifles firing cartridges of large powder capacity. Ranging from .40 to .50 caliber, Sharpes rifles were designed especially for big, tough game and were beautifully adapted to killing buffalo. The term "Big Fifty" came to be applied to various .50 caliber Sharpes rifles (and may have been applied to rifles of other calibers as well), although the true Big Fifty was the .50-170.[83] W. S. Glenn claims that the Sharpes Company developed a .45 caliber rifle especially for the buffalo-hunting trade after considerable experimentation and testing on the buffalo range.[84] The literature of the buffalo range, however, is replete with references to the Big Fifty, and J. Wright Mooar claims that it was in response to his insistence that such a weapon was both necessary and feasible that the .50 caliber Sharpes was produced.[85] The heavy slug backed by a heavy powder charge could be counted upon to penetrate bone and reach the vital organs of the buffalo, and on more than one occasion the extreme range of Sharpes rifles kept scalp-lifting Indians at a respectful distance.

Although the venture at Adobe Walls had cost them dearly, the merchants who served that isolated hunters' outpost did not lose heart—perhaps they had no choice—and as the hunters moved southward, so did the businessmen. Among the first of the northern hunters to arrive on the southeastern edge of the buffalo range were the enterprising Mooar boys, who pulled into Fort Griffin with twelve wagonloads of government freight. Upon receiving the goods, the commanding officer of the fort emphatically forbade the Mooars from going more than twenty miles beyond the fort, saying the government could take no responsibility for what the Indians might do. "We did not take the General very seriously," says Mooar, "and went 100 miles beyond the Fort." Other hunters came to Fort Griffin about the same time Mooar arrived, and in the fall of 1876 "about a dozen outfits of different sizes" pulled out of Fort Griffin for the hunting grounds.[86]

[82] Holden, "Robert Cypret Parrack," p. 36.
[83] West, "The Battle of Adobe Walls (1874)," p. 2.
[84] Strickland, ed., "Recollections of W. S. Glenn," pp. 23-24.
[85] Mooar to Haley, November 28, 1927.
[86] Mooar, "Frontier Experiences," pp. 90-91.

Along with the buffalo hunters from the north came the merchants who had served them at Dodge City and at Adobe Walls. A. C. Myers opened for business at Fort Griffin in 1876, while his German-born competitor, Charles Rath, arrived on the southern flank of the herd the same year. Bolder than Myers, Rath selected a site about fifty miles west of Fort Griffin on Double Mountain Fork of the Brazos. Around his establishment gathered other firms, and soon a typical frontier town, Rath City, developed. About eighty hunters followed Rath south, and although Rath City did not replace Fort Griffin, it did get a terrific share of the hide business—perhaps in excess of one million dollars' worth in 1877.[87] Thus enterprising frontier merchants, accepting the fact of high-risk enterprise, followed the hide men and facilitated the destruction of the buffalo by furnishing both ready access to supplies and convenient contacts with markets.

Finally, the buffalos' astounding incomprehension of danger contributed to their destruction because it made them especially susceptible to the still hunt. While Indians and *ciboleros* (Mexican buffalo hunters) regarded the thrill of the chase as intrinsically a part of the hunt as the kill, Anglo-American hide hunters sought efficiency, not thrills.[88] They, therefore, employed the still hunt, which meant taking a concealed position and killing buffalo as they came within range. Under favorable circumstances the still hunt produced what the hunters called "a stand." A hunter who "got a stand" was fortunate enough to find a number of buffalo grazing within a restricted area and to approach and conceal himself without alarming the game. From his hideout the hunter carefully picked his targets so as to kill any animals showing signs of alarm and fired deliberately so as to avoid overheating his rifle barrel and causing it to lose accuracy. If skillfully handled, the stand produced a large number of dead buffalo within a small area, which facilitated skinning and made skinners less susceptible to ambush. Dodge claims to have "counted 112 carcasses inside of a semicircle of 200 yards radius, all of which were killed by one man from the same spot, and in less than three-quarters of an hour." John R. Cook claims to have killed eighty-eight buffalo in a stand on Wolf Creek;

[87] Naomi H. Kincaid, "Rath City," West Texas Historical Association *Yearbook* 24 (1948): 40-44.
[88] For a description of Mexican buffalo hunting, see Fabiola Cabeza de Baca, *We Fed Them Cactus*, p. 42; Frank Collinson, *Life in the Saddle*, ed. Mary Whatley Clarke, pp. 60-66; and especially Charles L. Kenner, *A History of New Mexican-Plains Indian Relations*, pp. 98-114.

J. Wright Mooar claims a maximum kill of ninety-six in one stand; and Frank Collinson's "best score was 121 buffalo on one stand north of where Childress is now located."[89]

With so many factors, including his own nature, against him, the buffalo did not have a chance!

Although the attack upon Adobe Walls had turned out to be something of a swan song for the Indians of the southern Plains, they continued to jump their reservations in Indian Territory and to raid into Texas. As the buffalo hunt proceeded, their frustration mounted, and marauding Indians periodically fell upon isolated hunting parties. This was the fate of Marshall Sewell, an apparently well-thought-of hunter, who was ambushed while absorbed in hunting. Two scalp locks were lifted from Sewell and his body otherwise mutilated.[90] Responding to the Sewell killing and similiar occurrences the hunters organized a campaign against the Indians. Accordingly, in March 1877 forty-five well-armed men, supplied with, among other things, "corn for the horses, and 'corn' for the hunters,"[91] rode out of Rath City headed for the Staked Plains. Finding a large Indian encampment in Yellow House Canyon, the hunters attacked. The ensuing battle was dramatic though indecisive, but since the Indians withdrew, the hunters considered themselves to have won the day. Plainly, however, the whites got more of a fight than they had expected or wanted and did not press the engagement.[92]

---

[89] Dodge, *Hunting Grounds of the Great West*, pp. 135-136; Cook, *Border and the Buffalo*, pp. 163-167; Mooar to Haley, November 28, 1927; and Collinson, *Life in the Saddle*, ed. Clarke, p. 55.

[90] Cook, *Border and the Buffalo*, pp. 194-195.

[91] Collinson, *Life in the Saddle*, ed. Clarke, p. 103.

[92] See the following accounts of the Yellow House Canyon fight: ibid., pp. 101-106; Cook, *Border and the Buffalo*, pp. 205-232; and Strickland, ed., "Recollections of W. S. Glenn," pp. 42-63. All three authors participated in the Yellow House affair, and their accounts coincide in many particulars. They disagree on important points, however. Cook conveys the impression that the hunters fought with no less distinction than might have been expected from the Arthurian knights. Glenn claims that relatively few fought well, that many lacked the courage even to expose themselves enough to fire their weapons, and makes no effort to hide his contempt for those he considers to have been cowards. Frank Collinson characterizes the whole Yellow House incident as a "scalp hunt," and with refreshing honesty, proclaims, "many of the men went along for the very love of the sport of getting a scalp, and I am sure that I, too, belonged to that class." Only twenty-one years old at the time, Collinson rode toward the Staked Plains with a happy heart and even contemplated sending a scalp to his family back in England. In Collinson's view, the buffalo hunters were rather staunchly stoned by the time they charged the Indian camp and retreated without much encouragement from their leaders when the In-

Although the hunters considered the buffalo range to be safe after the Yellow House Canyon fight, it was not long until the Indians were raiding again, "coming to within five miles of Rath's, killing three more hunters, destroying several camps, and running off the stock."[93] On May 1, 1877, about one hundred Indians visited Rath City. One group of braves ran off the horses, and just at dawn fifty "of those reckless thieves" charged through the little community shooting, yelling, and generally playing havoc but injuring no one.[94] Though this incident seems to have been more of a stunt than a really serious raid, it goaded the hunters into a resolve to spend the summer of 1877 waging war to settle the Indian problem once and for all. This resolve got a number of hunters into one of the most hideous experiences ever endured by human beings on the Staked Plains—the infamous "Lost Nigger Expedition." A band of twenty-two hunters, led by Jim Harvey, agreed to guide the command of Captain Nicholas Nolan, who was under orders to pursue and destroy the raiding Indians. Nolan's command consisted of Negro troopers of the Tenth Cavalry. Tragedy resulted when Captain Nolan, apparently anxious to elevate himself in the opinion of his superiors, disregarded the advice of his buffalo-hunter guides as to the location of water. The command became lost and before water was finally located, suffered indescribably from thirst.[95]

Though the summer of 1877 was devoted to hunting Indians, the

---

dians met their charge with steady fire. "Oh, the wild ride they made," parodied Collinson upon the verse of another Englishman, "honor the light brigade, drunken buffalo hunters!" Collinson ends his account: "We didn't have an opportunity to be very heroic. If our men had been sober and properly led, we could have whipped half the entire Comanche tribe. But who could handle thirty or forty half-drunk buffalo hunters? We got licked and well licked."

The variations among these accounts are historiographically important. As the frontier passed, persons like John R. Cook and Billy Dixon acquired the trappings of civilization, including wives who recorded their husbands' memoirs and prepared them for publication. The nature of wives (deplorable in this case) being what it is, it is reasonable to suppose that there might be some variation between what actually happened to these ex-frontiersmen and what got into print. W. S. Glenn, on the other hand, remained rough-hewn and unaffected by advancing civilization, so that while his recollections suggest no latent literary genius, they have a ring of genuineness and are considered by this writer to be the best of the published buffalo-hunter memoirs. Frank Collinson took up writing of his frontier experiences late in life and found ready publication in *Ranch Romances*. Collinson is reliable and often delightfully honest, although it may be that he embellished a little bit for greater reader appeal, or perhaps because of the nature of an aged man's recollections of the high spirit and adventure of his youth.

[93] Cook, *Border and the Buffalo*, p. 233.
[94] Ibid., p. 242.
[95] Ibid., pp. 244, 259-285. Cook was one of the participating hunters.

hunters were back on the buffalo range in the fall. During the 1877-1878 season, the hunters took more than 100,000 hides,[96] and in 1877 Rath City had its million-dollar year.[97] As the final act in the great buffalo slaughter unfolded, settlers moved onto the range to establish homes. They, too, joined in the hunt for hides and for meat. Before the year of 1878 was very old, a herd of fifty head of buffalo was a rarity. By May the hunters were either leaving the range or settling down to become permanent residents of West Texas.[98] So ended an era.

Notwithstanding its brevity, the buffalo hunt was a significant phase of the history of the Texas Panhandle and adjacent territory. In the first place, the buffalo hunt worked to redirect the region toward the Anglo-American east and away from the Spanish southwest. The buffalo hunters, as has been shown, came directly from Kansas, although indirectly they came from the eastern United States and from Europe. The first numerically significant Anglo-Americans to enter the region, they were the first to enter because of something tangible located there. Although their occupation was interrupted, buffalo hunters were the first "residents" of the Panhandle. Several, such as Billy Dixon, the Cator brothers, and the Mooar brothers, became permanently associated with it or adjacent areas. James Hamilton Cator, in fact, may justifiably be considered the first permanent resident of the Panhandle.

Although the invasion of the Panhandle by the hide men fits into the occupational pattern of frontier advance outlined by Frederick Jackson Turner, contrary to the Turnerian pattern businessmen accompanied the vanguard of the Panhandle frontier, since they entered the region abreast of the hunters. Of the original three Panhandle towns, the buffalo trade was directly responsible for the origins of one, Mobeetie.

That the destruction of the buffalo spelled the doom of the Plains Indians has long been agreed. Since buffalo were the economic bedrock of the Plains Indians, the two disappeared together. When the buffalo were gone, the Indians became more tractable and, however grudgingly, they did retreat to the reservations.[99] The point was not lost in the 1870's, for when the Texas Legislature considered a bill to protect the buffalo, General Phil Sheridan addressed a joint session of the legislature strongly

[96] Ibid., p. 291.
[97] Kincaid, "Rath City," p. 40.
[98] Cook, *Border and the Buffalo*, p. 291.
[99] C. C. Rister, "The Significance of the Destruction of the Buffalo in the Southwest," *Southwestern Historical Quarterly* 33 (1929): 49.

urging that the buffalo hunters be left alone since they were doing more "to settle the vexed Indian question than the entire regular army has done in the last thirty years."[100] Sheridan exaggerated, for implicitly the Indian was doomed anyway. But the fact remains that the buffalo hunters played a major role in the sequence of events that destroyed the aboriginal Plainsmen.

Absence of the buffalo, moreover, cleared the way for subsequent development of the Panhandle region. With the buffalo gone, grass was available for cattle, and the way cleared for the next stage of regional evolution. In the longer range, the way also was prepared for the farmer, since there can be no doubt that significant numbers of wild buffalo are incompatible with any enterprise that requires fencing. The buffalo-hunting phase of regional history is, therefore, transitional—a sort of historical watershed— since the buffalo hunters changed forever the character of the primordial Panhandle and cleared the way for permanent occupation by an agricultural-industrial people. In this connection it is worth noting that the buffalo-hunting phase of regional history was enormously subsidized through the availability of public property (the buffalo) for private exploitation. Such policy, if it may be called that, was thoroughly consistent with the general pattern of economic development in the latter decades of the nineteenth century when private interests enjoyed a free hand in the grand larceny of a continent's natural resources.

The buffalo hunter has not been treated very generously, and William T. Hornaday seems to have sealed the historic reputation of the hunters when he wrote:

> Of all the deadly methods of buffalo slaughter, the still-hunt was the deadliest. Of all the methods that were unsportsmanlike, unfair, ignoble, and utterly reprehensible, this was in every respect the lowest and the worst. Destitute of nearly every element of the buoyant excitement and spice of danger that accompanied genuine buffalo hunting on horseback, the still-hunt was mere butchery of the tamest and yet most cruel kind.[101]

Although Hornaday's point of view as a naturalist and lover of wild things is understandable, it entirely misses the point. Hide hunters made no pretense of sportsmanship; hunting was purely a business enterprise,

---

[100] Quoted in Cook, *Border and the Buffalo*, p. 113. Even if the buffalo had been protected, it is very doubtful that such a law could have been adequately enforced.

[101] Hornaday, "The Extermination of the American Bison," Part II, p. 465.

and as entrepreneurs they conducted their business as efficiently as possible. J. Wright Mooar summed it up well when he said, "Buffalo hunting was a business and not a sport; it required capital, management and work, lots of hard work, more work than anything else."[102] Whether the destruction of a wild species as a business enterprise constituted a wise and moral use of the resource is another question, and Hornaday's denunciation can be fairly applied to much buffalo killing that passed for sport hunting. With that application of Hornaday's view this writer has no quarrel.

Perhaps the real tragedy of the buffalo lies in his basic incompatibility with industrial man. Some wild species, like whitetailed deer, adapt well, find a comfortable place, and flourish within his use of the land. Other species, such as the grizzly bear, find no place within industrial man's framework of land use and thus are eliminated. Buffalo would have competed with cattle for grass and could not have been fenced out of cultivated fields. They therefore were not compatible with widespread use of the Plains by numerous Anglo-Americans. Whether the destruction of the buffalo was wise or moral must be decided within the scope of one's own value system, but the choice is between two extremes: Would one prefer wild buffalo in significant numbers and wilderness, or buffalo in insignificant numbers and an Anglo-American civilization?

[102] Mooar, "Frontier Experiences," p. 91.

# 7. Military Conquest

Although the annihilation of the buffalo destroyed the commissary of the Plains Indians and may have, as General Sheridan thought, contributed more than any other single element to their subjugation, only an outright military defeat placed the Plains aborigines on reservations and kept them there. Post-Civil War America fought what may be reckoned, in the aggregate, a major war to accomplish this purpose, and the Texas Panhandle was the stage upon which one of the final acts in that tragic drama was played. In the 1860's and early 1870's the Panhandle was isolated, unoccupied, and forgotten in the pell-mell rush of the Anglo-American people across the continent, a kind of stepchild to the spirit of Manifest Destiny. Largely unknown to white men, except for the Canadian River Valley, the Panhandle remained a remote, sprawling fortress for the southern Plains tribes, a refuge where safety could be found, stolen stock and captives traded for firearms and whiskey, and from which raids deep into Texas and Mexico could be plotted and launched.

In that mystique of professional soldiering that admires excellence in one's enemy, the Plains warriors more than deserved the respect of their American military counterparts, for surely the surprise is not that the red men eventually lost, but that stone age people held out so well for so long against the forces of an industrial society. Their consummate utilization of the buffalo epitomizes the Indians' adaptation to the Plains environment. Their horsemanship and development of weapons represents no less complete accommodation of aboriginal culture to environmental conditions.

Almost from the moment of birth a Plains Indian child began to acquire equestrian skills, since the movements of a horse were among the very first sensations experienced by the offspring of horse nomads. Throughout boyhood the youngster was trained toward equestrian excellence—even his games were designed to develop it. By the time he was ready for his first hunt or war party, the young *llanero*'s horsemanship was so fine as to evoke unmitigated admiration from Anglo-Americans, who were themselves fine horsemen.

So important, indeed, were horses among the Plains tribes that personal wealth was measured by the size of one's horse herd; brides were purchased with horses; and one of the surest paths to social prestige—as well as economic security—was superior ability in the art of horse thievery. Training of horses achieved artistic attributes, their "labor" being specialized for warfare, buffalo hunting, or whatever particular task a given mount might be selected to perform. Among all the possessions of a Plains warrior, a fine war horse was his most prized.

Simple and effective, the weapons of the Plains Indians were designed expressly for hunting and warfare on horseback. Basic to the Plains warrior's personal arms were his bow and arrows. Kept short—about three feet ordinarily—so as to be manageable on horseback, the bow might be made of horn or of one of several varieties of wood, but the preferred material was bois d'arc or Osage orange because of its straight grain, strength, and resilience. Arrows were painstakingly made of several materials, but straight-grained juniper, which grows abundantly along the eastern escarpment of the High Plains, was best. So effective was the bow and arrow that at close range an arrow could be driven completely through the body of a buffalo, a notably tough animal. Up to ranges of about fifty yards, accuracy was remarkably great. Hitting a man-sized target at that range would appear to have been no great feat of marksmanship. Boys' games devised to inculcate good marksmanship and good horsemanship prepared the youngsters for their manhood roles as huntsmen and warriors. Among the Comanches more serious training was on an individual basis and under the supervision of a doting grandfather who, as companion and teacher, imparted to his grandson not only the techniques of war and the hunt, but

the lore and ways of the prairies and its customs, tribal history and tradition, and instilled pride in the heritage of the People.

Supplementing bow and arrows were war clubs and lances. Clubs consisted of stone heads weighing about two pounds attached with rawhide to
a wooden handle about fourteen inches long. Rather specialized weapons,
war lances were used largely to establish a reputation for extraordinary
courage. Never thrown as a javelin, lances were hand-held and delivered
with an underarm thrust which meant dangerous closeness to an enemy—
unless, of course, the horror-stricken enemy could be caught afoot in open
country—or to game. Lancing buffalo from horseback, intoxicatingly exciting though it may have been, also was fraught with danger, for the
slightest miscue by the horse or unanticipated move by the enraged buffalo might snap the shaft—with dreadful results for the lancer. In combat,
use of the lance, a strictly hand-to-hand weapon, committed the warrior to
win—or to die. Only the bravest or most ambitious fought with the lance,
but their glory was enormous.

For protection against enemy missiles—arrows or rifle balls—the Plains
warrior fashioned a shield of tough buffalo hide. Carried on the arm when
going into battle or suspended to protect the back when in retreat, the
shield effectively turned almost any projectile that did not strike at right
angles.[1]

Given the combination of superlative horsemanship and ingenious
weapons, the historic Plains Indians were splendid light cavalrymen with
few peers and no superiors. With the terror tactics of absolute fiends
frequently thrown in too, the Plains warriors were most dreadful enemies,
and endlessly frustrating to deal with. No less an authority than Randolph B. Marcy made the point beautifully when he described them as

... an enemy who is here to-day and there to-morrow; who at one
time stampedes a herd of mules upon the head waters of the Arkansas,
and when next heard from is in the very heart of the populated districts of Mexico, laying waste haciendas, and carrying devastation,
rapine, and murder in his steps; who is every where without being any
where; who assembles at the moment of combat, and vanishes when-
ever fortune turns against him; who leaves his women and children far
distant from the theatre of hostilities, and has neither towns nor maga-

[1] The foregoing discussion is based upon R. B. Marcy, *Thirty Years of Army Life on
the Border*, pp. 24-28; Ernest Wallace and E. Adamson Hoebel, *The Comanches:
Lords of the South Plains*, pp. 99-111, 126-217; and Walter Prescott Webb, *The Great
Plains*, pp. 60-68.

zines to defend, nor lines of retreat to cover; who derives his commissariat from the country he operates in, and is not encumbered with baggage-wagons or pack-trains; who comes into action only when it suits his purpose, and never without the advantage of numbers or position—with such an enemy the strategic science of civilized nations loses much of its importance, and finds but rarely, and only in peculiar localities, an opportunity to be put in practice.[2]

Perhaps the one great weakness in the military capabilities of the southern Plains Indians derives from their highly individualistic nature and the decentralized character of their social organization: they had little sense of grand strategy and produced little generalship. Certainly, there were many great captains—leaders who could organize and inspire war parties to audacious and devastating raids that left ghastly trails of grief and desolation. But the planning and execution of a campaign, the coordination of many raids to achieve one central objective, appears to have been quite beyond the capabilities of even such renowned and dreaded chieftains as Quanah of the Kwahadi Comanches or Satanta and Satank of the Kiowas. Great captains they were indeed, though among them there was no Tecumseh. From the American frontiersman's point of view, this deficiency of leadership probably was not clearly recognized, for the evil perpetrated upon the frontier was more than sufficient unto its day.

Their failure to take advantage of the opportunities offered them by the Civil War indicates the Indians' lack of strategic sense, although they did enjoy a relatively free hand in raiding upon the frontiers of both Confederate and Union states and territories. Such depredations upon the Santa Fe Trail, in fact, led to Kit Carson's invasion of the Panhandle in 1864 and the first battle of Adobe Walls. To the southeast, the Texas frontier lay dreadfully exposed, since the Confederacy could not fight two wars and Confederate Texas could do little better.

With the end of hostilities, the Texas frontier was even more vulnerable, for as the Confederacy collapsed even the pretense of frontier defense evaporated. Indians, doubtlessly encouraged by white renegades, swept into Texas, driving back the frontier line about one hundred miles during the first ten months of 1866—the worst ten-month period in the history of the Texas frontier. Helpless against this onslaught, the frontier population "forted up," that is, they gathered at centrally located places, built picket stockades for protection, and risked going out to attend stock or fields.

[2] Marcy, *Thirty Years of Army Life*, pp. 67-68.

Left unprotected, homes were at the mercy of marauding savages, and in the spring of 1867 charred rock chimneys dotted the face of West Texas as mute testimony to the dashed dreams of Texas pioneers. Helpless and nearly hopeless, frontier citizens sent sometimes semiliterate but always anguished pleas for aid to Austin and Washington.[3] Consider, for example, the letter of a Cooke County citizen to Governor James W. Throckmorton.

It is with feelings of the deepest anxiety that I address you on the present important chrsis, the most importent that ever our county has undergone since its organiseation. We feel truly that we are in the most chritical situation that we *have ever been* since *Cook County was organised*: of late we have been raded upon by large bands of Indians and White men togather whose depradations have been of the most horried character and they still threaten us almost daily, in so much, that nearly all the people have left the upper part of the county and Gainesville might now be called an extreme out post. . . . The very oldest of frontier settlers . . . have left their extreem frontier homes . . . not being able to withstand the tromendeous rades that are now being made against us. The raders are as well armed as we are, each man bareing from one to two sixshooters besids guns. . . . Of late our scouts have had several engagements with them, the raiders invariably getting the best of it. . . . Amongue these last raiders white men were seen distincly a monkst them as they pursued horses, and they were herd to speak plain English.[4]

In the aftermath of a struggle like the Civil War, energetic federal defense of the southwestern frontier developed slowly, while the pangs attending Reconstruction could hardly have accelerated the process, especially in Texas. Gradually, however, the old frontier forts were reoccupied by United States troops and some new ones were built. The most important forts in Texas were Fort Concho, at present San Angelo; Fort Griffin, in northern Shackelford County on the Clear Fork of the Brazos; and Fort

[3] For documentary evidence of these conditions, see *The Indian Papers of Texas and the Southwest, 1825-1916*, ed. Dorman H. Winfrey and James M. Day, IV, pp. 91-251. See also W. C. Holden, "Frontier Defense, 1865-1889," *Panhandle-Plains Historical Review* 2 (1929): 43-44; Rupert Norval Richardson, *The Frontier of Northwest Texas, 1846-1876*, pp. 269-270.

[4] W. H. Whaley to J. W. Throckmorton, September 26, 1866, in *Texas Indian Papers*, ed. Winfrey and Day, IV, pp. 112-113. On August 5, 1867, Governor Throckmorton wrote to Secretary of War E. M. Stanton that, since the end of the war, Indian raiders had killed 162 Texans, kidnapped forty-three, and wounded twenty-four. Twenty-nine captives had been reclaimed. See Throckmorton to Stanton, ibid., pp. 235-236.

Richardson, near present Jacksboro and the northernmost in the Texas cordon.[5] From Fort Richardson north, the line of defense gapped one hundred miles, for there was no other installation until one reached southwestern Indian Territory. For the Indians such a breach was as good as an engraved invitation to pillage Texas. They accepted.[6]

In Indian Territory the pre-Civil War forts—Arbuckle, on the Washita River near present Davis, Oklahoma, and Cobb, farther upstream on the Washita—ostensibly guarded the reservations until both were replaced by Fort Sill in 1869. Northwest of Fort Sill, at the confluence of Wolf Creek and the North Canadian, was Camp Supply and almost due north from Camp Supply, where the Arkansas River crosses the one hundredth meridian, Fort Dodge guarded western Kansas and the Santa Fe Trail. Far to the west of Fort Dodge lay Fort Lyon, Colorado, on the upper Arkansas about twenty miles above the site of Bent's Fort. Completing a ring of outposts around the Texas Panhandle was Fort Bascom on the Canadian River in present San Miguel County, New Mexico. Fort Bascom remained operational until December 1870, when it was superseded by Fort Union near present Watrous, New Mexico.[7]

These forts existed to protect civilian populations in adjacent areas—a mission in which they were less than a grand success—and it is important to notice that they *surrounded* the Texas Panhandle; not one was located *in* the region. They therefore mark something of a geographical demarcation between two fundamental phases of the Indian wars of the Southwest: One, the Indians depredated beyond the forts upon the frontiers of Texas, Kansas, Colorado, and New Mexico, *outside the ring of forts.* Having performed their raids, the warriors retreated to *within* the ring, that is, to their reservations or to the *terra incognita* of the Texas Panhandle and adjacent areas where the second phase, seeking out and destruction of Indian bands, had to be performed. The Panhandle therefore was both a hideout for marauding Indians and a battleground where they ultimately were defeated.

[5] Richardson, *Frontier of Northwest Texas,* pp. 270-278; Francis Paul Prucha, *A Guide to the Military Posts of the United States, 1789-1895,* p. 67 (Fort Concho), p. 77 (Fort Griffin), and p. 102 (Fort Richardson).

[6] Throckmorton to Stanton, August 5, 1867, in *Texas Indian Papers,* ed. Winfrey and Day, IV, p. 236; Richardson, *Frontier of Northwest Texas,* p. 278.

[7] Prucha, *Military Posts,* p. 7 (Fort Arbuckle), p. 66 (Fort Cobb), pp. 108-109 (Fort Sill), p. 110 (Camp Supply, which was redesignated Fort Supply in December 1878), p. 72 (Fort Dodge), p. 86 (Fort Lyon), p. 59 (Fort Bascom), and p. 113 (Fort Union).

If the post-Civil War years were bloody ones for the Texas frontier, Texans at least had the company of misery, for the Kansas frontier found life no less grim. As settlement crept westward along the Solomon, Saline, and Republican rivers, Cheyenne, Sioux, and Arapaho outrage turned into bloody resistance and brazen challenge to the military authorities. Serving to antagonize the Indians, particularly the Cheyennes, into even greater hostility, General W. S. Hancock's efforts to deal militarily with the Kansas phase of the problem failed dismally.[8]

Turning slowly, the wheels of the federal government, specifically those of the Congress, eventually ground out a response to the Indian crisis on the southwestern frontier. By an act signed July 20, 1867, Congress created the Indian Peace Commission to seek a peaceful settlement with the hostile Indian tribes. Should the commission fail, the president was authorized to call out troops "for the suppression of Indian hostilities."[9] Taking their mission seriously, the commissioners by October 11, were on the way from Fort Larned, Kansas, to Medicine Lodge Creek, about eighty miles south of the Arkansas, where members of southern Plains tribes were expected to congregate. The commissioners were accompanied by quite an entourage— not entirely welcome in all cases, one suspects—of reporters, buffalo hunters, Indian agents, politicians, sundry hangers-on, and an escort of five hundred Seventh Cavalry troopers and almost one hundred wagons loaded with supplies and gifts. Upon arrival, the commissioners found more than five thousand Indians. Taking great care to observe amenities and to cultivate good will, the commissioners eventually got down to issues and listened patiently as the Indians aired their grievances. A good deal of eloquent Indian oratory added up to two basic points, both of enormous importance to the red men: one, they resented white encroachment upon their country, and two, they wanted nothing to do with reservations, restrictive reservation life, and "the white man's road,"—a "road," as things turned out, that no self-respecting white man would ever tolerate.[10]

---

[8] William H. Leckie, *The Military Conquest of the Southern Plains*, pp. 30-56; hereafter cited as Leckie, *Military Conquest*. This study is the only effort to bring together the whole story of military operations and evolving Indian policy as they applied to the southern Plains. Since it goes far beyond the scope of this study, Leckie's work is essential thereto in providing the military and policy background against which the events specifically relating to the Texas Panhandle occurred.

[9] *United States Statutes at Large*, XV, p. 17; Leckie, *Military Conquest*, p. 58.

[10] Leckie, *Military Conquest*, pp. 59-61; Douglas C. Jones, *The Treaty of Medicine Lodge*, pp. 113-116. See the text of the speech of Chief Ten Bears of the Comanches in Wallace and Hoebel, *The Comanches*, pp. 282-284.

The three treaties eventually worked out on the Medicine Lodge provided for large reservations in Indian Territory for the signatory tribes; government subsidies of food, clothing, and agricultural equipment; agencies within the reservations; schools for the children and other services; and the right to hunt south of the Arkansas. Whites were forbidden to transgress reservation lands, and the Indians, in turn, were not to molest whites in any manner.[11] In other words, in their basic terms, the Medicine Lodge treaties provided for the very things the Indians passionately did not want! Moreover, the likelihood that the Indians understood what they were signing seems extremely remote and even if they had, it seems even more remote that they were psychologically capable of changing age-old cultural patterns so that the treaties could be complied with.[12]

The generally proper, if not cordial, atmosphere of the Medicine Lodge negotiations raised some hopes for peace in the Southwest. Probably unrealistic in the first place, these hopes soon fell victim to both circumstance and blundering. Instead of an earnestly desired peace, therefore, the southwestern frontier got a long drawn-out series of Indian wars. Settling none of the immediate differences between the races and contributing nothing toward the ultimate objective of a positive basis for peace, these hostilities visited untold bloodshed, tragedy, horror, and heartbreak upon both sides. Through these terror-stricken years, events built up to a climactic struggle between red man and white: the Red River War of 1874-1875.

In the first place, Indian raiding—an ancient and honorable way of life— did not stop just because of the Medicine Lodge treaties. The so-called Civilized Tribes in Indian Territory were easy targets and suffered badly; the temptations of the Texas frontier, just south of the Red River, were just too much, so that in 1868 Texans had little reason to believe that the Medicine Lodge negotiations had even been held; and some Indians did not recognize the Medicine Lodge treaties and most especially so the fierce, proud Kwahadi Comanches, who probably regarded the treaties with utmost contempt—and continued business in Texas as usual.[13]

---

[11] Charles J. Kappler, comp., *Indian Affairs: Laws and Treaties*, II, pp. 977-982, 982-984, and 984-989.

[12] This is not to imply lack of good faith on the part of the commissioners, who probably did as well as could have been done in the face of difficult and sensitive conditions. At the bottom of the matter would seem to lie the ubiquitous problem of communication—not just in a linguistic sense, in this case, although seven languages were used in the negotiations, but in the sense of total disparateness of comprehension as to what was culturally, indeed even morally, acceptable.

[13] See P. H. Sheridan, *Personal Memoirs*, II, pp. 283-290 for the general's impression of the Medicine Lodge treaties and their results.

On the opposite side of the Medicine Lodge treaties was the insufferable and perhaps inexcusable slowness with which the Congress acted upon them: House and Senate leisurely haggled over the financial obligations incurred by the treaties, and not until July 20, 1868, was $500,000 appropriated so that the government could meet its obligations under the treaties. Meanwhile, Indians who honestly wanted to keep their word were reduced to destitution because the government's agents in Indian Territory lacked the funds to house, feed, and clothe them. White settlers, meantime, hastily occupied tribal lands that had been surrendered. From the Indians' point of view, then, the Medicine Lodge treaties applied to them—but not to whites.[14]

Within an appallingly short time after October 1867, frontier conditions in the Southwest were as gruesome as they had ever been, perhaps more so. Into this chaos, however, came a new, young, and dynamic personality who would at least act: Major General Philip H. Sheridan, whom President Andrew Johnson appointed in August 1867 to command the Department of the Missouri.[15]

[14] Leckie, *Military Conquest*, pp. 63-67. Congressional dallying with the Medicine Lodge treaties, and especially with the really rather meager appropriations they required, almost tempts one to vile speculation. Granting deep congressional preoccupation with Reconstruction, it seems significant that Texas and Kansas were a long way from Washington and it was in Texas and Kansas that murder, rape, and burning were commonplace.

[15] Sheridan, *Memoirs*, II, p. 277; Leckie, *Military Conquest*, p. 63; Carl Coke Rister, *Border Command: General Phil Sheridan in the West*, pp. 33-34. An explanation of the military organization of the trans-Mississippi West, as it relates to this study, will be helpful at this point. Beginning in August 1866, the West, *excluding Texas*, which was considered politically a part of the South, was divided into the Division of the Pacific and the Division of the Missouri and each subdivided into Departments. Within the Division of the Missouri there were four Departments including the *Department* of the Missouri, which covered Missouri, Kansas, and the Territories of New Mexico and Colorado, and the Department of Arkansas, which contained Arkansas and Indian Territory. Never a part of any division, Texas, before March 1867, was combined with Florida and Louisiana into the Department of the Gulf. The First Reconstruction Act of March 2, 1867, in effect abolished the departmental structure as it applied to the South and substituted five Military districts, with Louisiana and Texas constituting the fifth. This arrangement aimed at effective military organization to facilitate Congressional Reconstruction, not primarily at protection of the region. On March 31, 1870, the Fifth Military District, as provided for in the First Reconstruction Act, became the Department of Texas, the terms of the act having been complied with and Reconstruction in Texas therefore over in a legal sense. Earlier in the month, on March 13, the Department of Arkansas was abolished and Indian Territory transferred to the Department of the Missouri. On November 1, 1871, Indian Territory was transferred to the Department of Texas, where it remained until July 10, 1874, when that part lying north of the Canadian River was

Sheridan's failure to take seriously the pleas of Texas' frontier citizens for protection was partly responsible for the president's decision to consign him to the outer darkness of the frontier, although the president was generally disenchanted with the general's tactless administration of the Fifth Military District. Without questioning Sheridan's integrity or goodness of intention, "he simply could not," says his biographer, "wield effectively the flat of his sword."[16]

Sheridan arrived at Fort Leavenworth, Kansas, in September 1867 to assume formally his new command under his immediate superior, another Civil War soldier with a no-nonsense reputation, Major General William Tecumseh Sherman, commanding general of the Division of the Missouri. Finding conditions relatively quiet because of the work of the Indian Peace Commission, Sheridan took leave of absence, visited in the East, and returned to Fort Leavenworth and the responsibilities of the Department of the Missouri in March 1868.[17] By this time the border was aflame and Sheridan found no lack of challenge for his unquestioned military capabilities. Improvising as best he could, the general fought an essentially defensive war through the spring and summer of 1868.[18] But by training, temperament, and experience, Sheridan was neither prepared nor content to wage strictly defensive warfare. With the arrival of fall, he assumed his customary aggressive posture.

In all seasons but one—winter—the land was the natural ally of the Plains Indians. Spring brought rains, green prairies, fat and frisky ponies, and, because of these, the thrill of the buffalo hunt and the warpath. Through the summer the land supported similar prosperity which, lasting into the fall, reached a heady climax in the great fall buffalo hunt, which provided winter food and raiment. Winter, however, was a time of immobility—occasionally perhaps a time of real suffering—for forage was sparse and the ponies thin, weakened, and incapable of carrying their far-ranging masters. As protection from winter's hardships, such places as the breaks of the

---

placed back into the Department of the Missouri, the remainder being similarly transferred the following March 11, 1875. The trans-Canadian Panhandle was attached to the Department of the Missouri from July 10, 1874, until March 11, 1875, when it was returned to the Department of Texas. See Prucha, *Military Posts*, pp. 153-155. The action described in this chapter, then, took place in the contiguous Departments of Texas and the Missouri.

[16] Rister, *Border Command*, pp. 30-34.

[17] Sheridan, *Memoirs*, II, pp. 281-283; Rister, *Border Command*, pp. 34-35, 40-41; Leckie, *Military Conquest*, p. 63.

[18] Sheridan, *Memoirs*, II, pp. 290-295; Leckie, *Military Conquest*, pp. 71-87.

Washita, the upper tributaries of the Red River, and Palo Duro and Tule canyons offered secluded, protected, well-watered, and well-wooded camps.

Moreover, unto everything there is a season, even among (maybe especially among) primitive, naturalistic people, and winter was a time for warmth and well-being of the various kinds derived respectively from one's tepee fire and buffalo robe, earnest talk with one's son, one's squaw, and the camaraderie of men who together have tasted the danger of battle, shared the exhilaration of victory, or chewed the tough bullet of defeat. Winter, therefore, by force of necessity (but partly because of social choice) more or less immobilized the Plains Indians and forced them to stay put—for a time. Only in winter, therefore, were they vulnerable to attack in fixed villages.

Aware of these ancient habits of their antagonists, Sherman and Sheridan determined to strike at a potential weakness. For white soldiers winter campaigning offered a dreadful ordeal, but the army had the technique of carrying its commissary into the field and, although exasperatingly awkward, the technique—not relying upon the land—could support a winter campaign. Hopefully a winter campaign would, for once, permit cavalry sabers to catch scalping knives in their scabbards!

More easily worked out in theory than in fact, Sheridan's plan required solutions to really intricate problems not the least of which was avoiding battle with Indians innocent of depredating. In Sherman's view the Kiowas, Comanches, and Kiowa Apaches were honestly trying to comply with the Medicine Lodge treaties and were therefore encouraged to stay close to their agencies at Fort Cobb. The Arapahos and Cheyennes, on the other hand, were to be punished and emerged as the main objects of the winter campaign. Separating, isolating, and controlling the innocents proved almost unattainable despite conscientious efforts.[19]

On November 1, 1868, Sheridan launched his basically simple but meticulously planned campaign, which involved nothing more than fielding several converging columns. From the west and across the Panhandle by way of the Canadian River from Fort Bascom came Major Andrew W. Evans with two infantry and six cavalry troops. Seven troops of the Fifth Cavalry under Brevet Major General Eugene A. Carr moved from Fort Lyon to the southeast toward Antelope Hills and united with a force

[19] Leckie, *Military Conquest*, pp. 88-94; Rister, *Border Command*, pp. 74-90.

under Brevet Brigadier General W. H. Penrose. The function of these two columns was to push the Indians hiding out along the Canadian and the streams of the eastern Panhandle toward Indian Territory, where hopefully the main forces could attack them. The largest force in the operation, led by Lieutenant Colonel Alfred B. Sully, included eleven troops of the Seventh Cavalry under Lieutenant Colonel George A. Custer, five infantry companies under Captain J. H. Page, and the Nineteenth Kansas Volunteer Cavalry commanded by Colonel Samuel Crawford, who had resigned the governorship of Kansas to take part. Sully's long and formidable column— including over four hundred wagons—pulled out of Fort Dodge on November 12, heading cautiously for the confluence of Wolf Creek and the North Canadian, where Camp Supply was established. Sheridan joined the column on November 21.[20] Already bitterly cold, the weather worsened, but at dawn on November 22, Custer and the Seventh Cavalry took the field to the strains of "The Girl I Left Behind Me."[21] Four days later the Battle of the Washita—surely the most spectacular engagement of the whole campaign—occurred when Custer's scouts discovered the Cheyenne camp of Black Kettle in the valley of the river just east of the one hundredth meridian. Planning his attack carefully and deploying his force in four columns to cut off retreat, the colonel was ready to strike just as dawn's first light appeared on November 26. Effecting almost complete surprise, the Seventh Cavalry executed a classic charge—complete with "Gary Owen." Black Kettle was killed, along with more than one hundred of his people, many captives and seven hundred ponies were taken, and enormous amounts of other property were destroyed. The Seventh Cavalry paid with serious losses, however, the greatest being that of Major Joel Elliott (for whom Fort Elliott was later named) and an eighteen-man detachment.

Custer erred seriously in failing to determine the extent of his adversary's strength, because, as he found out during the heat of battle, Black Kettle's camp was only the first of several Cheyenne, Arapaho, Kiowa, and Comanche camps scattered for ten miles along the Washita. As news of the events at Black Kettle's camp sped through the valley, warriors moved

[20] Sheridan, *Memoirs*, II, pp. 307-312; Rister, *Border Command*, pp. 91-100; Leckie, *Military Conquest*, pp. 95-97. The officers involved in these campaigns seem in almost every case to have carried both permanent and brevet rank. Where possible to determine, permanent rank is used throughout this study.

[21] One wonders what kind of girls these horse soldiers were attracted to, since so many seem to have been left behind.

upstream and the whites found themselves virtually surrounded by several times their own number of braves who occupied the hills surrounding the battlefield. Thinking quickly and boldly, Custer feigned an advance downstream as though he intended to sweep the whole valley. The warriors, taking the movement at face value, hastened to protect their own villages against an attack that Custer dared not attempt. Instead, when the sky was well dark, Custer reversed his march and pushed men and animals to the limits of endurance far up the Washita to where his supply train was located. Doubtless to Custer's enormous relief, it had not been molested.

At Camp Supply the Seventh Cavalry and its flamboyant commanding officer got a festive welcome—complete with "Gary Owen." Although pleased with his subordinate's victory, Sheridan was pointedly curious about Custer's failure to ascertain the fate of Major Elliott and his detachment. Likewise, misgivings, some very bitter, developed among Custer's own subordinate officers because of the Elliott affair.[22] On balance, Custer may be credited with having given the Cheyennes a frightful thrashing from which they would not easily recover and which must have given other hostiles a great deal to ponder as they sat about winter tepee fires—doubtless not so smug as customary. Further, the colonel brought off a risky but brilliantly conceived and superbly executed retreat when his position became untenable. Still, Custer came perilously close to finding his Little Big Horn on the Washita!

When Custer's prisoners revealed that other Cheyenne camps lay below Black Kettle's, Sheridan determined to sweep from the site of Black Kettle's camp down the Washita to Fort Cobb, slashing the camps as he went or forcing their occupants to the reservations. Custer would remain in command, but Sheridan would personally accompany and observe the operation. Exasperating delays through the last week of November kept the operation from starting until December 7, but on that date the well-trained (thanks to Custer) and now battle-tempered Seventh Cavalry, supplemented by ten companies of the Nineteenth Kansas Volunteer Cavalry, marched from Camp Supply. Three days of tough marching through deep

[22] George Armstrong Custer, *My Life on the Plains*, pp. 240-260, contains Custer's account of the Battle of the Washita. See also Sheridan, *Memoirs*, II, pp. 312-320; Leckie, *Military Conquest*, pp. 97-105; Rister, *Border Command*, pp. 101-112; and Jones, *Treaty of Medicine Lodge*, p. 40. Later investigation showed that Elliott had become surrounded, his whole detachment wiped out, and, as usual, the bodies dreadfully mutilated.

snow in subfreezing temperatures brought the column to the battle site of November 26. Here the grim fate of Major Elliott, his soldiers, other missing men, and white prisoners was learned.[23]

Pushing down the Washita toward Fort Cobb, Custer and Sheridan came upon hastily evacuated Kiowa and Arapaho villages. With their prey almost within grasp, the officers pressed forward toward a confrontation and a virtually certain military victory.

Victory was denied, however, for on the morning of December 17, 1868, a courier delivered a message from Brevet Major General W. B. Hazen at Fort Cobb saying that all Indians between the Seventh Cavalry and Fort Cobb were innocent of any current wrongdoing. Although thoroughly annoyed because of their conviction of the guilt of the Indians before them, Sheridan and Custer had little choice but to observe Hazen's injunction and avoid combat.[24] Perhaps a military showdown would have been in the long-range interest of the frontier, but Custer's fight on the Washita and the subsequent sweep from Camp Supply to Fort Cobb convinced almost all the Kiowas, Comanches, and Kiowa Apaches of the expediency of going to their reservations. The Cheyennes and Arapahos, however, holed up along the headwaters of the Red River and remained the main objects of the winter offensive.

The columns of Major Evans from Fort Bascom and General Carr from Fort Lyon served to harass the recalcitrant Arapahos and Cheyennes, and eventually harassment and negotiation persuaded most to come to their agencies at Camp Supply and Fort Sill.

Evans left Fort Bascom on November 18, 1868, with an expedition of 526 officers and men, including six troops of the Third Cavalry and a battery of mountain howitzers. Two days out of Fort Bascom a dreadful blizzard hit, but despite deep snow, sleet, and biting cold the troops slogged their way across the Panhandle, eventually setting up a supply depot on Monument Creek (a tributary of the Canadian, probably in Hemphill County), from whence many scouting parties scoured the eastern Panhandle for Indians. None were found. Leaving twenty men to guard his depot, Evans moved on down the Canadian on December 15. Ten days of searching finally brought Evans upon a substantial village of recalcitrant Comanches on the North Fork of the Red River. A sharp engagement on

    [23] Custer, *Life on the Plains*, pp. 284ff.; Sheridan, *Memoirs*, II, pp. 320-330; Leckie, *Military Conquest*, pp. 105-107; Rister, *Border Command*, pp. 114-116.
    [24] Sheridan, *Memoirs*, II, pp. 330-337; Leckie, *Military Conquest*, pp. 107-108; Rister, *Border Command*, p. 122.

Christmas Day, 1868, drove the Indians from their village, killed many of them, and destroyed vast amounts of dried buffalo meat, meal, sugar, coffee, and other property without which the Indians could not hope to sustain themselves through the winter. Moving on toward the Wichita, in still grimly cold weather, Evans sent couriers to Sheridan at Fort Cobb, and then on January 3, 1869, turned back westward toward his depot on Monument Creek, which took ten days to reach. Through hunger and exposure Evans' men were reduced to mere shells of soldiers and losses in livestock were appalling. But the village Evans destroyed was that of the Nokoni band of Horseback who had participated in particularly grisly raids in Texas the previous summer and fall. Some of Horseback's people made their way to Fort Cobb; others surrendered at Fort Bascom in such haste that they got there even in advance of Evans' return.[25]

Carr led seven troops of the Fifth Cavalry and one company of the Third Infantry from Fort Lyon on December 2 with orders to join Brevet Brigadier General W. H. Penrose, who had left Fort Lyon with five cavalry troops on November 10. The two forces were to establish a supply base on the North Canadian and then scour the country to the southeast. Carr's march went well for only three days when winter weather overtook him, so that it was not until December 23 and after much agony that he reached Penrose's sad camp, its supplies almost gone, on the North Canadian. Pushing southward and sending out scouting parties in a systematic search for Indians, Carr reached the main Canadian about twenty miles above Evans' supply base from which he replenished his stores to some extent. Although small search columns sought Indian haunts, frightful winter weather dogged their every pace and no Indians were found. Giving up on January 8, 1869, Carr marched for Fort Lyon, which he reached on February 19. He had lost 181 animals, two men from exposure, and had found no Indians.[26]

The operations of Evans and Carr had kept the Cheyennes and Arapahos on the prod. There was intense suffering among them. Their ponies died, and, in a strange twist of circumstances, roving troopers made hunting unsafe for the hungering Indians. Peace with the white people became an attractive proposition—now that tables had been turned. Sheridan, receiving intelligence that the Cheyennes and Arapahos wanted peace, sheathed his sword, hoping to achieve peace through persuasion.[27]

---

[25] Sheridan, *Memoirs*, II, pp. 336-337; Leckie, *Military Conquest*, pp. 114-118.
[26] Sheridan, *Memoirs*, II, p. 337; Leckie, *Military Conquest*, pp. 118-119.
[27] Sheridan, *Memoirs*, II, pp. 337-338; Leckie, *Military Conquest*, p. 119.

Despite good indications that the Cheyennes and Arapahos would come voluntarily to Fort Cobb and accept their reservations, several days of waiting produced no Indians and an impatient Custer. He requested authority to go into the field as a peace commissioner to persuade the Indians to come in. Although a very risky procedure, Custer proposed to take an escort of only forty men as proof of his honorable and peaceful intentions. Sheridan questioned both the efficacy and safety of the proposal, but did consent. Accompanying the soldier were the chiefs Little Robe of the Cheyennes and Yellow Bear of the Arapahos, through whose good offices Custer hoped to establish favorable communication with their tribes. It was in fact their voluntary appearance before Sheridan on January 1 that had raised hope that their people would come in. The Arapahos under Little Raven, finally found on Mulberry Creek, readily accepted Custer's offer of peace and, keeping their promise to Custer, were soon on their way to Fort Sill.[28]

Little Robe was permitted to go on alone to seek his people. When the chief failed to return, Custer moved on up the Red River far enough into the Panhandle to convince himself that the Cheyennes were not in the vicinity. He resolved, therefore, to return to Fort Sill and outfit a punitive expedition. Not until March 2, however, was Custer able to get into the field with eleven troops of the Seventh Cavalry, ten companies of the Nineteenth Kansas Volunteers, and the usual white scouts and Osage trailers. Skirting the southern end of the Wichitas, Custer led his command westward in a grueling, discouraging march that held scant promise of success. Custer had faith in his plan, however, and despite the privations it paid off, for Custer found the Cheyennes—in camps scattered for ten to fifteen miles along Sweetwater Creek! Custer was prepared to fight and doubtless was in the mood, but his recollection of the fate of white captives caught in Black Kettle's camp caused him to want to negotiate if at all possible. Although peaceable enough in attitude, the Cheyennes resorted to dilatory tactics that pushed Custer's patience to the utmost—and understandably so. Ultimately, the colonel seized four chiefs as hostages, one of whom was released to demand immediate surrender of white prisoners and prompt withdrawal of the Cheyennes to Fort Sill.

Meanwhile, Custer's problems with his Kansas Volunteers were almost as

[28] Custer, *Life on the Plains*, pp. 326-330; Sheridan, *Memoirs*, II, pp. 342-344; Leckie, *Military Conquest*, pp. 120-121.

severe as those with the Indians, for many of the Kansans had lost relatives and friends in Cheyenne raids. Out for blood, the volunteers fervently resented Custer's determination to avoid bloodshed. Ultimately Custer threatened to hang the three remaining hostage chiefs and attack the villages if the prisoners were not delivered by sunset of March 19. As nooses were being placed around the necks of the three chiefs, a small party appeared with two white women. The Indians tried to bargain for the release of their chiefs, but in their very persons Custer held the trump and the Cheyennes knew it. Custer's patience and adamance paid off, for now the great Cheyenne Chief Medicine Arrow agreed to get his people to their agency as quickly as possible, the hostage chiefs to remain hostage as a guarantee of compliance. Believing Medicine Arrow and his people honest, Custer considered his work done and marched to Camp Supply and then to Fort Hays, where the Kansas Volunteers were mustered out and where the battle proven and indescribably field weary troopers of the Seventh Cavalry could rest.[29]

At least in terms of immediate effects, Custer may be credited with a great deal of wisdom in handling this affair. First, he avoided a battle that surely would have cost the lives of white captives. Second, while he could probably have had a spectacular military victory, which would have looked good on his record, his avoidance of battle probably also avoided a hideous slaughter of noncombatant Cheyennes. Given their poor discipline and undisguised thirst for blood—understandable from their point of view—the Kansas Volunteers might well have produced another Sand Creek massacre. One was too many.

Though constituting no permanent solution to the Indian problem of the South Plains, Sheridan's winter campaign of 1868-1869 may be said to have achieved its immediate objective reasonably well. Several other developments worth noting occurred in connection with the offensive.

First, Fort Cobb was abandoned and a new and permanent post established within the Comanche and Kiowa reservation in order to watch better those tribes and to protect the Texas frontier. Originally known as Camp Wichita, the new post was located at the confluence of Cache and Medicine Bluff creeks on March 4, 1869, and beautifully situated relative to wood, water, forage, and defense. The post was formally named Fort

---

[29] Custer, *Life on the Plains*, pp. 345-375; Sheridan, *Memoirs*, II, pp. 344-346; Leckie, *Military Conquest*, pp. 121-126.

Sill on July 2, 1869, to honor Sheridan's classmate, Brigadier General Joshua W. Sill, who fell at the head of his brigade at Stone River, on December 31, 1862.[30]

To the Indians, Sheridan's winter campaign should have conveyed at least two important lessons: One, that they had no monopoly on guts; that the bluecoats, too, could fight fiercely and could and would endure the undeniable hardships and dangers of campaigning against them. Two, that winter was no longer a time of sanctuary and immunity.

Finally, Sheridan's plan of a system of columns converging upon the remote haunts of the hostiles, though hardly Napoleonic in concept or magnitude, was a sound approach to campaigning against the southern Plains tribes. The method would be used again, and more successfully, because its one basic flaw would be corrected.

The defect in Sheridan's strategy was the absence of forces pushing northward from Texas. Encirclement of the Panhandle and the adjoining areas where the action of 1868-1869 occurred was only a half-encirclement, so that various bands of hostiles simply moved southward out of the half-circle to the streams—the Pease and upper branches of the Brazos—along the edge of the Staked Plains to the south of the Red River. Over 250 lodges of Arapahos, Cheyennes, Apaches, and all the Kiowas and Comanches not on their reservations slipped to the south to hide out in the region not touched by Sheridan's cavalrymen.[31] Really decisive campaigning required that this strategic omission be corrected.

On the reservations Quaker agents assumed responsibility for those tribesmen who were driven, or voluntarily came, in. Responding to intensifying and justifiable criticism of Indian policy, the Grant administration appointed Indian agents from nominees submitted by various religious bodies who believed that fair treatment and kindness would induce the Indians to give up their "wild" ways and accept a "civilized" way of life.[32]

---

[30] Leckie, *Military Conquest*, pp. 111-112; W. S. Nye, *Carbine and Lance: The Story of Old Fort Sill*, pp. 99-101; and Prucha, *Military Posts*, pp. 107-108.

[31] Rister, *Border Command*, pp. 154-155.

[32] Laurence F. Schmeckebier, *The Office of Indian Affairs: Its History, Activities and Organization*, pp. 40-48, 54-55. The notion that kindness would induce the Indians to accept "civilization" perhaps indicates a basic reason why no really satisfactory settlement of the Indian problem could be worked out in the United States. The whites seem utterly to have been unable to grasp that, as the Indians saw the world, it was *their* way of life that was civilized. Even the astute Randolph B. Marcy, who admired the Indians in so many ways, found incomprehensible their responding to white "kindness" with more "atrocities." See C. C. Rister, "Documents Relating

On the whole, the Quaker agents among the southern Plains tribes were intelligent, courageous men who strove to the limit of human patience to deal effectively with their charges, to protect the Indians, and to maintain the peace of the southwestern frontier. Though their efforts in teaching the Indians met with some success, the Indians despised farming, and their good behavior was rather well confined to the reservation.[33]

Despite the best efforts of the Quakers, however, peace on the southwestern frontier was illusory, for the reservations often served only as bases for raids into Texas. The Kiowas, especially the bloodthirsty Satanta, were disaffected, but were ably backed by their long-time allies, the Comanches. Getting ample arms from illicit white traders, the reservation Indians, along with those who never came in, poured into Texas and made 1869 one of the state's bloodiest years. Utterly unable to protect the frontier, Major General J. J. Reynolds, commander of the Department of Texas, authorized frontier counties to raise militia, but the reservations bordering the Red River remained an open passageway to Texas. The year 1870 brought nothing better for Texas, while in 1871 Satanta and Satank, two of the most fiendish Kiowas, plotted ever greater bloodletting.[34]

Clearly, if this was peace, the Texas frontier could not stand much of it!

Texas cries for aid in defending themselves against these outrages finally brought a response from General Sheridan, who had succeeded to the command of the Division of the Missouri, and General Sherman, now general of the army. In what turned out to be a singularly important step, a Civil War tested young colonel, Ranald S. Mackenzie, was sent to command Fort Richardson in order that the most exposed portions of the frontier might be protected somewhat more effectively. Sherman, skeptical but nevertheless concerned, determined on a personal inspection of the Texas frontier. The general was accompanied by a couple of staff officers, an escort of fifteen cavalrymen, and the inspector-general of the army—who was none other than that old veteran of the Texas frontier, Randolph B. Marcy!

The Quaker agents and Colonel Benjamin H. Grierson, commanding officer at Fort Sill, discounted Texans' complaints as exaggerations and

---

to General W. T. Sherman [*sic*] Southern Plains Indian Policy 1871-1875," *Panhandle-Plains Historical Review* 9 (1936): 24.

[33] Rupert Norval Richardson, *The Comanche Barrier to South Plains Settlement*, pp. 323-339; Leckie, *Military Conquest*, p. 136.

[34] See the documents contained in *Texas Indian Papers*, ed. Winfrey and Day, IV, pp. 290ff; Ernest Wallace, *Ranald S. Mackenzie on the Texas Frontier*, pp. 25-26, 28; Leckie, *Military Conquest*, pp. 143-145.

insisted that the reservation Indians were behaving. Sherman's journey, beginning at San Antonio on May 2, 1871, seemed to support their view, since the inspectors traveled all the way from San Antonio to Fort Richardson (visiting Forts Mason, McKavett, Concho, and Griffin on the way) and saw not one Indian. This caused Sherman to believe Grierson and the Quakers were right, but Marcy knew better. In his judgment, there were fewer white people in the area along the route than he had found eighteen years earlier![3 5]

Actually Sherman reached Fort Richardson safely by the sheerest quirk of fate, for on May 18, the day the fort was reached, a war party of 150 Kiowas had quietly watched as the general's small party passed, restrained only by medicine which directed that the second, not the first, party to pass that day should be attacked. Arriving at Fort Richardson, Sherman received such hospitality as the remote outpost could provide, listened courteously to despairing pleadings of West Texans, and—still unconvinced—retired for the night.

Sometime during the night a wounded, horror-stricken man, Thomas Brazeal, arrived at the fort with news of the ambush of a wagon train about twenty miles west of the fort. Owned by Henry Warren, a government freight contractor, the train comprised of ten wagons and twelve men was jumped on the afternoon of the eighteenth by a party of about 150 Kiowas led by Satanta—apparently the ones who had let Sherman pass unmolested. Killing seven men, the Kiowas hideously butchered and mutilated the bodies and chained one member, Samuel Elliott, between two wagon wheels, cut out his tongue, and slowly burned him to death. Five men escaped, but the property was destroyed and forty-one mules stolen.[3 6]

Now taking the Texans seriously, Sherman ordered Mackenzie and Colonel W. H. Wood, commanding officer at Fort Griffin, into the field to verify Brazeal's story and, if true, to pursue the raiders into their reservations if necessary.[3 7] Preparing quickly for a thirty-day campaign, Mac-

---

[3 5] Rister, "Sherman [*sic*] Southern Plains Indian Policy," pp. 18-19. The bulk of this article is Marcy's diary kept during Sherman's inspection. See also Wallace, *Mackenzie*, pp. 28-29.

[3 6] Rister, "Sherman [*sic*] Southern Plains Indian Policy," p. 19; Wallace, *Mackenzie*, p. 30; Leckie, *Military Conquest*, p. 148; J. W. Wilbarger, *Indian Depredations in Texas*, pp. 552, 554-556; R. G. Carter, *On the Border with Mackenzie*, pp. 81-82. Carter, an eyewitness to the remains of Warren's wagon train, concluded from the appearance of Elliott's body that his death was caused by burning. But also see Nye, *Carbine and Lance*, p. 131, for a contrary interpretation of the evidence.

[3 7] Sherman to Mackenzie, May 19, 1871, and Sherman to Wood, May 19, 1871, in *Ranald S. Mackenzie's Official Correspondence Relating to Texas, 1871-1873*, ed.

kenzie hit the trail on the nineteenth amidst torrential rains. Shortly before nightfall the soldiers came upon the sickening proof of Thomas Brazeal's story—quite an initiation into the warfare of the Plains for the thirty-one-year-old Colonel Mackenzie. Placing the bodies in a wagon bed that served as a common coffin, the troopers buried the dead teamsters as decently as possible. Mackenzie then took up pursuit which turned into hopelessness and frustration since enormous rains obliterated the Indians' trail. On June 4, 1871, the column wound up at Fort Sill without having overtaken their quarry. At Fort Sill, however, the colonel discovered that Satanta, Satank, and Big Tree, three of the most feared Kiowas, were under arrest for the murders and were to be tried in Texas. Mackenzie at least had the consolation of taking the three back to Texas, although Satank was killed a short distance out of Fort Sill when he attempted to escape.[38]

Although important, the major significance of the Warren wagon train episode lies elsewhere than in the fate of the Kiowa chiefs. The specific point is the coincidental arrival of a new and dynamic personality, Ranald Slidell Mackenzie, who would play a leading role in the military operations in the Texas Panhandle. As Wallace aptly observes, "A new era in the history of the Texas frontier had begun."[39]

In the broad view of the Texas frontier experience, the Warren wagon train tragedy was just another incident not materially different from dozens of others. Because of its timing, however, the episode dramatized what every half-perceptive observer already knew: just as the Spaniards had learned centuries earlier that the Cross had to be supported by the sword, the Quakers would have to learn that their olive branch would be more attractive when proffered on the tip of a cavalry saber! Quaker Lawrie Tatum, with understanding, urged punishment for the Kiowas unless the forty-one mules stolen in the raid be returned forthwith. Having come to share these views, Sherman goaded the War and Interior departments into an amended Indian policy that would (1) withhold rations from the families of those who left the reservations to raid and (2) permit

Ernest Wallace, pp. 23-25. Documents pertinent to these events may also be found in C. C. Rister, "Documents Relating to General W. T. Sherman's Southern Plains Indian Policy, 1871-1875, II," *Panhandle-Plains Historical Review* 10 (1937): 48-60.

[38] Carter, *On the Border*, pp. 82-89; Wallace, *Mackenzie*, pp. 33-37. Satanta and Big Tree were tried, convicted, and sentenced to death. Governor E. J. Davis commuted the sentences to life imprisonment. The two eventually were freed. Later reimprisoned, Satanta died a suicide in the Texas penitentiary.

[39] Wallace, *Mackenzie*, p. 31.

troops to enter the reservations in pursuit of raiders or to recover stolen property. When possible, an agent was to accompany the military into reservations.

Mackenzie and Grierson agreed with Tatum that the Kiowas should be punished and thought that the Kwahadi Comanches, who had never come to the reservation, must be sought out and defeated. If the wild, free Kwahadis could be whipped, the soldiers believed, control of all the Indians would be easier. With the way cleared by the amendments in Indian policy, the two officers seized the initiative and planned a coordinated movement of their cavalry regiments, the Fourth and Tenth, from Fort Sill and Fort Richardson to scout the Red River and its upper tributaries for lurking Kiowas and Comanches. Rendezvousing at old Camp Radziminski on Otter Creek, the two colonels conferred on August 10, 1871. A few days later, the commands separated to scout the Salt Fork and North Fork of the Red River.[40]

Though starting out auspiciously, the campaign soon lost its steam—much to the chagrin of the energetic Mackenzie. The Kiowas complied with demands to return the mules stolen from Warren, and Kicking Bird led his "out" Kiowas to the reservation. Meanwhile, a change in military policy left Mackenzie gravely doubtful as to the propriety of campaigning outside of Texas.[41] Ultimately the colonel returned to the Otter Creek supply point on September 1. Meanwhile, however, Mackenzie had patrolled the rugged country between North and Elm forks of the Red and approached, if he did not enter, the Panhandle on Sweetwater Creek. He had experienced the searing, brutal heat of August in the region, had gagged on its highly mineralized waters as had the Marcy Red River expedition in 1852, and had become thoroughly acquainted with the tortures that could beset both man and beast while campaigning in this inhospitable region.[42] If the Kiowa campaign of 1871 achieved nothing else, it gave an officer of proven mettle experience in the sort of campaigning essential to eventual military resolution of the Indian problem in the South Plains.

[40] Leckie, *Military Conquest*, pp. 156-157. For the details of Mackenzie's role in these events, see Wallace, *Mackenzie*, pp. 36-41. Camp Radziminski, established in September 1858 at the base of the Wichitas, was abandoned in December 1859. See Prucha, *Military Posts*, p. 100.

[41] See Sherman's Order Relative to Mackenzie's Operations in *Mackenzie's Correspondence*, ed. Wallace, p. 38, and [J. J.] Reynolds to Adjutant General in ibid., p. 39.

[42] Carter, *On the Border*, pp. 122-148; Wallace, *Mackenzie*, pp. 42-44.

With the Kiowa matter apparently resolved, Mackenzie remained mindful of the Comanches, and he labored under no restrictions while campaigning in Texas.[43] Various Comanche bands, but particularly those under Mow-way and Para-o-coom, continually looted the Texas frontier and bragged openly to Tatum that they had no need of the government's generosity (the Comanchero trade kept them well supplied) and had no intention of retiring to reservations until and unless physically whipped. Upon his return to Fort Richardson, Mackenzie immediately prepared to do just that, and by September 25 had fielded eight companies of the Fourth Cavalry, two of the Eleventh Infantry, twenty Tonkawa scouts, and about one hundred pack mules. Striking westward across the Permian red beds, Mackenzie's column entered Blanco Canyon and overtook a Kwahadi camp led by none other than the renowned (then infamous) Quanah Parker. Chasing the Kwahadis out onto the Staked Plains, perhaps as far north as present Plainview, Mackenzie had the fleeing camp within his grasp only to have the prize stolen by a sudden blizzard. By mid-November, the components of the expedition were back at their respective bases along the edge of the Texas frontier.[44] Mackenzie's official report of the fall campaign of 1871 consists of four brief paragraphs; it lists one soldier and two Indians killed, sixty-six horses lost, but fails to mention that the colonel himself received a serious arrow wound in the thigh.[45] On the face of it, Mackenzie's operations in the fall of 1871 got less than imposing results—and Mackenzie made neither claims of success nor excuses for failure—but if the operation was not successful, it was significant. Wallace assesses the operation aptly when he says: "Mackenzie and his 4th Cavalry had penetrated the very heart of the hostile Indian country, even venturing onto the abysmal Llano Estacado in an area hitherto unexplored by the United States military. He had learned a great deal about Comanche customs and warfare, and concomitantly about the best ways of making war on these nomadic Lords of the South Plains—lessons that later helped him become one of the country's greatest Indian fighters."[46]

[43] Sherman's Order Relative to Mackenzie's Operations in *Mackenzie's Correspondence*, ed. Wallace, p. 38.
[44] Carter, *On the Border*, pp. 149-152, 154-206, is the best account of this campaign by a participant. The best secondary account is Wallace, *Mackenzie*, pp. 45-56.
[45] Mackenzie to Assistant Adjutant General, Department of Texas, November 15, 1871, in *Mackenzie's Correspondence*, ed. Wallace, pp. 41-42. See also "Wirt Davis' Account of the Battle of Blanco Canyon," in ibid., pp. 42-44. Captain Davis commanded Troop "F," Fourth Cavalry, during the 1871 campaign.
[46] Wallace, *Mackenzie*, p. 56.

Through the winter of 1871-1872 Mackenzie faced serious discipline and morale problems induced largely by the wretched living conditions at Fort Richardson. Illness was common, boredom omnipresent, and desertion frequent. Sensing that his troopers were not altogether to blame for their restlessness, Mackenzie dealt sternly but apparently sensibly with their infractions, resorting to severe measures only in extreme cases. More serious from Mackenzie's personal point of view was a quarrel with his superior, General J. J. Reynolds, who with proper bureaucratic indignation deplored the brevity and infrequency of Mackenzie's reports, resented Mackenzie's quaint notion that action took precedence over red tape, and most especially took offense when the fiercely honest Mackenzie accused his commander of fraud in the procurement of supplies. So offended was Reynolds, in fact, that he tried to institute court-martial proceedings against the colonel. Fortunately for Mackenzie, he had the unqualified confidence of Sherman and Sheridan while Reynolds received scant respect from either. They replaced the politically ambitious Reynolds with Brigadier General C. C. Augur, an experienced Plains soldier who would back their hard-driving field commander.[47]

While Mackenzie worked diligently through the winter to prepare for the campaigns of the forthcoming spring, his red antagonists plotted terror for the Texas frontier. With the return of green grass, the Comanches and later the Kiowas, who were for a time restrained for fear of recriminations against their imprisoned chiefs, resumed raiding and opened the season on April 20 with the massacre of a wagon train at Howard Wells in Crockett County. This time not one, but eight men, were burned to death. Soon other points in Texas felt the cruel steel of the scalping knife.[48] In the previous March, however, a seemingly inauspicious event had occurred that was to have far-flung implications.

Sergeant William H. Wilson, scouting from Fort Concho with a detachment of the Fourth Cavalry, jumped a band of Comancheros near Muchaque, a favored trading spot four and one-half miles southeast of present Gail, Borden County. Wilson's men killed two, wounded three, and captured one—Polonis Ortiz.[49] At Fort Concho, Ortiz talked freely—perhaps regarding a loose tongue as more comfortable if not more honorable than a

---

[47] Ibid., pp. 60-64. Regrettably, from an historian's point of view, Mackenzie was as reticent as Custer was verbose!

[48] Leckie, *Military Conquest*, pp. 161-163; Wallace, *Mackenzie*, p. 64.

[49] J. Evetts Haley, *Fort Concho and the Texas Frontier*, p. 195; Wallace, *Mackenzie*, p. 64.

stretched neck—and gave Major John P. Hatch, commander of the fort, a remarkable story of crossing the Staked Plains in a party of more than fifty men; of trading in guns, ammunition, and staples with the Kwahadis and Mescalero Apaches at Mucha-que; of stealing cattle in Texas for sale to established dealers in New Mexico, and most significantly and unbelievably to the Anglo-American mind, of well-watered trails across the Staked Plains![50]

Though not fully realized at the time, Polonis Ortiz—an obscure New Mexican whose pay for coming to Texas was to have been two cows—contributed uniquely to Anglo-American history in West Texas: he told Anglos how to cross the Staked Plains. Or, in broader terms, this ethnic descendant of Coronado conveyed to Anglo-Americans the ancient Spanish lore and knowledge of the Llano Estacado!

The resumption of Indian raiding in Texas in the spring of 1872, the actual capture of Comancheros at Mucha-que by Sergeant Wilson, and perhaps the loquacity of various Indians at the agencies about their Comanchero contacts seem to have impressed upon the military mind that there was actually a connection among these various facts of southwestern life. Texans, of course, learned nothing new, for these relationships had been clear to them for an agonizingly long time, but they had met little luck in convincing the military or other federal agents.[51]

At his Chicago headquarters General Sheridan must have read the report of Wilson and the statements of Ortiz with dismay, for on April 20, 1872, he wrote to Augur, "I fully authorize you to break up the illicit traffic with Indians on the Staked Plains and if any of the parties engaged in it are caught they should be turned over to the United States Civil authorities of the State of Texas."[52]

At Fort Richardson Mackenzie busied himself preparing for the campaigns to come—even to the extent of trying to spring good but indiscreet soldiers from court-martial sentences! Doubtless he had gotten wind of the

[50] John P. Hatch to Gordon Granger, March 31, 1872, in *Mackenzie's Correspondence*, ed. Wallace, pp. 45-46; Hatch to Assistant Adjutant General, Department of Texas, April 15, 1872, in ibid., pp. 47-48; Hatch to Gordon Granger, April 16, 1872, in ibid., pp. 48-51; and Polonis Ortiz to Hatch, May 21, 1872, in ibid., pp. 69-71. In these documents the routes, as given by Ortiz, are traced from point to point from Alamo Gordo twenty miles north of Fort Sumner to Mucha-que and from there to Fort Concho and from the Gallinos River to Quitaque by way of the tributary streams of the Canadian River and Tierra Blanca Creek.

[51] See Haley, *Fort Concho*, pp. 194-196, which makes the point very well.

[52] P. H. Sheridan to C. C. Augur, April 20, 1872, in *Mackenzie's Correspondence*, ed. Wallace, p. 53.

Ortiz incident, and, though not exactly verbose, his random correspondence with Augur's headquarters in San Antonio indicates clearly that the colonel intended to be ready for whatever the immediate future might bring.[53] The immediate future brought special orders from Augur placing Mackenzie in command of a major expedition for "breaking up the cattle stealing, and stopping the incursions of hostile Indians along the northern frontier of Texas."[54]

Pursuant to Augur's orders, Mackenzie established a supply camp on Freshwater Fork of the Brazos (Blanco, or White, River) and on July 9 began a thrust with Companies A, B, F, and L, Fourth Cavalry, toward the Red River where the aggressive colonel expected to find hostile Indians. Moving in a generally northerly direction, Mackenzie crossed the Red on the thirteenth and penetrated into the Panhandle as far as Mulberry Creek, near present Clarendon. Finding no Indians, Mackenzie turned back southward, reaching his supply camp on Blanco River on the morning of July 19.[55] Now convinced that the Indians would be found either on the North Fork of the Red or on Palo Duro Creek, Mackenzie prepared for another strike to the north. While awaiting arrival of supplies, however, Polonis Ortiz and Mackenzie's scouts found a large cattle trail leading westward into the Staked Plains. Since his orders were to break up cattle theft as well as to subdue Indians, Mackenzie changed his plan and determined to follow the new-found trail toward New Mexico—an operation Augur later endorsed and hailed as a singular achievement.[56]

As if nothing more significant than the regimental bugler sounding taps had occurred, Mackenzie's own reports tell little of what followed. One wonders, in fact, whether the colonel realized the historic significance or personal distinction of having led the first United States military force across the Staked Plains! Striking up the Blanco River on July 28 and ascending the High Plains Escarpment on the twenty-ninth, Mackenzie reached Double Mountain Fork of the Brazos, which he followed on to New Mexico, on the thirty-first. Hoping to catch and arrest sponsors of cattle thieves whom Ortiz had named, the colonel pushed as far northwestward as Puerta de Luna ten miles southeast of the present Santa Rosa. The

[53] Ibid., pp. 53-60.
[54] Augur's Special Orders for the Campaign of 1872, May 31, 1872, in ibid., pp. 71-73.
[55] "Mackenzie's Journal of Scout to Red River, July 9-19, 1872," in ibid., pp. 112-116; Wallace, *Mackenzie*, pp. 67-68.
[56] "Augur's Annual Report for 1872," in *Mackenzie's Correspondence*, ed. Wallace, p. 139.

thieves had fled, however, apparently because of an "invasion" of Texas cowmen who had come to retrieve stolen stock and perhaps mete out a bit of necktie justice. Thus thwarted, Mackenzie dropped back to Fort Sumner to rest, refit, and plan before returning to Texas.

After three days at Fort Sumner, Mackenzie moved northward to the head of Tucumcari Creek on the Fort Smith-Santa Fe Trail. Having learned that Colonel J. J. Gregg of the Eighth Cavalry had left Fort Bascom on August 7 to scout for Indians along the Fort Smith-Santa Fe Trail (i.e., along the Canadian River and its tributaries) Mackenzie determined to return to Texas by a route to the south that would take him over the Staked Plains—over another area unknown by Anglo-Americans, but familiar to a Comanchero like Polonis Ortiz!

Marching eastward, beginning on August 19, Mackenzie soon reached the western escarpment of the Staked Plains and a wagon road along Tierra Blanca Creek—just as Ortiz had described. Having spotted a small group of Indians on Palo Duro Creek, however, Mackenzie sent a cavalry detachment eastward along that stream while the main command followed Tierra Blanca Creek to the confluence of the two streams near present Canyon, where the detached cavalrymen rejoined the main column on August 23. While in the vicinity, Mackenzie's command examined Palo Duro and Cita canyons. Turning southeastward from the site of present Canyon, Mackenzie crossed to the head of Tule Canyon, following a well-marked road. The eastern escarpment was descended near present Silverton, and the main supply camp on the Blanco reached on August 31.[57]

Understandably disappointed, Mackenzie reported to departmental headquarters that he should "be obliged to recuperate my horses for probably 2 weeks, having been a very long distance and not very successful in accomplishing anything useful." Nothing useful? The colonel had just accomplished what no other Anglo-American commander had ever done and had established not one but two trails across the Staked Plains that were well watered, rich in grass, suitable for civilian and commercial use, and could be made safe "were my present command used for that

---

[57] Mackenzie to Assistant Adjutant General, Department of Texas, August 7, 1872, ibid., pp. 127-128; Mackenzie to Assistant Adjutant General, Department of Texas, August 15, 1872, ibid., pp. 129-130; Mackenzie to Granger, August 15, 1872, ibid., pp. 130-131; and Mackenzie to Assistant Adjutant General, Department of Texas, September 3, 1872, ibid., pp. 133-134. Wallace, *Mackenzie*, pp. 69-73, and map facing p. 66. Though the data are scant and scattered, Wallace has done an excellent job of tracing Mackenzie's activities.

purpose."[58] Moreover, Mackenzie had picked up much information about the Panhandle country, and especially the terrain surrounding Palo Duro Canyon, which would serve him well two years later.

From another point of view, however, Mackenzie's feeling that he had accomplished nothing useful is understandable because, after all, the destruction of marauding Indians was his primary mission and the officer was keenly aware of what was expected of him—and mostly perhaps of what he expected of himself. As much as it may have rankled, even Mackenzie had to appraise realistically the limits of men and animals, but on September 21—doubtless as soon as physically possible—the colonel was marching out of his supply camp toward the upper tributaries of the Red River. Surely hostiles would be found there. About a week later the command reached the Salt Fork, probably in present Donley County, and established a supply camp. Pressing northward early on the twenty-ninth, Mackenzie picked up a fresh Indian trail on McClellan Creek. Following the lead of the Tonkawa scouts, the bluecoats moved rapidly northward for twelve miles and came upon a substantial Indian village on the south bank of the North Fork.[59] This village, the largest of several in the vicinity, belonged to Mow-way of the Kotsoteka Comanches who, though not eager for reservation life, was anxious for peace with the whites and was on a peace mission when Mackenzie found his camp. So secure did these Kotsotekas regard themselves that they hardly looked up from their work when someone noticed a distant cloud of dust. They thought it was caused by their own people chasing buffalo!

Deploying his forces so as to strike the camp with his greatest concentration of force, but also to cut off escape routes, Mackenzie executed a perfect charge. Taken completely by surprise, the Kotsotekas put up a defense more valiant than effective and after a half-hour fight abandoned the village. An indefinite number of braves—but probably in excess of fifty—was killed; the village of 262 lodges and its property was burned; over one hundred captives, mostly women and children, were taken; and the horse and mule herd (variously estimated at from eight hundred to three thousand head) was captured. Evidence that members of Mow-way's band had plundered in Texas was abundant. Clearly, Mackenzie had won

[58] Mackenzie to Assistant Adjutant General, Department of Texas, September 3, 1872, in *Mackenzie's Correspondence*, ed. Wallace, pp. 133-134.

[59] Wallace, *Mackenzie*, p. 79, places the camp "on the south side of the North Fork of Red River, about seven miles from its junction with McClellan Creek, and five or six miles east of the present town of Lefors."

the victory he sought and which his superiors and the citizens of Texas expected of him.

On the night of September 29, 1872, Mackenzie bivouacked in sand hills about two miles from the battle site. The captured horses were secured (or so the colonel thought) in a depression about a mile away under guard of the Tonkawa scouts. The Tonks preferred sleep to guard duty, however, and during the night the herd was stampeded and even the mounts of guards driven away. On the night of the thirtieth the Comanches repeated the performance, getting back all but about fifty of the captured ponies. Even an officer of Mackenzie's caliber might err, but he would not again give Comanches a chance to steal back their horses.

Moving rapidly southward, Mackenzie's column reached the supply camp on the Blanco River on October 8, having been away eighteen days and marched 209 miles. The colonel recommended Medals of Honor, which were awarded, for a number of his troopers and sent 115 prisoners to Fort Concho, where they were held as hostages to secure the release of white prisoners and to encourage hostiles to come in to their reservations.

Mackenzie's only error in the operation was his failure to set the Comanches afoot, a step necessary to force them to stay on reservations. Nonetheless, his stellar victory on the North Fork sobered many hostiles, for their notion of the inviolacy of remote Panhandle hideaways was reduced to sheer myth. The captives at Fort Concho caused many to ponder whether maintaining the old, wild ways was worth continued separation from their families. Various bands drifted into the agency at Fort Sill, among them even the Kwahadis who came in for the first time. Perhaps at last the Texas frontier would know peace.[60]

Indeed, during the winter of 1872-1873 Texans experienced an unprecedented relief from Indian raiding, and for almost two years after Mackenzie's victory on the North Fork relative peace ensued. Notwithstanding the efforts of both red and white men of good will, however, the period was one of a great deal of tension which, among other things, brought the release of Satanta and Big Tree from the Texas penitentiary. Much opposed to their release, Agent Lawrie Tatum resigned when his Quaker

[60] The foregoing account of the Battle of the North Fork—or McClellan Creek as it is often called—is based on Mackenzie's official report, Mackenzie to Assistant Adjutant General, Department of Texas, October 12, 1872, in *Mackenzie's Correspondence*, ed. Wallace, pp. 141-145, and Wallace, *Mackenzie*, pp. 77-87. See also Carter, *On the Border*, pp. 377-389; Robert G. Carter, *The Old Sergeant's Story*, pp. 82-87; Leckie, *Military Conquest*, pp. 169-172; and Nye, *Carbine and Lance*, pp. 160-163.

superiors refused to support him. Understandable though it is, Tatum's resignation was unfortunate, for he seems to have had a genuine concern and compassion for *all* the parties to the Indian-white conflict; and while by no means abandoning his Quaker principles for a mailed fist, he had come to understand that with love there had also to be a firm hand. Almost coinciding with Tatum's resignation (effective March 31, 1872) was General Augur's decision to release the Comanche prisoners at Fort Concho, who were formally returned to their people on June 11.[61]

By January 1874, Fort Sill knew that hopes of peace were fading and the new year would bring new hostilities.[62] Several factors combined to bring the Indians off the reservations and onto the warpath in 1874. In the first place, the age-old raiding habits were egged on by what had become a traditional hatred of Texans, and the habit of raiding—even though many Indians knew they should not—was hard to kick. Moreover, raids into Texas had cost several Indian bands dearly and they craved revenge. As usual, the cost of war inflated the price of peace! Increasing realization that their access to ancestral lands was diminishing rapidly encouraged many to strike at the whites. These more or less standard, generalized animosities were greatly aggravated by 1874 through the activities of white horse thieves and whiskey peddlers among the tribes who both encouraged them to raid and stole their brains with sorry whiskey as well. Finally, of course, was the buffalo slaughter.[63]

Out of this cauldron of Indian frustration and bitterness arose the two young Comanche leaders, Quanah and Isa-tai, who plotted and led the attack on Adobe Walls.[64] Suffering not only a tactical defeat but inviting a strategic disaster as well, the hostiles spread out over the Plains after Adobe Walls for what was for many the last—and for some a fatal—fling at the old ways of life. This brought military retaliation, defeat, and confinement to the hated reservations.[65]

Known as the Red River War, the military operations of 1874 and 1875

[61] See Leckie, *Military Conquest*, pp. 173-184, for an account of developments relative to the government's Indian policy and events around Fort Sill agency that led ultimately to the collapse of peace in 1874.

[62] Ibid.; Nye, *Carbine and Lance*, pp. 187-189.

[63] Leckie, *Military Conquest*, pp. 186-187. An especially good account of the whiskey peddlers and their relationship to the Indians is Robert C. Carriker, *Fort Supply, Indian Territory: Frontier Outpost on the Plains*, pp. 56-84.

[64] See chapter 4, pp. 160-164.

[65] G. Derek West, "The Battle of Adobe Walls (1874)," *Panhandle-Plains Historical Review* 36 (1963): 31.

were characterized by Sheridan as "not only comprehensive, but . . . the most successful of any Indian Campaign in this country since its settlement by the whites."[66] Adobe Walls initiated a series of Indian depredations that quickly ended the Quaker "peace policy." Sherman and Sheridan, in July 1874, laid the basis for an offensive campaign against hostile Indians, which was agreed to by the War and Interior departments[67] and specifically implemented by the Secretary of War on July 20. In essence the new policy comprised two basic parts: (1) enrollment and careful protection of innocent and friendly Indians at their reservations, and (2) pursuit and destruction of hostile Indians without regard for reservation or departmental boundaries.[68]

Following the pattern established in Sheridan's winter campaign of 1868-1869, the offensive of 1874 utilized five columns converging on the general area of the Texas Panhandle and specifically upon the upper tributaries of the Red River where the hostiles were thought to be. Unlike the 1868-1869 efforts, however, the 1874 strategy aimed at full encirclement of the region, thereby plugging virtually all gaps through which escape might be effected.

From Fort Dodge Colonel Nelson A. Miles moved southward toward the Washita, Antelope Hills, and the headwaters of the Red; Major William A. Price moved eastward across the Panhandle from Fort Union; Lieutenant Colonel John W. Davidson marched westward from Fort Sill; Mackenzie led his now famed Fourth Cavalry northward from Fort Concho; and finally Lieutenant Colonel George P. Buell struck a westward course from Fort Richardson, plugging the open area between the columns of Mac-

---

[66] Quoted in Carter, *On the Border*, p. 525. By "this country" Sheridan apparently meant the southwest or southern Plains. Accounts of the Red River War may be found in the following: Carter, *On the Border*, pp. 473ff.; Haley, *Fort Concho*, pp. 240-243; Leckie, *Military Conquest*, pp. 185-235; Leckie, "The Red River War, 1874-1875," *Panhandle-Plains Historical Review* 29 (1956): 78-100; Nye, *Carbine and Lance*, pp. 187-235, which emphasizes the Indians' side of the story; and Wallace, *Mackenzie*, pp. 115-168. The documentary record of this remarkable phase of regional history is War Department, Adjutant General's Office, File No. 2815-1874, the whole of which is available on microfilm at the Panhandle-Plains Historical Museum. The significant documents from this file have been published by the Panhandle-Plains Historical Society in Joe F. Taylor, ed., *The Indian Campaign on the Staked Plains, 1874-1875.*

[67] Sherman to Sheridan, telegram, July 15, 1874; Sheridan to Sherman, telegram, July 16, 1874, War Department, Adjutant General's Office, File No. 2815-1874, hereafter cited as W.D.A.G.O. File No. 2815-1874.

[68] W. W. Belknap, Secretary of War, to Sherman, July 20, 1874, ibid. The secretary's communication was telegraphed to Sheridan on the same day it was received by Sherman. See also, Leckie, *Military Conquest*, pp. 198-199.

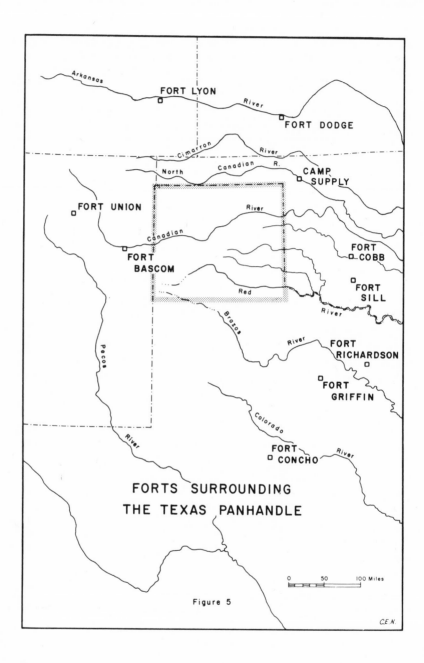

FORTS SURROUNDING
THE TEXAS PANHANDLE

0    50    100 Miles

Figure 5

C.E.N.

kenzie and Davidson. Although many infantrymen participated, these columns were principally cavalry and each was self-sustaining and capable of subdivision into smaller units so as to search greater areas.[69]

Organizing his expedition in early August 1874, Miles marched from Fort Dodge to Camp Supply, Indian Territory, which was to serve as his operational base. At Beaver Creek, Miles detached about fifty men under Lieutenant Frank D. Baldwin, who led Miles' Indian scouts, sending them to Adobe Walls, where they arrived on August 18 to aid the buffalo hunters still there. On the very next day, Baldwin clashed with a raiding party that attacked two hunters—killing one—within sight of the buildings. Upon seeing Baldwin's troops, the Indians fled. The soldiers pursued them, but gave up after a wild twelve-mile chase south of the Canadian. On August 20 Baldwin moved downstream to rendezvous with Miles' main column. At the mouth of Chicken Creek, Baldwin's troopers jumped a small group of hostiles, attacked them, killed one, and wounded one before moving on to meet Miles about twelve miles west of Antelope Hills. Significantly, Baldwin crossed several fresh trails leading southward.

Miles' own movement along the edge of the eastern Panhandle from Camp Supply drove the hostiles—Cheyennes, Kiowas, and Comanches—away from eastern Panhandle streams to the southwest and the supposed sanctity of the forbidding terrain adjacent to the Staked Plains. As they fled, the hostiles burned the prairie behind them to inhibit Miles' pursuit in the most effective way possible—that is, by destroying the all-important forage.

On the evening of August 26, 1874, on Sweetwater Creek, Miles' scouts found a large Indian trail leading westward. Though it was several days old, Miles, sensing its heat, determined to follow. On the twenty-seventh, Miles found an abandoned village on the Sweetwater, turned south, and marched thirty-one miles, crossing the North Fork of the Red and following up McClellan Creek. The ruggedness of the terrain and appalling intensity of August heat so inhibited his movement that the colonel left his train to follow as best it could, while the combat troops pushed ahead to pursue an expanding Indian trail. With only ammunition and light rations, the troopers moved more effectively, covering thirty-four miles on the twenty-ninth, camping that night on the Salt Fork.

[69] Sheridan to Sherman, September 5, 1874, W.D.A.G.O. File No. 2815-1874; Department of Texas, Special Orders No. 113, July 23, 1874, ibid.; Department of the Missouri, Special Orders No. 114, July 27, 1874, ibid.; Leckie, *Military Conquest*, pp. 205-206.

The ever-freshening trail led Miles' column southwestward for twenty miles on the thirtieth. As the column approached a line of bluffs near the Staked Plains, Lieutenant Baldwin's advanced guard suddenly was set upon by about two hundred braves. As cool a soldier as ever campaigned upon the Plains, Baldwin deployed his scouts and repulsed the charge about as quickly as it had occurred. Miles promptly brought up the main column, skillfully deploying its units to attack from four to six hundred warriors who occupied excellent defensive positions in rugged bluffs extending in an irregular line five to seven miles long.

Though seeming clearly to have had the best of the tactical situation, the warriors melted before the audacity and skill with which Miles' troopers, backed by Gatling guns, charged. For the next five hours the bluecoats chased the routed braves from ridge to ridge and from ravine to ravine for about twelve miles up the valley of the main Red. The Indians gradually dispersed until their trail, which led about eighteen miles up Tule Creek, was finally lost.

From Tule Creek the whipped Indians, whose property losses were staggering, scattered over the Staked Plains, where, on August 31, 1874, Miles pursued them for over thirty miles. Wisely, however, the colonel pushed no farther because of his exhausted men and animals, depleted supplies, the dreary condition of the drouth-parched land, and the great distance that now separated the command from its supply base. Indian casualties included seventeen dead whose bodies were found, although Miles believed that twenty-five Indian dead was a realistic estimate. Miles' troopers suffered only two men wounded, a sergeant and a Delaware scout.[70]

Because of his seriously depleted supplies, Miles sent his thirty-six wagon supply train, escorted by Captain Wyllys Lyman, back to Oasis Creek (a tributary of the Canadian just inside eastern Hemphill County), where he

[70] The foregoing account is based on Miles' reports. See Miles to Assistant Adjutant General, Department of the Missouri, August 25, 1874, September 1, 1874, and March 4, 1875, and Miles to General John Pope, September 5, 1874, W.D.A.G.O. File No. 2815-1874; and Nelson A. Miles, *Personal Recollections and Observations*, pp. 163-170. Taylor, ed., *Indian Campaign*, p. 23, footnotes 10 and 11, places this action on the north side of Prairie Dog Town Fork on a tributary stream, which Miles calls "Battle Creek," between Mulberry and Tule creeks. The current Texas State Highway Department map of Briscoe County shows a Battle Creek flowing into Prairie Dog Town Fork from the northwest, just inside the eastern boundary of Briscoe County. This points to the area lying just east of the mouths of Palo Duro and Tule canyons in northern Briscoe County as the scene of the first big engagement of the Red River War.

had requested a supply depot be placed to support his operations.[71] Though Miles' request had not been honored, Lyman was able to get a train from Camp Supply to meet him at Commission Creek (a stream on the north side of the Canadian in present Ellis County, Oklahoma), loaded his thirty-six wagons, and started southward. On September 9 Lyman's train was attacked on the divide between the Canadian and the Washita, and in the initial onslaught was nearly overwhelmed. Quick reaction and cool resistance by the troopers repulsed the assault, however, and Lyman was able to move about twelve miles southward almost to the Washita, where he placed his wagons in a defensive "corral"—unusual in Indian warfare—withstanding a siege that lasted until the morning of the fourteenth.

Critical not only from his own standpoint, Lyman's situation jeopardized Miles' troops to the south, who desperately needed the supplies the besieged train carried. After about thirty hours under siege, Lyman penned an almost indecently formal plea for help to the commanding officer at Camp Supply. The Captain wrote:

Sir:
I have the honor to report that I am corralled by Comanches two miles north of the Washita. . . .[72]

If Lyman was cool, however, he needed someone even cooler to deliver his plea. A magnificiently courageous man, Scout William F. Schmalsle, volunteered for the dangerous mission and despite the best efforts of the Indians to catch him, the scout reached Camp Supply at 9 o'clock on the morning of September 12. A relief column including an ambulance and surgeon arrived to aid Lyman very early on the morning of September 14 and the attacking Indians, about four hundred Kiowas and Comanches in Lyman's estimate, withdrew. At 9 o'clock that same morning Lyman moved out, crossing the Washita and soon met elements of Miles' Sixth Cavalry.[73]

Apparently for reasons of routine communication, Miles sent the reliable

[71] Miles to Assistant Adjutant General, Department of the Missouri, August 25, 1874, W.D.A.G.O. File No. 2815-1874. Logistical support for the units engaged in the Red River War was an exceptional undertaking in itself. See Carricker, *Fort Supply*, pp. 85-106.
[72] Lyman to Commanding Officer, Camp Supply, September 10, 1874, W.D.A.G.O. File No. 2815-1874.
[73] This account is based on Ernest R. Archambeau, ed., "The Battle of Lyman's Wagon Train," *Panhandle-Plains Historical Review* 36 (1963): 89-101, which contains Lyman's full report, Lyman to Adjutant General, U.S. Army, September 25, 1874.

Frank Baldwin and three scouts, Lem Wilson, Harry Wing, and William F. Schmalsle, to Camp Supply. Leaving Miles' camp on McClellan Creek at 8 P.M. on September 6, Baldwin's small party traveled until 4:30 on the morning of the seventh and made camp in a secluded spot on Whitefish Creek, intending to hide out during the daylight hours.[74] An Indian soon appeared, however, not more than fifty yards away. He was shot, but his fellows, occupying surrounding hills, soon made the whites' position untenable. Realizing that their only hope lay in gaining higher ground, Baldwin and his scouts mounted and charged, probably catching the enemy entirely by surprise, and broke the Indians' line. Gaining a high point, the men dismounted and drove the Indians back and "out of range of Wing's Sporting Rifle, in whose skilled hands sad havoc was made in their ranks." Eventually, the Indians had had enough. While Baldwin suffered no casualties at all, he was certain of having killed or wounded at least eight Indians. "Throughout the engagement the men . . . were as cool as though . . . shooting buffalo," says Baldwin, "and I can but say that this was one of the most desperate skirmishes I ever participated in." Actually, even from Baldwin's sparse and unembellished report, one may easily infer that this was one of the most desperate and heroic Indian fights in all South Plains Indian warfare.

Making their way northward, the four men reached the Washita at 4 o'clock on the afternoon of September 8 and stumbled upon a sizeable Kiowa village. Realizing that he had been detected and wanting to push his luck no further, Baldwin took to a ravine to escape and ran into a young Indian guarding livestock. Taken entirely by surprise, the young Kiowa was captured. Pushing hard into the night, the party reached "the train camp [apparently on Oasis Creek] on the north bank of the Canadian" shortly after midnight. Remaining on the Canadian until 6 P.M. on the

---

Archambeau describes this engagement, known also as the Battle of the Upper Washita, as "the most prolonged Indian battle in Panhandle history and one of the most violent. At no other time during the extensive campaign against the Indians in 1874," observes Archambeau, "did so large a unit find itself in such difficulty." Taylor, ed., *Indian Campaign*, p. 31, footnote 20, aptly characterizes this action as "an unusual situation. The Indians usually hit, exploited a weakness if one developed, fell back shortly if one did not. These, on the other hand, had stayed with the train for around 30 hours at the time of the writing of the dispatch." Taylor refers to Lyman's dispatch to Camp Supply.

[74] According to current Texas Highway Department county maps, Whitefish Creek rises along the Donley County-Gray County line and flows in a southeasterly direction into the Salt Fork. The action here described thus took place in northeastern Donley County.

ninth, Baldwin pulled out for Camp Supply, which he reached at 10 A.M. on the tenth, having traveled through the night.

Thinking that his prisoner might be useful to Miles, Baldwin turned the young captive over to Lyman for return to expeditionary headquarters.[75] For unknown reasons, Scout Schmalsle also joined Lyman at this point.

Miles' scouts' efforts to communicate with Camp Supply seem to have been plagued with trouble. Baldwin and Lyman had had to fight for their lives and had come out very well, but the most desperate fight of all was the Buffalo Wallow Fight. The colonel sent Scouts Amos Chapman and Billy Dixon, who had given up buffalo hunting to work for the army as a scout, Sergeant Z. T. Woodhall, and Privates Peter Rath, John Harrington, and George W. Smith with dispatches to Camp Supply. Following standard procedures of traveling at night, the party left Miles' headquarters camp on McClellan Creek late on September 10, intending to hole up during daylight to avoid the war parties that infested the Panhandle. Their precautions turned out to be not quite adequate, for about six o'clock on the morning of the twelfth, a party estimated at 125 Kiowas and Comanches who had just jumped the reservation attacked the scouts on the divide between the Washita and Gageby Creek. Four of the whites were wounded in the initial firing, but they made their way to a providentially close buffalo wallow and, in between Indian charges, dug madly to deepen the wallow and build a bit of protection about its edges with the dirt. Dixon felt the Indians "delayed riding us down and killing us at once, which they could easily have done, and prolonged the early stages of the fight merely to satisfy their desire to toy with an enemy at bay, as a cat would play with a mouse before taking its life."[76]

Chapman and Smith were hit and unable to reach the buffalo wallow. Dixon eventually managed to carry Chapman in, but assuming Smith to be dead, made no effort to retrieve his body. Later, however, when Rath went to Smith to salvage his firearms, Rath was astonished to find Smith alive. Although Rath and Dixon managed to get the unfortunate soldier into the

---

[75] This account is based on Baldwin's report of the incident, Baldwin to 1st Lieutenant G. W. Baird, 5th Infantry, September 10, 1874, W.D.A.G.O. File No. 2815-1874. Nye, *Carbine and Lance*, p. 214, identifies Baldwin's captive as an eighteen-year-old Texas boy who had been captured and adopted by the Kiowas and named "Tehan"—Texan! Nye claims also that Kiowas, searching for the boy, stumbled upon Lyman's wagon train instead. In any case, Tehan, professing to be happy over his "rescue," deceived his guard and escaped.

[76] Olive K. Dixon, *Life of "Billy" Dixon*, p. 201.

buffalo wallow, they realized that a bullet through his lung had made a fatal wound.

About three o'clock in the afternoon a thunderstorm dumped torrents of rain upon the countryside, filling the pit with a grim mixture of water and blood—which provided lifegiving liquid to the thirsting men. Although the rain plus a bitterly cold norther added immeasurably to the miseries of the defenders, it also drove off the attackers, who disliked fighting in such weather. Through the long, dreadful night of the twelfth, the men in the buffalo wallow, with absolutely no protection or food, fashioned beds from tumble weeds. The piteous Smith finally drifted into sleep and some time during the night died. Next morning, Dixon set out for help and soon ran into Major William R. Price, whose command had entered the Panhandle from Fort Union. Price's surgeon examined the wounded, but made no effort to treat them, and Price otherwise neglected to aid the beleagured, exhausted, starving men. A few of Price's troopers shared their hardtack and dried beef. Agreeing to inform Colonel Miles of the situation, Price rode away. When Miles' troops reached the scene, Smith was buried in the buffalo wallow and Amos Chapman was taken to Camp Supply, where his wounded leg was amputated.[77]

Several factors contributed to the success of the fight put up by the white men. One was the Indians' failure to utilize the element of surprise that they seem to have had, but as Dixon says, they preferred to play cat and mouse. Another element, of course, was the savage, implacable resistance of the whites, reinforced—again as Dixon indicates—by their knowledge of the fate of live captives in the hands of Indians. The thunderstorm and norther doubtless cooled the Indians' ardor for battle. But the main thing that saved the lives of the whites was their ability to sell them very dearly. The Indians were just not willing, it would seem, to pay the price of overrunning the white men—such a victory would cost too much.

[77] The best account of the Buffalo Wallow Fight is Dixon's. See Dixon, *"Billy" Dixon*, pp. 199-220. Dixon makes a number of interesting observations, among them (p. 209): "I was strongly tempted to take my butcher knife, which I kept at razor edge, and cut off my hair. In those days my hair was black and heavy and brushed my shoulders. As a matter of fact, I was rather proud of my hair." Miles was so impressed by the courage of the men that he wrote an account of the incident directly to the adjutant general of the army. See Miles to Adjutant General, U.S.A., September 24, 1874, W.D.A.G.O. File No. 2815-1874. The Buffalo Wallow Fight occurred in present Hemphill County about four miles inside its southern boundary and about mid-point between its eastern and western boundaries. The six participants were awarded Medals of Honor.

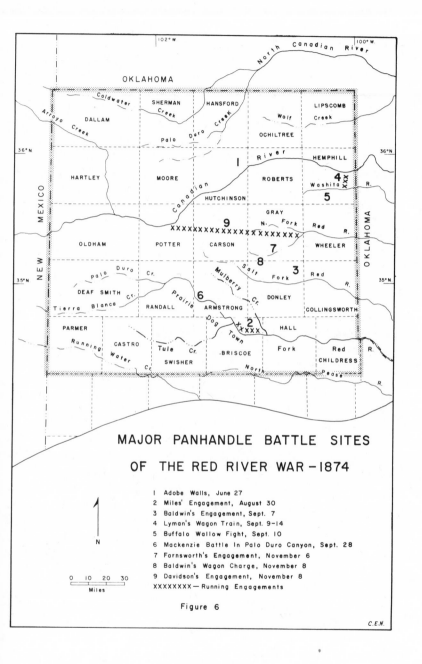

MAJOR PANHANDLE BATTLE SITES

OF THE RED RIVER WAR – 1874

1  Adobe Walls, June 27
2  Miles' Engagement, August 30
3  Baldwin's Engagement, Sept. 7
4  Lyman's Wagon Train, Sept. 9-14
5  Buffalo Wallow Fight, Sept. 10
6  Mackenzie Battle In Palo Duro Canyon, Sept. 28
7  Farnsworth's Engagement, November 6
8  Baldwin's Wagon Charge, November 8
9  Davidson's Engagement, November 8
XXXXXXXX — Running Engagements

0  10  20  30
Miles

N

Figure 6

C.E.N.

The western column from Fort Union under Major William R. Price moved out on August 24, 1874, with the three companies of the Eighth Cavalry supplemented by a fourth company at Fort Bascom. Crossing the Panhandle south of the Canadian, Price followed the old Fort Smith-Santa Fe road. Sending his train to a point near Adobe Walls, Price established a supply camp there and moved his main column to the southeast, expecting either to find Indians or to join Miles, which he did on September 7. After conferring with Miles, Price moved northward plagued by driving rains and swollen streams to intercept his train, which he had ordered to move southward. On September 12 Price encountered a large band of Indians between Sweetwater Creek and the Dry Fork of the Washita. Though hampered by fagged animals and mud, Price attacked, driving the Indians from ridge to ridge just as Miles had done on the Red River a few days earlier. Eventually the enemy dispersed, melting into the Plains. Price claimed a victory although a body count was not possible. Price lost no men.

On September 13 Price encamped on the Sweetwater. Here Billy Dixon found him. There is no strictly factual conflict between the accounts of Dixon and Price, but Price seems to have felt that he did all that he reasonably could have done for the Buffalo Wallow men.

Continuing his search for his train, Price passed very close to the Battle of Lyman's Wagon Train, heard the firing, but made no effort to go to Lyman's aid, preferring to move on northward to make contact with his own train.[78] Although judgments are difficult, Price seems terribly casual toward the pitiful plight of the survivors of the Buffalo Wallow Fight and the sound of firing from Lyman's grave situation. In any case Price's command was made a part of Miles' from September 20 until December 28, when Price was ordered back to New Mexico.[79]

Miles' operations in the Panhandle were hampered to some degree by logistical problems made more difficult by heavy rains and flooding streams. Still, various units under Miles' direction were thrown into the field to scout the streams of the northern and eastern Panhandle where the Indians were wont to hide.[80] The effect of these operations was to give the tribes not one day's respite, to keep them constantly on the move, and

[78] Price to Assistant Adjutant General, Department of the Missouri, September 23, 1874, W.D.A.G.O. File No. 2815-1874.
[79] Miles to Assistant Adjutant General, Department of the Missouri, March 4, 1875, W.D.A.G.O. File No. 2815-1874.
[80] Ibid.

ultimately to drive them southward upon the columns that would approach the Panhandle region from Forts Concho and Richardson.

The column of the Tenth Cavalry under Lieutenant Colonel J. W. Davidson, which was to approach the Panhandle from Fort Sill, got into the field on September 10, 1874—much later than had been anticipated. Because of heavy rains, Davidson kept to the divide between the Washita and the North Fork, seeking any hostiles who had evaded Miles. Thereafter, Davidson scouted Sweetwater and McClellan creeks, captured a couple of Indians, turned southwest, and marched along the edge of the Staked Plains to the breaks of the Red River hoping to find hostiles or to establish contact with Mackenzie, whose location was unknown to anyone operating from the north. Finding neither hostiles nor friendly forces, and with his men and supplies approaching exhaustion, Davidson turned eastward toward his base at Fort Sill, which he reached in mid-October after having marched about five hundred miles.[81]

Throughout the documents relating to the operations, speculation persists that the Indians were being driven southward where they would be hit by the columns of Mackenzie and Buell. Similarly, however, there is constant wondering as to the whereabouts of the Texas columns. Given the crude communications of the time, these units simply could not keep up with each other on a regular basis. Actually, however, the grand strategy of the Red River War was working out very well. Substantial areas of the Plains had been cleared of hostiles; many had in fact been driven onto or near the Staked Plains where the Mackenzie or Buell commands could strike them; while many others, seeing that time had run out on their old ways, voluntarily surrendered at their agencies.[82]

Mackenzie's part of the 1874 operation began on August 23 from Stone Ranch, a point on the North Concho about sixteen miles above the fort. Passing through country that had become familiar during the 1871-1872 campaigns, Mackenzie reestablished his old supply camp on Blanco River before moving northward to intercept the enemy. Toiling up the escarpment west of Quitaque, Mackenzie's column was hampered by cold weather and much rain and mud, but on September 26 camp was made near the head of Tule Canyon. When scouts reported hostile Indians in the vicinity, Mackenzie carefully secured his horses against an attack that he

---

[81] Davidson to Assistant Adjutant General, October 10, 1874, W.D.A.G.O. File No. 2815-1874.

[82] For an evaluation of the results of the campaign at this point see Leckie, *Military Conquest*, p. 218.

felt surely would come during the night. About 10:30, just as the colonel expected, Indians arrived and charged about the camp raising a frightful din. But the horses, properly secured, did not stampede. The attackers remained about through the night, though, and at daylight Mackenzie made only so much of an effort to run them down as was necessary to confuse them as to his real intentions.

Instead, apparently having knowledge from his advance scouts of a great encampment in Palo Duro Canyon, Mackenzie marched directly for that place on the twenty-seventh. Resting only briefly during the night of September 27, Mackenzie took the trail again about 4:00 A.M. on the twenty-eighth. As dawn just faintly lit the eastern sky, the column arrived at the edge of the Palo Duro. Peering intently, the bluecoats could distinguish the outlines of many lodges. It was broad daylight, however, before the cavalrymen found a snake-like trail to the floor of the canyon. Stumbling and crawling, they reached the canyon floor and formed an assault line. Such commotion could have done little else but alert the Indians (although it took a surprisingly long time), who promptly took to the canyon walls, using the rocks and ravines for protected firing positions. Since digging them out would doubtlessly have cost heavy casualties, Mackenzie declined to try. Actually, it was not necessary, because with the Indians driven from their village and their property abandoned, Mackenzie could accomplish his objective satisfactorily simply by systematically destroying the Indians' property. Moreover, the horse herd was captured! When by midafternoon the work of destroying the village was completed, Mackenzie, who had taken strict precautions to protect his trail out of the canyon, withdrew. Marching rapidly, Mackenzie's troopers reached the supply camp near Tule Canyon about 1 A.M. on September 29, when the men of the Fourth Cavalry collapsed into hard-earned sleep. Having earlier learned not to give a Comanche a chance to steal back his captured horse, Mackenzie ordered the destruction of 1,050 captured ponies.

Mackenzie's destruction of this great Indian camp, which included Comanches, Kiowas, and Cheyennes, left its occupants facing grim winter circumstances: their horses were killed; lodges, clothing, and robes burned; and winter food stores destroyed. For most, making their forlorn way to their agencies was the only alternative left, humiliating though it was. For some, of course, there would be no compromise, and for them Mackenzie and his fellow officers would offer equally uncompromising warfare.[83]

[83] The best primary accounts of the Palo Duro Canyon fight are Carter, *On the Border*, pp. 473-496; Robert G. Carter, *The Old Sergeant's Story*, pp. 103-112; and

Having routed the enemy from the security of Palo Duro Canyon, Mackenzie set off in relentless pursuit determined to give the Indians no respite. Leaving his camp near the head of the Tule, the aggressive colonel marched northwestward to the site of present Canyon, turned back northeastward so as to circle the head of Palo Duro Canyon, and scouted the divide between Prairie Dog Town Fork and Mulberry Creek. Eventually reaching Prairie Dog Town Fork, which was briefly scouted, the command cut back toward Quitaque and the Blanco River supply camp, which was reached apparently on October 23, 1874. After a rest of several days, Mackenzie resumed field operations, marching from waterhole to waterhole resolutely searching out small Indian bands and offering them no relief from pursuit and harassment. Finally, in early December, Mackenzie gave up the chase and broke up the expedition.[84]

Although there was still mopping up to be done in the Texas Panhandle, Mackenzie's attack in the Palo Duro was the last of the large engagements of the Red River War. Wallace probably assesses Mackenzie's role accurately when he says:

The Red River war was at a successful end, and to Mackenzie be-

---

Charles A. P. Hatfield, "The Comanche, Kiowa, and Cheyenne Campaign in Northwest Texas and Mackenzie's Fight in the Palo Duro Cañon, September 26, 1874" (MS, Panhandle Plains Historical Museum). Hatfield mistakenly places the date on September 26 instead of the twenty-eighth. Doubtless the finest secondary account, and probably the most accurate and complete of all accounts, is Wallace, *Mackenzie*, pp. 128-146, which is expertly assembled from a careful sifting of widely scattered and obscure data. Wallace places the scene of this action just below the junction of Palo Duro and Blanca Cita canyons and "about five miles below the present limits of the state park." (See p. 138 and especially note Wallace's map of Mackenzie's 1874 operations facing p. 146). As this writer sees the evidence, Wallace's location of the action is correct. Mackenzie's correspondence is almost devoid of reference to this action, and he apparently filed no final report of his 1874-1875 operations. See Mackenzie to Augur, November 27, 1874; Mackenzie to Augur, December 2, 1874; Mackenzie to Augur, December 2, 1874 [*sic*], W.D.A.G.O. File No. 2815-1874. See also Nye, *Carbine and Lance*, pp. 221-225. The lore of the Mackenzie fight has been of considerable interest within the Panhandle region, and the event has probably been emphasized to the detriment of others of equal significance. A serious local expert, however, was the late Bruce Gerdis of Tulia. See Bruce Gerdis, "The Mackenzie Battle" (MS, Gerdis Papers, Panhandle-Plains Historical Museum); Gerdis to Mrs. Arline Ogden, May 24, 1935, (MS, ibid.); Gerdis to Frank Collinson, January 12, 1938 (MS, ibid.); and Works Progress Administration, Federal Writer's Program, Swisher County, Texas, "Notes" (MS, Earl Vandale Collection, Archives, University of Texas at Austin).

[84] Carter, *On the Border*, pp. 497-525; Wallace, *Mackenzie*, pp. 150-166, and map facing page 146.

longed the major credit. In four months of hard campaigning the Colonel and most of his 4th Cavalry had marched well over 900 miles, had fought one battle and four skirmishes. . . . The number of casualties inflicted in the four months of serious campaigning is amazingly, almost unbelievably, small. The psychological and economic results on the Indians, however, rather than casualties were the factors that undermined Comanche and Kiowa resistance.[85]

While Mackenzie pushed upward from the south, Lieutenant Colonel George P. Buell, who led the Fort Richardson column, entered the Panhandle along the course of the Salt Fork. On October 9, 1874, Buell attacked a village near the Staked Plains, killed one warrior, destroyed the village, and sent its occupants fleeing. Successively, Buell destroyed villages of fifteen, seventy-five, and finally four hundred lodges. The fugitive Indians turned northward to the head of McClellan Creek and the North Fork with Buell hard on their trail.[86]

Although far from any source of supply, Buell felt he had significant numbers of hostiles on the run and, while pleading with Miles for supplies, was determined to stay in the field almost regardless of consequences. "I [am] determined . . . to continue the pursuit until these Indians are either captured or run into their reservation taking all chances of suffering."[87]

The combined forces of Mackenzie and Buell threw the hostiles right back into the teeth of renewed campaigns by Miles and Davidson. Davidson moved due west from Fort Sill on October 21, 1874, throwing out scouts widely. On October 30, Sheridan opined, because of Davidson's immediate success, that "the Indian war in this action is rapidly collapsing." One of Davidson's subordinates, Major G. W. Schofield, attacked a Nokoni camp on Elk Creek in western Indian Territory and captured sixty-nine warriors and two thousand horses, while word reached Sheridan that Lone Wolf's Kiowas were racing another column of troops to Fort Sill in a desperate effort to surrender before being overtaken in the field.[88] Davidson himself pushed on into the Panhandle and on November 8 struck a Cheyenne camp on the North Fork. Chasing them for ninety miles to the

[85] Wallace, *Mackenzie*, p. 165.
[86] R. C. Drum, Assistant Adjutant General, to William D. Whipple, Headquarters of the Army, October 24, 1874, W.D.A.G.O. File No. 2815-1874. Drum and Whipple were the subordinates of Sherman and Sheridan, respectively, between whom this dispatch passed.
[87] Buell to Miles, October 18, 1874, W.D.A.G.O. File No. 2815-1874.
[88] Whipple to Adjutant General of the Army, October 30, 1874, W.D.A.G.O. File No. 2815-1874.

Canadian, Davidson forced these Cheyennes to abandon many mounts and much property, but was unable to force them to stand and fight. Severe winter weather forced Davidson to give up the chase and turn back to Fort Sill.[89] Implicitly, Davidson's men suffered enormously, but what these Cheyennes went through must have been indescribable.

Sheridan's optimism that the Red River War was rapidly closing was not unfounded, for the Comanches and Kiowas lost their taste for battle and streamed abjectly into their agencies—"their animals were confiscated, their warriors confined, and their chiefs were put in irons."[90] This left the Cheyennes to be forced in, and Nelson A. Miles led the final operations that defeated them and ended the Red River War. Following the tactics that had paid off in subduing the Kiowas and Comanches, Miles marched his units relentlessly over the eastern Panhandle, especially scouring the water courses where the fugitives, sooner or later, had to go.[91]

On October 13 a considerable body of Indians was discovered between Gageby and Sweetwater creeks. Acting quickly, Miles launched a combined infantry and cavalry force under Captain A. R. Chaffee to pursue the hostiles. Chaffee hit them by surprise on the fourteenth "as to compel them to abandon their entire camp-property, lodges left standing; all of this was destroyed, and the Indians pursued by circuitous routes to within a short distance of the Cheyenne agency."[92]

Intelligence reports indicated to Miles that the main body of the remaining hostiles had been driven south of the Canadian and west of Adobe Walls. Accordingly, the colonel determined to get a column to their *west* and drive the Indians eastward upon a force he would place near the head of the Washita. Miles, along with Major C. E. Compton's command of three cavalry companies, two of infantry, a small artillery unit, and Lieutenant Frank Baldwin's scouts, marched from Adobe Walls to accomplish the objective of driving the hostiles eastward toward the command of Major Price, who was left at the Washita River supply camp. Miles' strategy succeeded amazingly well, it would seem, as he did in fact get west of the hostiles and sent various groups scurrying southward or eastward from their haunts along the edge of the Staked Plains.[93]

---

[89] Davidson to Augur, November 23, 1874, W.D.A.G.O. File No. 2815-1874.
[90] Leckie, *Military Conquest*, p. 226.
[91] Miles to Assistant Adjutant General, Department of the Missouri, March 4, 1875, W.D.A.G.O. File No. 2815-1874.
[92] Ibid.
[93] Ibid.

As the harassed Indians moved eastward, they were hit in several engagements in the Panhandle. A force under First Lieutenant H. J. Farnsworth, for example, while scouting south from the vicinity of Adobe Walls, engaged a force of about one hundred Cheyennes on McClellan Creek on November 6, 1874. Farnsworth apparently had no warning of the presence of the Cheyenne warriors, but they must have been ready for him since they seem to have picked the site of battle and to have been otherwise prepared. The engagement began about 1:30 in the afternoon and continued until Farnsworth retreated under the welcome cloak of darkness. Although inflicting some casualties, Farnsworth lost one man killed and had several wounded. The suffering of his wounded and his nearly exhausted ammunition made retreat the only acceptable course for the lieutenant to follow, and it would seem that he was fortunate to have gotten out of the engagement as satisfactorily as he did.[94]

Two days after Farnsworth's engagement, the indomitable Lieutenant Frank Baldwin—who was anything but a reckless impetuous soldier, and who had a penchant for getting into tight places and a genius for getting out—fought a more successful action. Leaving Miles' main camp on the Red River on November 4, 1874, Baldwin was to escort twenty-three wagons with one troop of cavalry and one of infantry to a supply camp on the Washita. Early on the morning of November 8, on McClellan Creek, Baldwin's scout, the ubiquitous William F. Schmalsle, reported a large Cheyenne village just a mile or so ahead. Baldwin, who had complete discretion as to whether he would engage any hostiles, decided to attack and improvised tactics on the spot. Placing his infantrymen in the empty wagons, Baldwin deployed his horse soldiers on either side of the wagons, which were placed in two lines, and ordered a frontal assault. So utterly surprised were the Cheyennes that they broke and fled, leaving their property behind and racing out onto the Staked Plains where Baldwin pursued them for about twelve miles. In the village, Baldwin's men found two white girls, Adelaide and Julia German, aged five and seven, whose family had been attacked by Cheyennes in Kansas earlier in the fall. From the little girls it was learned that two other German daughters were also captives.[95]

[94] Farnsworth to Field Adjutant, 8th Cavalry, November 7, 1874, W.D.A.G.O. File No. 2815-1874.

[95] Miles to Assistant Adjutant General, Department of the Missouri, March 4, 1875, W.D.A.G.O. File No. 2815-1874; Miles to Assistant Adjutant General, Department of the Missouri, November 9, 1874, ibid.; Miles to Pope, November 17, 1874, ibid.;

Unceasing harassment by the troopers drove more and more Indian bands into their agencies. But if the Indians were worn out, so were the soldiers, so that in much of November and December Miles had to pull most units back to Camp Supply, Fort Dodge, and Fort Bascom leaving only three cavalry companies and four of infantry in the field.[96] After a brief rest, however, the colonel was afield again for a final sweep of the Texas Panhandle and especially to purge the upper Red River of any hostiles who might remain there. Beginning his search on January 2, 1875, from an indeterminate point on the Canadian River, Miles marched southward along the edge of the Staked Plains, crossed Prairie Dog Town Fork, and went to the head of Tule Canyon. Turning downstream, Miles' column reached the confluence of Tule Creek and Prairie Dog Town Fork. Continuing downstream, Miles' scouting parties closely examined the area between the Red River and Elm Fork.

Meanwhile, a detachment under Major C. E. Compton marched southwestward from a supply camp on the Washita, carefully scouting the streams south of the Washita and the area adjacent to the Staked Plains. Following the south side of the Wichita River [*sic*], Miles proceeded on to Fort Sill and then back to a supply camp on the North Fork, which was reached on February 3. Miles' last scout—made in dreadfully severe winter weather—convinced the hard-driving colonel that there were no hostile Indians between the Arkansas and Red rivers, although, regrettably, some had, he believed, escaped to the northwest and a larger number had crossed the Staked Plains to New Mexico.[97]

Miles' estimate was correct, for soon numerous Indian groups, including some of the most recalcitrant, arrived at Fort Sill; and in the spring,

---

Alice Blackwood Baldwin, *Memoirs of the Late Frank D. Baldwin*, pp. 70-76; Miles, *Personal Recollections*, pp. 174-175; Leckie, *Military Conquest*, pp. 227-228. The two other German sisters, Sophia and Catherine, were later rescued. Five members of the family were murdered when the four girls were captured.

A most remarkable soldier, Frank Baldwin participated in twenty-eight engagements in an active career that spanned the period from the Civil War through the Philippine Insurrection. He is one of only five men to win two Medals of Honor (one of which was awarded for the wagon train charge on McClellan Creek) and was recommended for a third during the Civil War. See Baldwin,' *Baldwin's Memoirs*, p. 199. Relative to the wagon-train charge on McClellan Creek, Taylor, ed., *Indian Campaign*, p. 203, interestingly observes, "This charge is presumed to be the first time that infantrymen were deployed in wheeled vehicles in actual combat."

[96] Miles to Assistant Adjutant General, Department of the Missouri, March 5, 1875, W.D.A.G.O. File No. 2815-1874.
[97] Ibid.

Mackenzie, who now commanded that post, negotiated the surrender of the Kwahadi Comanches. Thus closed the Panhandle phase of the Red River War of 1874-1875. With his sense of integrity as fierce as ever, Mackenzie, in his new role as protector of the Indians, worked as avidly championing their rights as he had earlier worked to defeat them.[98]

In the overview of the military phase of the history of the Texas Panhandle, several generalizations emerge. In the first place, one cannot escape appreciation for the character and professional competence of the troops, both officers and men. Leaders such as Sheridan, Mackenzie, Miles, Buell, and Davidson understood preeminently that nomadic Indians had to be defeated in the field and on their own terms. In other words, these able officers understood in a modern sense the essence of a war of mobility. Moreover, their troopers delivered when their officers demanded performance beyond the limits of ordinary human capability. For not only were the fall and winter of 1874 and 1875 unusually brutal, it is apparent from the documents that detachments from the various commands were constantly on the move, virtually lacing and interlacing the eastern Panhandle and adjacent areas back and forth dozens of times over. The more spectacular engagements tend to overshadow the fact that the major work of subjugating the Indians was done by suffering, shivering, bone-weary troopers who wore the Indians out by giving them absolutely no peace— and in so doing got not one moment of relief from the everlasting toil of marching and countermarching over the Plains.

This is not to say that the engagements were not important; obviously they were. Noteworthy, however, is the fact that the fighting cost surprisingly little in soldiers' lives. Indian casualties were higher and probably greater than the number of bodies actually counted. Also, of course, there is no way of knowing how many died as an indirect result of military action and destruction of property. Still, it is worth a great deal, it would seem, that the military conquest of the Texas Panhandle saw nothing like the Sand Creek massacre, which reflects credit upon the white soldiers who defeated the Indians of the region. While such men as Mackenzie, Miles, Buell, Davidson, and their subordinates were tough, relentless soldiers out to win a most difficult war, nothing suggests that they were bloodthirsty or derived any sort of pleasure from inflicting casualties. Furthermore, while recognizing that warfare—any warfare—is by nature

[98] Carter, *On the Border*, pp. 527-528; Leckie, *Military Conquest*, pp. 228-235; Wallace, *Mackenzie*, pp. 169-171.

dirty and brutal, any construction of the military action against the Indians in the Texas Panhandle as a deliberate act of genocide is unmitigated foolishness.

Since the Indians had achieved a degree of civilization that had no need for either a military or civilian bureaucracy requiring constant written reports, reconstruction of their side of the story relies largely on circumstantial evidence. Nothing in the military documents suggests, however, that the southern Plains tribes were unworthy opponents militarily. Quite the contrary! Moreover, since the Indian bands were the fugitives during that frightful fall and winter of 1874-1875, their suffering must have passed the point of comprehension as ponies, tepees, buffalo robes, and food were destroyed. And human grief must have surpassed physical suffering as the ranks of warriors were thinned. Persons who suffered from Indian "atrocities" understandably may have applauded their fate. The dispassionate view of retrospect, however, decrees admiration for the tenacity, courage, and ingenuity that characterized the Indians' defense of their homeland. If their methods were "barbaric," then one may legitimately separate his compassion for personal human tragedy from recognition that a proud race merely defended home, family, and value system with whatever methods were available. What self-respecting people would not?

Of overriding importance is the fact that subjugation of the Indians was completed *before* a permanent civilian population entered the region. This means that in the process of settlement the Texas Panhandle experienced no conflict between Indians and a civilian population as had normally been the case in the American frontier experience. None of the agony of the Mohawk Valley, trans-Appalachia, or for that matter most of the remainder of West Texas attended Panhandle settlement. For that happy circumstance the Panhandle pioneer could thank the federal government, which fielded its army to eliminate Indians so white civilians could go about appropriating the region without fear of the scalping knife!

Finally, with the end of the military phase of regional history, the process of reorientation of the Panhandle toward Anglo-America was essentially completed, so that it remained only for Anglo-Americans physically to occupy the land.

As a kind of exclamation point to the Red River War, the only permanent United States military post in the Panhandle was established. The site, about two miles southeast of the head of Sweetwater Creek in Wheeler County, was selected by Major James Biddle, Sixth Cavalry, but

226                                        The Texas Panhandle Frontier

Major H. C. Bankhead, Fourth Cavalry, actually supervised the installation on June 5, 1875. First known as New Cantonment, the name of the post was officially changed at General Sheridan's behest to Fort Elliott on February 21, 1876, to honor Custer's loyal subordinate, Major Joel Elliott, who fell in the Battle of the Washita a little over six years earlier.[99]

Guarding the western edge of Indian Territory and keeping the Indians from reentering the Panhandle was Fort Elliott's primary mission. To that end the fort's troopers conducted countless patrols, chased down infinitely more rumors than raiders, and apprehended far more lawless whites than renegade Indians.[100] In fact, the fort may not have been necessary as a restraining influence on the Indians; on the other hand, its presence was known to them and perhaps it served admirably, as many locks do, to keep honest men honest.

Fort Elliott contributed to regional development mainly by supporting civilian occupation. It provided the first postal and telegraph service to the Panhandle and for several years the only such services.[101] Symbolizing governmental authority, the fort contributed some measure of stability to an infant society. Although army officers had no authority to enforce civil law, more flagrant violators were apparently taken in hand occasionally by the military.[102] The economic development of Mobeetie, the "Mother City" of the Panhandle, owed much to Fort Elliott's presence, for the fort employed many civilians; relied on local production and services to supply many of its needs; provided various services, most importantly medical care, to the civilian community whose entrepreneurs of assorted levels of respectability happily relieved the bored soldiers of their meager pay.[103]

To express the foregoing in broader terms, under the benevolent umbrella of Fort Elliott—a federal agency—occurred much of the initial settlement of the Panhandle. Unsurprisingly, (and traditionalists may be consoled that some things never change), the Mobeetie business community raised their anguished howls all the way to the White House when in 1890 the army abandoned the obsolete post. By presidential order,

[99] James M. Oswald, "History of Fort Elliott," *Panhandle-Plains Historical Review* 32 (1959): 3-8. This study was done originally as James Marlin Oswald, Fort Elliott, Texas Frontier Post (M.A. thesis, West Texas State College, 1958). See also W. S. Mabry, "The Location of Fort Elliott," *Panhandle-Plains Historical Review* 5 (1932): 87.
[100] Oswald, "Fort Elliott," pp. 31-33.
[101] Ibid., pp. 25-26.
[102] Ibid., pp. 39-40.
[103] Ibid., pp. 27, 28, 23-24, 34.

however, all Fort Elliott property was transferred to the Department of the Interior for disposal. Although kept intact for another decade, the post buildings eventually were sold at public auction on March 20, 1900.[104] Although insignificant in the broad scheme of American development, the passing of Fort Elliott rather symbolizes the profound transitions in American life that came with the twentieth century. Regionally speaking, the demise of Fort Elliott removed the last symbol of the victory it was established to secure—the victory of brave white men over brave red men who fought, among other reasons, for possession of a land no white man really wanted until there was little else left to grab!

[104] Ibid., pp. 51-55.

# 8. Anglo-American Occupation

As the United States observed its one-hundredth birthday in 1876, Colorado, well to the northwest of the Texas Panhandle, entered the Union as the Centennial State. Kansas, which suffered as fearfully as Texas from Indian wars, had been a state since 1861. New Mexico, to the west of the Panhandle, while remaining a territory until 1912, had sufficient population and importance to occupy some status in the national consciousness. In Texas, with the election of Democratic Governor Richard Coke over Republican Edmund J. Davis in 1874, Reconstruction ended and gradually Texans turned from licking their wounds—both real and imaginary—to facing the needs of a state rapidly emerging from the frontier into a new age.

Having previously received meager attention from anyone, including the remainder of Texas, the Panhandle obtained a sort of legal or legislative acknowledgement in 1874 when the region was divided between and attached to the Jack and Clay land districts. Divided geographically into counties created by legislative enactment in 1876, the region remained attached to Clay and Jack counties for "judicial, surveying and all other purposes" pending arrival of a permanent population necessary to organize county government.[1]

The previous chapters of this study have traced the activities of Spanish and Anglo-American traders, travelers, explorers, hunters, and soldiers who entered the Panhandle for some purpose other than occupation of the land. Perhaps—indeed probably—other adventurers of various sorts visited the region, but since they left few evidences their presence remains interestingly but purely conjectural. Chapter 4 discussed the presence of the New Mexican *pastores* along the western Canadian beginning in 1876, although there is an outside chance that some were present earlier.[2] As indicated in chapter 6, several buffalo hunters remained in the region as permanent residents after the hide trade played out.[3] Overlapping too, to some degree, were the buffalo hunting, military, and grazing phases of regional development. All of this complicates the fixation of a definite time, place, and identity for the first permanent settling of any person in the Panhandle. So, while purists may debate the point, the generally accepted date of 1876 as the beginning year of permanent Panhandle settlement is both convenient and essentially valid historiographically.[4]

With the Indians expelled, the Panhandle was a cartographic void—a part of a large vacant area in the southern Great Plains lying approximately between the 99th and 104th meridians.[5] Except in the sense of being unoccupied, however, the region was hardly any longer a frontier. Occupation involved merely the filling of a territorial vacuum, which proceeded rapidly, so that the Panhandle frontier soon phased into a process of regional development, a story beyond the scope of this study.

Development of the Panhandle region diffused from three germinal centers: Mobeetie in Wheeler County, Tascosa in Oldham County, and Clarendon in Donley County—none of which were destined for permanent

---

[1] See chapter 4, pp. 89-90; H. P. N. Gammel, comp., *Laws of Texas*, 1822-1897, VIII, pp. 164-165, 1070-1073, 1076-1078.

[2] Chapter 4, p. 101-103.

[3] Chapter 6, p. 174.

[4] Moreover, much of the problem of identification depends on definition of terms, so beyond what I have said in these paragraphs, I decline any invitation to verbal or literary brawling over exactly who the first Panhandle settler was or precisely where or when he settled.

[5] See the map of population distribution in the United States as of 1880 in U.S. Bureau of the Census, *Report on Population of the United States at the Eleventh Census: 1890*, Part I, following p. xxvi.

leadership in regional affairs—but, significantly, each was situated on a major watercourse.

Originating as the "Hidetown" of the buffalo hunters, Mobeetie attracted a population and enterprises that supported the hunting trade.[6] Establishment of Fort Elliott stimulated further growth, and thus created a population base and center of social cohesiveness from which settlement could emanate.[7] Mobeetie—the Indian term for Sweetwater Creek upon which the town was situated—looked to Dodge City for commercial contacts and an outlet to the outside world via the Jones-Plummer Trail,[8] which doubtlessly carried an enormous volume of freight in creaking wagons pulled by straining, sweating oxen and mules driven by cursing, short-tempered skinners. But through her trade with Dodge City, Mobeetie supported the development of cattle ranches within a radius of one hundred miles by providing the staples—"bacon, beans, flour, whiskey, and other necessities"—essential to the growing cattle industry.[9] Frontier town that it was, Old Mobeetie had its rough characters engaging in rough trades catering to rough customers, but probably many of the less respectable population were more rowdy than mean.[10]

Given Mobeetie's status as the commercial center for Fort Elliott and surrounding ranches, political organization came quickly. Accordingly, Wheeler County in 1879 was the first of the Panhandle counties to be organized.[11] With a center of government in the Panhandle region, the Texas Legislature promptly (in 1879) redefined the Tenth Judicial District to comprise several northwest Texas counties, including Wheeler County, to which were attached the unorganized counties of the entire Panhandle "for judicial purposes and for purposes of organization."[12]

A little over one hundred miles west of Mobeetie, another center of population developed at Tascosa from the nucleus of New Mexican sheep-

[6] Interview, John Woods to L. F. Sheffy, December 28, 1929, Panhandle-Plains Historical Museum. "Old" Mobeetie lay about one mile south of the present town.
[7] James M. Oswald, "History of Fort Elliott," *Panhandle-Plains Historical Review* 32 (1959): 38.
[8] L. F. Sheffy, "Old Mobeetie—The Capital of the Panhandle," West Texas Historical Association *Yearbook* 6 (1930): 5, 7.
[9] Ibid., pp. 11-13.
[10] Pat Bullis, "Ranging the East Panhandle" (MS, Earl Vandale Collection, Archives, University of Texas at Austin), 10; R. H. Conlyn Diary, 1883 (MS), ibid., pp. 22-23.
[11] "Counties, Cities and Towns of Texas," *Texas Almanac*, 1970-1971, p. 348.
[12] Gammel, comp., *Laws of Texas*, IX, pp. 60-61.

men led by Casimero Romero, who arrived in November 1876.[13] Shortly after Romero, other sheepmen settled along the Canadian.[14] Possibly some were former Comancheros whose commercial activities had been rudely terminated by the Red River War. The first Anglo-American resident of Tascosa or vicinity doubtlessly was Henry Kimball, an ex-soldier from Fort Union who reputedly camped at the site of Tascosa while visiting the Canadian as a member of a hunting party. Finding the spot rich in game and fish and exquisitely beautiful, the soldier resolved to return to live, which he did at the expiration of his enlistment in 1876. A blacksmith in the army, Kimball brought his equipment along, continued his trade, and operated the only smithy Tascosa ever had.[15]

The cattle industry stimulated Tascosa's growth beyond the initial handful of *pastores*, and new business firms opened, including a new saloon, a hotel, and a general store. A whole new business area—Hogtown—opened a discreet distance from the places where respectable business enterprise operated. Increasing growth of Tascosa and Oldham County, expanding economic activity, a booming livestock industry, and an increasingly complex social order made more convenient access to legal institutions desirable. Consequently, in November 1880 the citizens voted to organize Oldham County under the direction of the Wheeler County commissioners, and the first Oldham County officers took their oaths of office on January 12, 1881.[16]

[13] José Ynocencio Romero, "Spanish Sheepmen on the Canadian at Old Tascosa," ed. Ernest R. Archambeau, *Panhandle-Plains Historical Review* 19 (1946): 46-47.

[14] Ibid., pp. 48, 52-54, 96. See Chapter 4, pp. 101-102.

[15] John Arnot, "Tascosa Trail" (MS, Earl Vandale Collection, Archives, University of Texas at Austin), p. 5.

[16] Ibid., pp. 16-18; John Arnot, "My Recollections of Tascosa Before and After the Coming of the Law," *Panhandle-Plains Historical Review* 6 (1933): 63-64; "Counties, Cities and Towns of Texas," *Texas Almanac*, 1970-1971, p. 322. The organization of Oldham County under the guidance of Wheeler County authorities illustrates the operation of the system of land districts devised by Texas for government of sparsely populated counties and their eventual political organization under the supervision of established governmental entities. Apparently Tascosa was rougher than Mobeetie, and in Hogtown dwelt the sort of folk who probably justified the name. Really heinous violence visited Tascosa with some frequency; nevertheless excessive emphasis should be avoided since for every day that some grim crime or exciting shoot-out occurred, there must have been hundreds of sleepy days when the townsfolk wondered if ever again the monotony of daily routine would be broken. It is plausible to this writer, having surveyed the literature, that Tascosa, perhaps because of its Latin character, was a more playful town than the purely Anglo-American communities— although Anglo-Americans found it within themselves to be pretty playful on occa-

Forty-five to fifty miles to the southwest of Mobeetie, Clarendon, the last of the original trio of Panhandle towns, was consciously promoted—as contrasted to Mobeetie and Tascosa, which just more or less evolved. The Rev. L. H. Carhart, a Methodist minister with more energy and imagination than his ministerial duties could absorb, promoted Clarendon through a partnership with his brother-in-law, Alfred Sully of New York. By purchasing railroad land scrip, the promoters acquired title to 343 sections of Panhandle land centering in Donley County. In 1878 Carhart acquired financial backing through an English "stock company," the Clarendon Land Investment and Agency Company.[17]

The original site of Clarendon (about five miles north of the present location) was on a flat at the junction of Carroll Creek and the Salt Fork where, on October 1, 1878, Carhart established a "Christian Colony."[18] The townsite was laid out, and construction of buildings from natural materials—rock, adobe, sod, and pickets—immediately begun. Since Dodge City supplied Clarendon, the high cost of transportation prohibited the importation of construction materials such as lumber.[19] At least some of Clarendon's business contacts were with or through Sherman, Texas, however, since Carhart already had business contacts there. Stagecoach communication with Tascosa and Mobeetie was soon established.[20]

The original settlers of Clarendon, according to Carhart's nephew, were simply a group of friends who, for unexplained reasons, shared a desire to move to the isolated community in the Texas Panhandle. Carhart's subsequent efforts to attract settlers were economically motivated, although the town's citizenry at one time included *seven* Methodist ministers.[21] What-

---

sion. The most extensive treatment of Tascosa's history is John Lawton McCarty, "The History of Tascosa, Texas" (M.A. thesis, West Texas State Teachers College, 1945), or, in its published form, McCarty, *Maverick Town: The Story of Old Tascosa.*

[17] Interview, Whitfield Carhart to B. P. Brents, June 15, 1936, (Earl Vandale Collection, Archives, University of Texas at Austin), pp. 1-2. Whitfield Carhart was a nephew of L. H. Carhart. Besides colonizing Clarendon, the Clarendon Land Investment and Agency Company developed the Quarter Circle Heart ranch, which apparently did well until the disastrously cold winter of 1885, but declined thereafter and went into receivership in 1889. The last of its lands were disposed of upon court order in 1905 or 1906. Ibid., p. 6.

[18] Willie Newbury Lewis, *Between Sun and Sod*, p. 69. Common belief says that Clarendon was named in honor of Carhart's wife, Clara; but Whitfield Carhart thought it possible that the name was borrowed from Clarendon, England, "as a compliment to the English stockholders." Carhart to Brents, June 15, 1936, p. 2.

[19] Lewis, *Between Sun and Sod*, pp. 69-70.

[20] Carhart to Brents, June 15, 1936, pp. 5-8.

[21] Ibid., pp. 1, 3.

ever his motives, however, Carhart attracted a substantial—substantial numerically but mainly morally—population, and Clarendon grew.[22] Because Clarendon must have been more socially rigid than either Mobeetie or Tascosa, it showed little of the color of its sister pioneer towns. Carhart, ever the aristocratic moralist, "sought to attract . . . only one class, people of education and of strict adherence to the Methodist faith."[23] Clarendon, therefore, probably deserved the appellation "Saints' Roost" conferred upon it by less reverent folk of the region. But the pioneer Panhandle at least presented an environmental choice to newcomers: Clarendon for climate; Tascosa for society.

In 1880 Carhart surrendered local administration of the colony to his attorney brother-in-law, Benjamin Horton White, who by training, experience, and temperament was far better suited to the task than the promoter-preacher. White, universally liked and respected, gave the Clarendon area exceptionally effective leadership.[24]

Clarendon's development and the expansion of ranching in the vicinity prepared the way for the organization of Donley County, which in 1882 became the third organized county in the Panhandle.[25]

Legislative response to the evolving Panhandle and its political needs was prompt. After the organization of Oldham County in 1880, the Tenth Judicial District was reorganized and a new judicial district, the Thirty-fifth, provided for the Panhandle.[26] Only two years later, the Thirty-fifth Judicial District was again rearranged to take into account the organization of Donley County.[27] Similarly, in 1883 the legislature created the

[22] Lewis, *Between Sun and Sod*, pp. 70-75.
[23] Ibid., p. 86.
[24] Ibid., pp. 85-87.
[25] "Counties, Cities and Towns of Texas," *Texas Almanac*, 1970-1971, p. 272. Vigorous controversy often attended county organization. See L. F. Sheffy, *The Life and Times of Timothy Dwight Hobart, 1855-1935*, pp. 106-117. Large ranchers generally opposed organization because of the attendant complexities—like taxes. In more general terms these controversies may merely manifest a natural political instability reasonably expected in an infant society. Close scrutiny of this phase of regional history might produce a worthwhile study in the emergence of local political institutions.
[26] Gammel, comp., *Laws of Texas*, IX, p. 100. Ochiltree, Hemphill, Lipscomb, Roberts, Gray, Donley, Collingsworth, Childress, Hall, Briscoe, Armstrong, Carson, Hutchinson, and Hansford were attached to Wheeler County "for judicial purposes until organized." Sherman, Moore, Potter, Randall, Swisher, Castro, Parmer, Deaf Smith, Hartley, and Dallam counties were attached to Oldham County.
[27] Ibid., p. 336. For judicial purposes Sherman, Moore, Potter, Castro, Parmer, Deaf Smith, Hartley, and Dallam counties were attached to Oldham County. Carson, Ran-

234                                           *The Texas Panhandle Frontier*

Wheeler, Oldham, and Donley land districts (whose boundaries coincided with those of the newly arranged Thirty-fifth Judicial District) for purposes of surveying and maintaining records and files of surveys.[28]

Development of the livestock industry or cattle and sheep ranching, like the political evolution of the Panhandle, emanated from three rather specific geographical points. To be sure, regional political and economic development correlate closely. The first of the economic centers, along the western Canadian, derived from the New Mexican sheepmen whose activities have been discussed and need not be belabored. The other two, developed by Anglo-American cattlemen, involved the activities of two of the Panhandle's prominent pioneer citizens, Charles Goodnight, a southerner who spent the Civil War years trying to protect the Texas frontier, and T. S. Bugbee, a Maine yankee who, during that most tragic struggle, wore the uniform of the United States.

Goodnight had had a spectacular career before arriving in the Panhandle, and the early seventies found him on the Arkansas above Pueblo, Colorado, engaged in ranching, farming, and other enterprises.[29] The economic disaster wrought by the Panic of 1873 and increasing crowding of the southern Colorado range caused Goodnight to look elsewhere and ultimately to point his herds toward the Panhandle.[30] Thus the winter of 1875 found the Goodnight outfit on the Canadian River in eastern New Mexico, but in the following spring the cowman moved on downstream into the Panhandle, summering on Alamocitos Creek, an Oldham County tributary of the Canadian. Later, however, New Mexican sheepmen invaded the land, and Goodnight agreed to move on to the Palo Duro—which was his original intention anyway—and leave the Canadian to the *pastores*; they in turn agreed to keep their sheep away from the Palo Duro. So in the fall of 1876 Goodnight led his cattle into the canyon and drove the buffalo off the range to make room for his cattle.[31] Thus began the great livestock enterprise which was to become the famed JA Ranch.[32]

Thomas Sherman Bugbee, a descendant of Roger Sherman of Connecticut, who signed the Declaration of Independence, was a native of Perry,

dall, Armstrong, Swisher, Floyd, Briscoe, Hall, and Childress counties were attached to Donley County, and Collingsworth, Gray, Hutchinson, Hansford, Ochiltree, Roberts, Hemphill, and Lipscomb counties were attached to Wheeler County.
[28] Ibid., p. 358.
[29] J. Evetts Haley, *Charles Goodnight: Cowman and Plainsman*, pp. 260ff.
[30] Ibid., pp. 273-278.
[31] Ibid., pp. 278-283.
[32] Ibid., pp. 295ff.

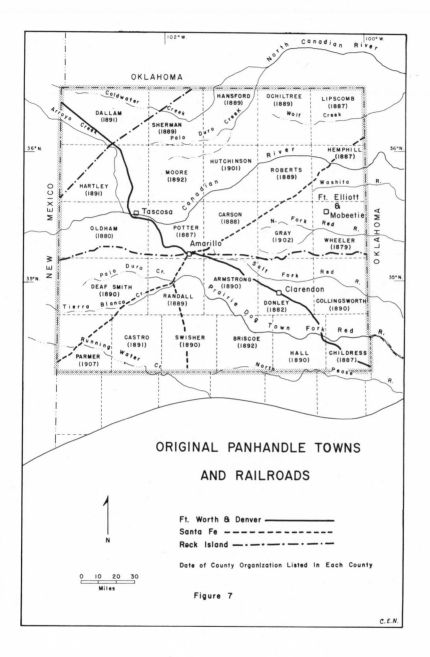

ORIGINAL PANHANDLE TOWNS

AND RAILROADS

Ft. Worth & Denver ————————
Santa Fe — — — — — — — — —
Rock Island —·—·—·—·—·—·—

Date of County Organization Listed In Each County

N

0   10   20   30
Miles

Figure 7

C.E.N.

Maine. Twenty years old when the Civil War came, Bugbee became a member of the Tenth Maine Regiment and was present at Cedar Mountain where his regiment lost 547 of 760 men! Later fighting at Second Bull Run, Antietam, Fredericksburg, Chancellorsville, Gettysburg, and Lookout Mountain, Bugbee lastly participated in General Nathan P. Banks' abortive efforts to invade Texas from Louisiana.[33]

Experiencing the restlessness and loss of identity that often come to men after a war, Bugbee soon quit a job as a streetcar conductor in Washington, D.C., and worked his way westward. Employed as a teamster, Bugbee got from St. Joseph, Missouri, to Salt Lake City; made money freighting on his own in Idaho; and in a cattle venture drove $11-steers from Texas to Idaho, where they became $45-steers. In Kansas in 1872 Bugbee married Mary C. Dunn; four years later the couple and their two small children headed southward to the Texas Panhandle. Losing many cattle and most of their personal and household property crossing the Cimarron River, the Bugbees pushed on southward and established the Quarter Circle T ranch—the Panhandle's second—making their home in a dugout on Bugbee Creek in Hutchinson County. Like Goodnight, Bugbee had to drive buffalo from his range to make way for cattle and hired men for that specific task.[34]

While such pioneers as Romero, Goodnight, Carhart, and Bugbee are to be reckoned as being men of courage, vision, and determination, they are, in the broader view of regional history, significant symbolically as well as personally. Upon their heels came others attracted by the unbelievably rich range lands of the Texas Panhandle, and who, like the vanguards,

[33] Helen Bugbee Officer, "A Sketch of the Life of Thomas Sherman Bugbee—1841-1925," *Panhandle-Plains Historical Review* 5 (1932): 10-11. Bugbee was a man of unusual as well as exciting experiences. Having left Washington on the night President Lincoln was assassinated, Bugbee was arrested at Boston on suspicion of having murdered the president. With blue eyes and curly black hair, the young veteran who had cast his first presidential vote for and enormously admired Lincoln, bore a resemblance to John Wilkes Booth. Bugbee was released when he produced his discharge papers. Unknowingly, Bugbee led a substantial contingent of Union veterans to the Panhandle. A special census of Union veterans and their widows taken in 1890 counted 223 veterans and seventeen widows in the northern-most thirty-three Texas counties. See Lowell H. Harrison, "Union Veterans in the Texas Panhandle," *Panhandle-Plains Historical Review* 37 (1964): 37. Harrison includes reproductions of the rolls for the Panhandle counties (pp. 43-60) and an alphabetical index of names appearing thereon (pp. 60-62). Most of these men arrived after 1880.
[34] Officer, "Life of Bugbee," pp.11, 15-16; L. F. Sheffy, "Thomas Sherman Bugbee," *Panhandle-Plains Historical Review* 2 (1929): 130-132. John Arnot, "The First Cattleman on the Canadian and Adjacent Territory" (MS, Earl Vandale Collection, Archives, University of Texas at Austin), p. 15.

brought stock, families, capital, and enterprise. With the way having been prepared by an active national government and now supported by a generous state government, they occupied and exploited the lush Panhandle ranges in a remarkably short time.

The first systematically recorded evidence of what was so quickly happening in the Texas Panhandle was the federal census of 1880.[35] As computed by Archambeau, the Panhandle's total population as reflected in the census schedules was 1,607 persons. Of these, Anglo-Americans numbered 1,198. Three hundred fifty-eight persons were "Spanish" and fifty-one were Negroes. All lived along live water and slightly over half (820) resided in the eastern counties of Hemphill and Wheeler, doubtlessly reflecting the impact of Fort Elliott on population patterns, and Donley, which contained Clarendon.

Though the population of the three eastern Panhandle counties was predominantly Anglo, Mobeetie and Fort Elliott counted thirty-six of the fifty-one Negroes resident in the region—again doubtlessly reflecting the fort's influence. No Negroes were among the rural population of Wheeler County. Outside Wheeler, no county counted more than three Negroes in its population, and no pattern of distribution is detectable.

The second highest population concentration lay in the counties along the western Panhandle boundary, Hartley, Oldham, and Deaf Smith. These counties' population totaled 417 persons, seventy percent of whom were Spanish. In Oldham County, Spanish population outnumbered Anglo-

---

[35] Considering the isolated, infant character of the Panhandle, the 1880 census would seem to have been done reasonably well. The published data, however, are most disappointing. The data purporting to record places of residents' nativity (U.S. Bureau of the Census, "Native and Foreign Born Population by Counties," *Statistics of the Population of the United States at the Tenth Census: 1880*, pp. 528-530), which should be exceptionally illuminating, fails, for example, to report any Panhandle resident from any state outside the South—an egregious error that might lead the unwary investigator into drastically inaccurate conclusions. Fortunately, a study based on the manuscript schedules is available and includes reproductions of the originals. See Ernest R. Archambeau, "The First Federal Census in the Panhandle, 1880," *Panhandle-Plains Historical Review* 23 (1950): 23-132. A supplementary study is Seymour V. Connor, "Early Ranching Operations in the Panhandle: A Report on the Agricultural Schedules of the 1880 Census," *Panhandle-Plains Historical Review* 27 (1954): 47-69. This study will rely on the work of Archambeau and Connor rather than the Census Bureau's published data for 1880, and except where otherwise indicated, the following discussion is based on Archambeau's and Connor's reproductions. Even when working with the reproduced schedules and rolls, one must be aware of the lack of standardized counting procedures and the uneven quality of the enumerators' work. What can be gotten from these data is not an absolute, literally true picture, but a reasonably accurate idea of emerging patterns and trends.

American 218 to sixty-one and fifty-six to forty-four respectively in Hartley County. This preponderance of Spanish-speaking population in the three western counties reflects, obviously, the influx of New Mexican sheepmen beginning late in 1876. The remaining population in 1880 was scattered about indiscriminately over the other counties.[36]

The major economic enterprise of the Texas Panhandle in 1880 was, of course, ranching, as clearly reflected by the principal occupations listed: "Stockman," "Sheepherder," "Cattle herder," "Herding cows," "Raising cows," "Ranchero," and the like. Contrary to popular impression, however, the number of sheep exceeded the number of cattle by about ten thousand head, with Hartley County reporting the greatest number of each—26,900 cattle and 72,316 sheep. The concentration of sheep in Hartley County correlates closely with the high number of Spanish-speaking persons in Hartley and Oldham counties.[37] Outside the western counties consequential numbers of sheep ranged in Donley (14,620 head), Hall (10,900 head), and Potter (9,030 head) counties.[38] In Donley and Hall counties Spanish names are almost exclusively related to sheep herding, although a number of Anglo names are similarly associated. Potter County lists no one occupationally connected with sheep.[39]

[36] Carson, Castro, Dallam, Moore, Parmer, and Sherman counties reported no population. Remaining concentrations of people correlate with some fairly obvious—or at least plausible—cause. Thirty-one persons in Armstrong County may well reflect the Goodnight-Adair partnership, effected June 18, 1877 (see Haley, *Goodnight*, p. 301), which founded the JA Ranch; fifty persons in Hutchinson County may relate to T. S. Bugbee's Quarter Circle T; while the thirty-two who lived in Roberts County may be accounted for by H. S. Cresswell's Bar CC. See Clinton Leon Paine, "The History of Lipscomb County" (M.A. thesis, West Texas State Teachers College, 1941). On the other hand, the agricultural schedules of the 1880 census indicate the presence of a number of small livestock operations that may have involved more people than the larger outfits, as for example in Lipscomb County, which listed sixty persons in 1880. See Connor, "Agricultural Schedules, 1880 Census," pp. 51-68. Occupations listed in the census rolls as published by Archambeau correlate with known activity. The "urban" populations of Mobeetie and Clarendon, as distinguished from the rural populations of Wheeler and Donley counties, reflect greater occupational diversity and clearly indicate the more complex demands of even simple towns, and in the case of Mobeetie, the needs of Fort Elliott. Swisher County, interestingly, reported a population of four persons—all Anglos engaged in "hunting Mustangs."

[37] Connor, "Agricultural Schedules, 1880 Census," p. 69. According to Connor's study, the Census Bureau accounted for 72,316 sheep in Hartley County while accounting for only 308 in Oldham County. This obvious discrepancy must derive from counting the sheep as being present in the county of the owners' residence. Connor's computations indicate that the twenty-six county Panhandle region contained 97,236 cattle and 108,234 sheep.

[38] Ibid.,

[39] Archambeau, "1880 Census," pp. 56-60, 62, 70-71.

In geographic, ethnic, and cultural origins the pioneer population of 1880 was amazingly diverse. From New Mexico and Colorado, and in a few cases from Mexico, came the Spanish-speaking population concentrated in the western counties.[40] The numerically predominant Anglo-American population came from almost all over the continental United States, with Texas contributing the largest number of persons from a single state. Only one in nine families of Texas origin came directly from the settled parts of the state, however.

Not counting Fort Elliott's military personnel, the number of Anglo adults over age fifteen was divided by place of birth 364 to 365 between former Union and former Confederate states and territories. From the northeast came fifteen persons from Maine, thirty-two from New York, twenty-three from Massachusetts, and twenty-five from Pennsylvania. From the mid-west Ohio and Illinois contributed forty-three and forty-five respectively.

While eleven different nations were represented among the foreign-born population, persons from English-speaking countries predominated, there being twenty-eight Irishmen, twenty Englishmen, fifteen Canadians, and seven Scots counted in the 1880 census. Nine Germans constituted the only significant concentration of non-English-speaking foreign-born.[41] In 1880 the Texas Panhandle was a man's country and especially a young man's country, with far more persons falling in the twenty to twenty-nine age group than in any other.[42]

The 1880 agricultural census schedules point toward relatively small, individually operated Panhandle ranches.[43] Presumably the operators supplied their own capital or personally borrowed it. Portending rapid and fundamental changes, the Goodnight-Adair partnership and Carhart's Clarendon Land Investment and Agency Company set the pattern of almost overnight and drastic alteration in the nature of the Panhandle livestock industry.

Left alone, the first Panhandle ranchers worked their cattle on open range and free grass, marketing their stock at Dodge City and evidently doing well financially. Word of their success spread far and wide—its extent apparently growing in direct proportion to the distance it traveled from the Panhandle. Indeed, all the factors for a booming cattle business

[40] Ibid., pp. 121-125; 111-120; 126-130; 131-132.
[41] Ibid., pp. 31-32.
[42] Ibid., pp. 30, 33-36.
[43] Connor, "Agricultural Schedules, 1880 Census," pp. 51-68.

were present. An expanding industrial economy in the United States; attendant concentrations of urban population who had to be fed from outside sources; technological advances that facilitated the marketability of beef; cheaply bought cattle and rich, free grass to graze them on; and minimal production costs all combined to point toward an economic bonanza that absolutely could not lose!

L. F. Sheffy beautifully summarizes what happened:

> It was natural . . . that eastern and foreign capital on a large scale should seek a share of profit from this lucrative cattle trade. No section of country offered greater opportunity than did Northwest Texas. The buffalo had just recently been killed out and the Indians had been removed to the reservations and, as rumor had it, there was free grass in abundance and land could be bought for a song. Corporations were formed in the North and East, bonds and debentures were sold in England and Scotland and, by the middle of the eighties, many large corporate concerns had entered into the business of cattle ranching in Northwest Texas. A scramble was made for both land and cattle.
>
> Since most of the water and grass lands had been preempted by the small cattlemen, these large companies eagerly sought to buy them out at liberal prices, tally book count and range delivery, without even making an actual count of the number of cattle purchased.

"This rush of foreign and eastern capital to Northwest Texas," continues Sheffy, "soon brought about a complete transformation in the ranching business."[44]

The transformation to which Sheffy refers, of course, is the transition

---

[44] L. F. Sheffy, "British Pounds and British Purebreds," *Panhandle-Plains Historical Review* 11 (1938): 59-60. Sheffy quotes T. D. Hobart, who was thoroughly familiar with the Panhandle cattle business, as having told him on June 6, 1934: "They actually came into the Panhandle and bought cattle that had been dead for two or three years. Texas ranchers put up all kinds of jobs on these foreigners [*sic*], like running the cattle around a hill and counting them two or three times. . . . One company's manager, who evidently became too liberal in his purchases, received the following wire from his company in St. Louis, 'Buy only necessities, for God's sake don't buy everything you see.' " Sheffy's is the pioneer study of its kind and remains the best specifically relevant to the Texas Panhandle. More up to date, however, are several others that deal with various or more general aspects of foreign investment in the Western American cattle industry. Lowell H. Harrison, "British Interest in the Panhandle-Plains Area, 1878-1885," *Panhandle-Plains Historical Review* 38 (1965): 1-43, is an excellent account of British periodical literature and its impact upon British interest and consequent investment in Panhandle-Plains cattle ventures. Besides being a fine, scholarly contribution to the literature of regional history, Harrison's article also proves that P. T. Barnum was right! See also Herbert O. Brayer,

from individual, local enterprise to corporate enterprise capitalized from alien sources. On the whole the precise mechanics of the transition held little good for any of the parties.[45] Although Panhandle-Plains ranching appeared an attractive investment for the reasons noted above, many con-

---

"Influence of British Capital in the Western Range-Cattle Industry," *Journal of Economic History* 9, supplement (1949): 85-98; Richard Graham, "The Investment Boom in British-Texas Cattle Companies, 1880-1885," *Business History Review* 34 (Winter 1960): 421-445; W. Turrentine Jackson, "British Interests in the Range Cattle Industry," in *When Grass Was King*, ed. Maurice Frink, pp. 135-332; W. G. Kerr, "Scotland and the Texas Mortgage Business," *Panhandle-Plains Historical Review* 38 (1965): 53-71; and J. Fred Rippy, "British Investments in Texas Lands and Livestock," *Southwestern Historical Quarterly* 58 (January 1955): 331-341.

[45] The literature of Panhandle-Plains ranching is extensive. The following are competent studies of various ranches in or near the Panhandle region: Josie Baird, "Ranching on the Two Circles Bar," *Panhandle-Plains Historical Review* 17 (1944): 8-67; Jesse J. Dyer, "A Survey of the J. Buckle Kingdom," ibid., 16 (1943): 59-89; Margaret A. Elliott, "History of D. B. Gardner's Pitchfork Ranch of Texas," ibid., 18 (1945): 12-78; Lee Gilmore, "The Mill Iron Ranch," ibid., 5 (1932): 57-66; Knox Kinard, "The History of the Waggoner Ranch," ibid., 16 (1943): 11-49; C. B. McClure, "A History of the Shoe Nail Ranch," ibid., 11 (1938): 69-83; C. Boone McClure, "A Review of the T-Anchor Ranch," ibid., 3 (1930): 64-77; Margaret Sheers, "The LX Ranch of Texas," ibid., 6 (1933): 45-57; and Estelle D. Tinkler, "A History of the Rocking Chair Ranche," ibid., 15 (1942): 1-88.

Among book-length studies the following ranch histories and biographies are especially worthwhile: Harley True Burton, *A History of the JA Ranch*, treats the first Anglo-American ranch established in the Panhandle and the first to be backed by foreign capital while Haley, *Goodnight*, is the definitive biography of the man who is generally considered to have been the first Panhandle cowman and the builder of the JA. William Curry Holden, *The Spur Ranch*, and its later and expanded version, William Curry Holden, *The Espuela Land and Cattle Company: A Study of a Foreign-Owned Ranch in Texas*, deals with one of the most important of the ranches financed by foreign capital, as does W. M. Pearce, *The Matador Land and Cattle Company*. While the Spur and Matador ranches were located just south of the region to which this study is devoted, both are closely related geographically to the Panhandle and are significant in a consideration of foreign investment in ranching, since both succeeded financially. See also W. C. Holden, *Rollie Burns*. The famous XIT ranch, which once occupied or dominated the six western Panhandle counties as well as the four below them is treated extensively in J. Evetts Haley, *The XIT Ranch of Texas and the Early Days of the Llano Estacado*, and Louis Nordyke, *Cattle Empire: The Fabulous Story of the 3,000,000 Acre XIT*. Cordia Sloan Duke and Joe B. Frantz, *6,000 Miles of Fence: Life on the XIT Ranch of Texas*, is composed of cowboy memoirs and tells a ranch story from the point of view of the men who did the work! J. Evetts Haley, *George W. Littlefield, Texan*, and Sheffy, *Timothy Dwight Hobart*, deal with the careers of prominent figures in the livestock industry of the Panhandle. Autobiographical is William Timmons, *Twilight on the Range: Recollections of a Latter Day Cowboy*, which especially relates to large-scale ranching in its declining years and suggests something of the relationship between Panhandle ranching and the development of the industry in the northern Plains—a matter that merits scholarly inquiry.

ditioning factors—unrecognized in the East and Europe—pointed toward a far less sanguine reality. In the first place, severe winter cold, summer drouth, or both, could summarily wreck the most promising season. Evidently unknown or ignored, these basic facts of Plains life turned more than one investment into a frozen—or parched—asset.

Contributing substantially to the losses was pure ignorance of the cattle business. Because of ignorance—or in addition to it—inefficient management, absentee management, and plain incompetence, few investors made money.[46] Besides, general economic conditions affecting the industry had deteriorated badly in 1887. Though caused substantially by drastic overexpansion in the early bonanza days, these conditions were worsened by other economic circumstances far beyond the western cattleman's control.[47] If the real cattlemen (as distinguished from speculators) who really knew what they were doing sometimes felt themselves the victims of some devious economic conspiracy, their feelings are certainly understandable.

Economic failure in the range cattle industry occurred *despite* the subsidization of the business through the use of open range, free water, and free grass—all public property available to the industry. What cannot really be determined about this phase of regional history may be the most important aspect of the whole story: what damage was done the land through overgrazing and poor land management is anybody's guess. This writer guesses that the damage probably was as horrendous as might be expected from any immature, ill-disciplined, unregulated, and exploitive industry.[48]

---

[46] Sheffy, "British Pounds and British Purebreds," p. 63.

[47] XIT Ranch, Annual Report, 1887 (MS, XIT Papers, Panhandle-Plains Historical Museum).

[48] The range industry likely was as wasteful of grass, soil, and water resources as some farming was later to be. Subsequent developments have shown that well-developed Plains soils can be cultivated (through proper agricultural technology) without damage. The old-time cowboy's lament that "God never intended the finest grazing land in the world to be plowed," is understandable as an emotional outburst over the passing of a beloved, exciting, individually free way of life. With this, the writer entirely sympathizes. Professionally evaluated, however, the statement is bad history. It is probably bad theology, too.

The idealization of the open-range cattle baron as the epitome of free enterprise is not consistent with the facts. On the one hand he was "free" in the sense of being unregulated, but his business was underwritten by a benevolent government—Texas in the Panhandle's case. While, as has been shown, this subsidy—grass—did not guarantee success, this writer has yet to find anyone familiar with the cattle business who would deny the helpfulness of feed provided by government.

Looking at the open range cattle industry as a *way of life* as distinguished from a business, it certainly was characterized by an enviable atmosphere of freedom from convention; personal individuality ran rampant. This kind of individuality is easily

Eventually the great ranches made money by disposing of their main capital asset—land—to farmers, for having bought land cheaply the ranches could sell profitably with relative ease.[49] And right here may be the key to their real importance: the large ranches became agencies for the distribution of land to an agricultural population and development of the region as an agricultural center. This writer claims to suggest nothing historiographically revolutionary or even original because the late L. F. Sheffy— who was easily the Panhandle's finest historian—clearly understood this relationship, as shown by his major publications.[50] This aspect of Panhandle-Plains history, however, remains largely unexplored and a vast field with enormous potential for scholarly inquiry.

Granting an initial hostility to farmers on the part of foreign-owned ranches and the probability of local discord, conflict between pastoral and agricultural economic interests should be carefully confined to bounds of historical perspective and not distorted as a causative factor in regional history. In the Texas Panhandle, farmer-rancher brawling is far more a vehicle for fiction than a phenomenon of demonstrable historicity.

Though not doing much for the investors, widespread and heavy investment in Panhandle ranching stimulated "side-effect" developments essential to regional growth. Among these were such essentials as railroads, drilled wells, windmills, barbed-wire fencing, and agricultural experimentation.[51]

The decade of the 1880's, clearly the era of the cattlemen, brought an almost unbelievable drop in the number of sheep in the Panhandle. Where-

---

exercised when there is little population and no institutions to prescribe acceptable behavioral standards. The courage required of the free-living cowboy was, therefore, largely of a *physical* character—and there is no intent here to impugn it. But by contrast, individuality in an organized, conventional society is hard to come by since an abundance of institutions—newspapers, churches, schools, chambers of commerce, and an assortment of various other organizations—stand ever ready to prescribe acceptable thought and behavioral patterns and to "discipline" deviation therefrom. To be an individualist in a developed society—such as the Texas Panhandle now is— requires a measure of *moral* courage almost never demanded of those who lived in an undeveloped society such as the Panhandle was in the 1880's.

[49] Sheffy, "British Pounds and British Purebreds," p. 63.

[50] Sheffy, *Hobart*, and Lester Fields Sheffy, *The Francklyn Land & Cattle Company: A Panhandle Enterprise, 1882-1957*. Since Sheffy's death an excellent monograph on the "colonization" of ranch lands just south of the Panhandle has appeared. See David B. Gracy II, *Littlefield Lands: Colonization on the Texas Plains, 1912-1920*.

[51] Sheffy, "British Pounds and British Purebreds," pp. 63-65; L. F. Sheffy, "The Experimental Stage of Settlement in the Panhandle of Texas," *Panhandle-Plains Historical Review* 3 (1930): 78-103.

as the woolies outnumbered the cattle in the census count of 1880, there were only 10,157 in 1890. Hartley County, where sheep were concentrated in 1880, counted only 3,200 a decade later.[52] In 1900 the census enumerators found 17,658 sheep in the region, with 12,360 in Castro County, while Hartley, Oldham, and Deaf Smith counties counted absolutely none.[53]

The cattle count, by contrast, jumped from 97,236 head in 1880 to 250,046 (excluding oxen and milch cows) in 1890.[54] Distribution of cattle by counties indicates concentrations in Dallam, Hartley, and Deaf Smith counties on the west; Armstrong and Potter counties in the south central area; and Collingsworth, Wheeler, Lipscomb, and Ochiltree counties on the east. The census count gives only a generalized idea of distribution, however, because cattle are obviously counted as present in the counties of ranchers' headquarters, not in counties where they in fact grazed.[55]

Explaining the decline in sheep raising in terms of the rise of the cattle industry is substantially valid because it was through cattle, not sheep, that wealthy investors expected to become even wealthier. More specific contributing factors are these: Roughly half of Hartley, Oldham, and Deaf Smith counties—the former domain of sheepmen—became part of the XIT ranch through Texas' trade of three million acres of public land for a new capitol at Austin.[56] Cattle, not sheep, concerned the XIT and adjacent ranches.[57] The XIT, moreover, had title to its lands while the New Mexican sheepmen depended, apparently exclusively, on free range.

Unusually severe weather in the 1880's made sheep raising a tenuous enterprise—and certainly did not enhance the cattle business. According to one observer, the "New Zealand Sheep Company," an English-Scotch con-

---

[52] U.S. Bureau of the Census, "Sheep and Wool on Farms by Counties," *Report of the Statistics of Agriculture in the United States at the Eleventh Census: 1890*, pp. 267-269.

[53] U.S. Bureau of the Census, "Number and Total Value of Specified Domestic Animals on Farms and Ranges, June 1, 1900," *Twelfth Census of the United States Taken in the Year 1900: Agriculture*, Part I, pp. 480-485.

[54] U.S. Bureau of the Census, "Neat Cattle and Dairy Products by Counties, 1890," *Statistics of Agriculture, Eleventh Census, 1890*, pp. 307-310.

[55] For example, Armstrong County lists 44,109 head while Randall lists 349 and Donley 302; Potter County lists 44,193 while Oldham and Moore list none and Carson County only 343.

[56] Frederick W. Rathjen, "The Texas State House," *Southwestern Historical Quarterly* 60 (April 1959): 433-438.

[57] As late as 1930 the western High Plains remained essentially a large land unit grazing area. See Elmer H. Johnson, *The Natural Regions of Texas*, p. 141.

cern lately arrived from New Zealand, put 100,000 sheep on Alamocitos Creek in the late seventies. An extreme winter in 1880-1881 drove the sheep out on the High Plains to the southwest. Their *pastores* died (presumably freezing to death trying to protect their sheep), and "worlds" of sheep were lost.[58] Similarly, the winter of 1885-1886 brought unusually bad snowstorms.[59] Finally, some evidence indicates that cattlemen (inferentially in the late seventies or early eighties) more or less forcibly expelled—"There was some hard feeling."—New Mexicans who grazed sheep along the Canadian during the spring.[60]

In the middle 1880's the Panhandle depended still upon Dodge City as a commercial outlet and source of goods. Trail drives from Panhandle ranches took cattle to Dodge for shipment, while Dodge City merchandise was hauled over the back-trail to supply the ranches.[61] Although freighting admirably supplied the needs of a simple society, real regional development required more efficient transportation, namely, railroads.

The railroad need first was met by the Fort Worth and Denver City Railway, which commenced construction near Fort Worth on February 27, 1882. Progressing slowly toward the Panhandle, the rails reached "New" Clarendon—which was moved about five miles southward from the original townsite to get on the railroad—October 31, 1887.[62] Not only the location but also the character of Clarendon changed. No longer the hand-picked, homogeneous group of moralists so adored by Carhart, Clarendon's population now contained "strange faces and strange people . . . everywhere. The name was unchanged but that was all."[63]

[58] Interview, Harry Ingerton to J. Evetts Haley, June 19, 1937, Earl Vandale Collection, Archives, University of Texas at Austin.

[59] Interview, John Woods to L. F. Sheffy, December 28, 1929, Panhandle-Plains Historical Museum.

[60] Interview, J. E. McAllister to J. Evetts Haley, July 1, 1926, Panhandle-Plains Historical Museum. Doubtlessly McAllister knew whereof he spoke, but the occurrence of cowman-sheepman violence was surely very limited and, like the rancher-nester matter, should be kept in perspective.

[61] John Arnot, "Ranches" (MS, Earl Vandale Collection, Archives, University of Texas at Austin), n.p. For a general account of freighting in the Panhandle, see Billy N. Pope, "The Freighter and Railroader in the Economic Pattern of Panhandle History" (M.A. thesis, West Texas State College, 1956), especially pp. 4-11 and 30-44.

[62] Ida Marie Williams Lowe, "The Role of the Railroads in the Settlement of the Texas Panhandle" (M.A. thesis, West Texas State College, 1962), pp. 14-15, 18. Lewis, *Between Sun and Sod*, p. 223. The definitive history of the Fort Worth and Denver is Richard C. Overton, *Gulf to Rockies: The Heritage of the Fort Worth and Denver-Colorado and Southern Railways, 1861-1898*. See especially pp. 131-216.

[63] Lewis, *Between Sun and Sod*, p. 223.

By the end of 1887 Fort Worth and Denver rails threaded their way up the High Plains Escarpment through northern Armstrong County to Amarillo, carefully avoiding the abrupt declivity of the Staked Plains. Moving northwestward through Potter, Oldham, Hartley, and Dallam counties, the Fort Worth and Denver reached New Mexico Territory in January 1888. Through service—Fort Worth to Denver—opened on April 1, 1888.[64]

Through a subsidiary company, the Texas Townsite Company, the railroad developed several towns along its route, especially through the eastern Panhandle. Widely advertising the virtues, advantages, and blessings of the Texas Panhandle, the Texas Townsite Company successfully sought population, attracted settlers, and created business for the Fort Worth and Denver.[65] Almost simultaneously, Santa Fe rails entered the Panhandle from the northeast and terminated at Panhandle—then called Panhandle City.[66] Like the Fort Worth and Denver, the Santa Fe became an active "colonization" agency for the region.[67]

Although some counties showed little population growth by 1890, the impact of the Fort Worth and Denver and perhaps of the Texas Townsite Company showed clearly in others. Aggregate population for the twenty-six-county region climbed from 1,607 persons in 1880 to 9,452 in 1890.[68] Childress, Donley, Armstrong, and Potter counties—all cut by Fort Worth and Denver rails—jumped conspicuously. How much responsibility for this population pattern may be attributed directly to the Texas

[64] Lowe, "Railroads and Panhandle Settlement," pp. 15-16.
[65] Ibid., pp. 19ff.
[66] Ibid., pp. 41-42.
[67] Ibid., pp. 42ff. By 1910 railroad construction through the Panhandle was complete. Besides the Fort Worth and Denver, the Santa Fe crossed the Panhandle to the southwest having built from Panhandle through Amarillo and into New Mexico at Clovis and also connected Amarillo to the South Plains through Canyon, Plainview, and Lubbock. The Rock Island crossed the region's northwestern corner and its east-west axis through Amarillo. The three roads thus intersected at Amarillo—doubtlessly one of the most significant reasons for Amarillo's early emergence as the metropolitan center of the region. Since their success depended upon an economically viable region, all three railroads assiduously promoted settlement and agricultural development.
[68] Population density per square mile was .06 person in 1880; .37 person in 1890; and with a total population of 21, 274 persons in 1900, .83 person per square mile. Panhandle population in 1910 totaled 89,285 persons, a density of 3.5 persons per square mile. See U.S. Bureau of the Census, "Composition and Characteristics of the Population for the State and for Counties, 1910," *Thirteenth Census of the United States Taken in the Year 1910: Population, Nebraska-Wyoming*, pp. 804-851.

Townsite Company is conjectural, but the impact of the railroad on regional development is inescapable.

Very quickly in its development, therefore, the Panhandle established a precedent for concentration of population along major arteries of transportation, or the "sutland" and "yonland" concept of population distribution as defined in Carl F. Kraenzel's perceptive study of the Great Plains, which modern *llaneros* (if they know what that term means) ought to take very seriously.[69]

Despite its sparsity of population the Texas Panhandle by 1890 clearly was the possession of domiciled Anglo-Americans and with accuracy the Superintendent of the Census could announce in his report of that year: "Up to and including 1880 the country had a frontier of settlement, but at present the unsettled area has been so broken into by isolated bodies of settlement that there can hardly be said to be a frontier line."[70]

Since the census reports rarely achieve prominence among the reading public, the superintendent's observation escaped notice until Frederick Jackson Turner's essay, "The Significance of the Frontier in American History" appeared in 1893.[71]

In drawing conclusions and comparisons between the Turnerian frontier concept and what happened in the restricted area of the Texas Panhandle, two important premises should be kept in mind: (1) the frontier that Turner *really* knew was that of the eastern woodland, not that of a semiarid, treeless frontier as obtained in the Texas Panhandle; and (2) Turner tried imaginatively and courageously to draw broad historical interpretations from a broad phase of national experience—always a risky thing to do—while the Texas Panhandle frontier is but a brush stroke on Turner's much larger canvas.

Subject to the foregoing qualifications, the following comparisons between the Turner thesis and the Panhandle frontier may be drawn.

(1) If a mere unoccupied area qualifies as a frontier, then the Panhandle frontier supports Turner's notion that in 1880 "the frontier was found in these mining camps and ranches of the Great Plains."[72]

---

[69] Carl F. Kraenzel, *The Great Plains in Transition*, pp. 196-197.

[70] U.S. Bureau of the Census, *Report on the Population of the United States at the Eleventh Census, 1890*, Part I, p. xxxiv.

[71] This essay is Chapter I in Frederick Jackson Turner, *The Frontier in American History*, pp. 1-38.

[72] Ibid., p. 9.

(2) Turner perceived a series of occupational stages—"fur trader, miner, cattle-raiser, and farmer"—as advancing the frontier. Says Turner: "Each passed in successive waves across the continent. Stand at Cumberland Gap and watch the procession of civilization, marching single file—the buffalo following the trail to the salt springs, the Indian, the fur-trader and hunter, the cattle raiser, the pioneer farmer—and the frontier has passed by. Stand at South Pass in the Rockies a century later and see the same procession with wider intervals between."[73]

Although the details do not coincide, Panhandle history supports the basic Turnerian idea of the frontier advancing through a series of distinct occupational stages. In the case of the Panhandle frontier the stages—not strictly occupational in the sense of profit-seeking in every case—reduce to a procession of (a) adventurers who entered the region for differing purposes (chapter 4); (b) scientific explorers (chapter 5); (c) buffalo hunters who may legitimately be construed as part of the fur trade (chapter 6); (d) military conquerors sent by the national government (chapter 7); and (e) physical occupiers of the region—Anglo-American civilians (chapter 8).

(3) While Turner regarded the frontier experience as strongly Anglo-American, the Texas Panhandle frontier was emphatically multinational. The region was Spain's frontier for almost three centuries and Mexico's for a quarter century after Spain's withdrawal. Further, the region was touched by the frontiers of France and England, since the pulsations of imperial competition vibrated across the Panhandle. The Texas Panhandle frontier, therefore, more nearly fits into the multinational concept of the frontier as is implicit in the works of Francis Parkman and Herbert Eugene Bolton than into a uninational concept.

Finally, the obvious historiographical question asks, what does the Panhandle frontier say about Walter Prescott Webb's great interpretive work, *The Great Plains*? The general answer is that so far as this study goes, Panhandle history strongly supports Webb. There are only a few exceptions. In chapter 2 Webb's interpretation of the Plains Indians as unusually vicious and cruel was challenged, and this writer holds that no reliable evidence supports that characterization. In Webb's defense it should be said that his conclusions were not unreasonable on the basis of the evidence available when he wrote *The Great Plains*, for he had nothing like the excellent ethno-anthropological studies available to present scholars. As to the question of the origins of the cultural characteristics of the

[73] Ibid., p. 12.

historic Plains Indians, also raised in chapter 2, this writer contends that the weight of current scholarly opinion supports Webb beyond a reasonable doubt.

With respect to the Spaniards and the Great Plains, Webb is essentially correct. Actually, the Spaniards were somewhat more successful explorers than even Webb credited them with being, as demonstrated by the latter-day triumphs of Vial, Mares, and Amangual. Militarily the Spaniards did win a few rounds in their combats with mounted Plains warriors, but Webb is hands down right in his beautifully expressed contention that the Spaniards ultimately were helpless to deal with "a people who could not be conquered, would not be converted, had no property to confiscate, and steadfastly refused to produce any."[74]

Exploration of the Panhandle fits easily into the generalized pattern of exploration and trail marking described by Webb, although he apparently did not recognize the importance of national government as the agent behind this highly important phase of western American development.

Relative to the ultimate conquest of the Plains Indians by Anglo-Americans, Webb seems to consider destruction of the buffalo as the key factor. The buffalo, says Webb, "was life, food, raiment, and shelter to the Indians." This is absolutely right. "The buffalo and the Indians lived together," continues Webb, "and together passed away."[75] This also is right, but it ignores the military conquest of the Plains Indians—that they were physically whipped in the field. Immediately granting that the military phase of Plains history is outside the conceptual framework of *The Great Plains*, the cause and effect relationship among military operations, annihilation of the buffalo, and subjugation of the Plains Indians remains to be established. On the basis of his study of what happened in the Texas Panhandle, this writer concludes that while destruction of the buffalo herds materially weakened the Indians' hold upon the land, they were eleminated as obstacles to white settlement only through defeat by military forces.

As to the cattle kingdom, its history in the Texas Panhandle gives no reason to alter Webb's interpretation of its general relationship to the history of the Great Plains and the American West.

---

[74] Walter Prescott Webb, *The Great Plains*, p. 88.
[75] Ibid., p. 44.

# BIBLIOGRAPHY

Manuscripts

Arnot, John. "A History of Tascosa." Earl Vandale Collection, Archives, University of Texas at Austin.

———. "Ranches." Earl Vandale Collection, Archives, University of Texas at Austin.

———. "Tascosa Trail." Earl Vandale Collection, Archives, University of Texas at Austin.

———. "The First Cattlemen on the Canadian and Adjacent Territory." Earl Vandale Collection, Archives, University of Texas at Austin.

Bullis, Pat. "Ranging the East Panhandle." Earl Vandale Collection, Archives, University of Texas at Austin.

Conlyn, R. H. "Diary, 1883." Earl Vandale Collection, Archives, University of Texas at Austin.

Gerdis, Bruce. "The Mackenzie Battle." Gerdis Papers, Panhandle-Plains Historical Museum, Canyon, Texas.

Hatfield, Col. Charles A. P. "The Comanche, Kiowa, and Cheyenne Campaign in Northwest Texas and Mackenzie's Fight in the Palo Duro Cañon, September 26, 1874." Panhandle-Plains Historical Museum, Canyon, Texas.

Lowe, Ida Marie Williams. "The Role of the Railroads in the Settlement of the Texas Panhandle." M.A. thesis, West Texas State College, 1962.

McCarty, John Lawton. "The History of Tascosa, Texas." M.A. thesis, West Texas State Teachers College, 1945.

McGee, H. T. "Some Panhandle and Plains History." Earl Vandale Collection, Archives, University of Texas at Austin.

Oswald, James Marlin. "Fort Elliott, Texas Frontier Post." M.A. thesis, West Texas State College, 1958.

Paine, Clinton Leon. "The History of Lipscomb County." M.A. thesis, West Texas State Teachers College, 1941.

Pope, Billy N. "The Freighter and Railroader in the Economic Pattern of Panhandle History." M.A. thesis, West Texas State College, 1956.

War Department. Adjutant General's Office, File No. 2815-1874. "Military Correspondence Relating to the Red River War, 1874-1875." Microfilm Collection, Panhandle-Plains Historical Museum, Canyon, Texas.

Works Progress Administration, Federal Writer's Program, Swisher County, Texas. "Notes." Earl Vandale Collection, Archives, University of Texas at Austin.

XIT Ranch. "Annual Report, 1887." XIT Papers, Panhandle-Plains Historical Museum, Canyon, Texas.

Government Documents

Abert, James W. *Journal of Lieutenant James W. Abert, from Bent's Fort to St. Louis in 1845*, 29th Cong., 1st sess., Sen. Exec. Doc. 438 (1846).

Baker, E. T., Jr.; A. T. Long; R. D. Reeves; and Leonard A. Wood. *Reconnaissance Investigation of the Ground-Water Resources of the Red River, Sulpher River, and Cypress Creek Basins, Texas*. Texas Water Commission Bulletin 6303, July 1963.

Carter, William T., Jr. *Reconnaissance Soil Survey of the Panhandle Region of Texas*. Washington: Government Printing Office, 1911.

*Congressional Globe*. 32nd Congress, 2nd sess. XXVI, 1853. Washington: John C. Rives, 1853.

Gould, Charles N. *The Geology and Water Resources of the Eastern Portion of the Panhandle of Texas*. U.S. Geological Survey, Water Supply and Irrigation Paper No. 154. Washington: Government Printing Office, 1906.

——. *The Geology and Water Resources of the Western Portion of the Panhandle of Texas*. U.S. Geological Survey, Water Supply and Irrigation Paper No. 191. Washington: Government Printing Office, 1907.

Hodge, Frederick Webb, ed. *Handbook of American Indians North of Mexico*. Bureau of American Ethnology, Bulletin 30. 2 parts. Washington: Government Printing Office, 1912.

Hornaday, William T. "The Extermination of the American Bison." *Annual Report of the United States National Museum*. Part II. Washington: Government Printing Office, 1889.

Johnson, Willard D. "The High Plains and Their Utilization." *Twenty-first Annual Report of the United States Geological Survey*, Part IV. Washington: Government Printing Office, 1901.

——. "The High Plains and Their Utilization." *Twenty-second Annual Report of the United States Geological Survey*, Part IV. Washington: Government Printing Office, 1902.

Kappler, Charles J., comp. *Indian Affairs. Laws and Treaties*. 2 vols. Washington: Government Printing Office, 1904.

Malloy, William M., comp. *Treaties, Conventions, International Acts, Protocols and Agreements between the United States of America and Other Powers, 1776-1909*. 2 vols. Washington: Government Printing Office, 1910.

Marcy, Randolph B. *Exploration of the Red River of Louisiana, in the Year 1852*. Washington: Beverley Tucker, Senate Printer, 1854.

——. "The Report of Capt. R. B. Marcy's Route from Fort Smith to

Santa Fe." *Reports of the Secretary of War*, 31st Cong., 1st. sess., Sen. Exec. Doc. No. 64 (1850).

Mooney, James. "Calendar History of the Kiowa Indians." *Seventeenth Annual Report of the Bureau of American Ethnology, 1895-1986*. Part I. Washington: Government Printing Office, 1898.

Simpson, James H. "Report and Map of the Route from Fort Smith, Arkansas, to Santa Fe, New Mexico, made by Lieutenant Simpson." *Report from the Secretary of War*, 31st Cong., 1st sess., Sen. Exec. Doc. No. 12 (1850).

Texas Board of Water Engineers. *Reconnaissance Investigation of the Ground Water Resources of the Canadian River Basin, Texas*. Texas Board of Water Engineers Bulletin 6016, September 1960.

U.S. Bureau of the Census. *Report on the Productions of Agriculture as Returned at the Tenth Census: 1880*. Washington: Government Printing Office, 1883.

——. *Report of the Statistics of Agriculture in the United States at the Eleventh Census: 1890*. Washington: Government Printing Office, 1895.

——. *Report on the Population of the United States at the Eleventh Census: 1890*. 2 parts. Washington: Government Printing Office, 1895.

——. *Statistics of the Population of the United States at the Tenth Census: 1880*. Washington: Government Printing Office, 1883.

——. *Twelfth Census of the United States Taken in the Year 1900: Agriculture*. 2 parts. Washington: United States Census Office, 1902.

——. *Twelfth Census of the United States Taken in the Year 1900: Population*. 2 parts. Washington: United States Census Office, 1901.

——. *Thirteenth Census of the United States Taken in the Year 1910: Population, Nebraska-Wyoming*. Washington: Government Printing Office, 1913.

U.S. Department of Agriculture. *Climate and Man*. 1941 Yearbook of Agriculture. Washington: Government Printing Office, 1941.

——. *Soils and Men. 1938 Yearbook of Agriculture*. Washington Government Printing Office, 1938.

U.S. Department of Commerce, Weather Bureau. *Climatography of the United States No. 86-36, Decennial Census of United States Climate—Climatic Summary of the United States—Supplement for 1951 through 1960, Texas*. Washington: Government Printing Office, 1965.

*United States Statutes at Large*. 40th Cong., 1st sess., XV, 1867. Boston: Little, Brown, 1869.

*The War of the Rebellion: A Compilation of the Official Records of the Union and Confederate Armies*. 130 vols. Washington: Government Printing Office, 1880-1901.

Whipple, A. W. "Report of Explorations of a Railway Route, Near the Thirty-Fifth Parallel of North Latitude, from the Mississippi River to the Pacific Ocean." *Reports of Explorations and Surveys, to Ascertain the Most Practical and Economical Route for a Railroad from the Mississippi River to the Pacific Ocean.* Vol. III, 33d Cong., 1st sess., House of Representatives, Exec. Doc. No. 91 (1856).

Winship, George Parker. "The Coronado Expedition, 1540-1542." *Fourteenth Annual Report of the Bureau of* [American] *Ethnology, 1892-1893*, Part I. Washington: Government Printing Office, 1896.

Books and Pamphlets

Bladwin, Alice Blackwood, *Memoris of the Late Frank D. Baldwin.* Los Angeles: Wetzel, 1929.

Bancroft, Hubert Howe. *History of Arizona and New Mexico, 1530-1888,* Facsimile of 1889 ed. Albuquerque: Horn and Wallace, 1962.

Bandelier, A. F. *The Gilded Man.* New York: D. Appleton, 1893.

——, and Fanny R. Bandelier. *Historical Documents Relating to New Mexico, Nueva Viscaya, and Approaches Thereto, to 1773.* Translated and edited by Charles Wilson Hackett. 3 vols. Washington: Carnegie Institution of Washington, 1923, 1926, 1937.

Bandelier, Fanny, trans. *The Journey of Alvar Nuñez Cabeza de Vaca and His Companions from Florida to the Pacific, 1528-1536.* New York: A. S. Barnes, 1905.

Bannon, John Francis, ed. *Bolton and the Spanish Borderlands.* Norman: University of Oklahoma Press, 1964.

Basso, Keith H., and Morris E. Opler, eds. *Apachean Culture History and Ethnology.* Anthropological Papers of the University of Arizona Number 21. Tucson: University of Arizona Press, 1971.

Beck, Warren A. *New Mexico: A History of Four Centuries.* Norman: University of Oklahoma Press, 1962.

Berthrong, Donald J. *The Southern Cheyennes.* Norman: University of Oklahoma Press, 1963.

Bishop, Morris. *The Odyssey of Cabeza de Vaca.* New York: Century, 1933.

Bolton, Herbert E. *Coronado: Knight of Pueblos and Plains.* Albuquerque: University of New Mexico Press, 1949.

——. *Texas in the Middle Eighteenth Century.* Berkeley: University of California Press, 1915.

——. *The Spanish Borderlands.* New Haven: Yale University Press, 1921.

——, trans. and ed. *Athanase de Mézierès and the Louisiana-Texas Frontier, 1768-1780.* Cleveland: Arthur H. Clark, 1914. Two volumes.

———, ed. *Spanish Exploration in the Southwest, 1542-1706*. New York: Barnes and Noble, 1946.

Burton, Harley True. *A History of the JA Ranch*. Austin: Von Boeckmann-Jones, 1928.

Cabeza de Baca, Fabiola. *We Fed Them Cactus*. Albuquerque: University of New Mexico Press, 1954.

Carriker, Robert C. *Fort Supply, Indian Territory: Frontier Outpost on the Plains*. Norman: University of Oklahoma Press, 1970.

Carroll, H. Bailey, ed. *Gúadal P'a: The Journal of Lieutenant J. W. Abert, from Bent's Fort to St. Louis in 1845*. Canyon: Panhandle-Plains Historical Society, 1941.

———. *The Texan Santa Fe Trail*. Canyon: Panhandle-Plains Historical Society, 1951.

Carter, R. G. *On the Border with Mackenzie*. Washington: Eynon Printing, 1935.

———. *The Old Sergeant's Story*. New York: Frederick H. Hitchcock, 1926.

Carter, W. T. *Soils of Texas*. Texas Agricultural Experiment Station Bulletin No. 431. College Station, 1931.

Castañeda, Carlos E. *Our Catholic Heritage in Texas, 1519-1936*. 7 vols. Austin: Von Boeckmann-Jones, 1936-1958.

Chittenden, Hiram Martin. *The American Fur Trade of the Far West*. 2 vols. Stanford: Academic Reprints, 1954.

Collinson, Frank. *Life in the Saddle*. Edited by Mary Whatley Clarke. Norman: University of Oklahoma Press, 1963.

Cook, John R. *The Border and the Buffalo*. Topeka, Kansas: Crane, 1907.

Custer, George Armstrong. *My Life on the Plains*. Norman: University of Oklahoma Press, 1962.

Dixon, Olive K. *Life of "Billy" Dixon*. Dallas: Southwest Press, 1927.

Dodge, Richard Irving. *Our Wild Indians: Thirty-three Years' Personal Experience among the Red Men of the Great West*. Hartford, Conn.: A. D. Worthington, 1882.

———. *The Hunting Grounds of the Great West*. London: Chatto and Windus, 1878.

Driver, Harold E. *Indians of North America*. Chicago: University of Chicago Press, 1961.

Duke, Cordia Sloan, and Joe B. Frantz. *6,000 Miles of Fence: Life on the XIT Ranch of Texas*. Austin: University of Texas Press, 1961.

Fenneman, Nevin M. *Physiography of Western United States*. New York: McGraw-Hill Book Company, 1931.

Folmer, Henry. *Franco-Spanish Rivalry in North America, 1524-1763*. Glendale: Arthur H. Clark, 1953.

Foreman, Grant, ed. *Marcy and the Gold Seekers*. Norman: University of Oklahoma Press, 1939.

Frink, Maurice, ed. *When Grass Was King*. Boulder: University of Colorado Press, 1956.

Fulton, Maurice Garland, ed. *Diary and Letters of Josiah Gregg: Southwestern Enterprises, 1840-1847*. Norman: University of Oklahoma Press, 1941.

Gammel, H. P. N., comp. *Laws of Texas, 1822-1897*. 10 vols. Austin: Gammel Book Company, 1898.

Gard, Wayne. *The Great Buffalo Hunt*. New York: Alfred A. Knopf, 1959.

Goetzmann, William H. *Army Exploration in the American West*. New Haven: Yale University Press, 1959.

———. *Exploration and Empire: The Explorer and the Scientist in the Winning of the American West*. New York: Alfred A. Knopf, 1966.

Gracy, David B., II. *Littlefield Lands: Colonization on the Texas Plains, 1912-1920*. Austin: University of Texas Press, 1968.

Graves, Lawrence L., ed. *A History of Lubbock*. Lubbock: West Texas Museum Association, 1962.

Gregg, Josiah. *Commerce of the Prairies: The Journal of a Santa Fe Trader*. Reprint edition. Dallas: Southwest Press, 1933.

Hackett, Charles Wilson, trans. and ed. *Pichardo's Treatise on the Limits of Louisiana and Texas*. 4 vols. Austin: University of Texas Press, 1931-1946.

———, and Charmion Clair Shelby. *Revolt of the Pueblo Indians of New Mexico and Otermín's Attempted Reconquest, 1680-1682*. 2 vols. Albuquerque: University of New Mexico Press, 1942.

Haley, J. Evetts. *Charles Goodnight: Cowman and Plainsman*. Boston: Houghton Mifflin Company, 1936.

———. *Fort Concho and the Texas Frontier*. San Angelo: San Angelo *Standard-Times*, 1952.

———. *George W. Littlefield: Texan*. Norman: University of Oklahoma Press, 1943.

———. *The XIT Ranch of Texas and the Early Days of the Llano Estacado*. Chicago: Lakeside Press, 1929.

Hallenbeck, Cleve. *Alvar Núñez Cabeza de Vaca: The Journey and Route of the First European to Cross the Continent of North America, 1534-1536*. Glendale: Arthur H. Clark, 1940.

———. *Land of the Conquistadores*. Caldwell, Idaho: Caxton, 1950.

Hamilton, Holman. *Prologue to Conflict: The Crisis and Compromise of 1850*. Lexington: University of Kentucky Press, 1964.

Hammond, George P., and Agapito Rey. *Don Juan de Oñate: Colonizer of*

*New Mexico, 1595-1628.* 2 vols. Albuquerque: University of New Mexico Press, 1953.

———. *Narratives of the Coronado Expedition 1540-1542.* Albuquerque: University of New Mexico Press, 1940.

———. *The Rediscovery of New Mexico, 1580-1594.* Albuquerque: University of New Mexico Press, 1966.

Hodge, Frederick Webb, and Theodore H. Lewis, eds. *Spanish Explorations in the Southern United States, 1528-1543.* New York: Barnes and Noble, 1946.

Holden, W. C. *Rollie Burns.* Dallas: Southwest Press, 1932.

Holden, William Curry. *The Espuela Land and Cattle Company: A Study of a Foreign-Owned Ranch in Texas.* Austin: Texas State Historical Association, 1970.

———. *The Spur Ranch.* Boston: Christopher Publishing House, 1934.

Hollon, W. Eugene. *The Great American Desert: Then and Now.* New York: Oxford University Press, 1966.

Hopkins, David M., ed. *The Bering Land Bridge.* Stanford: Stanford University Press, 1967.

Johnson, Elmer H. *The Natural Regions of Texas.* University of Texas Bulletin No. 3113. Austin: University of Texas, 1931.

Jones, Douglas C. *The Treaty of Medicine Lodge.* Norman: University of Oklahoma Press, 1966.

Kendall, George Wilkins. *Narrative of the Texan Santa Fe Expedition.* 2 vols. New York: Harper and Brothers, 1844.

Kenner, Charles L. *A History of New Mexican-Plains Indian Relations.* Norman: University of Oklahoma Press, 1969.

Kraenzel, Carl Frederick. *The Great Plains in Transition.* Norman: University of Oklahoma Press, 1955.

Krieger, Alex D. *Culture Complexes and Chronology in Northern Texas with Extension of Puebloan Datings to the Mississippi Valley.* University of Texas Publication No. 4640. Austin: University of Texas Press, 1946.

Lavender, David. *Bent's Fort.* Garden City, N.J.: Doubleday, 1954.

Leckie, William H. *The Military Conquest of the Southern Plains.* Norman: University of Oklahoma Press, 1963.

Lewis, Willie Newbury. *Between Sun and Sod.* Clarendon: Clarendon Press, 1938.

Loomis, Noel M. *The Texan-Santa Fe Pioneers.* Norman: University of Oklahoma Press, 1958.

———, and Abraham P. Nasatir. *Pedro Vial and the Roads to Santa Fe.* Norman: University of Oklahoma Press, 1967.

Lowie, Robert H. *Indians of the Plains.* New York: McGraw-Hill, 1954.

McCarty, John L. *Maverick Town: The Story of Old Tascosa*. Norman: University of Oklahoma Press, 1946.

McNitt, Frank. *The Indian Traders*. Norman: University of Oklahoma Press, 1962.

Malone, Dumas, ed. *Dictionary of American Biography*. 11 vols. New York: Charles Scribner's Sons, 1961.

Marcy, Randolph B. *Adventure on Red River*. Edited by Grant Foreman. Norman: University of Oklahoma Press, 1937.

———. *The Prairie Traveler: A Handbook for Overland Expeditions*. New York: Harper and Brothers, 1859.

———. *Thirty Years of Army Life on the Border*. New York: Harper and Brothers, 1866.

Mayhall, Mildred P. *The Kiowas*. Norman: University of Oklahoma Press, 1962.

Miles, Nelson A. *Personal Recollections and Observations*. Chicago: Werner, 1896.

Moorehead, Waren King. *Archaeology of the Arkansas River Valley*. New Haven: Yale University Press, 1931.

Nash, Roderick. *Wilderness and the American Mind*. New Haven: Yale University Press, 1967.

Newcomb, W. W., Jr. *The Indians of Texas: From Prehistoric to Modern Times*. Austin: University of Texas Press, 1961.

Nordyke, Louis. *Cattle Empire: The Fabulous Story of the 3,000,000 Acre XIT*. New York: William Morrow, 1949.

Nye, W. S. *Carbine and Lance: The Story of Old Fort Sill*. Norman: University of Oklahoma Press, 1942.

Overton, Richard C. *Gulf to Rockies: The Heritage of the Fort Worth and Denver-Colorado and Southern Railways, 1861-1898*. Austin: University of Texas Press, 1953.

Pearce, W. M. *The Matador Land and Cattle Company*. Norman: University of Oklahoma Press, 1964.

Prucha, Francis Paul. *A Guide to the Military Posts of the United States, 1789-1895*. Madison: State Historical Society of Wisconsin, 1964.

Richardson, Rupert Norval. *The Comanche Barrier to South Plains Settlement*. Glendale: Arthur H. Clark, 1933.

———. *The Frontier of Northwest Texas, 1846-1876*. Glendale: Arthur H. Clark, 1963.

Rister, Carl Coke. *Border Command: General Phil Sheridan in the West*. Norman: University of Oklahoma Press, 1944.

———. *Fort Griffin on the Texas Frontier*. Norman: University of Oklahoma Press, 1956.

Roe, Frank Gilbert. *The Indian and the Horse.* Norman: University of Oklahoma Press, 1955.

——. *The North American Buffalo: A Critical Study of the Species in Its Wild State.* Toronto: University of Toronto Press, 1951.

Schmeckebier, Laurence F. *The Office of Indian Affairs: Its History, Activities and Organization.* Baltimore: Johns Hopkins Press, 1927.

Sheffy, Lester Fields. *The Francklyn Land & Cattle Company: A Panhandle Enterprise, 1882-1957.* Austin: University of Texas Press, 1963.

——. *The Life and Times of Timothy Dwight Hobart, 1855-1935.* Canyon: Panhandle-Plains Historical Society, 1950.

Sheridan, P. H. *Personal Memoirs.* 2 vols. New York: Charles L. Webster, 1888.

Taylor, Joe F., ed. *The Indian Campaign on the Staked Plains, 1874-1875.* Canyon: Panhandle-Plains Historical Society, 1962.

*Texas Almanac, 1970-1971.* Dallas: *Dallas Morning News*, 1970.

Tharp, Benjamin Carroll. *Texas Range Grasses.* Austin: University of Texas Press, 1952.

Thomas, Alfred Barnaby, trans. and ed. *After Coronado: Spanish Exploration Northeast of New Mexico, 1696-1727.* Norman: University of Oklahoma Press, 1935.

——, trans. and ed. *Forgotten Frontiers: A Study of the Spanish Indian Policy of Don Juan Bautista de Anza, 1777-1787.* Norman: University of Oklahoma Press, 1932.

——, trans. and ed. *Teodoro de Croix and the Northern Frontier of New Spain, 1776-1783.* Norman: University of Oklahoma Press, 1941.

——. *The Plains Indians and New Mexico, 1751-1778.* Albuquerque: University of New Mexico Press, 1940.

Thornbury, William D. *Regional Geomorphology of the United States.* New York: John Wiley, 1965.

Thwaites, Reuben Gold, ed. *Early Western Travels, 1748-1846.* 32 vols. Cleveland: Arthur H. Clark, 1905-1907.

Timmons, William. *Twilight on the Range: Recollections of a Latter Day Cowboy.* Austin: University of Texas Press, 1962.

Turner, Frederick Jackson. *The Frontier in American History.* New York: Henry Holt, 1947.

Twitchell, Ralph Emerson. *The Leading Facts of New Mexico History.* 2 vols., facsimile edition. Albuquerque: Horn and Wallace, 1963.

Wallace, Ernest. *Ranald S. Mackenzie on the Texas Frontier.* Lubbock: West Texas Museum Association, 1964.

——, ed. *Ranald S. Mackenzie's Official Correspondence Relating to Texas, 1871-1873.* Lubbock: West Texas Museum Association, 1967.

———, and E. Adamson Hoebel. *The Comanches: Lords of the South Plains*. Norman: University of Oklahoma Press, 1952.

———, and David M. Vigness, eds. *Documents of Texas History*. Austin: Steck, 1963.

Ward, Robert DeCourcy. *The Climates of the United States*. Boston: Ginn, 1925.

Webb, Walter Prescott. *An Honest Preface and Other Essays*. Edited by Joe B. Frantz. Boston: Houghton Mifflin, 1959.

———. *The Great Plains*. Boston: Ginn, 1931.

Wedel, Waldo R. *Prehistoric Man on the Great Plains*. Norman: University of Oklahoma Press, 1961.

West Texas State University Geological Society. *Geology of Palo Duro Canyon State Park and the Panhandle of Texas*. Canyon: West Texas State University Geological Society, 1966.

Wilbarger, J. W. *Indian Depredations in Texas*. Austin: Pemberton Press, 1967.

Willey, Gordon R. *An Introduction to American Archaeology: North and Middle America*. Englewood Cliffs, New Jersey: Prentice-Hall, 1966.

Winfrey, Dorman H., and James M. Day, eds. *The Indian Papers of Texas and the Southwest, 1825-1916*. 5 vols. Austin: Pemberton Press, 1966.

Wissler, Clark. *North American Indians of the Plains*. New York: American Museum of Natural History, 1934.

———. *The American Indian*. New York: Oxford University Press, 1922.

Wormington, H. M. *Ancient Man in North America*. Denver: Denver Museum of Natural History, 1957.

Journals

Archambeau, Ernest R. "The Battle of Lyman's Wagon Train." *Panhandle-Plains Historical Review* 36 (1963).

———. "The First Federal Census in the Panhandle, 1880." *Panhandle-Plains Historical Review* 23 (1950).

———. "The Fort Smith-Santa Fe Trail along the Canadian River in Texas." *Panhandle-Plains Historical Review* 27 (1954).

———, ed. "Lieutenant A. W. Whipple's Railroad Reconnaissance Across the Panhandle of Texas in 1853." *Panhandle-Plains Historical Review* 44 (1971).

Arnot, John. "My Recollections of Tascosa Before and After the Coming of the Law." *Panhandle-Plains Historical Review* 6 (1933).

Baird, Josie, "Ranching on the Two Circles Bar." *Panhandle-Plains Historical Review* 17 (1944).

Bolton, Herbert E. "The Spanish Occupation of Texas, 1519-1690." *Southwestern Historical Quarterly* 16, no. 1 (July 1912).

Brant, Charles S. "Kiowa Apache Culture History: Some Further Observations." *Southwestern Journal of Anthropology* 9, no. 2 (Summer 1953).

———. "The Cultural Position of the Kiowa-Apache." *Southwestern Journal of Anthropology* 5, no. 1 (Spring 1949).

Brayer, Herbert O. "The Influence of British Capital on the Western Range Cattle Industry." *Journal of Economic History* 9, no. 2 (November 1949, supplement).

Bryan, Frank. "The Llano Estacado: The Geographical Background of the Coronado Expedition." *Panhandle-Plains Historical Review* 13 (1940).

Cabe, Ernest, Jr. "A Sketch of the Life of James Hamilton Cator." *Panhandle-Plains Historical Review* 6 (1933).

Carroll, H. Bailey, ed. "The Journal of Lieutenant J. W. Abert from Bent's Fort to St. Louis in 1845." *Panhandle-Plains Historical Review* 14 (1941).

Connor, Seymour V. "Early Ranching Operations in the Panhandle: A Report on the Agricultural Schedules of the 1880 Census." *Panhandle-Plains Historical Review* 27 (1954).

Conrad, David E. "The Whipple Expedition on the Great Plains." *Great Plains Journal* 2, no. 2 (Spring 1963).

Day, James M. "A Preliminary Guide to the Study of Buffalo Trails in Texas." West Texas Historical Association *Yearbook* 36 (October 1960).

Donoghue, David. "The Location of Quivira." *Panhandle-Plains Historical Review* 14 (1940).

———. "The Route of the Coronado Expedition in Texas." *Southwestern Historical Quarterly* 32, no. 3 (January 1929).

Dyer, Jesse J. "A Survey of the J. Buckle Kingdom." *Panhandle-Plains Historical Review* 16 (1943).

Elliott, Margaret A. "History of D. B. Gardner's Pitchfork Ranch of Texas." *Panhandle-Plains Historical Review* 18 (1945).

Gilmore, Lee. "The Mill Iron Ranch." *Panhandle-Plains Historical Review* 5 (1932).

Graham, Richard. "The Investment Boom in British-Texan Cattle Companies, 1880-1885." *Business History Review* 34, no. 4 (Winter 1960).

Grant, Ben O. "Life in Old Fort Griffin." West Texas Historical Association *Yearbook* 10 (October 1934).

———, and J. R. Webb, contribs. "On the Cattle Trail and Buffalo Range, Joe S. Combs." West Texas Historical Association *Yearbook* 11 (November 1935).

Gunnerson, Dolores A. "The Southern Athabascans: Their Arrival in the Southwest." *El Palacio* 63, nos. 11-12 (November-December 1956).

Hackett, Charles Wilson. "Retreat of the Spaniards from New Mexico in 1680, and the Beginnings of El Paso, I." *Southwestern Historical Quarterly* 16, no. 2 (October 1912).

——. "Retreat of the Spaniards from New Mexico in 1680, and the Beginnings of El Paso, II." *Southwestern Historical Quarterly* 16, no. 3 (January 1913).

——. "The Revolt of the Pueblo Indians of New Mexico in 1680." *Quarterly of the Texas State Historical Association* 15, no. 2 (October 1911).

Haley, J. Evetts. "The Comanchero Trade." *Southwestern Historical Quarterly* 38, no. 3 (January 1935).

Harrison, Lowell H. "British Interest in the Panhandle-Plains Area, 1878-1885." *Panhandle-Plains Historical Review* 38 (1965).

——. "Damage Suits for Indian Depredations in the Adobe Walls Area, 1874." *Panhandle-Plains Historical Review* 36 (1963).

——. "The Two Battles of Adobe Walls." *Texas Military History* 5, no. 1 (Spring 1965).

——. "Union Veterans in the Texas Panhandle." *Panhandle-Plains Historical Review* 37 (1964).

Holden, W. C. "Coronado's Route across the Staked Plains." West Texas Historical Association *Yearbook* 20 (1944).

——. "Frontier Defense, 1865-1889." *Panhandle-Plains Historical Review* 2 (1929).

——. "Robert Cypret Parrack, Buffalo Hunter and Fence Cutter." West Texas Historical Association *Yearbook* 21 (October 1945).

——. "The Buffalo of the Plains Area." West Texas Historical Association *Yearbook* 2 (June 1926).

——. "West Texas Drouths." *Southwestern Historical Quarterly* 32, no. 2 (October 1928).

Hughes, Jack T. "Lake Creek: A Woodland Site in the Texas Panhandle." *Bulletin of the Texas Archeological Society* 32 [for 1961] (1962).

——, "Little Sunday: An Archaic Site in the Texas Panhandle." *Bulletin of the Texas Archeological Society* 26 (1955).

Hunter, J. Marvin. "The Battle of Adobe Walls." *Clarendon News*, September 18, 1924.

Johnston, C. Stuart. "Prehistory in the Texas Panhandle." *Panhandle-Plains Historical Review* 10 (1937).

"J. W. McKinley's Narrative." *Panhandle-Plains Historical Review* 36 (1963).

Kelley, Jane Holden. "Comments on the Archeology of the Llano Estacado." *Bulletin of the Texas Archeological Society* 35 (1964).

Kerr, W. G. "Scotland and the Texas Mortgage Business." *Panhandle-Plains Historical Review* 38 (1965).

Kinard, Knox. "The History of the Waggoner Ranch." *Panhandle-Plains Historical Review* 16 (1943).

Kincaid, Naomi H. "Rath City." West Texas Historical Association *Yearbook* 24 (October 1948).

Leckie, William H. "The Red River War, 1874-1875." *Panhandle-Plains Historical Review* 29 (1956).

Mabry, W. S. "Early West Texas and Panhandle Surveys." *Panhandle-Plains Historical Review* 2 (1929).

———. "Some Memories of W. S. Mabry." *Panhandle-Plains Historical Review* 11 (1938).

———. "The Location of Fort Elliott." *Panhandle-Plains Historical Review* 5 (1932).

McClure, C. B. "A History of the Shoe Nail Ranch." *Panhandle-Plains Historical Review* 11 (1938).

———. "A Review of the T-Anchor Ranch." *Panhandle-Plains Historical Review* 3 (1930).

———, ed. "The Battle of Adobe Walls, 1864." *Panhandle-Plains Historical Review* 21 (1948).

McGann, Thomas F. "The Ordeal of Cabeza de Vaca." *American Heritage* 12, no. 1 (December 1960).

Mooar, J. Wright. "Frontier Experiences of J. Wright Mooar." West Texas Historical Association *Yearbook* 4 (June 1928).

———. "The First Buffalo Hunting in the Panhandle." West Texas Historical Association *Yearbook* 6 (June 1930).

Officer, Helen Bugbee. "A Sketch of the Life of Thomas Sherman Bugbee: 1841-1925." *Panhandle-Plains Historical Review* 5 (1932).

Oswald, James M. "History of Fort Elliott." *Panhandle-Plains Historical Review* 32 (1959).

Paul, J. C. "Early Days in Carson County Texas." *Panhandle-Plains Historical Review* 5 (1932).

Rathjen, Frederick W. "The Texas State House." *Southwestern Historical Quarterly* 60, no. 4 (April 1957).

Richardson, Rupert N. "The Comanche Indians at the Adobe Walls Fight." *Panhandle-Plains Historical Review* 4 (1931).

Rippy, J. Fred. "British Investments in Texas Lands and Livestock." *Southwestern Historical Quarterly* 58, no. 3 (January 1955).

Rister, C. C. "Documents Relating to General W. T. Sherman [*sic*] Southern Plains Indian Policy 1871-1875." *Panhandle-Plains Historical Review* 9 (1936).

———. "Documents Relating to General W. T. Sherman's Southern Plains Indian Policy, 1871-1875, II." *Panhandle-Plains Historical Review* 10 (1937).

———. "Fort Griffin." West Texas Historical Association *Yearbook* 1 (June 1925).

———. "The Significance of the Destruction of the Buffalo in the Southwest." *Southwestern Historical Quarterly* 33, no. 1 (June 1929).

Romero, José Ynocencio. "Spanish Sheepmen on the Canadian at Old Tascosa." Edited by Ernest R. Archambeau. *Panhandle-Plains Historical Review* 19 (1946).

Schroeder, Albert H. "A Re-Analysis of the Routes of Coronado and Oñate into the Plains in 1541 and 1601." *Plains Anthropologist* 7, no. 15 (February 1962).

Shaeffer, James B. "The Alibates Flint Quarry, Texas." *American Antiquity* 24, no. 2 (October 1958).

Sheers, Margaret. "The LX Ranch of Texas." *Panhandle-Plains Historical Review* 6 (1933).

Sheffy, L. F. "British Pounds and British Purebreds." *Panhandle-Plains Historical Review* 11 (1938).

———. "Old Mobeetie—The Capital of the Panhandle." West Texas Historical Association *Yearbook* 6 (June 1930).

———. "The Experimental Stage of Settlement in the Panhandle of Texas." *Panhandle-Plains Historical Review* 3 (1930).

———. "The Spanish Horse on the Great Plains." *Panhandle-Plains Historical Review* 6 (1933).

———. "Thomas Sherman Bugbee." *Panhandle-Plains Historical Review* 2 (1929).

Sjoberg, Andree F. "Lipan Apache Culture in Historical Perspective." *Southwestern Journal of Anthropology* 9 no. 1 (Spring 1953).

Skinner, Morris F., and Ove C. Kaisen. "The Fossil *Bison* of Alaska and Preliminary Revision of the Genus." *Bulletin of the American Museum of Natural History* 89, article 3 (1947).

Strickland, Rex W., ed. "The Recollections of W. S. Glenn, Buffalo Hunter." *Panhandle-Plains Historical Review* 22 (1949).

Studer, Floyd V. "Archeology of the Texas Panhandle." *Panhandle-Plains Historical Review* 28 (1955).

———. "Discovering the Panhandle." *Panhandle-Plains Historical Review* 4 (1931).

Suhm, Dee Ann, and Alex D. Krieger. "An Introductory Handbook of Texas Archeology." *Bulletin of the Texas Archeological Society* 25 (1954).

Tinkler, Mrs. Estelle D. "The History of the Rocking Chair Ranche" [*sic*]. *Panhandle-Plains Historical Review* 15 (1942).

Tunnell, Curtis D., and Jack T. Hughes. "An Archaic Bison Kill in the Texas Panhandle." *Panhandle-Plains Historical Review* 28 (1955).

Webb, Walter Prescott. "The American West, Perpetual Mirage." *Harper's Magazine* 214, no. 1284 (May 1957).

Wedel, Waldo R. "After Coronado in Quivira." *The Kansas Historical Quarterly* 34 no. 4 (Winter 1968).

———. "Coronado's Route to Quivira, 1541." *Plains Anthropologist*. 15, no. 49 (August 1970).

West, G. Derek. "The Battle of Adobe Walls (1874)." *Panhandle-Plains Historical Review* 36 (1963).

Williams, J. W. "Coronado: From the Rio Grande to the Concho." *Southwestern Historical Quarterly* 63, no. 2 (October 1959).

Winfrey, Dorman H. "Mirabeau B. Lamar and Texas Nationalism." *Southwestern Historical Quarterly* 59, no. 2 (October 1955).

## Newspaper

Fort Smith *Herald*, November 22, 1848. Photostated clippings, Archives, University of Texas at Austin.

## Interviews

Bussell, R., to L. F. Sheffy, undated, Panhandle-Plains Historical Museum, Canyon, Texas.

Bussell, R. "Dick," to J. Evetts Haley, July 19, 1926, Panhandle-Plains Historical Museum, Canyon, Texas.

Bussell, Richard, to L. F. Sheffy, December 27, 1929, Panhandle-Plains Historical Museum, Canyon, Texas.

Carhart, Whitfield, to B. P. Brents, June 15, 1936, Earl Vandale Collection, Archives, University of Texas at Austin.

Carroll, H. Bailey, to Frederick W. Rathjen, September 24, 1959, in private possession of the author.

East, James, to J. Evetts Haley, September 27, 1927, Earl Vandale Collection, Archives, University of Texas at Austin.

Hayes, Mose, to J. Evetts Haley, June 10, 1930, Earl Vandale Collection, Archives, University of Texas at Austin.

Ingerton, Harry, to J. Evetts Haley, June 19, 1937, Panhandle-Plains Historical Museum, Canyon, Texas.

McAllister, J. E., to J. Evetts Haley, July 1, 1926, Panhandle-Plains Historical Museum, Canyon, Texas.

Mooar, J. Wright, to J. Evetts Haley, November 28, 1927, Panhandle-Plains Historical Museum, Canyon, Texas.

Mooar, J. Wright, to J. Evetts Haley, January 4, 1928, Panhandle-Plains Historical Museum, Canyon, Texas.

Mooar, J. Wright, to Frank P. Hill, J. B. Slaughter, and Jim Weatherford, May 15, 1936, Panhandle-Plains Historical Museum, Canyon, Texas.

Simpson, George A., to L. F. Sheffy, November 30, 1929, Panhandle-Plains Historical Museum, Canyon, Texas.

Woods, John, to L. F. Sheffy, December 28, 1929, Panhandle-Plains Historical Museum, Canyon, Texas.

## Depositions

Cator, James H. October 11, 1892, Indian Depredation Case No. 4593. Photocopy, Panhandle-Plains Historical Museum, Canyon, Texas.

Cator, James H. October 11, 1892, Indian Depredation Case No. 4601. Photocopy, Panhandle-Plains Historical Museum, Canyon, Texas.

Langton, James. January 28, 1896, Indian Depredation Case No. 4593. Photocopy, Panhandle-Plains Historical Museum, Canyon, Texas.

Masterson, William B. June 24, 1893, Indian Depredation Case No. 4593. Photocopy, Panhandle-Plains Historical Museum, Canyon, Texas.

Rath, Charles. October 10, 1892, Indian Depredation Case No. 4593. Photocopy, Panhandle-Plains Historical Museum, Canyon, Texas.

Wright, R. M. Undated, Indian Depredation Case No. 4593. Photocopy, Panhandle-Plains Historical Museum, Canyon, Texas.

## Letters

Archambeau, E. R., to Lester Wood, August 10, 1963. Copy, Archambeau Papers, Panhandle-Plains Historical Museum, Canyon, Texas.

Gerdis, Bruce, to Mrs. Arline Ogden, May 24, 1935. Copy, Gerdis Papers, Panhandle-Plains Historical Museum, Canyon, Texas.

Gerdis, Bruce, to Frank Collinson, January 12, 1938. Copy, Gerdis Papers, Panhandle-Plains Historical Museum, Canyon, Texas.

# INDEX

Abert, James William: background of, 112-113, 144; skills of, 113-114, 121; on Plains, 115; on Kiowas, 117, 120; on Comancheros, 118; contributions of, 121, 122-123, 130, 132, 133, 140, 142, 143, 144
—expedition: route of, 114-121 *passim*; contacts of, with Indians, 115, 117-121 *passim*; hardships of, 117, 118-119, 121
Abert, John: origins of, 113
Abert, John James: career of, 113
Acoma: Alvarado expedition at, 58
Adair: and livestock industry, 239
*adelantado*: Óñate as, 63
adobe: use of, in Panhandle, 102
Adobe Walls: location of, 157; business at, 157-158, 160, 171; life at, 158, 160, 161; and buffalo hunters, 158-159, 160, 166; demise of, 160, 168; and military activity, 209, 216, 221; mentioned, 180, 221, 222
—Battle of: significance of, 96-98, 100, 164; events of, 161-165; results of, 166, 168, 172, 207; mentioned, 158, 206
Agassiz, Louis: and J. Marcou, 141
agate: observation of, 117. *See also* Alibates Flint Quarries
Agate bluffs: naming of, 117
Ágreda, Mother María de Jesús de: and Jumanos, 66
agriculture: and cotton production, 15; and grain production, 15, 38, 40, 43; and irrigation, 43, 102
Agua de Piedras. *See* Rocky Dell Creek
Agua Pintada. *See* Rocky Dell Creek
Aguayo, Marquis de Miguel de: and Spanish-French relations, 74, 75
Alamocitos Creek: Goodnight on, 234; sheep on, 245
Albuquerque, New Mexico: proximity of, to Isleta, 66
Algonquin linguistic family: in relation to Shoshonean, 47
Alibates Flint Quarries: history of, 39 and n., 117

Alvarado, Don Hernando de: expedition of, 57-58
Amangual, Francisco: expedition of, 80-81, 82, 249
Amarillo, Texas: naming of, 83; Wild Horse Lake in, 92; and Comanchero trade, 95; and railroad, 246
Amarillo Creek: Marcy crossing of, 128
Amarillo soil association: of High Plains, 13, 16
Anglo Americans: immigration of, 27, 177; and Spanish, 75, 76; commerce of, 80; and Llano Estacado, 81-82, 203; in Panhandle, 83, 94-95, 101, 104, 128, 143, 174, 176, 225, 229, 231, 239, 247; and Indians, 100, 194 and n.; and Canadian River Valley, 132; and P. Ortiz, 201
Antelope Creek: Gregg party at, 92; Marcy crossing of, 128
Antelope Creek Focus: location of, 27, 41; peoples of, 27, 42, 53; culture of, 41-44, 45
Antelope Hills: location of, 13; as landmark of expeditions, 65, 118, 120, 125-126, 141, 187, 207, 209; resources at, 126
Antelope Peak: as located by Marcy, 128
Antietam, Battle of: Bugbee at, 236
Anton Chico: mentioned, 72
Apaches: background of, 45; relations of, with Spanish, 45, 65, 68, 75; names of, 46; raiding by, 46, 70, 75, 98; strength of, 46-47; domain of, 66, 73, 194; relations of, with French, 75; with K. Carson party, 98; Carleton on, 99. *See also* Faraone Apaches; Jicarillo Apaches; Kiowa Apaches; Lipan Apaches; Mescalero Apaches; Poloma Apaches
Arapahos: hostilities of, 98, 161; relations of, with military, 183, 187, 190, 191, 192, 194; village of, 188, 190; and Yellow Bear, 192
Archaic Period: tradition of, 29
archaeology: of Plains, 28 and n., 29, 32-34

282
Index

tary operations, 190, 198, 204, 205, 209, 217, 223
—Prairie Dog Town Fork: physical features of, 9, 10, 138; as boundary, 10, 89; expeditions on, 79, 138, 144; buffalo hunters at, 159; and military operations, 219, 223
—Salt Fork: course of, 10-11; Marcy at, 135-136, 138; buffalo hunters on, 159; military operations on, 198, 204, 209, 220
Red River Basin: water resources in, 20 and n., 21
Red River War: events leading to, 184-206 *passim*; military operations of, 206-207, 209-214, 216-224; and military post, 225; and Comancheros, 231
Republican River: Spanish at, 80; settlement along, 183
reservations: Indian confinement to, 190, 192-195 *passim*, 198, 206; and Indian hostilities, 195, 206
Reynolds: at Fort Elliott, 167
Reynolds, J. J.: military career of, 195, 200
Right of Revolution: and Texas territorial claims, 84
Rio Colorado. *See* Canadian River
Rio Conchos. *See* Concho River
Rio de la Magdalene. *See* Canadian River
Rio Grande: Spanish at, 61, 62, 68, 73, 80; as boundary, 84
Rio Mora Creek: and Long expedition, 106 and n.
Rio Negro. *See* Washita River
Rio Palo Duro. *See* Red River
Rita Blanca Creek: settlers on, 102
rivers: of Panhandle, 6, 8
Roberts County: physical features of, 3 and n., 6, 8; archaeological finds in, 30; population in, 238n.
Robinson, Tobe: in Mooar party, 158
Rocking Chair Mountains: location of, 13
Rocky Dell Creek: Gregg party on, 92
Rocky Mountains: and Panhandle geology, 4, 28
Rodríguez, Agustín: expedition of, 61-62
Rodríguez-Chamuscado expedition: explorations of, 61-62 and n.
Roger Mills County, Oklahoma: Washita River in, 10
Rogers, Julian: on Marcy expedition, 125

Romero, Casimero: as Panhandle settler, 101-102, 103, 231, 236
Rough Broken Land: location of, 16, 24

Sabeata, Juan: and Spanish aid, 68
St. Louis: route to, from Santa Fe, 79, 80
St. Louis-Santa Fe route: and commerce, 80
St. Paul-Abilene soil association: of Eroded Plains, 13, 16
St. Vrain, Ceran: and Fort Adobe, 93
Salas, Juan de: and Jumanos, 66, 67
Saldivar Mendoca, Vicente de. *See* Mendoca, Vicente de Saldivar
Saline River: settlement on, 183
Salt Fork. *See* Red River, Salt Fork
San Angelo, Texas: and Jumanos, 66, 68; and Fort Concho, 181
San Antonio: and Apaches, 75; and Spanish, 77, 79, 80, 81; routes to, 78-79; military operations at, 196, 200
San Antonio River: Spanish on, 73
Sand Creek Massacre: mentioned, 193, 224
Sandoval, Agapito: as Panhandle settler, 101, 102
San Isidoro Mission: establishment of, 66
San Juan Bautista: location of, 73
San Lorenzo River. *See* Platte River, North
San Miguel County, New Mexico: fort in, 182
San Pedro Springs: settlement of, 73
San Saba River: presidio on, 80
Santa Bárbara: significance of, 61
Santa Fe: Spanish at, 67, 77; and Indians, 71, 72, 75; trade in, 76, 90; routes to, 77-78, 79, 80-81; contact of, with Texas, 77, 78, 79, 80, 85, 87; United States forces in, 87
Santa Fe railroad: in Dodge City, 157; in Panhandle, 246
Santa Fe Trail: protection of, 96, 182; travelers on, 123; Indian attack on, 180
Santa Rosa, New Mexico: Puerta de Luna near, 202
Sarsis: and Kiowas, 49
Satank: as Kiowa leader, 180, 195; arrest of, 197
Satanta: as Kiowa leader, 180, 195, 196; arrest of, 197; release of, 205